THE ULTIMATE
◆ *Encyclopedia of* ◆
BEER

This edition published in 1995 by Smithmark Publishers, a division of U.S. Media Holdings, Inc., 16 East 32nd Street, New York, NY 10016.

SMITHMARK books are available for bulk purchase for sales promotion and premium use. For details write or call the manager of special sales, SMITHMARK Publishers, 16 East 32nd Street, New York, NY 10016; (212) 532-6600.

Produced by Carlton Books Limited,
20 St Anne's Court,
Wardour Street, London W1V 3AW

ISBN 0-8317-1899-4

Printed and bound in Great Britain

10 9 8 7 6 5 4 3 2 1

Project Editor: Martin Corteel
Project Art Direction: Zoë Maggs
Picture Research: Charlotte Bush
Design: Ian Loats
Production: Garry Lewis

AUTHOR'S ACKNOWLEDGEMENTS

Thanks to (in Britain) Ted Bruning, Iain Loe, Research Manager of the Campaign for Real Ale, and Tim Hampson of the Brewers and Licensed Retailers Association; and in the United States Benjamin Myers for help with facts, figures, beers, pubs and pub games. Thanks to Robin Appel for advice on malt and English Hops for advice on hops. Thanks to all the brewers worldwide who responded to letters, phone calls, faxes and who, unsolicited, sent samples of beer that made me, briefly, popular with my neighbours. Thanks to Susan Nowak, bon beer viveur, author of the *CAMRA Guide to Good Pub Food*, for help with beer and food recipes. Special, heartfelt thanks to Martin Corteel and Charlotte Bush at Carlton Books for their patience and forbearance.

SOURCES AND FURTHER READING

Delos, Gilbert, *Beers of the World*, Paris, 1994.
Eames, Alan, *A Beer Drinker's Companion*, Harvard, 1986; and articles in *Ale Street News*, New Jersey.
Jackson, Michael, *Michael Jackson's Beer Companion*, London, 1993.
Jackson, Michael, *Pocket Beer Book*, London, 1994.
Lees, Graham, *The CAMRA Good Beer Guide to Munich and Bavaria*, St Albans, 1994.
Pepper, Barrie, *The Bedside Book of Beer*, St Albans, 1990.
Taylor, Arthur, *The Guinness Book of Traditional Pub Games*, London, 1992.
Webb, Tim, *The CAMRA Good Beer Guide to Belgium and Holland*, St Albans, 1992.
Wheeler, Graham, *The CAMRA Guide to Home Brewing*, St Albans, 1993.
Yenne, Bill, *Beers of the World*, London, 1994.

THE ULTIMATE
•*Encyclopedia of*•
BEER

THE
Definitive Guide
TO THE
WORLD'S
GREAT
BREWS

Roger Protz

SMITHMARK

CONTENTS

INTRODUCTION

*T*HIS IS MORE THAN JUST A BOOK. IT IS A CELEBRATION –
A CELEBRATION OF THE WORLD'S OLDEST ALCOHOLIC DRINK, WITH
ITS ORIGINS IN EGYPT AND BABYLON SOME THREE THOUSAND YEARS BC.

Most of the people of the world drink beer and most of us take it for granted. We will argue the merits of a chateau-bottled claret or a vintage Burgundy but will tip a glass of beer down our collective throat without giving a moment's thought to its aromas and flavours and the mighty skills of maltsters and brewers that went into its creation.

The aim of the Ultimate Encyclopedia is to put beer into context and heighten its appreciation and enjoyment. It is more than just a world guide to beer. For the first time within one volume you will find the history of beer, from its Old World origins to the present day, taking in the role of the church in medieval Europe, the arrival of the hop plant, the development of commercial brewing, and the pale ale and lager revolutions of the nineteenth century.

There is a detailed but untechnical description of the ways in which beers are brewed, the ingredients used and the two branches of the beer family – ale and lager.

The main section of the book is a country-by-country account of the beer styles available, their history and a selection of the finest brews on offer. The World A to Z does not set out to be comprehensive – the sheer size of such an undertaking would require a jumbo jet to carry it in – but points readers, both experienced beer drinkers and those coming fresh to the joys of the drink, to brands that are brewed true to style and offer the most tongue-tingling pleasures.

The best place to drink good beer is in public, where you can share the pleasures of a toothsome brew. To this end, the Ultimate Encyclopedia offers some of the best hostelries – pubs, bars, cafés and kellers – throughout the world. They are places chosen because they offer first and foremost good beer. They may not be the prettiest, with thatched roofs and roses round the door, the stock in trade of most pub guides, but in the belief that a bar based on good beer will also offer a good welcome, good service and good cheer. And because beer is often underrated as a companion to food, the book suggests some dishes that will benefit from the use of beer both in cooking and on the dining table.

The Ultimate Encyclopedia does not naively pretend that all is well in the world of beer. A business section looks at who owns whòm, at the tendency to monopoly, takeover and closure that threaten choice and variety. But as the experience of Britain proves, with its dynamic consumer movement the Campaign for Real Ale, beer lovers can refashion a whole industry, wrench quality from oblivion and ensure that brewers listen to drinkers and not just their accountants and the gurus of the graph.

Above all this is a book about pleasure, the simple and time-honoured pleasure of savouring a fine glass of beer, the world's oldest and arguably greatest drink.

Cheers!

ROGER PROTZ
St Albans, May 1995

7

THE ART AND SCIENCE OF BEER-MAKING

*B*EER IS AS OLD AS CIVILIZATION. THE METHODS THAT PRODUCE SOME TYPES OF ALE HAVE SCARCELY CHANGED FOR CENTURIES. MODERN LAGER BREWING HAS INTRODUCED NEW TECHNOLOGIES AIDED BY YEAST CULTIVATION AND REFRIGERATION. BUT THE ESSENTIALS OF MAKING BEER – TURNING BARLEY INTO MALT, EXTRACTING THE SUGARS, BOILING WITH HOPS AND FERMENTING WITH YEAST – REMAIN TODAY ESSENTIALLY THE SAME AS WHEN EARLY MAN FIRST DISCOVERED THE JOYS AND MYSTERY OF BREWING

When water was turned into wine, it was described as a miracle. But making beer from barley is rather more difficult, since a harvest of golden grain produces beer only as a result of profound and natural chemical reactions, and enormous skill from maltsters and brewers. Along the way other cereals may be blended in, while the remarkable hop plant imparts quenching bitterness and tempting aromas. In Germany, the biggest beer-drinking nation in the world, they do their best to keep it simple. The ingredients that can be used in brewing are controlled by a sixteenth-century law called the *Reinheitsgebot*, or "Purity Pledge", so German beer drinkers can be certain that only malted barley or wheat, along with hops, water and yeast, go into their favourite tipple. In the rest of the world, however, unravelling the contents of a glass of beer is more complicated. Many brewers use "adjuncts", either because they are cheaper, or because they help to produce the right balance of flavours. Germans turn their noses up at "impure" beers from abroad, but English pale ales and milds, as well as Belgian Trappist beers and Irish stouts would change character noticeably if brewers

Blowing in the wind ... beer starts with barley, the finest and sweetest grain that produces sugar-rich malt for the brewer

were not able to use special sugars and unmalted cereals to give their creations their own unique colours and tastes.

In a few regions of the world, where it is difficult to grow barley, brewers are forced to use the raw ingredients available – such as rice in the Far East, or sorghum in Africa. Barley, though, is the preferred grain for brewing. In the Ancient World of Egypt, Mesopotamia and Sumeria, the first brewers found that, while wheat made excellent bread, it caused problems if it was the only grain used in the beer-making process. Barley, on the other hand, makes relatively poor bread, but was found to be the ideal grain for brewing. Even today, with the dramatic revival of interest in wheat beers, wheat makes up only one per cent of the total grain used in brewing world-wide. Today, all "wheat beers" use between 30 and 50 per cent malted barley in their composition.

Cereals such as barley and wheat developed from tall grass. Barley, though, is unusual because it has a husk. The early brewers soon found that this husk acted as a natural filter in the first stage of brewing. This is known as "mashing", when the natural sugars are extracted from the malt. Other cereals, such as wheat, have no husk and so can clog up pipes and machinery in brewing vessels. The other important advantages of barley are that it has the highest "extract" of fermentable sugars, and also produces a cleaner-tasting beer. Wheat, on the other hand, has a distinctive, fruity tartness that does not blend well with the bitterness of hops, while oats and rye have to be used in small proportions or they will impart to the beer a flavour that is either too creamy or too grainy. Some specialist ale brewers in Britain, however, have rediscovered oats and are using small amounts in stouts that are radically different in flavour to the dry Irish style.

Making malt

Many people make the mistake of assuming that brewing is a simple process – unlike wine-making, that needs enormous skill. The opposite is the case. If you crush grapes, the natural yeasts on their skins will ferment the sugary liquid. But nothing happens if you crush an ear of barley. It needs the gentle craft of the maltster to take the raw grain and turn it into malt. During the malting process, natural chemical reactions begin to turn the starches in the barley into fermentable sugars.

THE BARLEY OF CHOICE

Brewers choose malt with great care, preferring to stick to a tried and trusted variety that they know yeast will work with in harmony. Change the barley, and the yeast will react badly or even refuse to ferment and produce alcohol. Brewers, if they can acquire it, prefer two-row barley. The name refers to the number of rows of grain within each ear. The finest two-row barley grows close to the sea on rich, dark soil and is known as "maritime barley" as a result. The East Anglia region of England, the Scottish Lowlands, and Belgium produce some of the finest varieties of two-row maritime. In warmer climates – the Mediterranean countries and the United States – six-row barley is more common. As well as having six rows of grain in each ear, the barley has a thicker husk; this contains tannins known as polyphenols. Both the husk and the

tannins can cause a haze in finished beer and brewers who use six-row barley tend to blend in substantial amounts of adjuncts, such as corn and rice, to counter this haze. Six-row barley is also particularly rich in enzymes that will convert the starches in corn and rice, as well as the malt, into sugar. American "lite" lagers are often made from six-row with large amounts of adjuncts. But master brewers in Germany and the Czech Republic, the birthplaces of modern lager brewing, will only use two-row barley. Pale ale brewers agree with them. They feel that six-row gives an astringent and harsh character to beer.

But whether it is two-row or six-row, only a small proportion of barley is suitable for brewing. It must be low in nitrogen to avoid hazy beer, and with the wide-spread use of pesticides and fertilizers, nitrogen is a growing problem. Ale brewers tend to prefer winter barleys – sown in the autumn and able to withstand frosts and snow – for their robust character, while lager brewers use spring varieties which possess softer, lighter qualities.

Under pressure from farmers and big brewers, seed merchants have developed new varieties of barley that have a high "yield". This means that they produce more grain per acre than some of the more famous barleys, such as Maris Otter in England and Golden Promise in Scotland, though traditional brewers are willing to pay a premium price for low-yield varieties of barley, since they produce the best flavours and ferment in harmony with yeast. Changing the barley variety can result in a "stuck" fermentation.

Barley is a hardy cereal that grows in many climates. This field is in Spain. Brewers prefer "maritime" varieties that grow close to the sea

MAKING MALT

ROASTED MALT, SUCH AS BLACK AND CHOCOLATE MALT, AS WELL AS UNMALTED ROASTED BARLEY, TASTES AND SMELLS REMARKABLY LIKE COFFEE. IN FACT, MANY INSTANT "COFFEES" CONTAIN LARGE AMOUNTS OF ROASTED MALT. THIS HABIT STEMS FROM WORLD WAR TWO, WHEN REAL COFFEE BEANS WERE DIFFICULT TO GET.

A hand's turn ... in a traditional maltings, the germinating grain is laid out on a warm floor and turned regularly to aerate it

THE MALTINGS

When the brewer and the maltster are satisfied with the quality of the barley, it goes to a maltings to start the long journey that will end with beer. At the maltings, the grain is washed thoroughly to remove dirt, agro-chemicals and other impurities. This is done by "steeping", or soaking, the grain with water in a deep trough or, in modern maltings, in large metal tanks. During this process, a primitive type of fermentation occurs as bacteria attack wild yeasts on the grain and the water bubbles and froths alarmingly. The water is changed frequently to flush away both bacteria and any wild yeasts that could interfere with the natural development of the grain. At the same time, the grain is absorbing moisture – vital if germination is to start – and the moisture level of the grain will increase from 14 to 40 per cent.

At the end of steeping, the water is drained and the grain is left to stand for several hours. In a traditional floor maltings, the grain is spread on a floor to form a "couch". In a modern maltings, the grain goes into large revolving drums. In either system, the grain will begin to germinate, and it must be turned or raked frequently to allow it to breathe. Germination and the biochemical changes that take place within the grain lead to a build up of heat that must be carefully controlled or the grain will suffocate.

MODIFICATION

What happens to the grain is known as "modification". The embryo of the grain, the acrospire, starts to grow while tiny roots break through the husk. The grain is composed of two parts, the starchy endosperm and a tough, outer, aleurone layer that protects the endosperm and also contains proteins. The growth of the acrospire causes natural chemical reactions to transform the proteins into enzymes and so make the starches soluble. While the acrospire becomes soft, the rootlets grow at great speed. The maltster tests the degree of modification by a simple test: he puts some grain in his mouth and chews it. If it is soft and "friable", then modification has gone far enough and the barley has become what is known as "green malt".

An ale brewer will want a fully modified malt with as much of its protein as possible turned to enzymes. This enables him to use a simple infusion mashing system that turns starches into brewing

As the barley starts to germinate, roots break through the husk. The maltster judges when germination has reached the required degree by chewing it

sugar. Lager brewers traditionally have used less modified malt with a lower rate of protein conversion, while a more complex decoction mashing system is needed to convert the sugar and avoid beer haze. The reason for the differences lies in the fact that lager brewers in central Europe didn't have access to maritime barley and so had to make do with inferior varieties. Today, all two-row barleys are of high quality, but many lager brewers – and German wheat beer brewers – prefer to stick with decoction mashing.

DRYING THE MALT

The green malt has to be heated to dry it and preserve the vital enzymes. In a modern maltings, this will be done inside a drum that is heated externally. A kiln in a traditional maltings is like a large chimney. A coke fire at the bottom heats the malt, which is spread out above on a mesh floor. The temperature is carefully controlled to produce the right type and colour of malt needed by the brewer. The first temperature stage, around 60 degrees C/150F, stops the process of germination. To produce white malt for lager brewing, the heat is increased slightly and held for 24 hours, while a marginally higher temperature is used for pale malt, the classic type for ale brewing. Malt destined for darker beers, such as English mild, will be kilned at an even higher temperature. The important factor is that the heat must be maintained at a level that will not kill the enzymes which will turn starch into sugar in the brewery. Heavily kilned malts will have no fermentable sugars and so are used solely for producing colour and flavour.

DARK MALTS

Dark malts – amber, chocolate and black – are produced in machines similar to coffee roasters. Unmalted roasted barley, used principally in dry Irish stouts, is also made in this way. Green malt is loaded into the roasters where temperatures range from 200 degrees C/430F to 210 degrees C/450F, depending on the colour required. Roasted malts have an intense, bitter flavour.

Special types of dark malt are made in a different way. Carapils and caramalt used in lager brewing, and crystal malt used for ale, are produced by loading green malt into a sealed kiln. The moisture cannot escape and, as the temperature is raised to 45 degrees C/150F, the enzymes convert starches

into sugar. The husks of grain contain soft balls of malt sugar. As the vents of the kiln are opened and the heat is increased, the sugar crystallizes and the colour deepens. Not all the starches are converted, however, and much of the sugar produced is dextrin rather than maltose. As dextrin cannot be fermented by brewer's yeast, it gives not only flavour and colour to the beer, but also "body", a roundness of fullness and flavour.

Brewers specify the colour of the malts they need by quoting a scale agreed by the European Brewing Convention. The scale applies either to the malt or to the colour of the finished beer. A classic pale-gold Pilsner will have around six to eight units EBC, an English pale ale using crystal malt will register between 20 to 40 units, while dark beers in the porter and stout category will be as high as 300 units on the scale. In the United States, brewers use a system known as Degrees Lovibond to measure colour. Under this system, pale lager will have 1.6 degrees, a pale ale three degrees, and a stout 500 degrees.

Pale or dark, the maltster has now taken raw grain and turned it into an ingredient rich in soluble starches. The first and staple ingredient in making beer is now ready to go the brewery.

A roasting machine at specialist maltsters French & Jupps. It produces black and chocolate malts for dark beers

UNTIL MALT COULD BE CURED BY COKE OR COAL, IT WAS DRIED OVER WOOD FIRES. HORNBEAM WAS THE MOST POPULAR TYPE OF WOOD. BUT BECAUSE WOOD FIRES ARE HARD TO CONTROL, THE MALT WAS OFTEN CHARRED AND HAD A DISTINCTIVE SMOKY FLAVOUR. SOME GERMAN BEERS ARE STILL MADE WITH SMOKED MALT.

Hops

Europe. In Britain, the hop, *humulus lupulus*, was eaten as a delicacy by the Romans, but was not used in brewing at the time. Knowledge of the hop and hop cultivation were then taken into the Caucasus and Germany as part of the great migration of people that followed the collapse of the Roman empire. By the early ninth century, hops were being grown in the Hallertau region of Bavaria. Brewers who used other plants, or a mixture of herbs, plants and spices known as "gruit", fiercely resisted the hop, while in many countries the church controlled the gruit market and could rail against the demon hop from the pulpit.

The hop arrived late in England in the fifteenth century and was banned by such luminaries as Henry VIII and the aldermen of Norwich and Shrewsbury. But eventually the superiority of hopped beer put paid to ale and gruit. Though the term "ale" is still widely used in the British Isles and the United States to define a top-fermenting style, today all ales are brewed with hops.

PITY THE POOR MALE

Left to itself, the hop will trail across the ground and grow wild in hedgerows. Hop farmers train it to climb up poles, its thick stalk or bine wrapping round the pole. This gives the plant maximum exposure to sun and light. The hop plant is dioecious: the male and female plants grow separately. Except in the British Isles, the male hop has a short and miserable existence. Lager brewers want unfertilized hops that will give aroma to their beers, but they avoid too much bitterness and shy away from any suggestion of astringency. In most countries the male hop is ruthlessly persecuted to stop it mating with female hops. Classic ale producers, on the other hand, want an earthy, peppery aroma and flavour in their beers and a deep and intense bitterness. As a result they use fertilized female plants and encourage the male to enjoy a healthy sex life.

The flower of the hop – the cone – contains resins known as alpha acids (or humulones) and beta acids (or lupulones), as well as oils. Alpha acids give bitterness to beer, while the oils impart flavour. The beta acids and tannins in the cone help to stabilize the beer and also have vital disinfectant qualities to ward off infections. The hops grown in such famous European regions as the Hallertau in Bavaria and Žatec (Saaz in German) in the Czech

Wine makers are fortunate. Everything they need to make wine is contained within the grape, including natural preservatives that single the grape out from other fruits. Brewers, however, have to balance malt, with its biscuity sweetness, with plants or herbs that not only add aroma and bitterness, but also prevent bacterial infections during the brewing process. For centuries brewers tackled the problem of how to offset both the poor keeping qualities of ale and its cloying sweetness by adding a variety of herbs and plants. These included yarrow, rosemary and bog myrtle. But from around the eighth century AD, hops started to be used in brewing in central

Republic are known as "noble hops" because of their superb aroma but comparatively gentle bitterness. Modern varieties, known as "high alphas", have been developed to give twice the level of bitterness to beer compared to noble varieties. Many brewers are wary of high alphas as they feel they give a harsh and astringent character to their brews. They prefer to blend in different varieties to achieve the right balance of aroma and bitterness. English ale brewers, for example, use the Fuggle for bitterness and the Golding for aroma. Both are named after their original growers.

HOPS AROUND THE WORLD

The major hop-growing areas of the world are the United States and British Columbia in North America, Kent and Worcestershire in England, Bavaria in Germany, Žatec in the Czech Republic, and Styria in former Yugoslavia. Hops are also grown in Poland and China, while the Pride of Ringwood variety from Tasmania is highly regarded and is much in demand from brewers of organic beer. Recently, leading growing areas, such as the German Hallertau and the English counties, have seen their hops attacked by pests and diseases, so new strains that are resistant to attacks from the likes of downy mildew and red spider mite have been developed. The United States is expected to dominate world hop-growing within a few decades as a result of the ideal climates in Idaho, Oregon and Washington state which produce such varieties as Cascade, Chinook, Cluster and Willamette. All hops give an appealing citric character to beer, and this is most apparent in American varieties – the Chinook in particular imparts a powerful aroma and flavour of grapefruit.

PICKING THE HOPS

Hops are picked in the early autumn. (Before mechanization, hop picking provided a short paid holiday for working-class families who lived close to the hop fields. In England, special trains were used to take London Cockneys and "Brummies" from Birmingham to pick hops in Kent and Worcestershire respectively.) Hops have a high water content and they must be dried and packed quickly to stop them going mouldy. Drying is usually carried out close to the hop fields – in England it is done in attractive oast houses topped by cowls that keep a steady draught of warm air

circulating over the hops. When they are dry, the hops are compressed into sacks and stored in dark, cool areas in breweries to avoid oxidation and photosynthesis.

Brewers with traditional equipment prefer whole hops, while breweries with modern hop whirlpools use pelletized hops that have been milled to a powder and reduced under pressure into pellets. Hop oils and hop extracts, produced by boiling hops with hydrocarbons or in an alkaline solution, are not popular with craft brewers, since they feel they give an unpleasant harshness and bite to the beer.

IBUS

The bitterness of beer is measured by an internationally-agreed scale, International Bitterness Units, or IBUs. They are sometimes known as EBUs (from European Bitterness Units), but the scale is now used in North America as well. The measurement is based on the level of hop acids and the quantity of hops used in a beer. IBUs do not give an indication of hop aroma or flavour, since they have to be balanced against the alcoholic strength of a beer and the amount of malt used. A "lite" American lager may have around 10 IBUs, whereas a genuine Czech Pilsner will have 40. An English mild ale will have 20 units, an India Pale Ale 40 or higher, an Irish stout 55 to 60 and a barley wine 65.

A traditional oast house in Kent where hops are dried

AS THE USE OF HOPS SPREAD, THE RUSSIAN ARCHDUKE VASILI II BANNED THEIR USE IN BREWING, WHILE IN ENGLAND, HENRY VIII INSTRUCTED HIS COURT BREWER TO USE NEITHER HOPS NOR BRIMSTONE IN HIS ALE. THE BREWERS' COMPANY WAS SET UP IN LONDON IN 1437 TO DEFEND THE INTERESTS OF ALE BREWERS AND DEMANDED THAT "NO HOPS, HERBS OR OTHER LIKE THING BE PUT INTO ANY ALE OR LIQUOR WHEREOF ALE SHALL BE MADE – BUT ONLY LIQUOR [WATER], MALT AND YEAST."

Water

A plentiful supply of water is essential to the brewing process. But brewers never call it water – "liquor" is the term used. Lager brewers soften their liquor while pale ale brewers require hardnesss

Even the strongest beer is made up of 90 per cent water. Yet, brewers apart, we tend to ignore the role of water in brewing, except when we accuse brewers of "watering" their beer. In fact, every brewer in the world has to water the beer, otherwise there would be nothing to drink. In a brewery, water is treated with a care bordering on religious fervour. For a start, it is never called water but "liquor": water is the stuff used for washing floors and equipment.

HARD VERSUS SOFT

The quality of the brewing liquor is essential to the clarity and taste of the beer. It encourages malt and hops to give up their sugars, aromas and flavours, and it also stimulates yeast to vigorously turn sugars into alcohol. The purity of water destined for brewing helps to produce a beer that is free from infections, while its hardness or softness will help determine the "mouthfeel" of finished beer. Brewers who want to produce a genuine Pilsner beer will need a soft water, while a pale-ale brewer will want a water that is hard and rich in mineral salts. The level of salts in the water of Pilsen in the Czech Republic, home of Pilsner beer, is 30.8 parts per million. Before the Industrial Revolution and the ability to make chemical changes to water, London's water was notoriously soft and was ideal for brewing milds, porters and stouts. In Burton-on-Trent, where the classic flinty English pale ales

were born, water is hard and salts add up to 1,226 parts per million. Centuries ago, when public water was unsafe to drink, breweries would be set up next to natural springs or wells, or water diviners would be paid to find a supply of fresh water that would not only provide clean brewing liquor, but could also be used to germinate barley.

All water, whether it comes from wells, rivers, or ponds, is the result of rain falling on to the earth. As it falls, it picks up gases that acidify it. Carbonic acid is the main acid in rain water. When it hits the ground, rain water drains through the top soil and finds it way through porous rocks and mineral layers until it settles on a water table of impervious rock. During that long, slow passage, the water will absorb mineral salts. The type and quantity of salts will depend on the rock formation in a given area. Soft water collects on insoluble rock, such as slate or granite, and is virtually free of minerals as a result. Water returns to the surface by forcing its way as a spring or flowing into a river, or bores will be sunk to pump it to the surface.

LIKES AND DISLIKES

Calcium bicarbonate is the most common cause of temporary hardness in water. It comes from chalk and is a nuisance in a brewery because the salts impede fermentation and reduce the effectiveness of other minerals. As those who live in a hard-water district will know, calcium bicarbonate leads to a heavy build up of deposits in kettles. Brewers remove as much of it as possible by boiling or filtration.

On the other hand, calcium sulphate – or gypsum – is as welcome as free beer in a brewery, since it encourages enzymes to turn starch into sugar during the mashing stage of brewing, maintains the correct level of acidity – the pH or "power of hydrogen" – in the unfermented beer, and ensures that the yeast works in a lively manner. The high levels of gypsum in the water of Burton-on-Trent enables brewers there to produce sparkling and clean-tasting pale ales of dazzling quality. The sulphury aroma on a true Burton beer is known locally as the "Burton snatch".

Yeast loves magnesium sulphate (Epsom Salts) and attacks the sweet sugars in the fermenters with enormous vigour thanks to the presence of magnesium. The salts also help to stabilize the sugar extract when it is boiled with hops. Edinburgh, which also became a leading pale ale centre, has water rich in mineral salts.

BURTONIZATION

At the other end of the brewing scale, great brewing centres, such as České Budějovice and Pilsen in the Czech Republic, and Munich in Bavaria, have soft waters with a neglible mineral content. This enables them to produce lager beers with a satiny, rounded smoothness. When London was a great centre for dark beers, the chlorine in the water accentuated the sweetness of the malt. But London is now, on a much reduced scale, a pale ale centre and brewers there "Burtonize" their liquor to match the hardness of Burton-on-Trent. The expression "Burtonization" is now used worldwide to describe the addition of mineral salts. Even brewers in Bavaria, speaking in German, use the term, though the amounts of gypsum and Epsom Salts added to Munich brewing liquor must be small as the lager beers of the city are noticeably soft in texture. But it is a sign of the importance that brewers attach to the quality of water that they have universally adopted a method to replicate the liquor of a small town in the English Midlands.

With the aid of modern technology, almost any water can be used in brewing. While it is pure Irish folk lore that Guinness in Dublin uses water from the River Liffey, there is nothing to stop the company from doing so. Brewers are meticulous in filtering liquor several times to remove any impurities. Many use double osmosis systems. It is a sad reflection on modern life that brewers in the East Midlands of England, home of pale ale, can no longer use some of the natural wells due to their high levels of nitrates. They have turned instead to the public water supply and as a result have to add back calcium and magnesium to achieve the right levels of hardness.

Guinness's Dublin brewery stands by the River Liffey, but the brewery uses pure water from the Wicklow Mountains to make the stout

15

Yeast

Yeast cells under a microscope: brewers test each batch of yeast to watch out for any infections that could cause a problem in the brewhouse

For centuries they called it "God-is-Good". Brewers didn't understand yeast, but they knew that if they saved the foam from one brew, it would magically turn sweet liquid into beer when used again. The earliest brewers probably did not even save the foam, but instead allowed deposits of yeast in their brewing vessels to ferment subsequent brews. Wild yeasts in the air would also attack the sugary liquid, while micro-organisms in storage containers added a lactic sourness. The production of lambic and gueuze beers by spontaneous fermentation in Belgium is a link with brewing's past.

It was not until the eighteenth century, with the pioneering work of the Dutch scientist Anton van Leeuwenhoek, followed by Louis Pasteur with his microscope in the following century, that the mystery of yeast was revealed. Today we know that yeast is a single-cell micro-organism – a fungus – that can turn a sugary liquid into equal amounts of alcohol and carbon dioxide by multiplying and reproducing itself. Pasteur's book *Etudes sur la Bière* changed brewing practice throughout the world. Prompted by the French scientist's work, brewers realized that yeast had to be cultivated and stored to remain pure and uncontaminated. They also had to keep their breweries scrupulously clean to avoid bacteria and wild yeasts infecting beer and turning it sour. With the aid of the microscope, brewers discovered that yeast was made up of several different, competing strains which fought each other and so impeded a successful fermentation. Gradually, yeasts were cultured, both to remove unnecessary strains and also to retain one or two that would attack brewing sugars with the most success. For example, Guinness in Dublin still uses Arthur Guinness's original yeast from the eighteenth century, though it has now been cultured down from five strains to one.

BANKING ON SUCCESS

Today, nothing is left to chance. Brewers realize how vital yeast is, not just to a clean fermentation, but also to the flavour and character of their beers. After each brew, the yeast is collected, pressed to remove any liquid, then stored in refrigerators.

Yeast is not neutral. It picks up and retains flavour from one brew to the next. So if a brewer wishes to produce a classic Pilsner or Pale Ale, he will need not just the right malt, hops and water, but also the correct yeast strain. He can take a

bucket to the brewery of his choice and ask for a supply, but he is more likely to go to a special yeast bank and buy a culture. All brewers keep samples of their yeasts in special banks.

A yeast infection is like a death in the family. If a brewery does get an infection, then it immediately orders a sample from a yeast bank. In Britain, the National Collection of Yeast Cultures, located in Norwich, has a vast range of cultures, as does Weihenstephan near Munich, VLB in Berlin and Jorgensen in Copenhagen. Craft brewers in the United States anxious to produce ales and lagers in the true style order their yeasts from these banks.

ALE AND LAGER YEASTS

There are two basic styles of brewer's yeast – ale and lager. Ale yeast, known by its Latin name of *Saccharomyces cerevisiae* – meaning literally "sugar fungus ale" – is a development of the type of brewing yeast that has been used since the dawn of time. It works at a warm temperature in the brewery, creating a vast blanket on top of the liquid. The temperature will start at around 15°C/59°F, but the heat created by fermentation will increase it to 25°C/77°F. Ale yeasts are used in the production of wheat beer and such German specialities as the Alt beers of Düsseldorf and the Kölsch beers of Cologne, as well as conventional British ales and Irish stouts. Although they are carefully cultured and scientifically analysed, these beers remain a throwback to the age before the industrial revolution. Unlike a pure, isolated, single-strain lager yeast, an ale yeast may be a two-strain variety and will not turn as many sugars into alcohol. As a result, there will be residual sugar in the finished beer and a certain hearty fruitiness to the aroma and palate.

Ale yeast is often used in open fermenters. The heavy blanket it creates on top of the liquid keeps oxygen at bay, and it is this tendency to rise to the top of the fermenting beer that has given ale yeasts the name of "top fermenters", while lager yeasts fall to the bottom of the vessel and are known as "bottom fermenters". The terms, however, are seriously misleading, because any brewer's yeast must work at all levels of the liquid if it is to convert sugars into alcohol. Better terms are "warm fermentation" for ale yeast and "cold fermentation" for lager strains.

In some modern ale breweries, fermentation takes place in enclosed conical fermenters. The

The magnificent elephant gate entrance to the Carlsberg Brewery in Helsinki where the first pure lager yeast strain was isolated

yeast gradually falls to the bottom of the vessel as though it were a lager strain. Brewers will replace such yeasts with a pure culture after just a few brews, otherwise it would not produce the correct ale characteristics.

Lager yeast is classified as *Saccharomyces carlbergensis*, as the first pure culture was isolated at the Carlsberg brewery in Copenhagen. Today it is more commonly called *Saccharomyces uvarum*. Lager brewing began in central Europe in the fifteenth century, when brewers in Bavaria stored – *lagered* in German – their beers in deep, icy caves to keep them in drinkable condition during the long, hot summers. The cold stopped wild yeasts attacking and infecting the brews, and also forced the brewer's yeast to work more slowly and precipitate to the bottom of the vessels.

GOLDEN PILSNER

In the nineteenth century, with the aid of ice-making machines and refrigerators, a brewer name Gabriel Sedlmayr II, working at the Spaten brewery in Munich, developed lager brewing on a commercial scale. These first commercial lagers, however, were dark. It was when a golden lager was produced in Pilsen, in neighbouring Bohemia, that the new method of brewing became an international craze and Pilsner a much-imitated – and ultimately, much-abused – style. Lagering became popular because the beer was more stable, with fewer flavour fluctuations from brew to brew. As a result of lower temperatures, brewers had better control over fermentation. The yeast turns more sugar into

alcohol, producing a dryer beer with little or no fruitiness. Fermentation is in two stages: primary fermentation starts at around 5–9°C/41–48°F and lasts for as long as two weeks, twice the time ale fermentation takes. The beer is then stored – lagered – at 0°C/32°F. During lagering, a secondary fermentation takes place, with the yeast slowly turning the remaining sugars into alcohol and carbon dioxide.

Today, there is a trend towards shorter lagering periods. Some "international" brands enjoy a brief honeymoon of just a couple of weeks in the lagering tanks. But classic lagers, such as the Czech Budweiser Budvar, enjoy three months lagering and emerge with clean, quenching palates, delicate aromas and a complex balance of malt and hops.

WILD FERMENTATION

There is a further type of fermentation in the world of brewing. It is confined to the Senne Valley area of Belgium, based in Brussels, where a handful of specialist brewers produce beers by wild, or spontaneous, fermentation. These lambic and gueuze beers are left to cool under the roofs of the brewhouses; during the night, airborne yeasts enter through open windows and attack the sugars in the solution. The two main yeast strains have been identified as members of the *Brettanomyces* family and are labelled *lambicus* and *bruxellensis*, though more than 30 wild strains have been identified in lambic breweries. The resulting beers, some fermented with fruit, are vinous and cidery and break down the boundaries between wine and beer.

ONE OF GABRIEL SEDLMAYR'S PUPILS AT THE SPATEN BREWERY IN MUNICH WAS JACOB CHRISTIAN JACOBSEN, WHO FOUNDED THE CARLSBERG BREWERY IN COPENHAGEN. SEDLMAYR DEVELOPED COMMERCIAL LAGER BREWING AND JACOBSEN TOOK A SAMPLE OF SPATEN YEAST BACK TO COPENHAGEN. HE KEPT IT IN A POT UNDER HIS STOVE PIPE HAT AND STOPPED THE COACH FREQUENTLY ON THE 600-MILE JOURNEY TO COOL THE POT IN STREAMS.

The strength of beer

% ALCOHOL BY WEIGHT	% ALCOHOL BY VOLUME
2	2.5
2.5	3
3	3.75
3.2	4
3.7	4.6
3.9	4.8
4	5
4.25	5.3
4.4	5.5
4.8	6
5.4	6.8
5.9	7.4
7	8.75
8.8	11
10	12.5
12	15

*A mash tun at Young's
Brewery in South London.
The grist – milled malt – and
hot liquor are mixed in the
tun and starches begin to
turn into malt sugars*

Alcoholic strength used to be expressed in many different and confusing ways. In Britain, beer was taxed on its "original gravity" before fermentation, while other European countries used degrees Balling or Plato. Fortunately, most countries have now adopted the system of Alcohol by Volume (ABV), which is, as the name suggests, a measure of the amount of alcohol in the finished beer. The only major exception is the United States, which prefers to use Alcohol by Weight (ABW). As alcohol is lighter than water, ABW figures are approximately 25 per cent lower than for ABV, so a 4 per cent ABV beer would be 3.2 per cent in the U.S. Not that you will find any indication of strength on an American label, though a Supreme Court ruling in spring 1995 will allow breweries to state alcohol ratings if they wish.

In the brewery

No two breweries are alike and many modern breweries blur the distinction between ale and lager. Some breweries use the same equipment for both types of beer, though ale and lager yeasts are kept strictly apart to avoid cross-fertilization. (The brewing processes for ale and lager described below are the classic methods for both styles.)

Both start in the same way, with the arrival of malt in the brewhouse. The malt is first screened to remove any small stones or other impurities that may have survived the malting process. It is then "cracked" in a malt mill to produce a rough powder called "grist", which gives us the expression "all grist to the mill". Most of the malt is ground to a fine flour, but it is also blended with coarser grits and the rough husks of the grain, which act as a natural filter during the mashing stage. The grist is then ready to start the brewing process.

Classic ale brewing

The first stage of ale brewing is an infusion mash. Grist and brewing liquor are mixed in a large circular vessel known as a mash tun, which may be made of copper, cast iron or stainless steel, and is covered by a lid that can be raised by pulleys. Balanced above the tun is a large tube, a nineteenth-century device called a Steel's Masher, after the Mr Steel who invented it. Exact proportions of grist and hot liquor are mixed by an Archimedes screw inside the masher and the mixture then flows into the mash tun. Temperature is crucial at this stage. If it is too high, the enzymes will be destroyed; too low, and the enzymes will work sluggishly and fail to convert some starches into sugar. The liquor, which has been stored in special tanks in the roof of the brewery, is heated to 75 degrees C/180F. This is known as "strike heat". It is higher than mashing temperature – 65 degrees C/150F – but the coolness of the grist will quickly reduce the temperature of the liquor to the desired level. If the temperature falls too low, more hot liquor can be pumped into the mash tun through its slotted base. The brewer has to avoid "cold spots" in the mash where the grist would turn into a paste, refuse to release its sugars and block every pipe and outlet.

ADJUNCTS

At this stage, the brewer may blend in other cereals with the malt. These are known as adjuncts, and are used to help clarify the beer, reduce nitrogen haze and give the right flavour balance the brewer seeks. The usual adjuncts in ale brewing are torrefied wheat or barley, which are similar to popcorn. The grain is scorched – torrefied – and the heat pops the endosperm and gelatinizes the starch. Flaked maize, another popular adjunct, is made by steaming or milling the grain to gelatinize the starch. Wheat flour is also widely used and gives a fine flavour to beer, but it can only be used in tiny amounts or it will clog up the brewing equipment. Adjuncts do not contain enzymes. It is up to the enzymes in the malt to convert the adjuncts' starches into sugar. All adjuncts have to be used in small amounts: add too much popcorn to beer and it will taste like breakfast cereal.

STARCHES TO SUGAR

The thick, porridge-like mixture is now left to stand in the mash tun for one or two hours as saccharification takes place. This means that starches turn to sugar as a result of enzymic activity. Enzymes are biological catalysts. The two most important ones in brewing are alpha-amylase, which converts starches into maltose and dextrins, and beta-amylase, which produces only maltose. Maltose is highly fermentable, while dextrin cannot be fermented by brewer's yeast and is important for giving "body" to beer. If all the sugars turned to alcohol, the beer would be high in alcohol, but thin in flavour.

The sugars dissolve into the liquor, producing a sweet liquid called wort, pronounced "wurt". The mash tun has taps fitted to the side and the brewer can run off a sample of the wort to check that saccharification is under way. He can usually tell just from the bready smell and taste of the liquid, but if necessary he can carry out a simple chemical test by mixing some wort with a few drops of iodine. If the iodine stays clear, sugar has been produced. If it turns blue-black, then starch is still present. It is important to stop the mashing process once saccharification has taken place, otherwise tannins in the wort will produce an unpleasant flavour, rather like stewed tea. Mashing is terminated by pumping more hot liquor into the tun to kill the enzymes.

The slotted base of the vessel is now opened and the sweet wort starts to filter through the thick cake of spent grain. Perforated tubes in the roof of the tun start to revolve and "sparge" the grains with more hot liquor to flush out any stubborn sugars that remain behind. Sparging was a Scottish invention and the word stresses the Old Alliance between Scotland and France, for sparge comes from the French word *esparger*, meaning "to sprinkle".

WASTE NOT, WANT NOT

Next, the hot sweet wort flows from the mash tun into a receiving vessel known as the "underback". Several vessels in a brewery have "back" in their name, an old word that is derived from the same root as bucket. In medieval breweries, wort would have been ladled from the mash vessel into a series of metal or wooden buckets. The spent grains left behind are not wasted and are sold to farmers as protein-rich cattle feed. In the brewing industry, nothing is wasted. Used hops are in great demand as garden fertilizer, while excess yeast is sold to companies that make yeast extract. Run-off from the mash tun takes two hours. The wort is then pumped from the underback to the coppers. Many modern "coppers" are made of stainless steel, but a genuine copper copper is a delight, a domed and burnished vessel, like a cross between a diving bell and a lunar module. In the days before hops were used in brewing, the wort had to be boiled in order to kill any bacteria. Today, boiling has a dual purpose: to ensure absolute purity of the wort, and to add the essential acids, oils and tannins of the hops. If an ale mash tun is like a giant tea pot, infusing malt and hot water, then the copper is akin to a coffee percolator. It has a central tube – the calandria – topped by a dome called a "Chinese hat". As the wort starts to boil, it gushes up the tube into the

YEAST EXTRACT IS SO POPULAR AS A SPREAD ON BREAD OR TOAST THAT THE LEADING BRITISH MANUFACTURER, MARMITE, BUILT ITS FACTORY IN BURTON-ON-TRENT IN ORDER TO LOCATE IT JUST A FEW YARDS FROM SOME OF THE COUNTRY'S LEADING ALE BREWERS AND SO GET CONSTANT SUPPLIES OF EXCESS YEAST.

The Marmite factory in Burton-on-Trent is cheek-by-jowl with Bass's Brewery. Spent yeast goes to Marmite to be turned into tasty and mineral-rich malt extract

Hops are added at several stages of the boil so that the maximum flavours and aromas are kept in the "wort"

This splendid Victorian copper is in the small museum at Young's Brewery

main body of the copper and begins what is known to brewers as a "good rolling boil".

Hops are then added through a porthole in the domed roof of the copper. They are not, however, added in one batch. Instead, the brewer will add them at stages, usually twice or three times. The almost magical qualities of the hop will kill any bacteria in the wort, destroy the enzymes to stop any further saccharification and force proteins in the wort to come out of suspension and coagulate at the bottom of the copper. If all the hops were added in one batch, many of the vital bittering and aroma qualities would be lost in the boil. So the brewer will add bittering hops in one or two stages and then will "late hop" just a few minutes before the end of the boil with aroma hops.

INVERT SUGAR

Some brewers will add sugar during the copper boil. Sugar is often considered to be an adjunct, but it has no starches that need to be attacked by enzymes, which is why it is added in the copper, not the mash tun. It is totally fermentable and the problem with brewing sugar is that if too much is used, then the finished beer will be high in alcohol but thin in body. Brewing sugar is called "invert sugar", as it has been inverted into its component parts of glucose and fructose. It comes in different colours, depending on the brewer's requirements, and is simply labelled Number One Invert, Number Two Invert and so on up the colour scale. Some of the sugars from both the malt and the invert will be caramelized during the boil, adding colour to the finished beer.

At the end of the boil, a powdered seaweed called Irish moss is added to the copper to clarify the wort by encouraging any remaining proteins and other detritus to settle at the bottom of the vessel. The spent hops act as a filter as the wort flows out through the slotted base of the copper into a hop back, where it is left to cool. The residue left behind is known as "trub". Mixed with the spent hops, it makes a rich compost for gardeners.

Some brewers will add further hops in the hop back to give additional aroma to the wort. Three famous ales from England – Adnams Extra and Greene King Abbot Ale, both from Suffolk, and Timothy Taylor's Landlord, from Yorkshire – circulate over a deep bed of hops in the hop back and have a pungent "hop nose" as a result. If pelletized hops rather than whole flowers are used, the hopped wort is pumped from the copper to a whirlpool, where the spent hops are removed by centrifugal force.

COOLING THE WORT

Before fermentation can begin, the temperature of the boiling hopped wort has to be lowered to 18°C/66°F. In a few breweries, the wort is left to cool in an open shallow vessel called a "cool ship", but there is always the danger that it can be attacked by wild, airborne yeasts as it cools. The vast majority of breweries use heat-exchange units known as paraflows. The wort is pumped through a series of plates that look like old-fashioned school radiators. Each plate containing wort is next to one filled with cold water. As the wort flows along the plates, it will get progressively cooler, until it is finally ready to be turned into alcohol.

PITCHING THE YEAST

The cooled wort is pumped into fermenting vessels and liquid yeast is then mixed or "pitched" into it. Before it is pitched, however, a sample of the yeast will have been checked under a microscope in the brewery laboratory. Yeast cells are invisible to the naked eye, but under the microscope they can be seen darting and diving around. What the brewery is looking for are white yeast cells. Blue cells are dead and would impede fermentation, while black rods among the yells indicate a yeast infection, which would require the entire batch to be poured down the nearest drain.

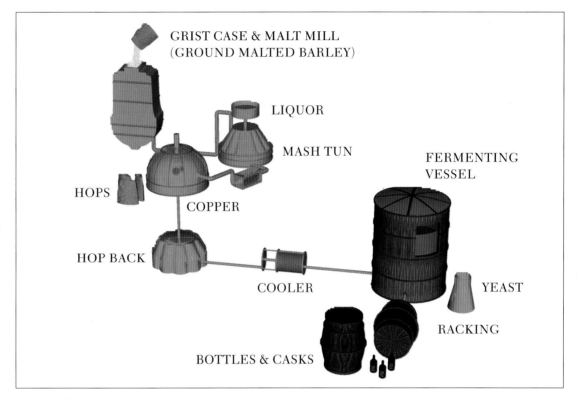

GRIST CASE & MALT MILL (GROUND MALTED BARLEY)

LIQUOR

MASH TUN

HOPS

COPPER

HOP BACK

COOLER

BOTTLES & CASKS

FERMENTING VESSEL

YEAST

RACKING

The traditional ale-brewing process: malt mill, mash tun, copper, hop back, cooler and fermenter, casks and bottles

Fermenting vessels vary from one ale brewery to the next. (Specialist fermenters unique to certain areas, such as Burton union and Yorkshire squares, will be covered in Chapter Two.) Most conventional ale breweries use open vessels, though nowadays there is a trend towards covering them in order to stop CO_2 escaping into the atmosphere. Depending on their age, fermenters may be built from wood, stone or various metals. Stainless steel is used to build modern vessels. Older ones are normally lined with polyproplene to avoid a build-up of bacteria and old yeast in cracks and other rough surfaces.

THE ROLE OF OXYGEN

Brewer's yeast respires in two ways: aerobically (with oxygen), and anaerobically (without oxygen). Pasteur described the ability of yeast to breathe without oxygen as *la vie sans air* — "life without air". Yeast works with oxygen at the start of fermentation. In fact, brewers agitate and aerate the wort to make sure there is plenty of dissolved oxygen present. The yeast works rapidly, with bubbles rising to the surface of the wort. Within a few hours, a brown slick covers the surface and within 24 hours this has grown to a dense, rocky

head that rises to peaks known as "cauliflowers". The yeast head is streaked with brown and black from proteins in the wort. The yeast head will be removed, or "skimmed off", from time to time to stop dead cells and detritus from impeding the work of the yeast in solution.

Enzymes in the yeast – maltase and invertase – turn sugar into alcohol and carbon dioxide. The converted sugars are assimilated by the yeast cells which at the same time are growing by dividing and fusing into fresh cells. Maltase enzymes produces glucose, while invertase turns sucrose into glucose and fructose. Dextrins cannot be fermented, neither can lactose – "milk sugar" – which is sometimes added to sweeten stouts. They remain to give body and sweetness to beer.

Fermentation causes the temperature of the wort to rise. Yeast is pitched at around 15°C/60°F, but during fermentation this will rise to 25°C/80°F. Fermentation also creates chemical compounds, known as "esters", which are present in the atmosphere above the vessels in the form of fruity aromas. Depending on the strength of the beer and the balance of malts, adjuncts and sugars, the aromas may be reminiscent of apples, oranges,

Yeast being "pitched" into a fermenter ... to turn the sugary wort into alcohol

Within a day or two the yeast will create a great blanket on top of the fermenting liquid. A brewer at McMullens tests the progress of the ferment

banana, pineapple, pear drops, liquorice or molasses. In some very strong beers, the esters can be reminiscent of fresh leather.

Eventually, the yeast will be overcome by the alcohol. After about seven days, the yeast cells will start to clump together and rise to the surface. This is known as flocculation. If it happens too early in the process, the brewer will have to aerate the wort again. When almost all the yeast has risen out of suspension, fermentation is at an end. Throughout the entire process, the brewer will check the transformation of sugar into alcohol by measuring the sweetness of the liquid with a hydrometer or saccharometer. Before the yeast is pitched, the wort may have a "gravity" of 1,040 degrees. Water has a gravity of 1,000 degrees, which means that 40 degrees of fermentable sugar is present in the wort. Since maltose, unlike brewing sugar, is not totally fermentable, the final gravity will be around 1,006 degrees, though stronger beers may have more sugar remaining.

GREEN BEER
Brewers, being fundamentalists as well as traditionalists, like to give the beer seven days or "two Sabbaths" in the fermenters. When fermentation is at an end, the wort has been turned into beer, but it is not yet ready to drink. It is known as "green beer" and has to spend several days in conditioning tanks to mature. Some of the rougher alcohols and fruity esters will be purged, producing a cleaner and drinkable beer. When it is ready to leave the brewery, the beer may go in two different directions. Packaged beer, either for bottle, can or keg, will be filtered to remove any remaining yeast and then pasteurized. Carbon dioxide is pumped into the container as the beer is packaged to give it both sparkle and a lively head when poured.

REAL ALE
The beer style unique to Britain, "real ale", does not go through any one these processes. Instead, it is racked from the conditioning tanks straight into casks, though additional hops for aroma and sugar for a secondary fermentation may also be added. The beer leaves the brewery in an unfinished state because final conditioning takes place in the pub cellar, where the yeast in the cask continues to turn the remaining sugars into alcohol. As the beer matures, it gains not only a small amount of additional strength, but also rounded and fruity

flavours. A glutinous substance known as "finings", made from isinglass, is added to attract yeast cells and other detritus to the bottom of the cask, leaving a clear beer above. Casks are vented by porous pegs hammered through a hole in the top of the cask to allow carbon dioxide to escape, though the cask has to be sealed when secondary fermentation is finished in order to keep sufficient gas in the beer to give it sparkle.

Classic lager brewing
The aim of a lager brewer is identical to that of an ale brewer: to extract the sugars from the malt, boil the wort with hops, ferment the hopped wort and produce beer. But the methods used are a variation on the theme, a variation that extends beyond the use of bottom-fermenting yeast, since it is based upon lower temperatures at almost every stage of production.

As lager malt is often less modified than ale malt, a decoction mashing system is used in which the grist is mixed with hot brewing liquor in a mash kettle at a starting temperature of around 38 degrees C/76F. Part of the mash will be pumped to a cooker, where it is heated to a higher temperature – between 43–56 degrees C/86–112F – and then returned to the kettle. Another portion of the mash will be pumped to the cooker and the temperature will rise to 65 degrees C/130F before being returned to the kettle. Returning the portions of heated mash to the kettle raises the temperature to around 50 degrees C/130F.

REST PERIOD
The central feature of the decoction system is that the main body of the mash has a "protein rest" at around 45–55 degrees C/90–110F for periods of an hour of more. This rest period allows excessive protein, contained in malt that is high in nitrogen, to be degraded by a process known as "proteolysis". The heating of portions of the mash at higher temperatures gelatinizes the starch present in poorly modified malt, so allowing it to be attacked by enzymes. Both protein and starch would cause haze in the finished beer if they were not tackled during mashing.

When double or triple decoction has taken place, the temperature of the kettle is raised to 75 degrees C/150F – the same as the mashing temperature in an ale brewery. At this heat, the mash is pumped to a third vessel, called a "lauter tun", which has a false bottom and clarifies the wort as it is run off. It also sparges the spent grain. Unlike an ale mash tun, though, this cannot be done in the mash kettle (which does not have a false bottom) because of all the pumping required to the cooker and back.

Different coloured malts will be used during mashing but, if the beer is being produced in Germany, the Czech Republic or other countries that adhere to the German Pure Beer Pledge, no cereal adjuncts will be used. Similarly, no brewing sugars are added during the boil in a wort kettle. These days, most lager brewers use pelletized hops and they are added in two or three stages during the boil. The hopped wort is then pumped to a whirlpool and centrifuged to remove the mushy pellets and other detritus.

FERMENTATION

Next, the hopped wort is cooled and pumped to fermentation vessels. Lager fermentation is in two stages. The first stage – primary fermentation – may take place in either a tall, conical, stainless steel vessel, or in a more traditional, horizontal one. Temperature ranges between 5–9°C/41–48°F. At such temperatures, the yeast will work much more slowly than an ale strain as it converts sugars to alcohol and CO_2. As a result, there is much less build up of yeast head and the purity of the single-strain variety creates few fruity esters.

Primary fermentation lasts for around two weeks. The green beer is then pumped to lagering tanks, where it is held at 0°C/32°F or just above. During this period of cold conditioning, which may last for several weeks or months, the yeast continues to turn sugars into alcohol as it precipitates at the bottom of the tank.

The finished beer will be clean and quenching, but it will deliberately lack the rounded, fruity quality of an ale, unless it is an exceptionally strong "bock"

beer that has been lagered for as long as a year. The cool temperatures and slow conditioning enable the brewer to remove most of the flavour characteristics that an ale brewer seeks, leaving a lighter, malt-accented beer with a delicate hop character. Neither dry hopping nor the use of isinglass finings is permitted under the *Reinheitsgebot*.

PASTEURIZATION

When lagering is complete, the finished beer will be filtered and often pasteurized. Louis Pasteur was a mixed blessing to the brewing industry. He solved the problems of infection in breweries and unravelled the mysteries of yeast. But he also introduced a heating method that can unbalance the subtle aromas and flavours of beer and give it hints of burnt toffee and cardboard. As the head brewer of the Brand brewery in the Netherlands once stated: "Pasteurization is for the cow shed, not the brew house". Grolsch, another leading Dutch lager brewery, does not pasteurize its beers. And what is good enough for them should be good enough for the rest of the world.

The final act in an ale brewery is to "rack" casks with beer in preparation for the journey to the pub cellar

The lager process: malt mill, brew kettles and lauter tun, copper, hop whirlpool, cooler, fermentation and lagering

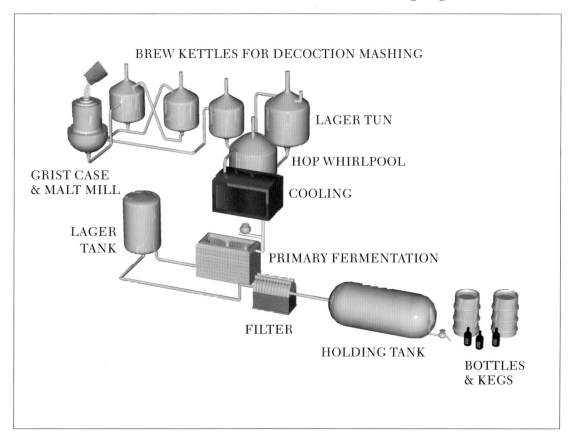

BREW KETTLES FOR DECOCTION MASHING

LAGER TUN

HOP WHIRLPOOL

GRIST CASE & MALT MILL

COOLING

LAGER TANK

PRIMARY FERMENTATION

FILTER

HOLDING TANK

BOTTLES & KEGS

The families of beer

Ale is the world's oldest style of beer, and modern ales are descendants of the beers brewed 3,000 years BC in Ancient Egypt and other parts of North Africa and the Middle East. The British Isles remains the major centre of ale brewing. Though lager has made considerable incursions into Britain and Ireland, around half the beer produced in those islands is in ale form. England is best known for bitter, a well-hopped beer that is best drunk in unpasteurized draught form in pubs. Bitter evolved from the India Pale Ales and other forms of pale ale introduced in the nineteenth century and brewed primarily in Burton-on-Trent, a town famous for its brewing since the twelfth century.

Sam Whitbread's brewery in London's where the brewing process was aided by one of James Watt's first steam engines

PORTER AND STOUT

Before the arrival of pale ale, the British Isles, like all other countries, produced brown and dark beers. Before the development of pale ale and lager, England's singular contribution to the history of beer was porter, a dark brown or black beer first brewed at the turn of the eighteenth century. In fact, the craze for porter created the modern commercial brewing industry. The strongest – stoutest – version of porter was called "stout". Although support for porter and stout declined in Britain as pale ale grew, it took deep root in Ireland and has never diminished. Irish ale and lager are both brewed in the Irish Republic, but dry stout remains the dominant beer. In Britain, mild ale, a dark brown and lightly hopped beer, which was

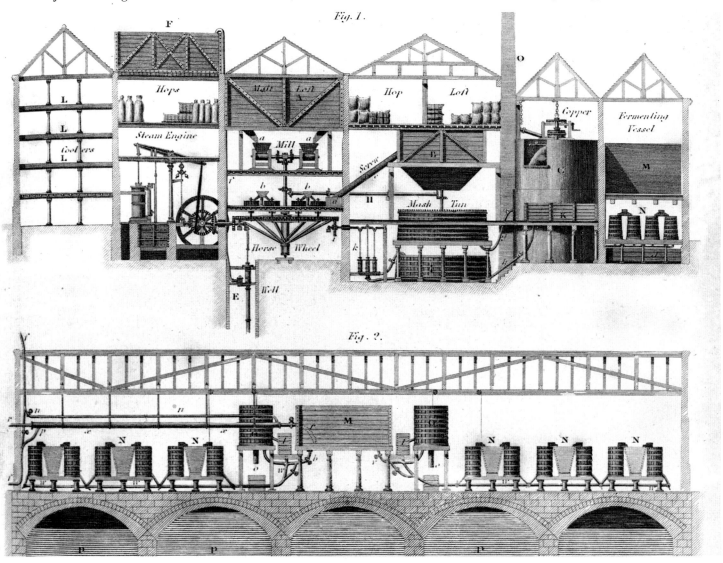

once blended into porter, has kept some support, especially in areas of heavy industry where workers need to refresh themselves with light and slightly sweet beer. Britain also enjoys a growing range of seasonal beers. Rich and fruity old and winter ales have been joined in recent years by spring, summer and autumn beers.

BELGIAN VARIETIES

In Belgium, ales are only a small proportion of a market dominated by such famous lager brands as Stella Artois and Jupiler. But the ale market is growing as both Belgians and the outside world have come to marvel at the enormous variety available in such a small country. Trappist monks, for example, brew ales of enormous complexity in their monasteries, while wheat beers, often flavoured with herbs and spices, have become cult drinks with the young. Pale ales and golden ales have enormous hop character, while in French-speaking Wallonia, seasonal or *saison* beers recall an earlier, bucolic time, when ale was brewed by farmers for their families and workers. In parts of Flanders, russet-coloured ales are stored in oak vats and have a sour and lactic taste. The most remarkable of all the Belgian ales are the wild beers of the Senne Valley, where lambic and gueuze beers are produced by spontaneous fermentation. When fruit – usually cherries or raspberries – is blended with these beers, they have a wonderful tart and quenching character. The success and interest in Belgian ales is creating a smaller revival in ale in the neighbouring Netherlands, dominated by the giant Heineken lager group.

GERMAN VARIETIES

Germany is the world's leading lager-brewing nation, producing beers of awesome quality, a long way removed from the light, bland, international interpretations in other countries. There are also powerful variations in the style, with malty versions in Bavaria, rounded but hoppier ones in Dortmunder, and intensely bitter beers in the north. Not all lagers are pale. In the Munich region in particular, dark lagers – *dunkel* – are still popular. The Germans also brew seasonal beers and strong beers. "Bock" means strong and the name is a corruption of the name of the town of Einbeck, where the style was first brewed many centuries ago. Bock also means "goat" in German and many

bock beer labels depict the animal. In the Munich area, exceptionally strong lagers have names ending in -ator, as in Celebrator or Triumphator. Seasonal beers are recalled in the Märzen (March) beers, brewed at the end of winter and stored until the autumn. Traditionally, it was Märzen beers that were served at the world-famous Oktoberfest in Munich. Other German specialities include the smoked beers of Bamberg, using wood-smoked malt, and beers in which the malt sugars are caramelized in the mash kettle by plunging in red-hot stones.

Germany also has some distinctive ales. Cologne has golden-coloured Kölsch beers, so treasured that they have the equivalent of an *appellation côntrolée* from the government, while nearby Düsseldorf has amber-coloured Alt – "old" – beers. Wheat beers have become vogue drinks, the spicy, fruity Bavarian style growing in recent years

Raspberries are the surprise addition to Belgian "wild" lambic beers. The fruit also ferments to make a light and quenching drink known as framboise or frambozen

And finally, enjoy a beer. After all the mashing, boiling and violent upheaval of fermentation, brewers can sit back and enjoy the fruits (or should it be the grains?) of their labours

little in common with the rich complexity of the genuine article.

In both Scandinavia and the Far East, lagers ranging from the bland to the complex are the norm, but there are small pockets of dark beer. The Japanese, for example, brew some flavourful dark beers, while Sweden and Finland brew porters produced by proper top fermentation.

BREWED IN THE USA

The history of American brewing has been dominated by both immigration and politics. The first settlers from England took an ale culture with them across the Atlantic, but ale took second place to lager when the second wave of immigrants from central Europe arrived. During the long years of Prohibition in the 1920s, quality ales and lagers largely disappeared, and the brew-

to 30 per cent of the beer market. In Berlin, the wheat beers are injected with a lactic culture to give them a mouth-puckering sourness.

THE GOLDEN PILSNER

Bohemia, now the Czech Republic, was the home of the first golden Pilsner lagers. The name comes from the great industrial city of Pilsen, also famous for the Škoda motor car. While Munich developed commercial lagering, the first pale beer of the style came from Pilsen at the height of the industrial revolution. Today, only two breweries brew genuine Pilsners, Pilsner Urquell – meaning "Original Source Pilsner" – and Gambrinus. Beers made in Prague or České Budějovice (Budweis in German) are termed respectively "Prague" beers or "Budweiser" beers. Outside the Czech Republic, though, brewers are not so punctilious. Any light lager is termed Pilsner or Pils, even though it has

eries that survived dominated the market with increasingly bland light or "lite" lagers. Today, however, there are more than 400 small craft breweries producing ales and lagers of enormous quality, while the one true American beer style – steam beer, a hybrid lager-cum-ale – has been rescued and resuscitated by the Anchor Brewery in San Francisco.

In Australasia, ale was supplanted by lager early in the twentieth century. Today, famous brands such as Foster's and Castlemaine XXXX dominate the market, but the success of one traditional ale brewery in Adelaide, Cooper's, has prompted a small ale revival in other parts of the country. There are now several brewpubs in Australia and New Zealand that are concentrating on ale brewing. As the twentieth century draws to a close, ale, against all the odds, is the world's most sought-after revivalist beer style.

THE BEER FAMILY

ALE (WARM FERMENTING) TYPES AND STYLES

BELGIUM:	Ales. Golden ales. Lambic and gueuze spontaneous fermentation/kriek and frambozen. Brown ales/brown kriek. Flemish red ales. Trappist ales. Abbey ales. Saison. Wheat beers.
THE CARIBBEAN:	Stout.
ENGLAND:	Mild (pale and dark). Sweet/"Milk" stout. Stout and porter. Bitter. Northern brown ales. Special bitter/India Pale Ale. Strong bitter. Summer ale. Harvest ale. Old ale/Winter ale. Barley wine.
FRANCE:	Bière de garde. Bière de Mars. Bière de Printemps.
GERMANY:	Alt. Kölsch. Wheat beer (Berlin/Bavaria). Stone beer.
IRELAND:	Irish ale. Irish red ale. Dry stout.
THE NETHERLANDS:	Aajt. Amber. Bock. Oud Bruin. Trappist ale. Wheat beer.
SCANDINAVIA:	Porter. Sahti/Juniper beer.
SCOTLAND:	Light/60 shilling. Heavy/70 shilling. Export/80 shilling. 90 shilling/Wee Heavy.
SRI LANKA:	Stout.
UNITED STATES:	Amber ale. Cream ale. Steam beer°. India Pale Ale. Porter/Stout. Wheat beer.

LAGER (COLD FERMENTING) TYPES AND STYLES

CZECH REPUBLIC:	Budweiser. Pilsner. Prague beer. Black lager.
GERMANY:	Munich Dunkel. Munich Helles. Dortmunder/Export. Bock/Double Bock. Märzen/Oktoberfest. Rauchbier. Black beer. German Pilsner.
JAPAN:	Alt. Dry beer. Black beer. American/German-style lager.
UNITED STATES:	Lite lagers. Malt liquor. Pilsner. Oktoberfest/märzen. Steam beer°. Bock/Double bock. Ice beer.
CANADA:	Ice beer.
MEXICO:	Vienna-style dark lager. Light lager.

NOTE

°Steam beer is a hybrid, made with a lager yeast but fermented at an ale temperature. Most other countries brew international-style lagers, based loosely on the Pilsner style.

SERVING BEER

TEMPERATURE IS CRUCIAL TO THE ENJOYMENT OF BEER. LAGER BEERS SHOULD BE KEPT IN A REFRIGERATOR AND SERVED AT 9°C/48°F. LIGHT AMERICAN AND AUSTRALIAN LAGERS ARE OFTEN SERVED AT A LOWER TEMPERATURE OF 6°C/42°F. ALES SHOULD NOT BE OVER-CHILLED OR THEY WILL DEVELOP A HAZE AND THEIR FRUITY FLAVOURS WILL BE MASKED. 12–13° C/54–56°F ARE RECOMMENDED. VERY STONG ALES, SUCH AS BARLEY WINES, SHOULD BE SERVED AT ROOM TEMPERATURE. DO NOT STORE BOTTLE-CONDITIONED BEERS IN A FRIDGE. KEEP THEM COOL AND ALLOW THEM TO STAND FOR SEVERAL HOURS (A DAY IS BEST) TO ALLOW THE SEDIMENT TO CLEAR.

CHAPTER 2

The World

FANCY A BEER? IT IS ONE OF THE OLDEST INVITATIONS IN THE WORLD AND ONE THAT SETS THE TASTEBUDS TINGLING. BEER, MORE THAN ANY OTHER DRINK, MEANS CONVIVIALITY, A PLEASURE SHARED. BUT SIMPLY TO ASK FOR "A BEER" IN A BAR OR A PUB IS TO RISK MISSING OUT ON THE DIVERSITY AND THE COMPLEXITY OF STYLES AVAILABLE ON THE WORLD STAGE. IF YOU ASK FOR "A BEER" IN AN ENGLISH PUB YOU MAY BE HANDED THE STOCK BITTER OR, IF YOU'RE UNLUCKY, THE STANDARD LAGER. AN INTERESTED BARPERSON, ON THE OTHER HAND, MAY ASK YOU TO SPECIFY. PERHAPS A MILD ALE, OR A PALE ALE, OR A SPECIAL BITTER, A PORTER, A STOUT, AN OLD ALE, A BARLEY WINE OR A WINTER WARMER? YOU BEGIN TO SEE THAT BEER IS NOT SUCH A SIMPLE THING; THAT NOT ALL BROWN LIQUIDS ARE THE SAME.

In Germany it would be absurd and mildly irritating to call for "ein bier, bitte" or, even worse, "a lager", which to the Germans is a brewing term and certainly not a definition of a style. Again, you would be asked to be specific: a Helles (light), or a Dunkel (dark), a strong Bock, an export, a Pils, a Weizen (wheat) beer or the two proud and idiosyncratic warm fermenting styles of Cologne and Düsseldorf, a Kölsch or an Alt.

Belgium packs within its small territory such a manifold range of beers that a waiter confronted by the demand for just "a beer" would respond by handing you a drinks menu conveniently divided into pale ales, Trappist, Abbey beers, red beers, white beers and fruit beers – and that is just scratching the surface of the choice available.

Even in the United States, where for generations the call for "a beer" was synonymous with asking for a standardized bland, mass-marketed lager, the explo-sion of small craft breweries – 500 by 1995 and that number expected to double by the turn of the century – the beer world has been turned on its head. A bar specializing in craft beers may offer you an India Pale Ale, an amber ale, a red ale, a "London" porter or an "Irish" stout. If lager beers are the specialities, they will be far removed from a Bud or a Coors. You may get a genuine Märzen, a Bock, a Celebrator, an Oktoberfestbier, a Dunkel, a Pilsner, or a Dortmunder.

In Australia, where for decades beer drinking was epito-mized by the "six o'clock swill" – as many schooners knocked back before the shutters came down – more liberal opening hours have encouraged greater emphasis on quality and a will-ingness to experiment. Craft breweries and brewpubs may not challenge the hegemony of such mass market brands as Castlemaine and Foster's, but choice is beginning to seep across the continent. The revival of ale, personified by the doughty Adelaide firm of Cooper's, founded by an emigrant from Yorkshire, has created interest in a beer style that pre-dates the lager revolution and proves that warm-fermented beer can be enjoyed in hot climates.

In countries considered to be quintessentially within the lager fold there are surprises. In Japan you will find black beers and stouts, cold-fermented it is true, but offering welcome choice in a country where pale lagers dominate. And in pockets of Scandinavia warm-fermented porters and stouts stick their heads above the ice floes.

The world of beer is not noted for its conformity. As beer makes inroads even into great wine-making countries such as France and Italy, drinkers are discovering a multiplicity of flavours and aromas. Fasten your seat belts for a fascinating ride.

A–Z of Beer

The Beers of Europe

*E*UROPE IS THE CRADLE OF MODERN BREWING. THE LAGERING OR STORING OF BEER – USUALLY IN ICY CAVES – DEVELOPED EMPIRICALLY IN CENTRAL EUROPE FROM MEDIEVAL TIMES AND THEN SPREAD LIKE A BUSH FIRE WHEN ICE MAKING MACHINES WERE INVENTED DURING THE INDUSTRIAL REVOLUTION. THE FIRST COMMERCIAL LAGERS IN MUNICH WERE DARK IN COLOUR. IT WAS PILSEN IN BOHEMIA – TODAY'S CZECH REPUBLIC – THAT PRODUCED THE FIRST GOLDEN LAGER AND GAVE THE WORLD A STYLE KNOWN AS PILSNER OR PILS. BRITAIN AND IRELAND REMAINED FAITHFUL TO ALE: PALE ALE OR BITTER IN BRITAIN AND DARK, ROASTY DRY STOUTS IN IRELAND WHILE BELGIUM OFFERS A REMARKABLE CHOICE OF ALES, INCLUDING SOME BREWED BY TRAPPIST MONKS.

AUSTRIA

Austria lost not only a great empire but a beer style as well. Today brewers will argue there was no such thing as a Vienna style based on "red" malt but history tends to prove them wrong. In far away Mexico, briefly and incongruously ruled by Austria, red-brown lagers such as Dos Equis and Negro Modela pay homage to a style that marked Vienna out from such all-conquering neighbours as Munich and Pilsner.

Anton Dreher was one of the great brewing innovators. He worked closely with Sedlmayr in Munich to develop commercial lager brewing in the nineteenth century. While the first Munich lagers were dark brown – Dunkel – Dreher's were amber-red. His signature was achieved by the use of a type of malt similar to the crystal used by British brewers in their bitters: unkilned and damp "green" malt is heated in a sealed drum until the starches in the endosperm turn into a

Birthplace of Vienna "red" beers... master brewer Anton Dreher perfected his beer style at Schwechat

sugary syrup. The grains are then kilned at high temperature which caramelizes some of the sugars and produces a reddish-tinged malt. As a proportion of the sugars are dextrins, which cannot be fermented by brewers' yeast, the malt gives body as well as colour and a delightful chewy, nutty flavour to finished beer. The type used in lager brewing is often called "caramalt".

Vienna lager beers were first produced by Dreher around 1841 from his brewery in Schwechat in the Vienna suburbs. The brewery still exists, a remarkable group of buildings, both bucolic and baronial, parts dating back to a hunting lodge built in 1750 for Archduchess Maria Theresa, ruler of most of Europe, who is thought to have used the lodge for less than courtly purposes.

In Dreher's day, Schwechat was a vast enterprise challenging Pilsner Urquell in size. He built other breweries in Bohemia (at Michelob, a name still in use as Anheuser-Busch's premium beer in the US), in Budapest and in Trieste. The Italian brewery still bears Dreher's name though it is now owned by Heineken. In his heyday of the 1870s, with the Industrial Revolution going full bore and the world of beer turned upside down as a result of new technologies, Dreher was exporting beer far and wide. But his Vienna company went out of business in the 1930s and the style of beer he had created became just a fading memory for elderly Viennese. Today Austrian beers tend to ape the Bavarian style across the border though they do not adhere to the *Reinheitsgebot*. Corn, wheat and rice are used as adjuncts and hop rates in general are not high. The result is pale, golden lagers that tend to be malty with a sweetish edge and only light bitterness.

The Schwechat Brewery is now part of Austria's biggest group, Bräu AG, short for Osterreichische Bräu-Aktiengesellschaft – the Austrian Brewing Corporation, with head offices in Linz. **Schwechat Lager** (5.2 per cent ABV) is malty and rounded while the premium **Hopfenperle** (5.3 per cent ABV) has more hop character and a dry finish. It has no connection with the Swiss beer of the same name. Bräu AG also brews under the Kaiser and Zipfer labels. **Zipfer Urtyp** – Original – (5.4 per cent ABV) has a fine perfumy hop aroma and finish with good balancing malt.

The second biggest Austrian group is Steirische Bräuindustrie of Graz. The name means Styrian Breweries and is based in the hop-growing region of Styria, though most hops today that carry the name come from a province of the same name from the former Yugoslavia. The most assertive and characterful beers from the group are brewed under the Gösser label. **Gösser Export** is 5.0 per cent ABV, brewed with pale malt, caramalt, maize and rice, with Hallertau, Spalt, Styrian and Goldings hops (20 IBUs). With just gentle hop bitterness, the beer has a rich malt and vanilla aroma and palate with some hop notes in the bitter-sweet finish.

Stiegl in Salzburg was founded in 1492, the year

Columbus landed in the Americas. The connection is celebrated by **Columbus** (5.3 per cent ABV) a rich, malty but well-hopped lager.

Ottakringer in Vienna dates from 1837 and is still family-owned. Its beers are among the most characterful in the country due to the generous use of Saaz hops. Its **Helles** (5.1 per cent ABV) is tart, quenching and aromatic while its Gold **Fassl Spezial** (5.6 per cent ABV) has a more pronounced maltiness balanced by perfumy hops.

The small Eggenburg Brewery in the town of the same name has a beer that panders to Scotch whisky drinkers while offering a colour akin to a genuine Vienna Red. **MacQueens Nessie Whisky Malt Red Beer** is a powerful 7.5 per cent ABV with 26.7 IBUs from Hallertau hops. The malt is imported from Scotland and imparts a delicious smoky, peaty character. The colour of the beer is amber and the finish is long and smoky with hop undercurrents. "It's like a whisky and soda," according to the brewer. He also makes an **Urbock 23°**, the number referring to its strength on the Plato scale which translates into 9.3 per cent ABV. It is lagered for an impressive nine months, has a rich fruity aroma, rounded malt and hops in the mouth and a big vinous and hoppy finish. It is made from Pilsner and Munich malts and Saaz and Hallertau hops (40 IBUs).

The Josef Sigl Brewery in Obertrum keeps the wheat beer tradition alive with a top-fermenting **Weizen Gold** (5.2 per cent ABV). It is hopped with

Hallertau and has a spicy cloves aroma, a tart and refreshing palate and a lingering bitter-sweet finish.

Two brewpubs of note are the Fischer Gasthof at Billroth Strasse 17, Döbling in Vienna, which offers a Helles and a Bock. In Nüssdorf, Baron Hendrik Bachofen von Echte has a fine brewery and restaurant in the cellars of his castle. He makes top-fermenting beers, including a Helles brewed with 30 per cent wheat malt, a malty Altbier and a chocolatey and dry Irish-style stout called Sir Henry's.

AUSTRIAN BREWERS
Braueueri Eggenberg,
Eggenberg 1, 4655 Vorchdorf.
Josef Sigl Brauerei,
A-5162 Obertrum SLBG.
Steirische Bräuindustrie,
Reininghausstrasse 1-7, A-802 Graz STMK.

From the heart of hop country... Gösser of Graz enjoys the pick of the crop in Austrian Styria

Eggenburg beers have a rich hop character and its MacQueens Nessie appeals to whisky drinkers with the use of peated malt imported from Scotland

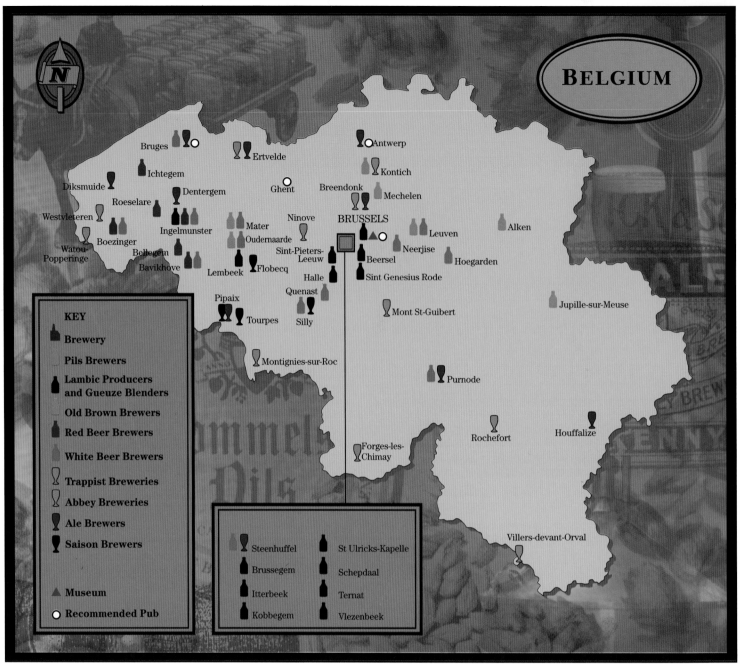

BELGIUM

KEY

- Brewery
- Pils Brewers
- Lambic Producers and Gueuze Blenders
- Old Brown Brewers
- Red Beer Brewers
- White Beer Brewers
- Trappist Breweries
- Abbey Breweries
- Ale Brewers
- Saison Brewers
- ▲ Museum
- ◯ Recommended Pub

Steenhuffel
Brussegem
Itterbeek
Kobbegem

St Ulricks-Kapelle
Schepdaal
Ternat
Vlezenbeek

BELGIUM

BELGIANS ARE PASSIONATE ABOUT BEER. IF YOU SHOW AN INTEREST IN THE SUBJECT, WAITERS OR BAR OWNERS TEND TO DIVE INTO CELLARS AND RETURN WITH DUSTY BOTTLES THEY HAVE BEEN SAVING FOR "A SPECIAL OCCASION". OFTEN THE BOTTLES ARE WRAPPED IN COLOURED TISSUE PAPER AND HAVE CHAMPAGNE-STYLE CRADLES AND CORKS. WITHOUT HESITATION OR FEAR OF BEING DERIDED, THEY WILL CALL SUCH OFFERINGS "GRAND CRU" OR THE BOURGOGNE (BURGUNDY) OF THE BEER WORLD. UNLIKE THE BRITISH, WHOSE COLLECTIVE STIFF UPPER LIP REFUSES TO ACKNOWLEDGE THAT THEY ALSO MAKE SOME AMAZING ALES, THE BELGIANS HAVE NO QUALMS ABOUT PROCLAIMING THEIR BEERS TO BE AS GOOD AS FINE WINE.

BELGIAN PILS

The choice in this small country is astonishing. But the recent revival of interest in Belgian ales – pale, golden, red, Trappist, Abbey, wheat and lambic – cannot disguise the fact that for everyday drinking the people consume vast amounts of Pilsner-style lagers. Purists may argue that only lagers from Pilsen in the Czech Republic should carry the appellation, but it cannot be said that the Belgian interpretations of the style are anything less than good. The two leading Pils brands, **Stella Artois** and **Jupiler**, come from the giant Interbrew group, the result of a 1980s merger between Stella Artois of Leuven and Piedboeuf of Jupille-sur-Meuse near Liège. The merger not only brought two leading breweries under one roof but also, as their places of origin suggest, managed to bridge the linguistic divide. Leuven – Louvain in

French – is a university city. In the sixteenth century there were 42 breweries in the city and not surprisingly the university developed a brewing faculty – the Academy of Brewing – that today offers laboratory and yeast cultivation facilities for Belgium's 150 breweries.

Stella Artois traces its origins to the Den Horen (the Horn) tavern that brewed beer from 1366 and began to supply the university from 1537. Sebastien Artois was an apprentice brewer at Den Horen, graduated as a master brewer and bought the brewery in 1717. His grandson Léonard busily expanded the business and bought two rival companies in Leuven. Den Horen Artois became one of the major commercial breweries in Europe and switched with enthusiasm to the new lagering methods in the late nineteenth century. Its first golden, cold-fermented beer was

called **Bock** but unlike German Bocks, which are high in alcohol, this was weaker than a genuine Pilsner. The company achieved greater fame and fortune in 1926 when it brewed a stronger 5.0 per cent Pils-style beer, Stella Artois, that is now Belgium's best-known – though not best-selling – Pils. It is exported widely and brewed under licence in several countries. Stella Artois is made with great dedication to traditional methods. The brewery has a six-storey maltings in Leuven, using the floor method rather than modern tanks. Brewers believe that malt spread out on warm floors and regularly turned and aerated produces a cleaner, sweeter beer. In the brewhouses – Artois once had a dozen but is consolidating them – the wort is boiled with Czech Saaz hops along with some German Northern Brewer and Tettnanger, as well as Styrians.

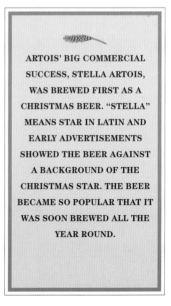

Bright star... Stella Artois started life as a Christmas beer and is now a famous international Pilsner-style lager

ARTOIS' BIG COMMERCIAL SUCCESS, STELLA ARTOIS, WAS BREWED FIRST AS A CHRISTMAS BEER. "STELLA" MEANS STAR IN LATIN AND EARLY ADVERTISEMENTS SHOWED THE BEER AGAINST A BACKGROUND OF THE CHRISTMAS STAR. THE BEER BECAME SO POPULAR THAT IT WAS SOON BREWED ALL THE YEAR ROUND.

Jupiler from the Interbrew stable is the Belgian leader in the Pils market

PRIMUS BEER IS NAMED IN HONOUR OF JAN PRIMUS, A MEDIEVAL DUKE OF BRABANT WHO HAD A GREAT CAPACITY FOR DRINKING. HIS NAME BECAME CORRUPTED TO GAMBRINUS AND HAS BEEN ADOPTED AS THE NAME FOR BREWERIES AND BEERS THROUGHOUT THE WORLD. ONE OF THE ORIGINAL BOHEMIAN PILS BREWERIES IN PILSEN IS CALLED GAMBRINUS.

The Saaz dominate, giving the finished beer (30 IBUs) an aromatic, slightly spicy aroma. Stella is lagered for around two months and is clean and quenching in the mouth with a finish that becomes dry as the hops emphasize their character. The Artois side of Interbrew also produces a stronger (5.7 per cent ABV) lager beer called **Loburg**, designed to counteract Danish "super premium" imports.

Jupiler (5.0 per cent ABV, around 25 IBUs) is the biggest-selling Pils in Belgium. The Piedboeuf family founded its brewery in 1853 in Jupille, believed to be the birthplace of Charlemagne and with a history of brewing that dates back to 1256. Jupiler's rise to popularity is impressive as it was launched as recently as 1966. It is an easy-

drinking, soft, malt-accented beer lacking the hop character of Stella. Interbrew also owns the **Lamot Pils** brand though the Lamot Brewery in Mechelen closed at the end of 1994.

Four-fifths of all Belgian Pils are accounted for by Interbrew and the second biggest brewing group, Alken-Maes, half-owned by Kronenbourg of France. **Cristal Alken** is the Pils favoured by connoisseurs. It was formulated in 1928 to suit the tastes of miners in the Limburg region. As a result it is more aggressively hoppy than other leading Belgian Pils. Alken is close to the German border and it could be the German Pils brewing tradition that has prompted Alken to make its beer a shade dryer and more positively bitter, though the brewers who formulated the beer claimed they were attempting to recreate a genuine Czech Pilsner.

Alken's partner, Maes (pronounced "Marse") is based in Flemish-speaking Waarloos near Antwerp. In common with Limburg, this was once a heavy industrial area and there were some mighty thirsts to quench. **Maes Pils** first appeared in 1946 with some help from a German brewer. The company survived a period of ownership by the British Watney group and retains a magnificent copper brewhouse. Brewing is firmly traditional, with a double decoction mash using mainly Czech malt, more Czech influence in the Saaz hops in the copper, and a slow, cool, two-to-three months' lagering.

There are around 100 Pils brands in Belgium. Even some specialist ale brewers also produce a Pils in order to have a

small slice of the substantial market. The most highly regarded Pils from a smaller brewer comes from Haacht near a village of the same name that is roughly equidistant from Brussels, Leuven and Mechelen. The Pils is called **Primus** and is a complex beer with a sweetish start leading to a refreshing palate and a dry finish with good hop influence. French and Dutch malts are joined by the ubiquitous Saaz and German varieties of hops.

SELECTED PILS BREWERS
Alken, Alken-Maes, Stationstraat 2, 3820 Alken.
Maes, Alken-Maes, Waarloosveld 10, 2571 Kontich-Waarloos.
Haacht Brouwerij, Provinciesteenweg 28, 2890 Boortmeerbeek.
Brasserie Jupiler, Interbrew, rue de Vise 243, 4500 Jupille-sur-Meuse.
Stella Artois, Interbrew, Vaartstraat 94, 3000 Leuven.

LAMBIC

Lambic, a beer produced by spontaneous fermentation as a result of action by air-borne yeasts, is a potent link with brewing's past. Before brewers understood the mysteries of yeast and tamed it to dance to their tune, they allowed wild strains either in the air or in brewing vessels to attack malt sugars and turn them into alcohol. With the aid of science and technology, ale brewers and later lager producers turned their back on such antiquated methods and produced their beers with the aid of carefully cultured yeast strains.

In the Payottenland area of Belgium centred on the Senne valley (Zenne in Flemish) a handful of dedicated brewers has remained faithful to a tradition that produces beers which, with their tart, vinous and even cidery characteristics, seem to break down all the barriers between cereal-based and fruit-based alcoholic drinks. They hark back to a period when all alcoholic drinks were bucolic, peasant

ones, made from the raw ingredients to hand in the surrounding fields.

Lambic (sometimes spelt "lambik") is the world's oldest beer style still made on a regular commercial basis. It has existed for some 400 years and it is fitting that its area of production almost exactly matches that part of Belgium dubbed by the tourist board "the Bruegel Route". For the paintings of the Bruegels, Pieter the Elder in particular, personify a rural idyll in which the consumption of a rough ale called lambic was at the heart of family and communal life. The recent revival of interest in lambic and its off-shoots – gueuze, faro, mars, kriek and frambozen – has prompted both the Belgian government and the European Union to protect the style and to lay down strict rules for its production.

Lambic is a country beer style. It declined as industry sprang up and the great city of

Brussels expanded into the Senne valley. City dwellers switched first to strong ales brewed in the conventional manner and then to the new Pilsner beers. Although two of the remaining lambic brewers are based in Brussels – Belle-Vue, owned by Interbrew, and the smaller craft brewery of Cantillon – it remains a rustic beer in its methods of production. As with farm brewers of earlier times, brewing does not take place during the summer months because of the impossibility of controlling the temperature of a spontaneously fermenting ale.

In order to qualify as a genuine lambic, the beer must be brewed with at least 30 per cent wheat in the mash. Unlike a classic Bavarian wheat beer, the wheat in a lambic is unmalted. Busy farmers understood that barley malt provided sufficient enzymes to convert starch to sugar without the need to malt their wheat as well. The barley malt is as pale as Pilsner malt. With the addition of wheat, the resulting mash is cloudy and milky white. The starting gravity is around 1050 degrees with a finished ABV of 4.5 to 5.0 per cent.

The hop rate is high but the hops used are four years old. They have lost their aromatic quality and have a deliberate "cheesy" smell. The varieties are used primarily for their antiseptic qualities. Lambic brewers

discovered, along with wheat beer producers in other regions, that the tart nature of fresh hops does not blend well with the spicy, fruity and slightly lactic character of wheat beer.

When the copper boil is over, brewing is left to nature. The hopped wort is pumped to a shallow, open fermenting vessel known as a "cool ship". The ship is always high in the roof of the brewery. Louvred windows are left open and a few tiles are even removed from the roof. During the night yeasts come in on the breeze and attack the inviting malt sugars in the ship.

After spontaneous fermentation, the green beer is transferred to oak casks where it is attacked by microflora. In the cellars cobwebs and spiders abound, as nothing must be done to alter the eco-structure. Spiders are important as they attack fruit flies which would otherwise feast on the beers, especially those to which fruit is added. The casks, made mainly from wood with a few of chestnut, are bought from port producers in Portugal. Belle-Vue,

> THE ORIGINS OF THE NAME LAMBIC ARE OBSCURE. IT COULD COME FROM THE VILLAGE OF LEMBEEK IN THE SENNE VALLEY, WHICH HAS HAD A BREWERS' GUILD SINCE THE FIFTEENTH CENTURY AND A SHRINE TO THE PATRON SAINT OF LAMBIC, SAINT VERONUS. AN ALTERNATIVE THEORY IS THAT THE WORD CAME ORIGINALLY FROM THE SPANISH. WHEN THE SPANIARDS CONQUERED THE LOW COUNTRIES THEY CALLED FARM BREWERIES AND DISTILLERIES THERE "ALEMBICS".

Cantillon is the classic lambic brewer in Belgium. The use of the Manneken Pis statue does little for the image of a brewery dedicated to style and ingredients

Cantillon's Kriek – cherry beer – uses the whole cherries and nothing but the whole cherries. The brewery scorns other makers who use fruit essence

THE ACADEMY OF BREWING AT LEUVEN UNIVERSITY HAS ISOLATED TWO MAIN STRAINS OF *BRETTANOMYCES* YEAST IN LAMBIC BREWING. THEY ARE CALLED *BRUXELLENSIS* AND *LAMBICUS*. THE TOTAL NUMBER OF STRAINS IN THE CELLARS AND INSIDE THE MATURATION VESSELS COMES TO 35.

the biggest producer of lambic, has 15,000 casks on five floors, ranging in size from 250 litres to 30 hectolitres.

Wild *Brettanomyces* yeasts give what brewers call a "horse-blanket" aroma to ale, a grainy, slightly musty character. But it takes some time for *Brettanomyces* to dominate other microflora active in lambic. The beer will stay and mature in cask for a few months, in some cases for as long as six years. A young lambic is yeasty and immature, and even after a year the beer will still have some "cheesiness" from the hops. At 18 months the beer takes on a sherry colour and *Brettanomyces* has started to dominate the aroma. An aged lambic of six years will have a pronounced vinous aroma, a deep sherry character in the mouth, and a sour and lactic finish.

GUEUZE

Lambic is usually served on draught and its most widely available form is known as gueuze. To counteract the green flavours of young lambic, gueuze is a blend of mature and young brews. The mature lambic gives gloss, depth, and a tart vinous

character to the beer while the young, which contains unfermented malt sugars, causes a second fermentation in the bottle. The blend is usually 60 per cent young to 40 per cent mature. The bottles are stoppered with Champagne corks and laid down horizontally in cellars for between six and 18 months. When a bottle is opened, the ale rushes, foaming into the glass: it is truly the Champagne of the beer world. As more alcohol has been produced during the bottle-conditioning, a gueuze will have around 5.5 per cent ABV. It is tart, cidery and refreshing. Some gueuze makers have tended to sweeten their beers in order to reach a wider but less appreciative audience and the resurgence of interest in the style has concentrated brewers' minds. In 1993, Belle-Vue responded to its critics by launching a **Séléction Lambic**, a bottle-conditioned gueuze of 5.2 per cent ABV with an intriguing aroma of roast chestnuts, sour and quenching in the mouth and with a dry and fruity finish. It was immediately awarded an appellation contrôlée by the European Beer Consumers' Union. As Belle-Vue, which also produces lambic under the De Neve label, dominates the market, its refound enthusiasm for traditional gueuze has helped to give credibility and longevity to the style.

THE ORIGIN OF THE NAME GUEUZE IS EQUALLY AS ELUSIVE AS LAMBIC. IT MAY COME FROM "GEYSER", AS THE BEER FOAMS AND GUSHES WHEN IT IS POURED INTO A GLASS. IN BRUSSELS IT IS PRONOUNCED EMPHATICALLY AS "GERSER".

KRIEK AND FRAMBOZEN

In a world where there is a sharp but wholly absurd dividing line between beer and wine, a "fruit beer" sounds bizarre, but the origins of fruit beer are functional and sensible. Before the hop was adopted both to make beer bitter and to act as a preservative, country brewers used all manner of herbs and spices to balance the malty sweetness of their brews. Brewers in the Low Countries found that cherries, which grow in abundance, added a further fermentation to their brews, increasing the level of alcohol and imparting a pleasing tartness. Fruit marries especially well with wheat beers, with their fruity flavours in which apple and banana predominate.

Kriek is the Flemish word for cherry. Raspberry beers are called both framboise in French and frambozen in Flemish. The preferred cherry is the small, hard Schaarbeek that grows around Brussels. Rather like "noble rot" grapes, the cherries are picked late so that the fermentable sugars are well developed. The cherries are not crushed but the skins are lightly broken and added at the rate of one kilo of cherries to five kilos of beer in the lambic cellars. Some young lambic is also added. The fruit sugars and the young beer encourage a new fermentation and the skins of the cherries add dryness to the beer. As fermentation proceeds, the yeasts even attack the pips which impart an almost almond-like quality. You can tell which casks in the cellar contain cherries as the brewers place some twigs in the open bung hole. These stop the cherries floating to the top of the beer, blocking the bung and preventing attack by fruit flies.

Fruit beers improve and deepen with age. A young kriek, with its luscious pink colour, will offer an aroma and palate of fruit whereas a year-old version will have developed a sour palate and a long, dry finish. At 18 months, a kriek will have taken on earthy, vinous characteristics. A frambozen of around one year will have a delicate perfumy aroma, bitter-sweet fruit in the mouth with a spritzy, refreshing finish.

The small craft lambic brewery of Cantillon in Brussels produces a magnificent range of beers. Its classic is considered to be **Rosé de Gambrinus**, a blend of kriek and frambozen. The brewery has further blurred the distinction between beer and wine by making a lambic that uses grapes as well as cereals. Cantillon has regular open days where visitors can taste the beers and see the brewing vessels. Cantillon and some of the other lambic brewers also occasionally make faro, a lambic produced by remashing the grains of the first brew and adding candy sugar to encourage fermentation. **Faro** is drunk on draught at around 4.0 per cent ABV as a good refreshing beer. The even lower-alcohol mars is no longer made.

LAMBIC PRODUCERS AND GUEUZE BLENDERS

Belgor Brouwerij,
Kerkstraat 17, 1881 Brussegem.

Belle-Vue,
Rue Delaunoy 58, 1080 Brussels. Owned by Interbrew: lambic, gueuze, kriek and frambozen.

Frank Boon BV,
Fonteinstraat 65, 1520 Lembeek: lambic, gueuze, kriek, frambozen and faro.

Cantillon Brouwerij,
Gheudestraat 56, 1070 Brussels: lambic, gueuze, kriek, frambozen and faro.

De Keersmaeker Brouwerij,
Brusselstraat 1, 1703 Kobbegem (owned by Alken-Maes, brews under the Morte Subite and Eylenbosch names): lambic, gueuze, kriek, frambozen and faro.

De Koninck Gueuzestekerij,
Kerstraat 57, 1512 Dworp (not related to De Konick of Antwerp): gueuze and kriek.

De Troch Brouwerij,
Langestraat 20, 1741 Ternat-Wambeck: lambic, gueuze and faro.

De Neve Brouwerij,
Isabellastraat 52, 1750 Schepdaal. Owned by Interbrew and linked to Belle-Vue; similar range of products.

Drie Fonteinen,
H. Teirlinckplein 3, 1650 Beersel: lambic, gueuze, kriek and frambozen.

Girardin Brouwerij,
Lindenberg 10, 1744 Sint-Ulriks-Kapelle: lambic, gueuze and kriek.

Hanssens Gueuzetekerij,
Vroenenbosstraat 8, 1512 Dworp: gueuze and kriek.

Lindemans Brouwerij,
Lenniniksebaan 257, 1712 Vlezenbeek: lambic, gueuze, kriek and frambozen.

Moriau Gueuzestekerij,
Hoogstraat 1, 1600 Sint Pieters-Leeuw: lambic, gueuze and kriek.

Timmermans NV,
Kerkstraat 11, 1711 Itterbeek: lambic, gueuze, kriek and frambozen.

Vander Linden Brouwerij,
Brouwerijstraat 2, 1500 Halle: lambic, gueuze, kriek, frambozen and faro.

Vandervelden Brouwerij,
Laarheidestraat 230, 1650 Beersel: lambic, gueuze and kriek.

Van Honsebrouck Brouwerij,
Oostrozebekestraat 43, 8770 Ingelmunster (produces lambic and fruit beers under the St Louis name: uses mainly syrups, not whole fruit.)

Wets Gueuzestekerij,
Steenweg op Halle 203, 1640 Sint Genesius Rode: gueuze, kriek and faro.

Back in the fold... Interbrew's Belle-Vue Brewery in Brussels made sweet and sticky versions of lambic and kriek but has found favour with new and more traditional versions

Liefman's of Oudenaarde brews a classic "old brown" beer, versions of which have cherries and raspberries added. The bottles are stylishly presented in tissue wrappings

BROWN ALE

The historic waterside Flemish city of Oudenaarde and the surrounding area are the home of brown ales. The best known of the **Old Brown (Oud Bruin)** ales come from Liefman's, a brewery dating from 1679. The fame of Liefman's spread in the 1970s when the owner died and the company was taken over by his former secretary, Rose Blancquaert-Merckx, known as "Madame Rose". With her son Olav she expanded the business and won worldwide acclaim for her brews. Madame Rose has now retired and Liefman's was bought by the Riva group in the early 1990s.

The brewing water of the region adds a special character to local beers. It is low in calcium and high in sodium bicarbonate, which suggests beers using the liquor are good for the digestion and may help explain their appeal to chefs. The basic Old Brown is brewed from a blend of Pilsner, Munich and Vienna malts and a little roasted barley. Hops are English Goldings, with some Czech and German varieties. The slow copper boil lasts for 12 hours. The 5.0 per cent ABV beer is fermented for seven days in open vessels and is then matured for four months. A stronger, 6.0 per cent ABV, version called **Goudenband** (Gold Riband) is a blend of the basic beer with one that has matured for six to eight months. The blend is primed with sugar, re-seeded with yeast and stored for three months. Goudenband can be laid down and will improve for several years, taking on a dark, sherry-like wineyness.

Once a year Liefman's makes both a kriek and a frambozen from fresh cherries and raspberries, with the basic oud bruin. The beers are stored and refermented for up to two months. The 7.1 per cent ABV Liefman's kriek has a delectable dry and tart fruitiness while the 5.1 per cent ABV frambozen has a lilting aroma of fresh fruit and is bittersweet on the palate. All the Liefman's beers come in tissue-wrapped bottles.

As a result of being incorporated into the Riva group, the Liefman's beers are now mashed and boiled at Riva's main brewery at Dentergem. The wort is then trunked to Oudenaarde for fermentation and maturation, where Olav Blancquaert remains firmly in charge. Riva also brews brown ales at its Het Anker brewery in Mechelen, a dry 5.5 per cent ABV **Bruynen** and the rich, chocolatey **Gouden Carolus**, a bottle-conditioned 7.8 per cent ABV dark ale full of spicy and fruity character. Among other brown ale brewers, the splendidly artisanal Roman, which dates from 1545, has a chocolatey 5.0 per cent ABV **Oudenaards** and an 8.0 per cent ABV **Dobbelen Bruinen** (double brown) packed with dark malt and hop flavours.

OLD BROWN BREWERS

Clarysse Brouwerij,
Krekelput 16-18, 9700 Oudenaarde.

Cnudde Brouwerij,
Fabriekstraat 8, 9700 Eine.

Het Anker Brouwerij,
Guido Gezellaan 49, 2800 Mechelen.

Liefman's Brouwerij,
Aalstraat 200, 9700 Oudenaarde.

Roman Brouwerij,
Hauwaert 61, 9700 Mater.

RED ALE

If the brown ales of East Flanders are a rare style, the sour red beers of West Flanders are even more esoteric. They are beers that are matured for long periods in unlined oak vats where micro-organisms attack the malt sugars and add a lactic sourness. Such beers are yet another fascinating link with brewing's past, when beers were deliberately "staled" and were then blended with younger ales. The major producer of sour red ale is Rodenbach of Roeselare. The Rodenbachs came from Koblenz in Germany. Alexander Rodenbach bought a small brewery in Roeselare in 1820.

The St George's Brewery in Roeselare is supplied with

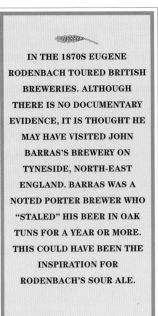

IN THE 1870S EUGENE RODENBACH TOURED BRITISH BREWERIES. ALTHOUGH THERE IS NO DOCUMENTARY EVIDENCE, IT IS THOUGHT HE MAY HAVE VISITED JOHN BARRAS'S BREWERY ON TYNESIDE, NORTH-EAST ENGLAND. BARRAS WAS A NOTED PORTER BREWER WHO "STALED" HIS BEER IN OAK TUNS FOR A YEAR OR MORE. THIS COULD HAVE BEEN THE INSPIRATION FOR RODENBACH'S SOUR ALE.

brewing water from underground springs beneath a lake in the grounds of the brewer's stately home. The brewery site is dominated by an old malt kiln now used as a museum. Beer is made from a blend of pale malts, both spring and winter varieties, and darker Vienna malt. Vienna malt is similar to English crystal and adds both the red/copper hue and body to the beer. Malt accounts for 80 per cent of the grist, the rest made up of corn grits. The hops are Brewers' Gold and East Kent Goldings, used primarily for their aroma. Too much bitterness would not marry well with the tartness of the beer. Primary fermentation takes seven days and is followed by a second fermentation in metal tanks. The "regular" **Rodenbach**, 4.6 per cent ABV, is bottled after six weeks and is a blend of young and mature beers. Beer destined for ageing is stored in tall oak tuns for a minimum of 18 months and as long as two years.

As the beer matures in the wood, *lactobacilli* and *acetobacters* add a sour and lactic flavour to the beer. The blended beer has a sour, vinous aroma, is tart in the mouth with more sour fruit in the finish. **Grand Cru**, bottled straight from the tuns, is 5.2 per cent ABV and 14 to 18 units of bitterness. It is bigger in body and flavour than the blended beer: woody, tannic, sour and fruity. Both beers have some sugar added to take the edge off the sourness and they are pasteurized. Devotees plead with Rodenbach to produce an unsweetened, bottle-conditioned Grand Cru. There is also a version of Grand Cru known as

Alexander Rodenbach to which cherry essence is added: yet another Belgian fruit beer.

Among smaller West Flanders breweries, **Bavik Petrus Oud Bruin**, 5.5 per cent ABV, is fermented in oak casks for 20 months and then blended with young beer. The brewery also produces a 7.5 per cent ABV **Triple Petrus**.

RED BEER BREWERS
Bavik-De Brabandere,
Rijksweg 16a, 8752 Bavikhove.
Bockor Brouwerij,
Kwabrugestraat 5, 8540 Bellegem (Ouden Tripel).
Leroy Brouwerij,
Diksmuidesweg 406, 8930 Boezinge (Paulus).
Rodenbach Brouwerij,
Spanjestraat 133, 880 Roeselare.
Strubbe Brouwerij,
Markt 1, 8270 Ichtegem (Ichtegems Oud Bruin).
Van Honsebrouck Brouwerij,
Oostrozebekestraat 43, 8770 Ingelmunster (Bacchus).

WHITE BEER

When Pierre Celis decided to brew a "white beer" in the 1960s he had no idea he would spark a small revolution in Belgium. For today white beers (bière blanche/witbier) have become cult drinks, not least among the young. Celis revived a beer style that was once very important in the Low Countries, and to do so he chose the small town of Hoegaarden near Leuven, where there had been 30 white beer producers in the nineteenth century. All had disappeared as a result of the onslaught of lager brewing. The region of Brabant, with rich soil that produces

barley, oats and wheat in abundance, encouraged farmers, peasants and monks to brew: monks were brewing in Brabant from as early as the fifteenth century. Herbs and spices were added to the brews to balance the sweetness of the grains.

White beer is wheat beer, a member of the ale family, brewed by top or warm fermentation: centuries ago it was fermented spontaneously. The grist is a 50:50 blend of barley malt and unmalted wheat. Pierre Celis used oats as well in his early days but they are no longer used. The units of bitterness in Hoegaarden are around 20: the brewer is not looking for excessive bitterness. The varieties are East Kent Goldings for aroma and Czech Saaz for gentle bitterness. Coriander seeds and orange peel

Rodenbach's striking old maltings is now a brewery museum

Hoegaarden white – wheat – beer has become a cult drink among the young of Belgium

are milled to coarse powders and added with the hops to the copper boil. After fermentation the green beer is conditioned for a month, primed with sugar, re-seeded with yeast and then bottled or kegged. **Hoegaarden** is 4.2 per cent ABV and has a rich, appetizing spicy nose with a clear hint of orange. It is tart and refreshing in the mouth followed by a clean, bitter-sweet finish. It will improve with age for around six months and takes on a smooth, honey-like character. Hoegaarden is served in a heavy, chunky glass and is cloudy from the yeast and protein left in suspension. The beer is a pale lemon colour with a dense white head of foam.

Among other wheat beer producers, the Riva group gives prominence to its **Dentergems Witbier** (5.0 per cent ABV), made without spices but with a pleasing apple-fruitiness. The Wallonian brewers have not been slow to spot a large niche in the market. Du Bocq's **Blanche de Namur** (4.5 per cent ABV) is named after a princess from the region (Snow White?) who became queen of Sweden. The beer has a herbal aroma and palate, while the small Silly Brewery's **Titje** (5.0 per cent ABV) is uncompromis-ingly spicy, tart and quenching.

WHITE BEER BREWERS
Bavik-De Brabandere,
Rijksweg 16a, 8752 Bavihove.
Brasserie Du Bocq,
Rue de la Brasserie 4, 5191 Purnode.
Brouwerij Riva,
Wontergemstraat 42, 8720 Dentergem.

Clarysse Brouwerij,
Krekelput 16-18, 9700 Oudenaarde.
De Gouden Boom Brouwerij,
Langestraat 45, 8000 Bruges.
Haacht Brouwerij,
Provinciesteenweg 28, 2980 Boortmeerbeek.
De Kluis Brouwerij,
Stoopkenstraat 46, 3320 Hoegaarden.
De Kroon Brouwerij,
Beekstraat 8, 3055 Neerijse.
Domus Brouwerij,
Tiensestraat 8, 3000 Leuven.
Brasserie Lefèbvre SA,
Rue de Croly 52, 1381 Quenast.
Leroy Brouwerij,
Diksmuideswg 406, 8930 Boezinge.
Palm Brouwerij,
Steenhuffeldorp 3, 2901 Steenhuffel (Steendonk Witbier).
Roman Brouwerij,
Hauwaert 61, 9700 Mater.
Brasserie de Silly,
Ville Basse A141, 7830 Silly.
Van Honsebrouck Brouwerij,
Oostrozebekestraat 43, 8770 Ingelmunster.

TRAPPIST ALES

When Trappist monks were hounded from France during the French Revolution they stoically headed north into the Low Countries to establish new centres of religious devotion. Their simple life included eating the produce from the surrounding fields and making their own alcohol to sustain them during Lent and to help keep them healthy. In France they had made wine liqueurs. In the Low Countries the absence of grapes forced them to make beer from cereals. Thus was born one of the world's great beer styles.

The encroaching secular life has closed many of the abbeys in the Low Countries. Today just five abbeys in Belgium and one in the Netherlands still make beer and they need help from lay brewers to sustain produc-tion. Unless sufficient numbers of young people can be attracted to the austere way of life, there is a real fear that true Trappist beers could cease to exist.

Chimay is by far the most famous of the Belgian Trappist breweries. Its ales are sold worldwide. The success of Chimay is a fascinating example of God and Mammon pooling their resources: the monks are in charge of brewing but a few miles from their abbey in a complex of utilitarian buildings a large secular staff skilfully markets their beers.

Chimay once had a fine, traditional copper brewhouse but expansion and demand led to a new functional modern plant being installed. Most of the vessels are behind tiled walls. The monks, following a dispensa-tion from the Vatican, are now allowed to talk but are disap-pointingly close-mouthed about the ingredients they use. The local water is soft and acidic and

Orval produces just one Trappist ale of awesome complexity and depth of flavours. Chimay (right) is the most famous of the Belgian Trappist brewers

is not treated for brewing. It is thought that malts are a blend of Pils and caramalt, with candy sugar used in the copper. German hops, possibly Hallertau, are blended, surprisingly, with some American Yakima. All the beers are primed with sugar for bottling. The three beers produced are known by the colour of their caps. **Chimay Red** is the original beer, 7.0 per cent ABV. It is copper-coloured with a fruity nose – blackcurrant is the dominant aroma – and great peppery and citric hop bitterness. Red is also known as **Première** when it is in large, Bordeaux-style bottles. **Chimay Blue** is 9.0 per cent ABV and is called **Grande Réserve** in large bottles. It has great depth of complex flavours, with spice and fruit from the hops and yeast. Dark malts give it a vinous character. **Chimay White** (8.0 per cent ABV) is sharply different to red and blue. It was first brewed in 1968 and, although the monks deny it, it is widely believed that white was introduced as a competitor to the beer from the nearby abbey of Orval. In common with all the true Trappist ales, Chimay's are bottle-conditioned. They will improve with age, red and blue taking on a port-wine character. They should be served at room temperature.

The Abbaye de Notre-Dame d'Orval is in the Belgian province

> TRAPPIST MONKS TAKE THEIR NAME FROM THE ABBEY THEY FOUNDED AT LA TRAPPE IN NORMANDY. THE TRAPPISTS WERE A BREAKAWAY FROM THE BENEDICTINES WHO IN TURN HAD SPLIT FROM THE CISTERCIANS.

of Luxembourg and is unusual in producing just one beer. The first abbey was built by Benedictines in 1070, but it was sacked and rebuilt several times: the present buildings date from the 1920s and 1930s. **Orval Trappist** ale is made from pale malt and caramalt, with candy sugar in the copper. German Hallertau and East Kent Goldings are the hop varieties: the brother brewers prize the earthy/peppery aromas of Goldings. The 5.2 per cent ABV beer in a club-shaped bottle has 40 units of bitterness. Following primary fermentation with an ale yeast, the beer has a second one lasting from six to seven weeks using several strains of lager yeast, circulating over a bed of Goldings. The beer is then bottled and seeded with the original ale yeast, which creates a third ferment. Not surprisingly, it is a highly complex ale, spicy with tart and quenching fruit, the finish becoming dry and dominated by hops.

Rochefort ales come from the Abbaye de Notre-Dame de Saint-Rémy in the Ardennes. There are three beers brewed from pale Pils and darker Munich malts, with dark candy sugar in the copper. Hop varieties are German Hallertau and Styrian Goldings. The beers are labelled Six, Eight and Ten from a now-defunct method of measuring alcohol. **Rochefort**

Six is 7.5 per cent ABV, pale brown in colour and with a soft, fruity and slightly herbal palate. **Rochefort Eight** (9.2 per cent ABV) is a rich and rounded ale, copper-coloured with a dark fruit character that recalls dates and raisins. **Rochefort Ten** is a mighty 11.3 per cent ABV. Hops meld with dark fruit, nuts and chocolate. The brothers point out that the strength of their beers and their malty/fruity character developed from their use as "liquid bread" during fasting.

There are two Trappist breweries in Flemish-speaking area. Westmalle ales comes from the Abdij der Trappisten north of Antwerp. The 9.0 per cent ABV **Tripel** is as pale as a Pils with just 13 units of colour, with 35 to 38 IBUs. The monks use French and Bavarian pale malts with Czech, German and Styrian hops. Candy

Westmalle, one of two Trappist breweries in the Flemish-speaking area, makes powerful ales with great hop character

Saintly ploughman's... several of the Trappist breweries, including Orval, also make cheese. Some use the brothers' ales in their recipes

> ORVAL IS A CORRUPTION OF D'OR VAL, THE GOLDEN VALLEY. ACCORDING TO LEGEND, A TUSCAN PRINCESS LOST HER RING IN A LAKE IN THE VALLEY AND VOWED TO BUILD AN ABBEY THERE IF THE RING WERE RETURNED TO HER. A TROUT BROKE THE SURFACE OF THE WATER WITH THE RING IN ITS MOUTH: THE IMAGE IS NOW THE LOGO OF THE BREWERY.

sugar is also added to the copper. The beer has a secondary fermentation in tanks lasting from one to three months and is then primed with sugar and yeast for bottle conditioning.

The Abdij Sint Sixtus in the hamlet of Westvleteren near Ypres (Ieper) is the smallest of the Trappist breweries and the least accessible. Visits are difficult but the full range of beers can be enjoyed in the Café De Vrede across the road. There is a malty/spicy **Green** corked **Dubbel** (4.0 per cent ABV), a **Red** (6.2 per cent ABV), fruity and hop-peppery, and the **Blue Extra** (8.4 per cent ABV) with great warming fruit and alcohol. The 10.6 **Abbot** is an explosion of raspberry and strawberry fruits (from the yeast, not from actual fruit) with a deceptively smooth drinkability.

TRAPPIST BREWERS
Abbaye de Notre-Dame d'Orval, 6823 Villers-devant-Orval.
Abbaye de Notre-Dame de St Rémy, rue de l'Abbaye 8, 5430 Rochefort.
Abbaye de Notre-Dame de Scourmont, rue de la Trappe 294, 6438 Forges-les-Chimay.
Abdij Trappisten van Westmalle, Antwerpsesteenweg 496, 2140 Malle.
Abdij Sint Sixtus, Donkerstraat 12, 8983 Westvleteren.

ABBEY BEERS

Abbey beers are modelled on Trappist ones. The original idea was a reasonable, even noble one: monks who no longer had the resources – money as well as manpower – licensed a commercial brewer to produce beer for them. But the success of genuine Trappist ales has encouraged scores of breweries to produce abbey beers, diluting the style as well as the intention.

> SOME OF THE TRAPPIST BREWERS, INCLUDING CHIMAY, ORVAL AND ROCHEFORT, ALSO SELL SOFT, CREAMY CHEESES, INCLUDING SOME MADE WITH THEIR BEERS.

The Norbertine abbey of Leffe has not brewed since the Napoleonic wars – the brothers struck a deal with the local brewer to make beers for them. In the way of the modern secular world, the brewery was taken over and Leffe beers finally ended up controlled by Interbrew and produced at its Mont St-Guibert plant. The abbey of Grimbergen, once in the country and now in the northern suburbs of Brussels, has followed a similar fate: its beers are now brewed by Maes, a subsidiary of Kronenbourg of France. The beers from the Benedictine abbey of Maredsous south of Namur are produced by the Moortgat Brewery in Breendonk.

The best of the Leffe beers is the bottle-conditioned **Triple** (8.4 per cent ABV) which was brewed for a time by De Kluis of Hooegaarden. As the future of the Mont St-Guibert plant is in doubt it cannot be said with certainty where the Leffe range will next turn up, though it will not be an abbey. Triple is golden in colour with an appealing citric lemon from the hops on the nose and palate and an aromatic finish. **Vieille Cuvée** (7.8 per cent ABV) is a one-dimensional darker ale while the 8.5 per cent ABV **Radieuse** has a strong hop presence.

Grimbergen beers, perhaps unintentionally mimicking the style of Benedictine liqueurs, are sweet in the mouth. The 10.00 per cent ABV **Optimo Bruno** is a deep amber colour with a pear-drop character on the palate. The 6.1 per cent ABV **Tripel** is darker and its aroma and palate are dominated by sweet fruits. The 6.2 per cent ABV **Dubbel** is copper-coloured with toffee and vanilla on the palate.

The Corsendonk range of abbey ales is brewed for the priory at Turnhout by Bios and Du Bocq. The 8.1 per cent ABV **Agnus Dei** has good citric lemon notes from the hops and more hop perfume in the finish. The 7.0 per cent ABV **Pater Noster** has a pleasant chocolate-and-raisins character.

SELECTED ABBEY BREWERS
Brasserie de l'Abbaye des Rocs, Chaussée Brunehaut 37, 7383 Montignies-sur-Roc. (Despite the name, this is a micro-brewery; there is no abbey on the site.)

Bios, Brouwerij van Steenberghe,
Lindenlaan 25, 9068 Ertvelde.
Maes,
Waarloosveld 10, 2571
Kontich-Waarloos.
Moortgat Brouwerij,
Breendonkdorp 58, 2659
Breendonk.
Sint Bernardus Brouwerij,
Trappistenweg 23, 8978
Watou-Poperinge. Licensed by
St-Sixtus to brew under its
name.
Brasserie St-Guibert,
rue de Riquau 1, 5870 Mont
St-Guibert.
Slaghmuylder Brouwerij,
Denderhoutembaan 2, 9400
Ninove.

ALES

The most famous of Belgium's
pale ales is **Duvel**. It looks like a
lager and many think it is
pronounced, in the French
manner, "Duvelle". But it is top-
fermented and is pronounced
Doovul in the Flemish manner.
The golden beer dates only from
the 1970s, but the Moortgat
(Moorgate) Brewery
was founded in
1871 as a
specialist ale
producer. When
sales of Pilsner
beers started to
take off in Belgium,
Moortgat remained
true to ales but
introduced Duvel
alongside its darker brews to
expand and protect its market.
Two-row Belgian and French
barleys are specially malted for
Duvel, which has a colour rating
of seven to eight, only a fraction
more than for a Pilsner. The
brewing process is complex and
intriguing. The ale is infusion-

mashed in the traditional
manner. Saaz and Golding hops
are added to the copper boil in
three stages to produce between
29 and 31 units of bitterness.
Dextrose is added before
primary fermentation to give
body to the beer. Two strains of
yeast are used in the first stage
of fermentation: the hopped wort
is split into two batches, which
are fermented by two different
yeast strains. A second fermentation takes place during cold
conditioning, which lasts for a
month. It is then primed with
dextrose and re-seeded with
yeast to encourage a third
fermentation in the bottle. The
end result is a beer of 8.5 per
cent ABV. It throws such a
dense, fluffy head that it has to
be poured into a large tulip-
shaped glass to contain both
foam and liquid. Duvel is such an
enormous success that several
rivals have been launched with
similar names, including **Judas**
from Alken-Maes, **Joker** from
Roman and **Rascal**
from du Bocq.
Belgium's biggest
selling pale ale is
Palm (5.2 per
cent ABV),
brewed by a
family-run
brewery in
Steenhuffel.
Spéciale Palm
has a citric aroma
from the hops, is bitter and
quenching in the mouth and has
a fruity/hoppy finish.

Antwerp is home to a superb
ale rightly called **De Koninck** –
"the king" (5.0 per cent ABV).
The brewery began life in 1833
as a brewpub and its owners
have resisted any suggestion that

they should move from ale to
lager. The copper colour of De
Koninck comes from pale and
Vienna malts. No sugars are used
in the brewing process. Saaz
hops are added three times
during the copper boil. Following
fermentation the beer has two
weeks' cold conditioning.

SELECTED ALE BREWERS
Bios, Brouwerij van Steenberghe,
Lindenplaan 25, 9068 Ertvelde
(Piraat, 9.7 per cent ABV).
De Block Brouwerij,
Nieuwbaan 92, 1880 Peizegem
(Satan Gold, 8.0 per cent ABV).
Brasserie du Bocq,
rue de la Brasserie 4, 5191
Purnode (St Benoit Blonde, 8.0
per cent ABV; Gauloise, 9.0
per cent ABV).
De Koninck Brouwerij,
Mechelsesteenweg 291, 2018
Antwerp.
Moortgat Brouwerij,
Breendonkdorp 58, 2659
Breendonk.
Palm Brouwerij,
Steenhuffeldorp 3, 2901
Steenhuffel.
Riva Brouwerij,
Wontergenstraat 42,
8898 Dentergem (Lucifer,
8.0 per cent ABV).
Straffe Hendrik,
Walplein 26, 800 Bruges
(Bruges Straffe Hendrik,
5.4 per cent ABV).

WALLONIA
Brewers in the French-
speaking region of Belgium
complain that, with the exception of the Trappist ales, their
contributions are overshadowed
by those from the Flemish areas.
But the saison or seasonal ales
of Wallonia are worthy of
respect, a beer style in their own

DUVEL MEANS "DEVIL" IN
FLEMISH. THE NAME IS SAID
TO HAVE BEEN INSPIRED BY A
BREWERY WORKER WHO
TASTED IT WHEN IT WAS
FIRST BREWED AND
DECLARED: "THIS IS A DEVIL
OF A GOOD BEER". THE NAME
IS LESS MENACING THAN THE
GUEUZE MORTE SUBITE,
WHICH MEANS "SUDDEN
DEATH".

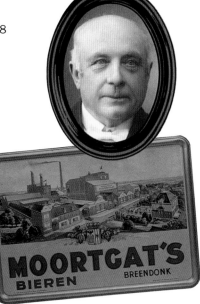

*Moortgat's Brewery – with
founder Jan-Léonard
Moortgat inset – produces
Duvel which looks like
a lager but is bottle-
conditioned and has
an aromatic "nose"
reminiscent of pears*

right. They date from the time when farmer-brewers produced strong beers in the winter and spring that would survive the long, hot summer months. Saisons are top fermenting, dark malts are often used and they are generously hopped. The classic of the style comes from Dupont at Tourpes. The brewery was founded on a farm with its own natural spring in the 1850s. The small brewhouse uses pale and caramalts with East Kent Goldings and Styrian hops. **Vieille Provision** (Old Provision) is 6.5 per cent ABV and has a peppery hop aroma and palate. Dupont also brews beers under the **Moinette** (Little Monk) label, a blonde and a brune, both at 8.5 per cent ABV. The blonde is hoppy and perfumy, the brune sweet and fruity.

There is nothing *Monty Python*-ish about the Silly Brewery. It is based in the village of Silly, on the river Sil. Like Dupont it is a farm-brewery that once ground its own grain. The 5.4 per cent ABV **Saison Silly** is brewed from French and Belgian malts with English Goldings hops. In common with several smaller saison brewers, the mash tun doubles as a hop back: after the copper boil, the hopped wort is pumped back to the mash tun for filtration. The beer is top fermented for a fortnight, then matured in tanks for a further two weeks. The finished beer is copper coloured with a pronounced earthy hop aroma and dark vinous fruit in the mouth. Silly also brews an "artisanal" **Double Enghien** – the name comes from the neighbouring village which had its own

A Christmas brew from Dubuisson, maker of Belgium's strongest beer

brewery – and a hoppy, perfumy and fruity **Divine** (9.5 per cent ABV).

SELECTED SAISON BREWERS

Brasserie Dupont,
rue Basse 5, 7911 Tourpes-Leuze.

Brasserie de Silly,
Ville Basse A141, 7830 Silly.

Brasserie à Vapeur,
rue de Marechal 1, 7904 Pipaix.

Brasserie Voisin,
rue Aulnois 15, 7880 Flobecq.

SPECIALITY BEERS

The strongest beer in Belgium is brewed by a small company in Wallonia called Dubuisson. In the style of the region, Dubuisson is a former farm in Pipaix. Dubuisson means "bush" in French and the name of the 12 per cent ABV beer, **Bush**, was Anglicised in the 1930s to cash in on the popularity of strong British ales in Belgium. The amber-coloured beer Bush is made from pale and cara malts, with Styrian and East Kent Goldings. It is sold in the US as **Scaldis**, the Latin name for the major Belgian river, the Scheldt, to avoid confusion with Busch beer brewed by Budweiser giant Anheuser-Busch.

"Mad beer" can surely not be a style yet it vies to become one as a result of the success of the Mad Brewers – De Dolle Brouwers – in Esen. The small brewery was on the point of closing in 1980 when some keen home-brewing brothers bought the site. Architect Kris Herteleer runs the enterprise with a ragbag of equipment: a pre-First World War mash tun, a copper

fired by direct flame, and an open wort cooler or cool ship. The main beer, **Oerbier** (Original Beer) is 7.5 per cent ABV and is brewed from six malts, including caramalt and black malt, with Belgian hops from Poperinge and English Goldings. It has a sour plums aroma – the yeast came originally from Rodenbach – is bitter-sweet in the mouth with a fruity finish. An 8.0 per cent ABV **Arabier** is bronze-coloured, with a fruity and spicy aroma and more ripe fruit on the palate and finish. **Boskeun** (Easter Bunny) is an 8.0 per cent ABV season ale sweetened with honey, while the 9.0 per cent ABV Christmas ale, **Stille Nacht**, is packed with fruit and a hint of sourness.

La Chouffe, in the Belgian province of Luxembourg, takes its name from the village of Chouffe which in turn is named after a legendary local gnome. The brewery was opened in the 1980s. As well as using Pils and pale malts, Kent Goldings and Styrian hops, the beers are spiced in the medieval fashion with coriander, honey and bog myrtle. **La Chouffe**, 8.5 per cent ABV, has a sweetish start but a dry and spicy finish. **McChouffe**, inspired by Scottish ales, is 8.8 per cent ABV, bottle-conditioned with a big spicy aroma and palate.

SELECTED SPECIALITY BREWERS

Brasserie d'Achouffe,
route de Village 32, 6666 Achouffe-Houffalize.

Brasserie Dubuisson,
Chaussée de Mons 28, 7904 Pipaix.

De Dolle Brouwers,
Roeselarestraat 12b, 8160 Esen-Diksmuide.

CZECH REPUBLIC

*I*T IS ONE OF THE GREAT UNSOLVED MYSTERIES OF THE WORLD OF BREWING: WHY DID PILSEN IN BOHEMIA BREW THE FIRST GOLDEN BEER BY THE METHOD OF COLD OR BOTTOM FERMENTATION? IT SEEMS REMARKABLE THAT THIS SMALL COUNTRY, LOCKED AT THE TIME INTO THE AUSTRO-HUNGARIAN EMPIRE AND, BEFORE THAT, PART OF THE GERMAN EMPIRE, WAS THE FIRST TO BREAK OUT OF THE DARK BEER STRAITJACKET BEFORE SUCH MIGHTY CITIES AS VIENNA AND MUNICH.

Good King Wenceslas I gave great support to the Bohemian brewing industry

CZECH & SLOVAK REPUBLICS

KEY

Brewery

Recommended Pub

Museum

The true answer is complex and rooted in history. Bohemia – which now with Moravia makes up the Czech Republic – has a long brewing tradition. A brewery was recorded in Cerhenice in 1118 and both Pilsen and Budweis had breweries from the thirteenth century. As in other European countries, monasteries dominated beer production for centuries until the power of the church waned.

From the thirteenth century many towns and cities had "citizens' breweries" – essentially co-operatives – while the aristocracy supplied beer from their castles. The Moravian capital, Brno, had been granted rights to brew beer from the twelfth century and King Wenceslas I (Václav I in Czech) decreed in 1243 that no one could brew within a mile of the Blue Lion inn in the city. Similar brewing

rights were given to Pilsen in 1295.

Hops had been grown in the region from as early as 859 AD. While the first Bohemian beers were spiced and flavoured with berries and leaves, the superiority of the local hops encouraged their early use in brewing. From the twelfth century there are records of hops from the region being shipped to the hop market in

Temple of brewing... moulded frieze above the entrance to the Pilsner Urquell brewery

Czechs consider that only beers brewed in Pilsen should carry the appellation

THE CLAIM THAT JOSEF GROLL CHANGED THE FACE OF BREWING BY ACCIDENT BY MAKING A PALE LAGER INSTEAD OF A DARK ONE IS ALMOST CERTAINLY FANTASY. PALE MALT WAS AVAILABLE AT THE TIME AND IT IS LIKELY THAT THE TAVERN OWNERS OF PRAGUE WANTED A BEER THAT LOOKED DIFFERENT TO THE DARK LAGERS OF BAVARIA.

Hamburg. Meanwhile Moravia had established a reputation for the quality of its malting barley, though for centuries wheat beer appears to have been the dominant style in what is now the Czech Republic.

For all its "Bohemian" associations with an unconventional lifestyle dominated by writers and artists living in Ruritanian surroundings, the real Bohemia was never a bucolic backwater. Tadeas Hájek wrote one of the first books on brewing technology in 1585, Professor C.J.N. Balling studied the role of enzymes in the mashing and fermentation processes while the Jecmen brothers developed the Czech method of bottom fermentation.

The history of Bohemian brewing fused with the present in 1842 when the new "Burghers' brewery" of Pilsen employed a German brewer to make beer for them. Josef Groll or Grolle was employed because he was an expert in the new method of cold fermentation and came from the old brewing town of Vilshofen in Bavaria. The reputation of Pilsen beer was poor at the time and the brewery, a co-operative of tavern keepers, needed good beer because they faced stiff competition from the new brown lagers from neighbouring Bavaria.

The golden Pilsner beer was a sensation. Its clarity in glass was immediately appealing while its complexity of aromas and flavours, at once rich and malty yet enticingly hoppy and bitter, entranced all who drank it. Its reputation spread at great speed, aided by canals and a new railway system that carried supplies to all the great cities of the Austrian Empire, across into Bavaria and up the Elbe to Hamburg and beyond. A Pilsen Beer Train left every morning for Vienna. It became a cult drink in Paris and by 1874 it had reached the United States.

The success of the first Pilsen lager brewery prompted a second to be built in 1869. The Gambrinus Brewery, funded among others by Škoda the car manufacturer, was named after Jan Primus, the thirteenth-century toping Duke of Brabant, and built on land adjacent to the other brewery. In the German fashion, the beers from the town of Pilsen were known as "Pilsners", just as the rival brews from Budweis were called "Budweisers". In 1898, the first Pilsen lager brewer registered "Pilsner Urquell" as its official name. It is the German for "Original Source Pilsner" (Plzeňsky Prazdroj in Czech). The document referred to the "absurdity and illogicality of using the word 'Pilsner' for beers brewed in towns outside of Pilsen".

IN THE 19TH CENTURY THE GERMAN HIGH COURT DECREED THAT BREWERS WHO USED THE TERM PILSNER HAD TO PUT THEIR TOWN OF ORIGIN FIRST TO AVOID CONFUSION WITH THE ORIGINAL.

It was all too late. With the exception of the British Isles, brewers throughout Europe rushed to emulate, replicate and too often denigrate the original with their versions of pale lagers. And Germans and Czechs emigrated in large numbers to the New World of the United States, taking with them the technology to brew bottom-fermenting beers.

The preponderance of German Pilsners tended to hide the originals. Drinkers could be forgiven for thinking the beer was a German style. The misunderstanding was heightened by the Cold War when Czechoslovakia disappeared from Western eyes. When it surfaced briefly during the "Prague Spring" of 1968 visitors from the West returned with the news that Czech beer was one of the wonders of the world. Beer had such deep roots in the Czech way of life that the Communist regime did not tamper with it. The breweries were state owned but a surprisingly large number were allowed to operate, providing a wide choice albeit within one general style. Even the fact that most of the breweries were starved of funds for modernization had its positive side as managements were forced to remain true to methods of production considered old fashioned, conservative and quaint in other countries. While other

Eastern bloc regimes forced breweries to use inferior ingredients so that the best barley and hops could be exported for hard currency, the Czech government stayed true to the German *Reinheitsgebot* for its premium beers. The Purity Law had been imposed on Bohemia and the other Czech regions when they were under German domination.

Now the walls are down and the West can marvel at Czech brewing. But the move to a market economy and the double-edged sword of modernization pose threats to the finest Czech traditions. There are around 70 breweries in the republic but the number is expected to fall as market forces take effect. Under the old regime the price of beer was kept low, but now prices are rising and consumption is falling.

INGREDIENTS

The quality of Czech beer is based on the ingredients used and the balance between them. The barley from the plains of Moravia and the Elbe produces a luscious sweet malt. Brewing liquor is soft and low in salts, allowing the sweetness of the malt and the aroma of the hops to best express themselves. The hop-growing area around the town of Žatec is in the North-west of Bohemia between Karlovy Vary (Carlsbad) and the capital, Prague. There is a smaller region north of Prague in Mustek. Žatec is known as Saaz in German and most Western brewers who buy the hops use the German name. Žatec hops grow in areas protected by mountains from high winds and rains. The soil is limestone and red clay. The hops are renowned for their fragrance, their softness, their ripe yet delicate aroma. They are not high in bittering acids but are rich in the tannins that give a distinctive piney, resiny aroma to beer. As a result of their aroma, Pilsner and other Czech beers have a late addition of hops towards the end of the copper boil.

STRENGTH

The strength of Czech beers is expressed in degrees Balling, devised by Professor Balling. Most exported beer is 12 degrees, which is equivalent to 4.5 to 5.0 per cent ABV. But for everyday drinking, Czechs choose 10-degree beers, around 4.0 to 4.2 per cent ABV. Eight-degree beers are consumed in large quantities in industrial areas, and they are low in alcohol, around 3.2 per cent ABV. Some speciality beers are stronger, with 13-, 14-, 16- and even 19-degree ratings. Twelve-degree beers are all-malt but adjuncts are permitted in 8- and 10- degree beers, usually unmalted barley, wheat and sugar. The proportion of adjuncts does not usually exceed 10 per cent of the total grist. Premium beers are lagered for long periods – three months for Budweiser Budvar – but 21 days is normal for the lower strength beers.

PILSNER

The **Pilsner Urquell** Brewery is a temple of brewing. At night its neon-lit name blazes out over the city. By day visitors enter through a great triumphal arch to be confronted by tall chimneys, an almost Moorish water tower, and a warehouse complex that looks remarkably like London's King's Cross railway station. A meeting room in the grounds, with polished oak and stained glass windows, is like a chapel. In the 1980s the brewery yard was filled by giant oak casks, brought up from deep sandstone cellars to be re-pitched, the air rich with the smoky, autumnal aroma of

More a triumphal arch than an entrance to the first Pilsner brewery.
Left, a postcard extols the pleasures of Bohemia's principal industrial city and greatest brewing centre

THE OLD PITCH-LINED OAK TUBS AND GIANT CASKS USED FOR PRIMARY FERMENTATION AND LAGERING IN THE PILSEN BREWERY ARE NOW ON SHOW IN A BREWERY MUSEUM ON THE SITE.

SEVERAL OF THE BOHEMIAN KINGS NAMED WENCESLAS (VÁCLAV IN CZECH) ATTEMPTED TO BAN CUTTINGS OF ŽATEC HOPS BEING TAKEN FROM THE COUNTRY AND PROPAGATED ELSEWHERE BECAUSE OF THEIR HIGH QUALITY AND RENOWNED AROMA.

Calling the bibulous to prayer... Pilsner Urquell's mosque-like water tower

fresh pitch. Both primary and secondary fermentation took place in pitch-lined oak vessels. Was it just the water or did the oak vessels help impart a comforting softness to the beer?

In the two brightly-lit, tiled brewhouses the mash is a thorough triple decoction system. Žatec hop flowers are added three times in direct-flame coppers. Until changes were introduced, the hopped wort went first to a vast, cool dimly-lit room packed with small oak tubs each set at a slight angle as though the vessels were about to raise imaginary hats. The angle was designed to allow brewers to clamber up and check the progress of fermentation. When primary fermentation was complete, the green beer was pumped to six miles of sandstone cellars where the beer was lagered for 70 days at a natural temperature of 0–3.5 degrees C/ 32–38F. The oak lagering vessels were barrel-shaped and arranged horizontally. The beer has 40 units of bitterness. Under the old lagering system, the original gravity was 1048 degrees with a finished alcohol of 4.4 per cent. This meant the beer was not fully attenuated – not all the malt sugars turned to alcohol.

The use of the past tense in describing fermentation and flavour profile is deliberate. For fundamental changes have taken place at the brewery since the fall of the old regime and the arrival of the market economy. Mashing and boiling remain the same but fermentation now takes place in modern stainless steel conical fermenters. The brewery claims that change had been under way since the 1970s but there had been no sight of conical vessels during the 1980s when Western journalists visited the brewery. It is more likely that the 10-degree version of the beer was brewed in modern vessels not open to inspection and the 12-degree beer was switched to them in the early 1990s following privatization.

In spite of claims to the contrary, the character of the beer has changed. The reason lies in the nature of conical fermenters. Unlike a horizontal lagering tank, where the yeast works slowly, almost lazily, turning remaining sugars into alcohol, a conical causes yeast to work more voraciously, hungrily attacking the sugars. The result is a more fully attenuated beer.

Pilsner Urquell now has more in common with a German version of Pilsner: it is drier and more assertively bitter. It will be a tragedy if the inexorable demands of the market economy lead to any further blurring of its distinctiveness.

The **Gambrinus** Brewery next door is now part of the same privatized company as Pilsner Urquell. The brewery has also switched to fermentation in stainless steel conicals. Oak vessels were not used at Gambrinus: stainless steel replaced cast-iron. It is 4.5 per cent ABV and has 33 IBUs with a fresh-mown grass aroma, a more delicate bitterness than Urquell and a malty/hoppy finish that becomes dry. The 10-degree version, made with a proportion of sucrose, is the most popular beer of that strength in the Czech Republic.

EBERHARD ANHEUSER WAS A GERMAN IMMIGRANT FROM BAD KREUZNACH NEAR MAINZ. HE WAS SO IMPRESSED WITH THE BEERS OF BUDWEIS IN BOHEMIA THAT WHEN HE WENT TO THE UNITED STATES HE JOINED FORCES WITH ADOLPHUS BUSCH, AN IMMIGRANT FROM MAINZ, TO BUY A BREWERY IN ST LOUIS, MISSOURI, AND BREW A BEER CALLED BUDWEISER.

BUDWEISERS

Deep in the south of Bohemia and close to the Austrian border, the town of České Budějovice, with its magnificent central square and a fountain topped by a statue of Samson, vies with Pilsen as the great brewing centre of the Czech Republic. Its two breweries are smaller but Budweis, to use the old German name, had 44 breweries in the

Beers from Česke Budějovice have for centuries been known as Budweisers

fifteenth century and was home to the Royal Court brewery of Bohemia. The royal connection allowed beers from the court brewery to be known as the "Beer of Kings" while all the town's brews became famous under the generic title of "Budweisers".

The standing of Budweiser beers can be seen in the decision of the American Anheuser-Busch company to give the name to its main product when it was launched in 1875 in St Louis, Missouri. Further confusion was added by the American sub-title "the King of Beers".

Twenty years later, in 1895, the Budejovicky Pivovar company started to brew. The name means the Budejovice Brewery and its beer is always known simply by the contraction "Budvar" at home. But it is exported as **Budweiser Budvar** and the clash of names has led to endless law suits and wrangles over copyright. Anheuser-Busch can claim that it has precedent over Budvar for the use of the name but this ignores the fact that the older surviving brewery in Ceské Budejovice, now called Samson, exported beer under the Budweiser name long before the American company took up the title. The Czech Budvar brewery cannot export to the United States using Budweiser on its labels while the American

giant has to call its beer simply "Bud" in such countries as Germany and Spain where the Czechs registered the title first.

Since the arrival of the market economy Anheuser-Busch has lobbied hard to win a stake in its smaller Czech rival. It has offered to buy 34 per cent of the shares, to inject capital to allow Budvar to expand, and to help Budvar market its beer world-wide. A-B has opened a St Louis Center in Ceské Budějovice, donated to Prague University and taken full-page advertisements in newspapers to tell the Czech people that its intentions are honourable towards Budvar. So far the Czechs are unimpressed and the brewery remains in state hands, though it is due to be privatized.

The Budvar Brewery is one of the most modern in the country. The old regime invested money in new plant to enable Budvar to export. Ironically, the beer had for years been hard to find in the Czech Republic as so much of it went for export. The brewhouse is magnificent, with large copper mash and brew kettles on tiled floors. A double decoction mash is used. Primary fermentation is in open vessels, lagering in horizontal ones. Lagering lasts for three months for the 12-degree beer, one of the longest

periods in the world. It is an all-malt beer, using Pilsner malt and Žatec hops. The original gravity is 1049 with a finished alcohol of 5.0 per cent ABV. The beer is well attenuated and has 20 units of bitterness. The balance of a Budweiser beer is therefore demonstrably different to that of a Pilsner. Budvar has a rich malt and vanilla aroma, it is quenching and gently hoppy in the mouth, while the finish has a balance of malt, hops and a deli-cate hint of apple fruit from the yeast.

The Samson Brewery was the result of a merger in 1795 of two breweries, Velky (Great) and Maly (Small). It became the Citizens' Brewery and moved to a new site in the town in 1847. It changed its name to Samson but exported for some time under the Budweiser name until the arrival of the Budvar Brewery. Samson's management felt it received a bad deal under the old regime as all the investment available went to Budvar. Today Samson is seeking independence and plans to stop sharing yeast with Budvar. It is a classic Czech lager brewery, with cast-iron mashing and boiling vessels, open squares for primary fermen-tation and horizontal ones for lagering. The management plans to install conicals but will continue to ferment its 12-degree beer in the old vessels to avoid any changes to the flavour profile. The premium product (4.3 per cent ABV) has a creamy note from the malt, some citric fruit from the hops and a well-balanced finish. An up-rated version is exported to Britain under the name of **Zámek** (Castle) at 4.5 per cent ABV.

Entrance to the Budvar Brewery… the company has been involved in law suits with Anheuser-Busch since the turn of the century over who has the right to use the brand name Budweiser

Staro-
pramen
means the
Old Spring
and is the
principal
brewery
in Prague

PRAGUE BEERS

Three of the Czech capital's four breweries merged in 1992 to form Prague Breweries. The biggest of the three in the group is the Staropramen (Old Spring) Brewery in the Smichov district, which started to brew in 1871. Its beer was praised by Emperor Franz Josef I and production soared. It is one of the biggest breweries in the Czech Republic, producing more than a million hectolitres a year. It is a classic lager brewery with secondary fermentation in horizontal tanks. In 1994 the British Bass group took a 34 per cent stake in Prague Breweries and said it would not change the brewing method as horizontal tanks were crucial to the flavour of the beer. The 12-degree **Staropramen** is 5.0 per cent ABV. It has superb hop aroma, is well-balanced in the mouth between malt and hops and the finish is dry and bitter.

The second partner in the group is the Holesovice Brewery which brews under the **Méstan** name. Méstan comes from the original title of the brewery when it was founded in 1895 as První Prazsky Méstanský Pivovar – First Prague Burghers' Brewery. Its 12-degree beer is aromatic, soft, malty and bitter in the finish. The third member of Prague Breweries, Braník, started production in 1900. Its 12-degree beer is notably fresh, clean and well-hopped. Since privatization the brewery has undergone substantial modernization. Fermentation now takes place in conical vessels and beer is canned for export.

The most celebrated beer in Prague comes from the world-famous beer hall, brewpub and beer garden known as U Fleků at 11 Kremencova in the New Town, the entrance marked by a large hanging clock. Beer has been brewed on the site since at least 1499: isotopic measurements of the remains of paintings on the wooden ceiling of the brew-house have dated them back to 1360. The present name of the establish-ment stems from 1762 when Jakub Flekovský and his wife bought it. In the Czech fashion, the tavern was known as U Flekovskych, which over time was shortened to U Fleků. In Czech "U" serves the same purpose as the French "chez" – "at the house of". The tiny brewhouse, with a capacity of 6,000 hectolitres, is the smallest in the republic. With its open "cool ship" fermenter, it is reminiscent of a Belgian lambic brewery but no wild fermentation is allowed here. New brewing vessels are made of copper and date from 1980. The one beer is a dark lager, **Flekovaky**, 13 degrees (4.5 per cent ABV). It is made from four malts: Pilsner pale (50 per cent), Munich (30 per cent), caramalt (15 per cent) and roasted malt (5 per cent). A double decoction mash is used and Žatec hops are added in three stages.

BRNO

The capital of Moravia has a long history of brewing, dating back to monastic times. The Starobrno (Old Brno) Brewery dates from 1872 when the family firm of Mandel and Hayek built the plant. Expansion was rapid, with exports moving from horse-drawn wagons to the railway in 1894. In the economically turbulent decades of the 1920s and 1930s, Starobrno bought several smaller breweries in the area. The plant was severely damaged by an air raid in 1944. It was nationalized in 1945 and during the course of re-building was considerably modernized. It now produces some 700,000 hectolitres of beer a year. Its 12-degree **Lezak Export** (Export Lager) is rounded and soft in the mouth, with a delicate hop aroma, and a gentle, bitter-sweet finish.

COUNTRY BREWERIES

"Baker, priest, farmer, butcher, all drink beer from Breznice" an old slogan says. Brewing in the town dates back to 1506 and the

> U FLEKŮ IN PRAGUE IS THE WORLD'S OLDEST BREWPUB. ONE WALL OF THE BREWHOUSE IS DECORATED WITH THE WORDS "GOD BLESS THE MOTHER WHO GAVE BIRTH TO A BREWER" AND A PAINTING SHOWING A BREWER BEING GIVEN A GIFT OF BARLEY AND HOPS BY GOD. REMARKABLY THIS RELIGIOUS ARTEFACT SURVIVED THE YEARS OF COMMUNIST RULE.

town brewery was in the hands of the aristocratic Kolowrat Krakowsky family for 150 years. The coats of arms of the family with the emblem of an eagle adorns the labels of today's Herold beer. The Breznice brewery produces 10- and 12-degree Herold pale lagers but its main claim to fame is the first wheat beer seen in the Czech lands for at least a century. **Pivo Herold Hefe-Weizen** is a cloudy wheat beer in the Bavarian style, 12 degrees, unpasteurized and bottle-conditioned with a spicy, fruity aroma, a rich palate with apple fruit, and a long quenching finish. The brewery also makes kits for home-brewing: the new Czech Republic is learning an early lesson in basic capitalism – when commercial beer becomes expensive, drinkers turn to home-brewing.

The entrance to the **Krušovice** Brewery is guarded by an old wooden lagering tank bearing the company symbol of a cavalier. Krusovice malts its own barley using a traditional floor maltings where the grains are turned by hand. The 12-degree beer is one of the most highly prized beers in the Czech Republic, a fine blend of sweet malt and aromatic Žatec hops, a quenching palate and a long, delicate finish with good hop notes.

The **Platan** Brewery in Protivín is one of the finest in the country. Platan means plane tree and an avenue of the trees leads down to a complex of brewing buildings surrounded by woodland. There has been brewing on the site since the late sixteenth century. The feudal Schwarzenberg family built a new brewery between 1873 and 1876 and adopted all the new methods for producing lager beer. The first cultivation plant for Bohemian yeast was set up in the brewery and the beer was so highly prized that it was sold not only in Prague and Pilsen but also in Vienna, Trieste, Zagreb, Berlin, Leipzig, Geneva and as far afield as New York and Chicago. The brewery was nationalized in 1947 but has now been restored to its original owners. The 12-degree beer is closer to a Budweiser than a Pilsner in style, due to Protivín's proximity to Česke Budějovice. It is soft and and malty in the mouth, with a rounded, well-balanced malt and hops finish.

Closer to Prague, the beer from **Velké Popovice** would be declared a world classic if it were better known. The original brewery was built by monks in 1727, using the master of Czech baroque architecture, Kilian Dienzenhoffer. The plant was extensively expanded in 1871 and brewing capacity has been extended further in recent years. It is planned to build capacity to more than one million hectolitres, making it one of the biggest Czech breweries. The brewery has always been able to draw on natural water supplies from surrounding woodland and today takes its supply from 12 wells. The 12-degree beer has an enticing citric aroma of oranges and lemons, which dominate the palate

and the finish, balanced by a sweet maltiness. The beer can be sampled in U Cernéha Vola, the Black Ox, in Prague, an ancient tavern opposite the Loretto church at 1 Loretanské námesti, Hradcany, Prague 1.

The **Žatec** Brewery is in the heart of the great hop-growing region north of Prague and enjoys the pick of the crop. The brewery was built in 1801 as a citizens' brewery on the site of a former castle. The ancient castle cellars are used to lager the beers. It is a small brewery producing 120,000 hectolitres a year, concentrating on quality and supplying surrounding towns.

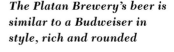

The Platan Brewery's beer is similar to a Budweiser in style, rich and rounded

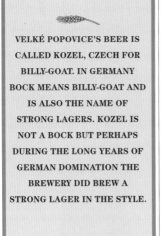

The Regent Brewery in Třebon produces a classic ruby-red lager

DARK LAGER

Bohemia did not turn its back on dark beers as a result of the success of golden Pilsners. Many breweries still produce dark beer (tmavé), all bottom fermented today though there have been occasional spottings of beers called "porter", an indication that in its day London porter had an impact as great as those of Pilsner.

The Regent Brewery in Třebon has one of the finest brewhouses in the country. The brewery was founded in 1379 and came to be owned by the Schwarzenbergs, who moved the plant into their castle armoury and had it rebuilt, complete with its own maltings, by the Italian master builders, the brothers De Maggi, the Viennese Martinelli and the Prague architect Bayer. It has been privatized since the "Velvet Revolution" and recent investment has restored the brewhouse to its former glory. The brewing process is meticulous: mashing and boiling takes twelve hours, followed by primary fermentation for up to 12 days and lagering, for the 12-degree beers, for 90 days. Although Regent makes splendid pale lagers – closer to Budweiser than Pilsen in style – its classic beer is **Dark Regent** (12 degrees: 4.8 per cent ABV). Brewed from pale, cara-

malt and dark malts, it is ruby red in colour, with an appealing aroma of hops and bitter chocolate, dark malt in the mouth, and a hoppy/malty finish reminiscent of cappuccino coffee.

The Breclav Brewery has a 12-degree dark **Breclav Speciál**, sweet with a burnt sugar, caramel character. As the Czechs are a little late in learning about Political Correctness, this sweet style of dark lager is often referred to as "women's beer". Černà Horà's 12-degree **Granát** is highly complex, with a sweet aroma but a dry finish and a

smooth palate. The name means "garnet", a reference to the beer's appealing red-black colour. The Bernard Brewery in Humpolec also has a **Granát** (11 degrees) made from pale and caramalt. **Nová Paka Granát** is 12 degrees and has a bitter coffee finish after a malty start and palate. Velké Popovice has a dark version of its **Kozel** billy-goat lager, malty and chocolatey.

The Ostravar Brewery is in the mining town of the same name. It was founded by Czechs in 1897 to rival another brewery controlled by Germans. The present brewery's 10-degree **Vranik** has a delicate bitterness and dark maltiness and avoids the sweetness of other brands. Gambrinus markets **Purkmistr** (4.7 per cent ABV) brewed for it by the Domazlice Brewery.

The most memorable dark beer comes from the Pardubice Brewery in eastern Bohemia close to the Slovakian border. The 19-degree **Pardubice Porter** (7.0 per cent ABV) has a fine roasted malt aroma with powerful hop notes, a big palate of dark fruit and bitter hops, and a long finish bursting with coffee, chocolate and hop notes.

SLOVAK REPUBLIC

Slovakia is a wine-making country with only a handful of breweries. The **Urpin Brewery** in Banská Bystrica produces a

fine interpretation of the Pilsner style using Pilsner malt and Žatec hops. The 12-degree beer has a marked hop aroma, a firm malty body, and a long finish, hoppy and becoming dry.

The Martin Brewery in the town of that name was formed in 1893 with Jan Mattus, former head brewer at the Pilsen Brewery, in charge. As well as 12- and 14-degree pale beers, both delicately hopped, the brewery also produces the strongest known beer in both republics, **Martin Porter**. The 20-degree beer, around 8.0 per cent ABV, has a complex bitter-sweet palate after a hefty start of dark malt and bitter hops. The finish is long and deep with a charred malt character. It is only brewed occasionally.

> THE OLD MINING TOWN OF OSTRAVA IN MEDIEVAL TIMES HAD A "TOWN BREWERY" THAT WAS NO MORE THAN A CO-OPERATIVELY OWNED MASHING VESSEL. CITIZENS WOULD MAKE WORT IN THE VESSEL AND THEN FERMENT IT IN THEIR HOMES.

SELECTED CZECH BREWERS

Bernard,
5 kvetna 1, 396 01 Humpolec.
Braník,
Udolni 212/1, 101 00 Prague 4.
Breznice,
262 72 Breznice.
Budějovicky Budvar,
Kar. Svetlé 4, 370 21 České Budejovice.
Černá Hora,
679 21 Cernà Hora.
Gambrinus,
U Prazdroje 7, 304 97 Pilsen.

Krušovice,
270 53 Krusovice.
Kutná Hora,
U Lorce 11, 284 1t Kutná Hora.
Nová Paka,
Marantova 400, 509 01 Nová Paka.
Ostravar,
Hornoplni 57, 728 25 Ostrava.
Pardubice,
Palackého 250, 530 33 Pardubice.
Platan,
Pivovarská 856, 393 01 Pelhrimov.
Plzeňské Prazdroj (Pilsner Urquell),
U Prazdroje 7, 304 97 Pilsen.
Regent,
Trocnovské nám. 379 14 Třebon.
Samson,
Lidická 51, 370 54 Ceské Budejovice.
Starobrno,
Hlinky 12, 661 47 Brno.
Staropramen,
Nádrazni 84, 150 54 Prague 5-Smichov.
Trutnov,
Krizikova 486, 541 01 Trutnov.
Velké Popovice,
Ringhofferova 1, 251 69 Velké Popovice.
Žatec,
Zizkovo nám. 78, 438 33 Žatec.

Note: In Czech, Prague is Praha, Pilsen is Plzen.

SLOVAK BREWERS

Martin,
Hrdinov SNP 12, 036 42 Martin.
Urpin,
Sládkovicova 37, 975 90 Banská Bystrica.

> THE CZECH PLAYWRIGHT VÁCLAV HAVEL, NOW THE PRESIDENT OF THE REPUBLIC, ONCE WORKED IN THE TRUTNOV BREWERY. THE CONDITIONS THERE INSPIRED HIM TO WRITE HIS PLAY *AUDIENCE*, SET IN A BREWERY.

EASTERN EUROPE

ITH THE EXCEPTION OF THE FORMER CZECHOSLOVAKIA, THE BEERS OF THE OLD EASTERN BLOC WERE HIDDEN FROM WESTERN EYES. ALL THE BREWERIES WERE STATE-OWNED AND THE SWITCH TO MARKET ECONOMIES WILL LEAD TO FUNDAMENTAL CHANGES. WESTERN BREWERS ARE HURRYING TO ESTABLISH BRIDGEHEADS AND TO BREW THEIR STRONGLY-BRANDED PRODUCTS LOCALLY.

Anton Dreher stored his Vienna lager in the rocky foundations of Pest

The beers brewed in Poland's capital, Warsaw, are notably full-bodied

HUNGARY

The great Austrian brewmaster Anton Dreher stamped his mark on Budapest. When Buda's twin city, Pest, was being constructed, large caves were dug in the rocky foundations and Dreher seized on them to lager his beer after he set up a company there in the middle of the nineteenth century, when Hungary was linked to Austria politically and economically. His Köbànya Brewery has survived and among its beers **Rocky Cellar** pays oblique homage to the founder. The 12-degree beer – approximately 5.5 per cent ABV – uses a substantial amount of adjuncts and is lightly hopped with 20 IBUs. More interesting brews are all-malt – a hangover perhaps from the days when the Bavarian *Reinheitsgebot* held sway – and include a 5.0 per cent **Köbànyai** with delicate hop bitterness and a dark and sweet beer with some sultana fruitiness called **Bak** (7.5 per cent ABV), a local interpretation of the German Bock, and a pale lager of 5.5 per cent called simply Budapest.

The Kanizsa Brewery in Nagy-kanizsa was founded in 1892 in an important barley and malting region. Production stopped during the Second World War and did not begin again until 1957. In 1984 the brewery went into partnership with Holsten of Hamburg and now brews the German group's beer under licence. Its own main brand is a malty lager called **Sirály** – Seagull – a rounded Export style called **Korona** and a Dunkel-type known as **Göcseji Barna**.

Belgium's Interbrew has a majority stake in the Borsodi group while Heineken has bought Komaromi near Budapest and will brew Amstel there.

POLAND

Poland is a major brewing country with a sizeable hop-growing industry in the Lublin region and a well-developed barley and malting industry. As a result its lager beers have both good malt character and a strikingly perfumy and resiny hoppiness.

The Zywiec Brewery in Cracow takes its name from the old Polish name for the city. Its brewing liquor comes from the Tatra Mountains and is close to the hop fields of Krasnystaw. **Zywiec Beer** is called Full Light and the inspiration is as much as Munich Hell as a Bohemian Pilsner. It has a soft malt and powerful, peppery hops aroma, is tart and quenching in the mouth, with a finish that becomes dry and bitter.

Okocim Brewery has a goat on its label, though this comes from the heraldic sign for the city of Okocim and is not a reference to a Bock beer. **Okocim Pils** is 5.1 per cent ABV, has a rounded malty aroma, with rich vanilla and hops in the mouth, and a big bitter-sweet finish.

The Warsaw Brewery (Browar Warszawksi) in the Polish capital produces two full-bodied lagers in the Pilsner and Export styles, **Stoteczne** and **Krolewskie**. Of most interest is a beer called **Porter**, a bottom-fermenting dark beer with plenty of dark malt and coffee character, a reminder that porter and stout were once exported in vast amounts from Britain to the Baltic states. When the Napoleonic Wars closed the trade to Britain, local brewers responded to demand with their own versions but preferred to use lagering techniques.

A fascinating top-fermenting beer comes from the Grodzisk Wiekopolski Brewery near Poznan. Called **Grodzisk**, the beer is a blend of malted barley cured over an oak fire, with some wheat and help from wild yeasts in fermentation. The result is a beer with a tart, refreshing sourness, some spice from the wheat and a smoky, oaky tang.

FORMER YUGOSLAVIA

With the regions and new states of the former Yugoslavia in turmoil, the brewing picture is complicated. Except in Muslim areas, the region has powerful brewing traditions dating back to the thirteenth century. Slovenia has been a major hop-growing area for centuries and the quality of the hops has stamped its mark on beers that are broadly in the German and Austrian moulds, though bottom-fermented dark beers and porters have been spotted occasionally. Austrian practices, from the time when the Austro-Hungarian empire

included the Slav regions, is evident in the use of the Plato scale to indicate strength. The Apatin Brewery was built in 1756 with financial support from the Imperial Chamber of Commerce in Vienna.

In Belgrade, Bip was founded in 1850. Its **Belgrade Gold** is a full-bodied malty lager of around 5.0 per cent ABV with a tart and citric hop character. Serbia's oldest brewery was built in Pancevo in 1722 and brews a **Standard** lager of around 4.5 per cent ABV and a stronger, malty/vanilla **Weifert** of 5.5 per cent.

The Trebjesa Brewery at Niksic was founded in 1896 and takes its brewing liquor from the natural spring waters of the surrounding mountains. Its main product is **Big Nik Gold Beer** – the name suggests it's a steal at the price.

ESTONIA

The Tartu Olletehas brewery launched a German-style Bock beer in 1995. Called **Rüütli Olu**, the 7.5 per cent alcohol beer is dark brown in colour and is lagered for 70 days. It is the strongest beer brewed in Estonia. It has a dark fruit and spicy hops character, is rich and warming and is promoted as the ideal beer for festivals.

RUSSIA AND THE UKRAINE

Russia is a major producer of beer but that is due to the sheer size of the country. Consumption is low and the favourite tipple is vodka. Just as the English attempted to stamp out the evils of gin-drinking by promoting beer, the Soviet regime encouraged brewing until Mikhail

Gorbachev clamped down on all forms of alcohol. Beer is now reviving and the country is open to imports, to such an extent that England's Newcastle Brown Ale has become something of a cult drink among the young.

For centuries the Russian people, especially in the countryside, drank a home-made porridge beer called *kvass*, and it survives as a cheap and nourishing drink. It is made from rye. Barley and wheat are sometimes added and the drink is sweetened with unfermented hedgerow fruits such as bilberries. It has never been made successfully on a commercial scale.

Commercial breweries were established early in the twentieth century and were nationalized following the Bolshevik Revolution. The industry was damaged severely during the Second World War and was rebuilt mainly with Czech expertise in the 1950s and 1960s. The Czechs were called in again to build additional plants in the 1980s but these were mothballed when Gorbachev called for a crackdown against drunkenness.

Snowed in... the Tartu Brewery in the depths of an Estonian winter. Tartu, once famous for producing "imperial" stout, has recently launched a German-style Bock beer

WHEN ZHIGULI WAS FIRST EXPORTED TO BRITAIN IT WAS PROMOTED WITH THE SLOGAN "THE BEER THAT GRABS YOU BY THE ZHIGULIS", A SUGGESTION THAT IT REACHED PARTS UNPLUMBED EVEN BY HEINEKEN. THE SLOGAN WAS SOON DROPPED.

Big Nik from Niksic in former Yugoslavia is brewed with pure mountain spring water

Stout brewed in London for the Baltic states was highly esteemed in the Russian court

It is estimated that there are some 16 brand-new and unused brewing plants dotted around the countries that made up the USSR.

The most popular beer in Russia comes from the Ukraine, its popularity underscored by its own beer garden in the Russian capital, the Zhiguli Cellar off Kalinin Prospekt. The Obolov Brewery in Kiev that makes **Zhiguli** (4.4 per cent) uses pale malt, brewing sugar and around 5.0 per cent rice with Klon hops. Bitterness units are low, around 17. The beer is conditioned for 45 days and has a light malt aroma and palate, with some delicate hops in the finish.

The Moscow Brewery, established in 1863, makes a 4.6 per cent **Moskovkoye Lager** broadly in the Pilsner style, and a fuller-bodied, almost amber **Radonej**. It has added **August** (4.5 per cent ABV), an all-malt beer named after the failed August coup that brought Boris Yeltsin to power. It is bronze coloured with a rich toffee/vanilla aroma, hops on the palate and a light but fruity and hoppy finish.

"RUSSIAN STOUT"

In the nineteenth and early twentieth centuries the Baltic states had a love affair with the dark porters and stouts brewed in Britain. The strongest versions became known as Imperial Stout as a result of their popularity with the Russian court. The Empress Catherine was a devotée and encouraged the beer to be given to the sick. Imperial stouts were brewed in London by several companies based along the Thames. They were black and viscous, and heavily hopped in order to withstand long sea journeys to the Baltic. The sole surviving example, **Imperial Russian Stout**, comes from the Courage group, which began life as Henry Thrale's brewery in London, founded in the seventeenth century. It was bought by a Scottish-American called Barclay, and became Barclay-Perkins before joining the Courage group founded by John Courage, a Scot of French Huguenot origins. There is a further convoluted ethnic twist to the story, for Imperial Russian Stout was exported to the Baltic for Barclay Perkins by a Belgian named Le Coq. Monsieur Le Coq produced a booklet in Russian extolling the healthy attributes of the beer. He boosted the popularity of Russian Stout by giving away cases of the beer to Russian soldiers injured in the Crimean War. At the turn of the century Le Coq bought a brewery in Tartu in what is now Estonia to brew both porter and stout for the Baltic market. His success was short-lived for the brewery was nationalized by the Bolsheviks in 1917. Records show that the brewery last brewed a bottom-fermenting porter in 1969.

Back in Britain, Courage still produces Imperial Russian Stout in small batches every other year. When it closed its London brewery, it moved production to its John Smith's subsidiary in Tadcaster in Yorkshire. In London the beer used to be conditioned in the brewery for 18 months before being released but now the consumer is expected to lay the beer down. The bottle-conditioned beer has a starting gravity of 1104 degrees and is declared 10 per cent ABV, though 11 has been reached. Its complex grist includes some Pilsner malt as well as pale, amber and black malts with some brewing sugar: perhaps the habit of using Pilsner malt stems from boats that had been full of stout returning to England with cargoes of European barley. It is hopped with the Target variety in the region of 24 pounds per barrel – four times the normal rate. Bitterness units are in the region of 50.

Next door to John Smith's Brewery, the distantly related but independent firm of Samuel Smith introduced an **Imperial Stout** (7.0 per cent ABV) in the 1980s, a superb bottled beer with great dark malt, winey fruit and hops character, more quenching than the Courage version.

Jim Pryor, who has brewed with Bass, Courage and Whitbread, and has visited Russia regularly to advise on brewing and pubs, launched **Vassilinsky's Black Russian Beer** in 1993, a bottled-conditioned 4.8 per cent beer brewed for him by McMullen of Hertford. It is more of a porter than a stout, made from pale, crystal, brown and black malts and Fuggles and Goldings whole hops (35 IBUs). It has a deep aroma of bitter chocolate, hazel nuts, hops and spices, there is full malt in the mouth and the big finish is a fine balance between earthy Fuggles hops, bitter chocolate and coffee and dark fruit and malt. Mr Pryor hopes his beer will encourage Russian brewers to experiment with dark beer again.

IMPORTANT ADDRESS
Kiev Obolon Brewery,
Bogatyrskaya Street 3,
Kiev 212.

FRANCE

THE FRENCH MAKE BEER. THE FRENCH DRINK BEER. IF THAT SOUNDS TRITE, IT IS BECAUSE THE INTERNATIONAL IMAGE OF FRANCE IS INEXTRICABLY LINKED TO WINE; BEER NEEDS TO BE DRAGGED FROM THE GIANT SHADOW CAST BY THE VINE. BEER IS DRUNK THROUGHOUT THE COUNTRY, OFTEN IN BARS AND CAFÉS CALLED BRASSERIES – BREWERIES. BEER WAS ONCE BREWED ALL OVER FRANCE, TOO. THE GAULS WERE FAMOUS FOR THEIR CERVOISE, FROM THE LATIN CERVISIA – ALE. AT THE TURN OF THE TWENTIETH CENTURY THERE WERE STILL 3,000 FRENCH BREWERIES, MANY OF THEM TINY AND RUN FROM FARMS, OPERATING IN NICE, LIMOGES AND TOULOUSE AS WELL AS IN BEER'S NORTHERN HEARTLANDS.

Today there are just 33 breweries left, plus a handful of micro-breweries. That marks a fall from 76 breweries in 1976. The decline of beer is remarkable in a country that is still largely rural and with a powerful agricultural lobby. But, outside the far North, beer was never treated as seri-ously as wine, was never so much part of the tapestry of life. It was a refresher, not a drink to savour or ponder. As a result, it became prey to industrialization. Today brewing is dominated to an astonishing degree by just two companies: Kronenbourg, part of the giant food and drinks group BSN, and Heineken. Kronenbourg controls 50 per cent of the market, Heineken 25 per cent. The Belgian Interbrew group also busily sells beer in France though it no longer brews there. Most of this production takes place in the North, mainly in Alsace-Lorraine, an area under German rule from 1871 to 1919 and also during the Second World War, experiences that stamped their mark on the

language, the cuisine and the beer. And even within the region, brewing is concentrated in Alsace and its capital, Strasbourg. The last independent brewery in Lorraine (Amos of Metz) closed in 1992. The last regional brewery of any size or note outside the North, Schneider of Puyoô, closed in 1990 and even here there was an obvious German influence. Heineken has a plant in Marseilles but it scarcely ranks as a French brewery.

Change is taking place, though. Consumption is increasing and there is a flow-ering of brewing of a quite different kind to the German-influenced lagers of Alsace. In the Nord-Pas de Calais region, strung out along the border with Belgium, ales are flourishing, albeit on a small scale. The brewers of the region, many of them new, small micros, concen-trate in the main on the style known as bière de garde, a top-fermenting beer that has powerful links with the farm-

house saison and vieille provi-sion ales of Wallonia. The sudden interest in French ales has not gone unnoticed and even the giants of French brewing are reviving such long-lost styles as Christmas and March beers.

ALSACE-LORRAINE

This is lager-brewing territory. The German influence is obvious in the names of breweries, cities, towns and villages as well as in the cuisine, in which pork dishes abound. But the beer is a long way removed from the influence

Strasbourg, great city of Alsace with a long brewing tradition that has been influ-enced by German techniques

A bit of a mouthful... French beer drinkers have shortened the long brand name for a lager that marked three centuries of brewing

of the German *Reinheitsgebot*. Twenty to 30 per cent of cereal adjuncts are not uncommon in the lagers of the region. Hopping rates are not high, with bitterness units in the low to middle 20s. The results are beers of between 5.0 and 6.0 per cent ABV that are pleasant, refreshing but in general unremarkable.

Kronenbourg is based in Strasbourg. It has a second brewery in nearby Obernai and its subsidiary Kanterbräu brews at Champigneulles in Lorraine, and Rennes in Britanny. The history of Kronenbourg is stamped on the label of one of its best-known brands **1664**, for that was the year when Jérôme Hatt started to make beer in a

tavern called Au Canon (Zur Karthaune in German) on the Place de Corbeau (the Raven) in Strasbourg, close by the Customs House on the banks of the Rhine (Le Rhin). Hatt had qualified as a master brewer and cooper and he quickly won acclaim for the quality of his beer, which would have been top-fermenting in those days. His tavern became the top meeting place for the Strasbourgeois (the tavern has survived but now sells beer from the Schützenberger Brewery).

In 1850 Frédéric-Guillaume Hatt moved the brewery to a new site in the suburb of Cronenbourg, meaning the crown or brow of the hill. In the Germanic fashion, the brewery took on the name of its place of domicile and the spelling was subsequently changed to Kronenbourg. It achieved national status in the 1920s with a bilingual beer called Tigre Bock which frustratingly no longer exists. In the 1950s Kronenbourg began to expand aggressively. It pioneered beer in 25-centilitre bottles and made a big play for supermarket sales with disposable containers. Kronenbourg 1664 was launched in 1962, two years short of the brewery's double centenary, and a second brewery known as "K2" was opened at Obernai in 1969. A year later Kronenbourg became part of the BSN group, which also acquired Kanterbräu. The brewing groups were merged in 1986.

The main brand is simply called **Kronenbourg**, with medieval lettering on a quartered red and white label that is supposed to emulate a shield but looks more like a rugby shirt. The beer is 5.2 per cent ABV, with 23 IBUs. The aroma is light, delicate, unobtrusive, with a clean palate and finish, and some hop and malt notes. The 5.9 per cent ABV 1664 has a more pronounced aroma but is disappointingly light for a beer of the strength. The version brewed under licence in Britain by Courage is 5.0 per cent ABV. A brown version, **1664 Brune**, is a percentage point stronger and has a pleasant chewy, dark caramel character. A 4.7 per cent ABV **Bière de l'Eté** is a light summer refresher while a Christmas beer, **Bière de Noël**, has a fuller golden colour with a hint of red – perhaps a dash of Munich or caramalt – and more body.

The Kanterbräu subsidiary came about as a result of series of mergers and takeovers. Its origins are as Les Grandes Brasseries de Champigneulles, founded in 1897 by Victor Hinzelin and Victor Trampitsch. Victor Trampitsch was a Slovenian who had learned his brewing skills in Pilsen, an impressive pedigree. Following the Second World War the company swallowed many other breweries in the region, becoming Société Européene de Brasseries

Beers of the Strasbourg region have clear German roots, but it was Alsace brewers who challenged the German Pure Beer Law

(SEB) before being bought up by BSN in 1970 and renamed Kanterbräu. At one stage SEB had 11 breweries but now only two operate. The main brand, Kanterbräu, takes its name from a German brewmaster, Maître Kanter, who came to France from Germany. A romantic interpretation of him, in broad-brimmed hat and holding a foaming jug of beer, adorns the beer labels. **Kanterbräu** (4.5 per cent ABV) is light in aroma and body. A stronger **Kanterbräu Gold** is in similar vein to 1664 while a recent revival of **Bière de Mars** (March Beer) is disappointingly thin. The group has had considerable success with **Tourtel**. It is a low-alcohol beer named after another closed brewery: surely the ultimate indignity.

The small town of Schiltigheim – "Schillick" to the locals – is called "ville des brasseurs" (brewers' town). It is home to four brewing companies that provide jobs for around 2,000 people. The Grande Brasserie Alsacienne d'Adelshoffen was founded in 1864 by the Ehrhardt brothers. It was renamed Strassburger Münsterbräu during the years of German control and was bought by the Fischer/Pêcheur group in

1922, though it has always been given a considerable degree of independence to run its own affairs. It has an everyday light lager in the Alsatian style but a more characterful **Adelshoffen Export** (4.5 per cent ABV). It is brewed from pale malt and maize (corn) with Hallertau and Styrian hops (20 IBUs). It has a clean malt aroma with some citric notes from the hops, a malty palate and a bittersweet finish that becomes dry. The company created enormous interest in 1982 with **Adelscott**, a beer made with some peated whisky malt. It cashed in on the French fascination with Scotch malt whisky. The beer is 6.6 per cent ABV, made from pale malt, whisky malt and maize. It is hopped with Alsace Brewers' Gold, Hallertau and Styrian varieties and has 16 to 20 IBUs. It is lagered for two months and has an appealing aroma of smoked malt, rich malt in the mouth and a light smoky finish.

Fischer/Pêcheur is the largest independent brewery in France. It hedges its bets with its name, having used both at various terms when under

French and German control but today is known simply as Fischer. It was founded in 1821 in Strasbourg by Jean Fischer, who moved to Schiltigheim in 1854. Its ebullient chairman, Michel Debus, caused a storm of controversy in 1988 when he instigated the court case against the German *Reinheitsgebot*. He is a great innovator, constantly creating new brands that have considerable public relations impact but are a dubious contribution to the greater appreciation of beer. He has produced an aphrodisiac beer **36.15 – La Bière Amoureuse**, flavoured with ginseng, a rum-flavoured beer, and non-alcoholic beers for dogs and cats called **Mon Titi** and **Mon Toutou**. A 6.5 per cent ABV kriek is an attempt to replicate a Belgian cherry beer, using a fruit concentrate rather than whole cherries.

Among the standard brews, **Fischer Gold** (6.4 per cent ABV) in a Grolsch-style swing-top bottle, has a perfumy aroma and good hop character, and a soft, malty, smooth bière de mars is brewed for the spring.

The brewery that became Schützenberger was founded in Strasbourg in 1740 but may be older. It was bought by Jean-Daniel Schützenberger in 1768. It

Imposing entrance to Météor's Hochfelden Brewery. It was licensed to use the term "Pils" by Pilsner Urquell. Schutzenberger's Patriator is a German-style Bock with a Tartan influence

was called the Brasserie Royale until the revolution of 1789 when it was hastily renamed Brasserie de la Patrie, which translated into Brauerei zum Vaterland – the Fatherland Brewery – under German rule. It moved to Schiltigheim in 1866. It is run today by Rina Müller-Walter, who succeeded her father. She is believed to be the only woman running a major brewing company in Europe. The company brews some rich and beautifully-crafted beers, a long way removed from the general Alsatian style. Its **Jubilator** and **Patriator** brews (7.0 per cent ABV) are pale and dark German-style double Bocks, with great hop character. The pale is smooth and perfumy, the brown rich and fruity. **Schutz 2000** was brewed to mark the two-thousandth anniversary of the founding of Strasbourg. It is an unfiltered,

bottle-conditioned beer (6.5 per cent ABV) bursting with rich, tart fruit and resiny hops. Another celebration beer, **Cuivrée** (house brew) marked the brewery's own 250 years. This is a luscious, 8.0 per cent Vienna-style strong lager, gold-red, malty and fruity, underscored by perfumy hops. There are seasonal March (5.2 per cent ABV) and Christmas (6.0 per cent ABV) brews.

The cuckoo in the Schillick nest is Heineken, which went on the rampage in Alsace in the 1970s and 1980s. It is based on the site of the old Brasserie de l'Espérance (ironically, the Great Expectations Brewery) which was founded in Strasbourg in 1746 and moved to Schiltigheim in 1860. It merged with four other breweries, including Mützig, to form Alsatian Breweries, Alba for short. In 1972 Alba was bought by Heineken, which then staged a mammoth three-way merger in 1984 with Union de Brasseries, famous in Africa and South-east Asia for its 33 brand, and Pelforth of Mons-en-Baroeul, whose pelican trade mark is recognized throughout France. The new group, with a quarter of French beer sales, went through several changes of name until the dominant partner exerted its influence. It is now Brasseries Heineken. As well as the Schillick plant, it has the

Pelforth Brewery near Lille and one in Marseille. The major emphasis goes into promoting the ubiquitous Dutch Heineken. The fate of other brands is less clear. It is likely that the Pelforth beers will continue because of their popularity in the Lille area. **Pelforth Blonde** and **Pélican** (4.8 per cent ABV) are standard French lagers but **Pelforth Brune** (6.5 per cent ABV) has plenty of rich dark chocolatey malt character. It is to be hoped that the characterful Mützig brands, **Mützig** (4.8 per cent ABV) and **Old Lager** (7.3 per cent ABV), both with rich malt and dry, hoppy finishes, will survive. The Pelforth plant produces **George Killian's Bière Rousse**, based on Killian's Irish Ale. It is sold in The Netherlands under the name of Kilyan.

Météor is in the Alsatian village of Hochfelden. Brewing dates back to 1640 and beyond: beer was supplied to a local abbey and to farms in the area. The present brewery was bought by the Metzger family of Strasbourg in 1844 and is now owned by their relations through marriage, the Haags. The name **Météor** was adopted in 1925 and the company launched a Pilsner-style beer under the name two years later. It signed an agreement with Pilsner Urquell to use the term "Pils", the only such agreement in the French brewing industry. The beer is 4.9 per cent ABV and is brewed with pale malt and corn grits. Hops used are Czech Saaz (Žatec) and Alsatian varieties. The beer, by local standards, is well-hopped, achieving 35 IBUs. A single decoction mash is used and the beer is lagered for one month. It has a toasty malt and hops aroma, with sweet malt and bitter hops in the mouth, and a long dry finish with more hops and some honey/vanilla notes. It lacks the depth and finesse of a true Pilsner but is a well-made and attractive beer. **Ackerland Blonde** (5.9 per cent ABV) is a rich and malty pale lager. A brown version, **Ackerland Brune** (6.3 per cent ABV), is packed with dark malt and hops character. The brewery has cashed in on the Scotch malt whisky craze with **Mortimer** (8.0 per cent ABV), an amber-coloured beer, fruity and lightly hopped.

NORD-PAS DE CALAIS

If Alsace is a triumph of modernization, of state-of-the-art brewing, then Nord-Pas de Calais is a time-warp where beer is made by ancient, hand-crafted methods. This is the region of "artisanal beer". Some lagers are produced, but in general the beers of border country recall a more ruminative and rural period when beer was made on farms and in homes as naturally as bread would be baked and the land tilled and harvested. It is a region of flat land, lowering skies and distant horizons where political borders do not impinge on the reality of everyday life, a region rich in Flemish as well as French traditions. The locals speak of "French Flanders" and cock a snook at history.

On the coat-tails of the Belgian revival, beer lovers have disovered the ales of French Flanders, Artois and Picardy once just a footnote in the brewing books, now a recognizable style in their own right. Between Calais and Lille there is a tradition known as "bière de garde". These were beers brewed on farms, usually in the winter, to provide important sustenance for farmers and all those who worked the land.

Many of the breweries are still small and are based on farms, though farming is no longer the major preoccupation as the interest in beer from Flanders grows. The beers are often pale as well as brown, but the original versions would have been dark. Wherever possible brewers use barley and hops from the region, which allows them to carry the appellation "Pas de Calais/Région du Nord" on their labels. From Ypres across the border in Belgium down into French Flanders, stretches a small and very ancient hop-growing area, while Flanders, the Champagne region and Burgundy produce malting barley of the highest quality.

The classic style is a strong beer of between 6.0 and 8.0 per cent ABV, malty and spicy from the use of well-cured malts. Mashing is often long to achieve some caramelization of the brewing sugars. Hop rates are not high, with IBUs in the 20s: the brewer is seeking roundness, fullness, a certain alcoholic warmth rather than a hard bitterness. Finished beers are stored for a month: centuries ago this would have been a far longer period.

Commercial success has brought problems in its wake. Some brewers have switched from the use of traditional top-working yeasts to lager cultures. They say this gives them greater control over fermentation and the beers are more stable once out in trade. But at the same time they are still fermenting at ale temperatures in order to achieve a fruity ale character. Nevertheless, it would be a tragedy if the true concept of a top-fermenting bière de garde is lost in the rush to embrace all the demands of the modern market with its insatiable belief in "shelf life".

The beer that breathed life back into the style is Jenlain. It became a cult drink with students in Lille in the 1980s and features prominently in festivals and celebrations in the city. Jenlain comes from the Brasserie Duyck in the village of Jenlain south-east of Valenciennes. Brewing started on a farm and in 1922 Félix Duyck, of Flemish stock, started brewing on the farm. The business is now run by his son Robert and grandson

A GROUP CALLED LE GHILDE DES ESWARDS CERVOISIERS IN THE NORD-PAS DE CALAIS HAS RECREATED THE TRADITION OF THE "ALE CONNERS" OF MEDIEVAL EUROPE AND ENGLAND, GOVERNMENT OFFICIALS WHO TESTED THE QUALITY OF BEER IN TAVERNS AND ALE HOUSES.

BIÈRES DE GARDE ARE "KEEPING BEERS". THE GERMANS WOULD SAY LAGER BUT THE FRENCH TRADITION IS QUITE DIFFERENT AND HAS MORE IN COMMON WITH THE SAISONS OF BELGIAN WALLONIA AND THE OLD ALES AND STOCK ALES OF ENGLAND.

Jenlain was the bière de garde that captured the attention of beer drinkers worldwide

Raymond. Production has grown to 90,000 hectolitres a year but brewing has remained traditional in copper vessels. Malts from Flanders, Champagne and Burgundy are used along with four hop varieties from Belgium, France, Germany and Slovenia. **Jenlain**, 6.5 per cent ABV, is russet-coloured, spicy and malty. It is a highly complex beer with great depth (25 IBUs). The Duycks did experiment with a bottom-fermenting yeast but latest information is that they have returned to proper ale brewing. They also brew a Christmas beer and a pale spring (Printemps) beer.

Beer was brewed in the region for coal miners as well as farm workers – Lille was once at the heart of the mining industry of northern France. The Castelain Brewery at Bénifontaine near Lens once made a special 2.0 per cent alcohol beer for miners, but all the pits have gone and the only reminder of the industry is the ghostly figure of a coal miner with his lamp on the label of the brewery's main brand Ch'ti. The name comes from Picardy dialect and means "c'est toi" – "it suits you". The brewery, part of a farm, was built in 1926 and was bought by the Castelain family in 1966. The handsome brewhouse with gleaming copper kettles produces 28,000 hectolitres a year. Yves Castelain uses Flemish and French barley and hops for pale and brown versions of Ch'ti as well as for an organic beer called Jade, Christmas and March beers, and an abbey-style beer called Sint Arnoldus. Yves Castelain has switched to lager yeast but ferments at 15 degrees

C/60F. The beers are fermented for 10 to 12 days and then conditioned for up to two months. **Ch'ti Blonde** is made from four malts, the **Ch'ti Brune** from eight, including Munich, cara-Munich and torrefied varieties. The 6.5 per cent ABV beers are rich and fruity, with the Brune in particular having a strong hint of raisins in the mouth. The 4.6 per cent ABV **Ch'ti Jade** has more hop character, pungent and perfumy, with sweet malt in the mouth and a fruity finish that becomes dry.

In the hills of French Hainaut, close to the Belgian border, the Bailleux family runs the Café Restaurant au Baron in Gussignies and also brews on the premises. All the products are true top-fermenting, bottle-conditioned bières de garde, though one is called a saison in the Belgian fashion. The **Cuvée des Jonquilles** does not, in spite of the name, use daffodils in the brewing process but it has an entrancing golden colour and flowery-fruity aroma and palate. The 7.0 per cent ABV beer is brewed in the spring, which explains the daffodil associations. Four malts and four hop varieties are used. The **Saison Saint Médard**, also 7.0 per cent ABV, has a fine cherry colour and a fruity aroma similar to a Belgian kriek but without the lambic sourness. There is also a chocolatey and spicy Christmas beer.

The Brasserie d'Annoeullin is in the small town of the same name between Lens and Lille. The brewery was once a farm and Bertrand Lepers' wife, Yvonne, comes from farmer-brewers at Flers. When they married they merged the two

breweries. The mash tun doubles as a copper after the wort has been clarified. The beer ferments in horizontal tanks in cellars that were once cattle byres. Primary fermentation lasts for a week, followed by two weeks' conditioning. The bière de garde is called, tongue-in-cheek, **Pastor Ale** with the sub-title "C'est une symphonie". It is 6.5 per cent ABV and is made from pale malt only. It has a rich gold colour, pronounced orange fruit and earthy hops on the aroma, more tart fruit in the mouth and a dry and fruity finish. A 7.3 per cent ABV **Angelus** is a wheat beer, using 30 per cent buck wheat in flour form. It is bronze coloured and has a powerful citric tangerine aroma backed by spicy hops, with more tart fruit in the mouth and a long, bitter-sweet finish: a magnificent beer.

The St Sylvestre Brewery at Steenvoorde, in the heart of the hop country, produces a gold bière de garde called **3 Monts** (8.5 per cent ABV). It is named after three local hills, worthy of celebration in such flat country. The beer is dry and winey with good hop character from local Brewers' Gold and German Tettnang.

The depth of support for beer in the region can be seen in the annual summer festival in Douai where ale is the main lubricant. The two legendary giants that lead the parade are known as Monsieur and Madame Gayant and the local brewery calls itself Les Enfants de Gayant. The enterprising brewery has a large portfolio of beers, including an Abbey beer and a 12 per cent ABV perfumy lager, **Bière de Démon**. Its interpretation of the bière de garde style is called Lutèce Bière de Paris – Lutèce comes from the Roman name for Paris, Lutetia. Brewers in Roman Paris were based in an area known as La Glacière, fed by the waters of the river Bièvre, named after beavers that bred there. Beer was stored in icy caves – an early form of lager brewing. The beer style was called **Brune de Paris**. The Lutèce Brewery was founded in Paris in 1920 on the site of an old Brasserie de Glacière and, although brewing has been switched to Douai, the style of the original beer is meticulously maintained. It is 6.4 per cent ABV and is made from pale, Munich, crystal and caramel-amber malts. Spalt and Saaz hops achieve 23 IBUs. The beer is conditioned for 60 days. It has a rich malt and fruit aroma, with malt and raisins in the mouth and a deep finish with hints of chocolate and liquorice.

Visitors to Lille can find instant refreshment when they leave the railway station in Les Brasseurs at 22 Place de la Gare. It is a large, beautifully-appointed brewpub, the first in a small chain owned by Patrick Bonduel in Northern France (other pubs are in Angers, Mulhouse, Paris and Strasbourg). The beers are all-malt and unpasteurized, brewed in a tiny brewhouse. Customers can order La Palette du Barman, four taster glasses of each beer. The Blonde has a malty, perfumy aroma with a bitter-sweet palate; the Ambré has a dark toasty character; the Brune has hints of sweet nuts and bitter chocolate; while the cloudy wheat beer – Blanche – has a tangy apples-and-cloves aroma,

citric fruit in the mouth and a dry finish with a powerful hint of apples. There are also March and Christmas seasonal beers.

SELECTED FRENCH BREWERS

Grande Brasserie Alsacienne d'Adelshoffen,
87 route de Bischwiller, 67300 Schiltigheim.

Brasserie d'Annoeullin,
4 Place du Général de Gaulle, 59112 Annoeullin.

Brasserie Bailleux,
Café-Restaurant Au Baron, Place du Fond des Rocs, Gussignies, 59570 Bavay.

Brasserie Castelain,
13 rue Pasteur, Bénifontaine, 62410 Wingles.

Brasserie Duyck,
113 rue Nationale, 59144 Jenlain.

Brasserie des Enfants de Gayant,
63 Fauborg de Paris, 59502 Douai.

Brasserie Fischer,
7 route de Bischwiller, 67300 Schiltigheim.

Brasseries Heineken SA,
19 rue des Deux-Gares, 92565 Rueil-Malmaison.

Kanterbräu SA,
Tour Chenonceaux, 92100 Boulogne.

Brasserie Kronenbourg SA,
86 route d'Oberhausbergen, 67067 Strasbourg.

Brasserie Météor Haag-Metzger & Cie,
6 rue du Général-Lebocq, 67270 Hochfelden.

Brasserie Saint Sylvestre,
1 rue de la Chappelle, 59114 Saint-Sylvestre-Cappel.

Brasserie Schützenberger,
8 rue de la Patrie, 67304 Schiltigheim.

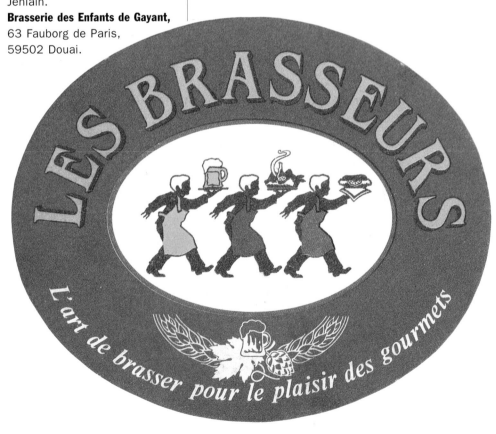

GERMANY

GERMANY IS THE WORLD'S GREATEST BEER NATION. BEER IS ROOTED IN THE LIFESTYLE AND CULTURE OF THE PEOPLE. IT UNDERSCORES EVERY CELEBRATION. AND IN THE CATHOLIC SOUTH, THE BAVARIANS SEEM TO FIND GOOD REASON TO CELEBRATE ALL YEAR ROUND. THEIR MUNICH OKTOBERFEST IS THE WORLD'S MOST FAMOUS BEER FESTIVAL BUT IT IS NOT SUFFICIENT TO SATIATE THE BAVARIANS. THEY HAVE WINTER BEERS, MARCH BEERS, MAY BEERS AND STRONG LENT BEERS THEY CALL "LIQUID BREAD".

WHILE MOST GERMAN BEERS ARE FILTERED BEFORE LEAVING THE BREWERIES, UNFILTERED BEERS EXIST IN SOME AREAS, FRANCONIA IN PARTICULAR. KRÄUSEN BEER MEANS THAT SOME PARTIALLY FERMENTED WORT HAS BEEN ADDED DURING SECONDARY FERMENTATION AND THE FINISHED BEER IS THEN SOLD WITHOUT FILTRATION. BEER THAT IS NOT KRÄUSENED BUT STILL UNFILTERED IS KNOWN AS KELLERBIER. BEERS MATURED IN OPEN OR PARTIALLY OPEN TANKS AND, AS A RESULT, LOW IN CARBONATION, ARE CALLED UNGESPUNDERD, LITERALLY "UNBUNGED". DAMPFBIER MEANS "STEAM BEER" AND IS USED BY BREWERIES THAT ONCE HAD STEAM ENGINES. MAISEL IN BAYREUTH HAS ITS STEAM ENGINES ON SHOW AND BREWS A DAMPFBIER IN THEIR HONOUR.

Greetings from the Oktoberfest, the world's most famous beer festival. Right, the 1516 Reinheitsgebot

It is not just "lager" that Germans drink. Ask for a lager in a German bar and you will get a puzzled look. You may be shown the storage area or the refrigerator instead of being served a cool, pale beer. Lager, from *lagerung* meaning "to store", is a stage in the brewing process. The term lager is mainly confined to exports to the British Isles where it is used to distinguish beers brewed by cold fermentation from warm-fermented ales. In Germany drinkers need to be more specific. Bavarians will call for a Hell or a Dunkel or, depending on the season of the year, they might demand a Märzen or a Bock. In the North, the call may be for an Export. And everywhere the shout for "a Pils" will bring forth a dry and bitter interpretation of the Bohemian Pilsner.

And Germans do not only drink beers made by cold fermentation. Members of the ale family of beer are growing in favour. Bavarian wheat beers are enormously popular

and have grown to around 30 per cent of the total beer market. Berlin has its own idiosyncratic version of wheat beer while Cologne and Düsseldorf proudly brew golden Kölsch and copper-coloured Alt beers.

REINHEITSGEBOT

The history of the *Reinheitsgebot*, the sixteenth-century Bavarian "Pure Beer Pledge", is covered in the history section. It is still in force throughout Germany. It stipulates that beer can only be brewed with malted barley and wheat, hops, yeast and water: sugars and "adjuncts" – cheap unmalted cereals – are outlawed. The pledge is adhered to with fierce pride by brewers who were angered by a decision of the European Court in 1987 to declare the pledge "a restraint of trade". The case was taken to court by French brewers based ironically in the former German region around Strasbourg. French and other European brewers were irritated that they could not export beer to Germany as they did not brew according to the *Reinheitsgebot*. But, despite a court ruling in favour of non-German brewers, imported beer has made little headway in Germany. The German brewers launched a campaign against what they call "chemi-beer", an attempt to suggest that beers from other countries are grossly inferior to their own and brewed using chemicals. While some poor quality packaged beers are sometimes brewed with the help of small amounts of chemicals to speed up

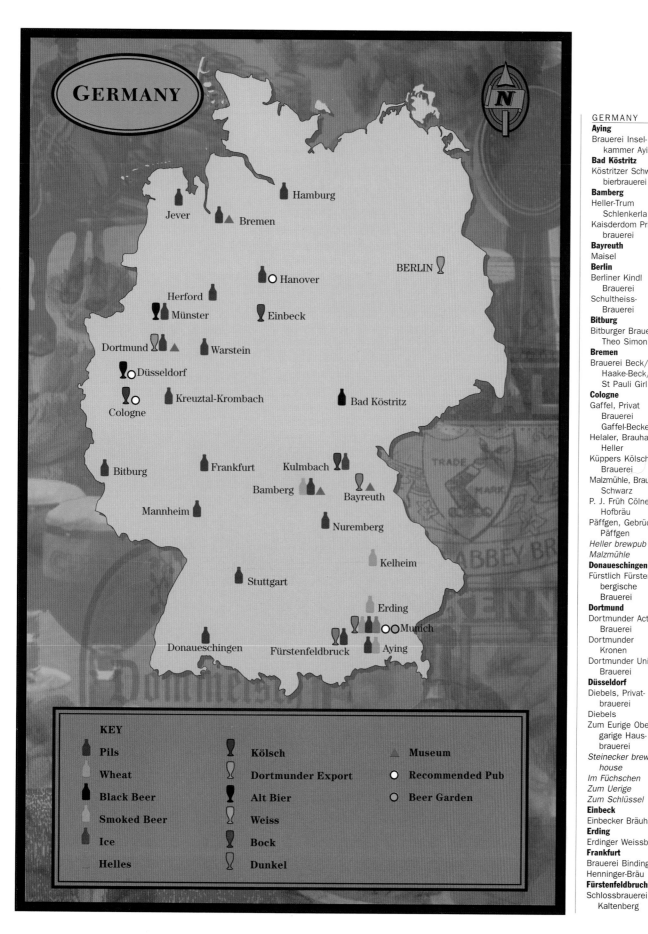

GERMANY

Jever · Hamburg · Bremen

Herford · Hanover · BERLIN
Münster · Einbeck

Dortmund · Warstein
Düsseldorf
Kreuztal-Krombach · Bad Köstritz
Cologne

Bitburg · Frankfurt · Kulmbach
Bamberg · Bayreuth
Mannheim · Nuremberg
Kelheim
Stuttgart
Erding
Donaueschingen · Fürstenfeldbruck · Munich · Aying

KEY

Pils	Kölsch	▲ Museum
Wheat	Dortmunder Export	○ Recommended Pub
Black Beer	Alt Bier	○ Beer Garden
Smoked Beer	Weiss	
Ice	Bock	
Helles	Dunkel	

CZECHS CLAIM THAT NOW THEY ARE DIVORCED FROM THE WINE-DRINKING SLOVAKS THEY ARE THE WORLD'S GREATEST BEER DRINKERS. BUT NO ONE CAN BEAT THE SHEER VOLUME OF BEER CONSUMED IN THE MUCH LARGER COUNTRY OF GERMANY. GERMANS PUT AWAY 148 LITRES PER HEAD A YEAR WHILE THE BAVARIANS MANAGE A STAGGERING 240 LITRES.

The powerful beers that sustained monks during Lent were known as "liquid bread"

fermentation and to create a thick head on beer, the use of chemicals or natural compounds is in the main confined to water treatment to enable brewers to harden or soften their brewing liquor. And nothing in the *Reinheitsgebot* stops German brewers treating their water.

Every brewery in Germany and many bars, too, display plaques announcing that the beers produced or on sale adhere to the *Reinheitsgebot*. Consumers are intensely loyal to their local breweries and the German brewing industry has been largely untouched by imports, though Czech beers, which are brewed to the Purity Pledge, are popular. It should be noted, however, that with the exception of Bavaria, German

beers brewed for export do not have to meet the requirements of the *Reinheitsgebot*.

BAVARIA

Germany has around 1,400 breweries. The country has so far not been overtaken by the merger mania of the rest of the world. Some 750 of the total are located in Bavaria. Every town and just about every village has a brewery, sometimes more than one, brewing to traditional recipes, producing seasonal specialities, ignoring the outside world and pressures to produce beers by faster and less perfect methods. Monasteries and even convents brew beer, often for just their own and visitors' consumption. Bavaria remains a largely rural region and brewing is a time-honoured, bucolic

ritual, as natural as baking bread, using the barley and the hops from the surrounding fields and pure, icy water from the Alps. The choice is literally staggering, around 5,000 different beers, in a wide variety of styles and strengths. By avoiding mergers, only a handful of brewers, mainly in Munich, are large, producing more than half a million hectolitres a year. Five hundred Bavarian breweries make no more than 10,000 hectolitres a year and some of those produce as little as 2,000 hectolitres.

The only major change in brewing practice in Bavaria has been the switch from warm to cold fermentation. The earliest empirical attempts to store or lager beer came in the great Bavarian capital of Munich. The city was founded in 1158 when a Bavarian duke built a bridge across the River Isar and Munich became a major trading town on the salt route from Austria to the north German ports. Munich – München in German, from Mönchen, "the monks' place" – is close to the foothills of the Alps and brewers stored their beers in deep caves to withstand the rigours of hot summers. The low temperatures encouraged yeast to settle at the bottom of the fermenting vessels and to turn malt sugars into alcohol much more slowly than conventional warm fermentation. The result was a cleaner-tasting, less fruity and more stable beer.

As massive industrial innovation swept across Europe in the late eighteenth and nineteenth centuries, brewers rushed to embrace all the new

technologies available to them. Steam power, temperature control, yeast propagation, better hop utilization, kilning of malt over coke fires and, above all, refrigeration led to fundamental changes in the way beer was brewed. Gabriel Sedlmayr the Younger, a member of the great Munich brewing dynasty that owns the Spaten group, travelled widely in Europe to learn his brewing skills. He returned to Munich in 1834 to put his knowledge into operation and to use new technology to develop lager brewing. From the late 1830s Sedlmayr became famous throughout the world of brewing as the man behind the new bottom-fermenting beer. He collaborated with Anton Dreher, another innovative brewer in Vienna, and the two worked with Carl von Linde, builder of ice machines, to develop a commercial refrigerator that would enable beer to be stored not in caves but in brewery cellars at near-freezing temperatures.

DARK LAGERS

The first Munich lagers were dark. Malting techniques must have been behind those in England, where pale ales appeared early in the nineteenth century. Coal was notoriously expensive in Bavaria and coke, made from coal, was vital to produce pale malt on a large scale. And continental varieties of barley, high in protein, were more difficult to work with, needing a triple-decoction mashing regime. So the revolutionary new beer that emerged from Sedlmayr's Spaten brewery was a dark copper-to-mahogany colour. The style survives and is called Dunkel, sometimes rendered as Dunkles, which means dark. Today the malt grist for the beer will be a careful blend of pale and darker malt. The latter is known worldwide as Munich malt, which has been kilned in the maltings to a high temperature but avoids the bitter, roasty character of a much darker English black or chocolate malt. A Munich brewer looks for sweetness from his malt which he can balance with aromatic Bavarian hops.

Spaten's **Ludwig Thoma Dunkel** is the classic Munich dark beer. It is 5.5 per cent ABV, with 47 colour units and a gentle 20 IBUs. It has a malty, slighty spicy aroma, a malt-and-coffee palate and a finish that begins bitter-sweet and becomes dry. Among the other Munich brewers, Augustiner's **Dunkel** is 5.0 per cent ABV, exceptionally dark with russet tints, a malty nose, a nutty palate and a dry finish. Hacker-Pschorr's **Dunkel** (5.2 per cent ABV) is rich, malty and chocolatey with a dry finish. The Hofbräuhaus, the world-famous "royal court brewhouse", with oompah bands and a large beer garden, has a distinctive 5.2 per cent ABV **Dunkel** with a complex malt and vanilla aroma, tart dark fruit in the mouth and a long finish with hints of hops, dark fruit and chocolate. Paulaner's 5.2 per cent ABV **Dunkel** is both extremely dark and well-hopped for the style, with an aromatic malt and hops aroma, dark fruit in the mouth and a dry and bitter finish.

Outside Munich, the Kaltenberg Brewery has turned its dark lager into a speciality. The brewery is based in a splendid neo-Gothic castle and is owned by an aristocratic brewer, Prince Luitpold of Bavaria. He is a member of the German royal family that lost power at the end of the First World War. When he took over the family castle and brewery in 1976, he decided to beef up the Dunkel and make it his leading brand.

The 5.6 per cent ABV **König Ludwig Dunkel** – named after a royal ancestor, King Ludwig – is well-attenuated, with most of the brewing sugars turned to alcohol. The mashing is an exhaustive triple decoction one and hops – Hersbruck and Tettnang – are added three times during the copper boil. The British practice of dry-hopping – adding a handful of hops to the beer in cask – is

Kaltenberg Castle near Munich is owned by Prince Luitpold, a renowned brewer

Kaltenberg's Dunkel lager is a classic of the style, with a coffee and dark fruit character from the malts

THE NAME OF THE GREAT MUNICH BREWERY SPATEN MEANS "SPADE". ITS SYMBOL IS A MALT SHOVEL BUT THE NAME IS ALSO A HUMOROUS REFERENCE TO A FORMER OWNER OF THE BREWERY CALLED SPAETH.

Maisel's Brewery is in Bayreuth with its strong Wagnerian associations

Kulmbach's EKU Brewery is famous for Kulminator 28, once the strongest beer in the world

LÖWENBRÄU MEANS LION'S BREW AND IS PROPERLY PRONOUNCED "LURVENBROI". THE MUNICH BREWERY WAS FOUNDED IN A TAVERN NEXT TO A CAGE WHERE THE DUKES OF BAVARIA KEPT THEIR LIONS. THERE ARE SEVERAL GERMAN BREWERS WHO USE LÖWEN IN THEIR TITLE AS A SYMBOL OF STRENGTH.

used for additional aroma: this is frowned on by most German brewers. The finished beer has 24 to 26 IBUs. The beer is kräusened during lagering, which means that some partially-fermented wort is added to the beer to encourage a powerful second fermentation. Lagering takes place in the castle cellars in pitch-lined wooden vessels. The beer has a pronounced bitter-hoppy character from aroma to finish, balanced by dark malt, coffee and bitter fruit. It is a splendidly refreshing beer.

Franconia, the northern region of Bavaria (Franken in German), is packed with breweries. The main towns of Amberg, Bamberg and Nuremberg have 18 breweries between them, nine of them in the half-timbered, medieval splendour of Bamberg. The relative isolation of Franconia, heightened by its proximity to East Germany and Czechoslovakia during the years of the Cold War, has made it a conservative region with a great belief in traditional values, including a devotion to dark lagers. Many of the breweries are tiny, no more than brew-pubs. A classic is the Hausbrauerei Altstadthof in Nuremberg, which means "the house brewery in the old town courtyard". Based in sixteenth-century buildings, the brewhouse has copper mashing and boiling vessels and wooden fermenters and lagering tanks.

Using organically-grown barley and hops, the 4.8 per cent ABV dark beer is red-brown in colour, has a yeasty and malty aroma, a creamy palate and a malty finish with some hints of dark fruit.

In Kulmbach, the Kulmbacher Mönchshof was once a monastic brewery, secularized at the end of the eighteenth century. Its speciality is **Kloster Schwarz Bier** – cloister black beer – a 4.7 per cent ABV brew known locally as "the black Pils" because of its unusual hoppiness for the style. It begins malty and yeasty on the nose but picks up hop character on the palate and finishes dry and bitter.

Also in Kulmbach, EKU, the brewery famous for its 13.5 per cent ABV Doppelbock, one of the strongest beers in the world, also makes a 4.8 per cent ABV **Rubin Dunkel**, rich and malty with a hint of tart fruit and a dry finish.

The Klosterbräu Bamberg is another brewery with monastic origins. It dates from the sixteenth century when it was owned by the local bishop and monks carried out the brewing. The dark beer, available in the tavern next door, has a tongue-twisting name: **Achd Bambärcha Schwärzla** (5.3 per cent ABV), Franconian dialect for "real Bamberg black". It is a dark brown, almost black beer,

hoppy on the nose, with coffee and dark fruit on the palate and a bitter-sweet finish.

In Bayreuth, with its Wagner associations, Maisel brews a 5.1 per cent ABV **Dunkel** with a pleasant nutty palate, dry finish and delicate hop bitterness.

PALE LAGERS

To call the pale lagers of Munich and Bavaria "everyday beers" is to diminish the quality and the respectable strengths of brews of between 4.5 and 5.0 per cent ABV. They are known as Helles or Hell for short, meaning pale. (The only exception is Franconia where the style is often referred to as *Vollbier*.) Helles beers sit just below Pilsners, which are slightly stronger and a shade dryer and more hoppy. Helles is the drink of the beer garden and the keller, refreshing, spritzy, malty and delicately hopped.

The first pale lager appeared from the Spaten Brewery in 1894. Paulaner, which now includes Hacker-Pschorr, busily promoted the style in the 1920s and 1930s. But Helles did not overtake Dunkel in popularity until the 1950s, rather as pale ale replaced mild in British beer drinkers' affections. Helles beers tend to be extremely pale while a Pilsner is golden. Spaten's **Hell** is 4.8 per cent ABV, its **Pilsener** – note the variation in spelling – is 5.0 per cent ABV. But the Pilsner has 38 IBUs, the Hell just 22. The Hell is a Bavarian classic, with an entrancing bitter-sweet, malt-and-hops aroma, malty in the mouth and finish that becomes dry but not bitter.

Augustiner's **Hell** (5.2 per cent ABV) is the most popular among Munich's beer lovers, perhaps as a result of its more robust strength, with a malty-creamy aroma, malt in the mouth and on the finish. Hacker-Pschorr's 4.9 per cent ABV **Hell** is darker with a fruity aroma and palate, and a dry finish (20 IBUs). Löwenbräu's **Hell** (5.3 per cent ABV) is soft and malty from aroma to finish. In sharp distinction, Paulaner's **Original Münchner Hell** (4.9 per cent ABV) has a dry edge to the finish and is much more generously hopped.

The oddest beer comes from Forschung at Perlach, an outer suburb of Munich. As well as brewing, the Jakob family also carries out research work for other breweries. The name of the 5.4 per cent ABV **Pilsissimus** suggests it is a junior version of a Pilsner but the strength belies this. It is copper coloured with a big floral hop aroma, soft malt in the mouth and a finish packed with great hop character.

Another brewery close to Munich, Bachmayer of Dorfen near Erding, brews a 4.7 per cent ABV **Hell** that is excep-

tionally pale with a fruity aroma and palate and a dry finish. The 4.8 per cent ABV **Hell** from Dimpfl in Fürth im Wald is golden in colour, sharp and tangy on the aroma, with a rounded maltiness offset by good hop character: the character of the beer is clearly influenced by its proximity to the Czech border.

Examples of Franconian **Vollbier** include Bärenbräu's 4.8 per cent ABV in Staffelstein, hoppy and dry, Brauhaus's crisp and quenching 4.6 per cent ABV offering in Amberg, the bitter-sweet 5.1 per cent ABV from Eichorn of Forcheim, and the apple-fruity 4.8 per cent ABV from Falkenloch of Neuhaus.

PILSNER

In spite of the geographical closeness of Bavaria and Bohemia, the brewing of golden lagers was slow to spread from their town of origin, Pilsen, to Munich. But now "Pils" is such a widespread style that most beer drinkers think of it as German rather than Czech beer. Unlike the more austere Pils of Northern Germany, with their flinty dryness, Bavarian versions have much in common with the genuine article from Pilsen: a rich maltiness offset by generous bitterness, using hops from the Hallertau that have a similar aromatic quality to Bohemian Žatec or Saaz varieties. Most Bavarian breweries include a Pilsener – the German interpretation of the spelling – in their portfolios. Drinkers invariably shorten the word to demand "ein Pils".

In Munich, Löwenbräu's **Pilsener** (5.4 per cent ABV) is

the hoppiest of the city's contributions to the style. With bitterness units in the high 30s from Hallertau and Saaz hop varieties, it has a superb citric aroma, a fine balance of malt and hops in the mouth and a shatteringly long finish packed with hop bitterness. Löwenbräu buys malt from Bavaria and also from the Champagne region of France. Paulaner's 4.8 per cent ABV **Pilsener** has a floral, aromatic hop nose, a big malty body underpinned by hops and a long, dry finish. In the manner of German winemakers, Paulaner describes the beer as "Extra Trocken" – Extra Dry. The world-famous brewing university of Weihenstephan ("Holy Stephen") at Freising on the Munich outskirts and close to the new airport is connected to a brewery of the same name. Its **Edelpils** (4.9 per cent ABV) is extremely dry with a fine perfumy hop aroma, a malty body and a dry and bitter finish.

Elsewhere in Bavaria, Aukofer of Kelheim brews a 4.8

At first a simple tavern beer, Löwenbräu grew to be one of the mighty Munich breweries

LÖWENBRÄU

Märzen beers are now giving way to less characterful Oktoberfest lagers

per cent ABV **Pilsener** with a complex hoppy aroma, bitter-sweet malt and hops in the mouth and long, lingeringly hoppy finish. In Franconia, Becher of Beyreuth produces a 4.7 per cent ABV **Pilsener** that, in the Franken fashion, is unfiltered, with a yeasty aroma balanced by good bitter hops. In Amberg, the Brauhaus 4.7 per cent ABV **Pilsener** has a big hop attack on the aroma and palate, with some malt in the mouth and big bitter finish. At Zapfendorf near Bamberg, the Drei Kronen – Three Crowns – brewery has a superb 4.8 per cent ABV **Pilsener** with a dense head, firm body, malty palate and long dry finish. EKU's **Pilsener** (4.9 per cent ABV) from Kulmbach has a rich, floral hop bouquet, bitter hops in the mouth backed by sweet malt and a bitter-sweet, malt and hops finish. In Bamberg, Mahrs's **Pilsener** (4.7 per cent ABV) is rich and malty balanced by aromatic hops, with a dry and bitter finish. In the heart of the great Hallertau hop-growing area, the Schlossbräu (Castle Brew) **Pilsener** is 4.9 per cent ABV and, fittingly, has a nostril-expanding hop aroma, more hops with balancing malt on the palate and a bitter finish.

MARCH BEER

In spite of the enormous interest in Bavarian beers both within and without the region, one style is under threat. Märzenbier means March beer, an ancient style from the days before refrigeration. March was the last month when it was safe to brew before the hot summer weather arrived. So in that month beers strong in alcohol and high in hops were made and stored for drinking during the summer, with any left over consumed in September and October. The Märzenbiers of Bavaria took on a special significance in the nineteenth century with the arrival of the Munich Oktoberfest in 1810, followed by the moves towards commercial lagering of beer in the 1830s. March beers became an Oktoberfest treat, a special beer to mark a special occasion. The beers at first were dark brown but when Gabriel Sedlmayr at Spaten began his work on cold fermentation he worked closely with Anton Dreher in Vienna where beers had a reddish tinge as a result of using a well-kilned amber malt. Spaten's Märzenbier became the benchmark for other brewers to copy, a reddish-brown brew developed by Gabriel Sedlmayr's brother Josef at his own Franziskaner Brewery in Munich (the two breweries were to merge in 1920). The 5.6 per cent ABV beer today, called **Ur-Märzen** (Ur being short for Urtyp, or Original) is lagered for three months, has 32.5 colour units and 21.5 IBUs. It is a malty beer but the maltiness is clean, quenching and slightly spicy, not cloying, underpinned by a delicate but firm hoppiness, with a bitter-sweet finish.

Sales of Märzenbier are declining – down to less than 10 per cent of the total Bavarian beer market – as a result of the changing nature of the Oktoberfest. The festival is now so renowned that it attracts a vast number of visitors from abroad, mainly from the English-speaking world: it is packed with Americans, Australians and New Zealanders. Most of them are unaware of the history of Märzenbier and come to Munich expecting to drink pale lagers. The brewers oblige and some Oktoberfestbiers, though of good quality, are in every way a pale shadow of the brews originally proudly stored for the occasion. Even Spaten, with its classic Märzen, also produces a separate Oktoberfestbier today.

Fortunately the Hofbräuhaus sticks to tradition. Its 5.7 per cent ABV **Märzen** is another classic brew, red-brown in colour, with a rich malty aroma, a light and quenching palate and a gently dry finish. Outside Munich, the Bräuhaus at Fussen close to the Austrian border has a suitably dark red **Märzen**, with a honey aroma, a rich and fruity palate and malty finish that becomes dry. The Eichorn Brewery at Forcheim has a much paler **Märzen** (5.7 per cent ABV) with an apple-fruit nose, malt and hops in the mouth and big bitter-sweet, well-balanced and complex finish. Fässla of Bamberg has a 5.3 per cent ABV **Märzen**, also known as **Zwergla**, that has a dark amber colour, a nutty palate, and firm hops in the mouth and the finish. Goss's interpretation of the style in Deuerling is a 5.5 per cent ABV pale amber brew, more hoppy than most, with malt and light fruit on the palate and a clean, quenching finish. The St Georghen Brewery in Buttenheim in Franconia produces a magnificent **Gold Märzen** (5.6 per cent ABV) which, despite the name, is a true amber colour with great hop attack on the aroma and palate, a rich and rounded maltiness with a dry finish and a hint of apple fruit. Wagner in Eschenbach plays all the right tunes with its 5.3 per cent ABV **Märzen**: rich malt arpeggio, spicy and fruity notes with a good hop glissando.

BOCK

Outside Bavaria the most popular theory for the origin of the term Bock is that it comes from the town of Einbeck in Lower Saxony. For centuries Einbeck has been associated with brewing strong beers, known as Einbecker beers and corrupted to just Beck (which has nothing to do with Beck's Brewery in Bremen). In the Bavarian dialect Beck became further corrupted to Bock. The style of beer had spread to the south as a result of a marriage in the seventeenth century between a duke of Brunswick in Lower Saxony and the daughter of an aristocrat from Bavaria. They were married in Munich and a century later there were

records of an "Oanbock" beer brewing brewed in the Hofbräuhaus, the royal court brewery, in the Bavarian capital.

The Bavarians will have none of these airy Northern theories. For them Bock is a local style, a strong seasonal beer associated with Lent and brewed by monks as "liquid bread" to help them sustain themselves during the fasting period.

The early Bocks would have been dark and warm-fermented. Today there are pale Bocks, amber Bocks and copper Bocks as well, and they are cold-fermented. They are strong in alcohol, ranging from 6.0 to 8.0 per cent by volume. There are several seasonal versions: winter Bocks, Maibocks for the early summer and even stronger Double Bocks for Lent. The Double Bocks are also known as Starkbier (Strong Beer) and are drunk on draught for Starkbierzeit, "Strong Beer Time", in Munich.

The classic Maibock comes from the Hofbräuhaus in Munich, where the first casks are tapped on May Day by the Mayor and Prime Minister of Bavaria who, like a bibulous double act, perform the same ceremony at the Oktoberfest. Although the beer is described as "Helles Bock" (pale Bock) it is a burnished amber colour with 7.2 per cent alcohol. It has a dense head of foam through which springs the punch of alcohol balanced by a rich nutty maltiness and floral hop background leading to a deep malty palate and a finish that becomes dry with malt, fruit and hops.

Hacker-Pschorr's 6.8 per cent ABV **Hubertusbock** is a

copper-coloured Maibock with hops and rich, dark fruit on the aroma, a massive malt and hops palate and a long bitter-sweet finish that becomes dry. The Union brewpub in Munich, owned by Löwenbräu, produces a 6.3 per cent unfiltered **Maibock** with a pronounced hoppy aroma, nutty in the mouth from the malt, and a bitter-sweet finish. South of Munich, the Ayinger Brewery in Aying brews a delicious 7.2 per cent **Maibock**, straw-coloured, with a rich, perfumy hop aroma, apple and apricot fruit in the mouth and a dry, superbly balanced finish.

Franconian interpretations of Bock include the Malteser Brewery's **Rittertrunk** Bock (6.5 per cent ABV) in Amberg, reddish-brown, malt and hops aroma and a fruity palate and finish, and Mönchshof of Kulmbach's **Klosterbock** (6.3 per cent ABV), amber-coloured, with a malty start and a long, bitter and dry finish.

Double Bock (Doppelbock in German) is not double the strength of a Bock but is an indication that the beer is stronger than an "ordinary" Bock. They are Lent beers and are meant to be sustaining, a meal in a glass and a blanket round the shoulders. They are usually dark, warming, rich, glowing, more heavily malty and less hoppy than a Bock. The benchmark Double Bock comes from the Paulaner Brewery in Munich. So famous is the beer that the company is officially

Calling a spade a Spaten ... an ultra-modern brewing complex on the site of the brewery where commercial lagering was developed in the nineteenth century

IN BAVARIA BOCK MEANS BOTH A STRONG BEER AND A BILLY GOAT, A SYMBOL OF POTENCY. MANY BREWERS USE A BILLY GOAT ON THEIR LABELS. THE BILLY GOAT IS ALSO THE SYMBOL FOR THE ZODIAC SIGN OF CAPRICORN AND SOME BOCKS ARE BREWED DURING CAPRICORN.

Ayinger brews a Bock called Fortunator with a rich Dundee-cake fruitiness

EKU's powerful Bock is the most famous beer from the region of Franconia

named Paulaner Salvator in order to incorporate the name of the beer in the title. The brewery was founded by monks of the order of St Francis of Paula in 1634, who naturally made a Lent beer. (This Saint Francis came from Calabria in Italy and must not be confused with the founder of the Franciscan order, St Francis of Assisi.) Beer from the monks' brewery was sold commercially from the late eighteenth century and early in the nineteenth a brewer named Franz-Xaver Zacherl began to develop the Salvator brand. Salvator means "Holy Father Beer". The impact of the Double Bock that honours him led to all other God-fearing brewers adding the letters "-or" to their versions of the style.

Paulaner Salvator Doppelbock is 7.5 per cent alcohol and is brewed from three malts and Hallertau hop varieties. It is a deep, dark brown in colour, has a big malty-fruity aroma with a good underpinning of hops, a malty, yeasty, fruit-bread palate and an intense finish packed with dark fruit, malt and hops. The beer is lagered for around three months. Löwenbräu's **Triumphator** is 7.0 per cent ABV and has an intriguing and complex aroma and palate of roasted malt, nutmeg and spices, hints of chocolate, and a big, fruity, bready finish.

Hofbräu offers a rich, warming, malty-hoppy **Delicator** (7.4 per cent ABV).

Ayinger brews a **Fortunator** (7.5 per cent ABV) with a Dundee-cake aroma and palate, warming and rich, with a dry finish. Eck in Böbrach brews a 7.0 per cent **Magistrator**, a slightly sinister name that suggests those who over-indulge will appear before the bench next morning. It is dark brown verging on black, with a deep malt and hops aroma, bitter chocolate in the mouth and a long bitter-sweet finish. With his determination to boost dark lagers, Prince Luitpold of Kaltenberg's **Dunkel Ritterbock** (6.8 per cent ABV) has a pronounced coffee aroma, a good balance of malt and hops in the mouth, and a dry, smooth finish. The monastic Klosterbräu Brewery in Ettal produces a 7.3 per cent **Curator**, reddish-brown, with a big malt aroma, a winey palate and a late burst of hops in the finish. The Klosterbräu at Irsee, South-west of Munich, uses the alternative **Starkbier** name for its strong Bock (6.8 per cent ABV). It is unfiltered with a yeasty, malty aroma, hops and fruit in the mouth and a dry, quenching finish.

The most famous Double Bock beers to drinkers outside Germany come from the EKU Brewery in Kulmbach. The letters stand for Erste Kulmbacher

Unionbrauerei: Erste means first and Union indicates a merger of two former breweries in 1872. Using local barley, Hallertau hops (Perle, Hersbruck and Tettnang) and mountain water, EKU brews a 7.5 per cent **Kulminator** with an appealing claret colour, big malt on the aroma and palate, and hops and dark fruit in the finish. Not satisfied with this rich brew, the brewery then packs even more malt into its mash kettles to produce **Kulminator 28**, known abroad as **EKU 28**. For many years the beer vied with **Samichlaus** of Switzerland as the strongest lager in the world, though the Swiss beer is now the acknowledged leader. But 13.5 per cent alcohol by volume at EKU tests to the limits the ability of conventional brewer's yeast to ferment malt sugars before being overcome by the sheer weight of alcohol it has produced.

The beer is brewed from only pale malt but the amount of malt and some caramelization of the malt sugars gives the beer an amber glow. The alcohol gives a glow as well, backed by rich malt on the aroma, some citric fruitiness on the palate and a long, deep, intense, rich and warming finish with more fruit, malt and hops (30 IBUs). The beer is lagered for nine months and towards the end of the storage period ice forms in the lager tanks. But the brewery does not claim this makes it an "Eisbock" in which the creation of ice crystals concentrates the beer: there is quite enough alcohol in EKU 28 without any additional help. Some afiçionados claim the beer is a cure for the common cold. It would certainly take your mind off it.

Close by, the Kulmbacher Reichelbräu brews a definably ice beer in the Bock style, known both as **Eisbock** and **Bayrisch G'frorns** ("Bavarian frozen"). The beer is 10.0 per cent alcohol and is made from five malts, including a dark variety and one that is deliberately slightly sour and lactic to avoid any cloying sweetness in the finished beer. It has 27 units of bitterness from Brewers' Gold, Perle, Hersbruck and Tettnang varieties. After primary fermentation, the beer is frozen for two weeks. Water freezes at a higher temperature than alcohol, forming ice crystals in the brew. The ice is removed, concentrating the alcohol. The beer is then kräusened with partially-fermented wort to start a strong second fermentation. The finished beer is warming, aromatic from both malt and hops, rich and fruity in the mouth, and with a long, rich finish with coffee from the dark malt and an alcoholic kick. Eisbock may have been the inspiration for the heavily-hyped Ice Beers developed in Canada. The Franconian version has the advantage of strength and a long lagering to give it great depth of character. The beer is brewed every year in August and September and stored until the last Saturday in March when a frozen cask is ceremonially broached at the Eisbock Festival in Kulbach's Rathaus – town hall.

FRANCONIAN SPECIALITIES

The smoked beers of Bamberg are a powerful link with brewing's past and a more tenuous link with Scotch malt whisky where the grain is cured over peat fires. In the Bamberg area, the beers get their smoky character from barley malt kilned over beechwood fires. Until the Industrial Revolution and the switch from wood to coke, it is likely that all beers had a slightly smoky note from the kilning of the malt.

Bamberg, with its impressive blend of Romanesque, Gothic and Baroque buildings, is a malting centre as well as being rich in breweries. Beechwood is gathered from the surrounding forests to supply fuel for the malting kilns. The classic smoked or Rauchbier comes from the Heller-Trum Brewery which started in the Schlenkerla tavern in the town in 1678, when the beer was lagered in caves in the nearby hill of Stephansberg. The need for more space in the tavern and a growing demand for the beer forced the brewers to move to new premises. The brewery yard is packed with beechwood logs. Inside, there is a smoke-house where the barley lies on a mesh above a beechwood fire that throws up marvellous aromas reminiscent of autumnal garden fires. The copper brew-

house uses a double decoction mashing regime with primary fermentation in open vessels followed by two months' lagering. The main beer produced is **Aecht Schlenkerla Rauchbier** (5.0 per cent ABV; 29–32 IBUs), dark brown in colour and with an intense smoked malt aroma and palate, with dry malt in the mouth and a deep smoked malt finish. The brewery also makes an autumn smoky Bock and a Helles which also has a hint of smoked malt.

The Christian Merz family's Spezial Brewery in Bamberg is a brewpub dating from 1536 that produces only smoked beers. Malt is made in a courtyard at the back of the pub. The Rauchbier is called, simply, **Lagerbier**. It is 4.9 per cent ABV with a light brown colour, with a malty-smoky aroma and palate, and a dry and fruity finish with a hint of burnt toffee. The Bürgerbräu-Kaiserdom Brewery has a full range of beers; its speciality is a 4.8 per cent **Rauchbier**, amber-coloured, with a malty/smoky aroma and palate leading to a dry finish.

Steinbier is a Franconian speciality even though the brewery using the method has moved from Neustadt, near Coburg, to Altenmünster in Southern Bavaria. Before metal kettles were widely used in brewing, it was dangerous to

The Heller-Trum Brewery (above) in Bamberg brews a smoked or Rauchbier (left). The malt for brewing is smoked over beechwood fires

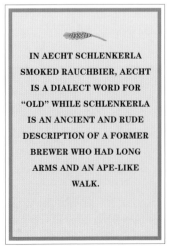

IN AECHT SCHLENKERLA SMOKED RAUCHBIER, AECHT IS A DIALECT WORD FOR "OLD" WHILE SCHLENKERLA IS AN ANCIENT AND RUDE DESCRIPTION OF A FORMER BREWER WHO HAD LONG ARMS AND AN APE-LIKE WALK.

73

*A colour lithograph of the
Hofbraühaus, Munich, 1911*

build fires under wooden vessels and it was a widespread custom in Northern Europe to lower hot stones into the mash. In 1982 Gerd Borges bought the brewery in Neustadt and decided to revive the fashion. Stones are brought from a nearby quarry and heated to white-hot temperature in an oven fired by beechwood logs. The stones are then lowered by the jaws of a small crane into a copper kettle. The mash boils, foams and steams while some of the malt sugars are caramelized and stick to the stones. When the stones have cooled they are placed in the maturation tanks where the caramelized sugar acts as a priming agent for a second fermentation. A top-fermenting yeast strain is used. **Steinbier** is 4.9 per cent alcohol, brown in colour, with a smoky aroma, toffee-like palate and a long, well-balanced malt, hops and dark fruit finish. The mash is a 50:50 blend of barley and wheat malts. Hersbruck and Tettnang hops are used and create 27 IBUs.

A version of the beer, using 60 per cent wheat malt, is called Steinweizen and is bottle conditioned.

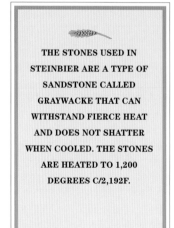

THE STONES USED IN STEINBIER ARE A TYPE OF SANDSTONE CALLED GRAYWACKE THAT CAN WITHSTAND FIERCE HEAT AND DOES NOT SHATTER WHEN COOLED. THE STONES ARE HEATED TO 1,200 DEGREES C/2,192F.

BAVARIAN WHEAT BEERS

The beer world has turned upside down in Bavaria. A top-fermenting type of ale that was doomed to extinction with the development of lager brewing in the nineteenth century is undergoing a revival of Biblical proportions. Wheat beer, derided for decades as a beer for pensioners, enjoyed spectacular growth in the 1980s and achieved cult status among the young. As a result of bottle-conditioning, which leaves a sediment rich in yeast and proteins, it is perceived by the "green generation" as being a healthier drink than lager beers.

In the fifteenth century the barons of Degenberg appropriated the right to brew wheat beer and passed the right on to the Wittelsbachs, the Bavarian royal family. Their Royal Court Brewery – the Hofbräuhaus – in Munich was opened in 1589 and by the early part of the next century was producing large quantities of wheat beer. At one stage there were around 30 royal brewhouses in Bavaria producing the style. The ordinary people had no choice in beer, for the royal family controlled the grain market and refused to release wheat for brewing. Wheat beer only

became available commercially in 1850 when the royal family licensed a Munich brewer named Georg Schneider to brew it in their Munich Hofbräuhaus. Perhaps the royals were losing interest in wheat beer and were casting envious eyes on Sedlmayr's new lager beers. Georg Schneider later moved a short distance to a brewery in Im Tal (the Dale), just off the the Marienplatz with its stunning Gothic town hall, the Rathaus. Even though lager beer was being developed in the same city, Schneider's wheat beer was a sensation and he had to buy a second brewery in Kelheim in the heart of the Hallertau hop-growing area to keep up with demand. The Munich brewery was destroyed by the British Royal Air Force in the Second World War. It has been rebuilt as a beer hall but no beer is brewed there now.

Many Bavarian brewers followed in Schneider's footsteps and brewed wheat beer as a sideline, something to have in their portfolio alongside mainstream dark and pale lagers. But now wheat beer accounts for 30 per cent of the vast Bavarian beer market and, along with low alochol (Alcoholfrei) beers, is the only growth sector. Although some brewers have introduced draught

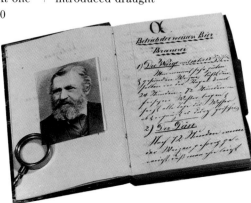

*The original recipe book
(right) for Schneider's wheat
beer brewed at Kelheim*

versions of wheat beer, they are usually bottled. A secondary fermentation in bottle gives the beers a high level of natural carbonation, creating a dense and foaming head and adding to the refreshing character. Wheat beers are made from a blend of wheat and barley malts: wheat malt by law must make up at least half of the grist. Barley malt is essential as it has a greater number of enzymes that turn starch into sugar and it also has a husk that acts as a filter during mashing. Wheat is a huskless grain and used on its own would clog up brewing vessels. The main contribution wheat malt makes to the beer is an appealing pale and hazy yellow colour and a characteristic aroma and flavour of spices and fruit: cloves is the dominant spice while apple and banana are typical fruit aromas.

The surge in popularity of wheat beer has encouraged some brewers to cut corners in its production. Ale yeasts for the second fermentation in bottle are being replaced by lager yeasts because of their greater stability and ability to give beer longer "shelf life". The use of lager yeasts removes some of the fruity and spicy flavours that only an ale yeast can impart. Some brewers even pasteurize the beer after primary fermentation before re-seeding with lager yeast and adding sediment to give a false impression of natural cloudiness. Most wheat beer producers make two versions: Hefe Weisse or Hefe Weizen, which means wheat beer with yeast, and a filtered version called Kristall or Ohne Hefe, without yeast. The unfiltered versions are by far the most popular and flavourful. Connoisseurs like to pour the beer slowly until the glass is almost full then twirl the bottle and deposit the sediment of yeast into the glass. The habit of placing a slice of lemon in the glass is declining. The reasons for doing this are lost in time but it may have played a similar role to the addition of fruit or herb syrup to Berlin wheat beers to reduce some of the acidity.

Schneider – the name means Taylor in English – is the wheat beer brewer by whom all others are judged. The Kelheim Brewery produces nothing but wheat beer, though the family owns a smaller plant near Regensberg where it brews lagers. The Kelheim Brewery, an odd but fetching blend of Spanish and Gothic architecture, was built in 1607 and is thought to be the oldest continuous wheat beer brewery in the world. It is run today by Georg Schneider V and his son, Georg VI, who will take over when his father retires. The brewery has open fermenters, a rare sight in Germany where brewers prefer to keep their beers locked away from possible air-borne infections. But the Schneiders will do nothing to interfere with the workings of the single-strain yeast culture, which has been used for as long as anyone can remember. Nothing is altered in the fermentation hall. Rather like whisky distillers who will replace one vessel with a slight kink with a new one with an identical kink built in to it, the Schneiders will replace one fermenter with another of exactly the same dimensions. They will not change the specification of their malts in case it upsets the temperamental yeast.

Schneider makes 300,000 hectolitres a year, 90 per cent of which is a 5.4 per cent **Weisse**. The rest is made up of an 8.0 per cent wheat Bock named **Aventinus** and a lighter beer called **Weizen Hell**. The brewery uses half a million tonnes of Bavarian barley and

Put him on a pedestal... a statue of Ludwig, King of Bavaria, suitably placed in front of a brewery

SCHNEIDER'S AVENTINUS STRONG WHEAT BEER TAKES ITS NAME FROM AVENTINE STRASSE IN MUNICH, WHERE THE BREWERY HAD A BOTTLING STORE. THE CONNECTION HAS BEEN UPGRADED AND THE LABEL NOW SHOWS THE IMAGE OF JOHANNES AVENTINUS, HISTORIAN OF THE BAVARIAN PEOPLE.

wheat. In the Weisse they are blended in the proportion of 60 per cent wheat to 40 per cent barley. Some Vienna and darker malts are added to give the beer its attractive bronze colour. Hersbrücker hops from the surrounding Hallertau are used in pellet form with a small amount of hop extract. The Weisse has 14 to 15 units of bitterness: hops in wheat beer are used primarily for their antiseptic and preservative qualities as too much bitterness will not blend with the spicy, fruity character of the beer. The local well water is softened by osmosis to remove some of the natural salts.

The modern brewhouse was built in 1988 with stainless steel mashing and boiling kettles standing on marble floors. A double decoction mash is used: portions of the mash are pumped from one vessel to another, heated to a higher temperature and then returned to the first vessel, raising the temperature of the entire mash. As modern continental European malts are "well modified", with the cell walls of the grain easily broken to enable the starches to be attacked by enzymes, double decoction mashing is probably not necessary but the Schneiders will not tamper with tradition. Mashing starts at 38 degrees C/100F, a lower temperature than a typical English infusion mash.

As the wort is pumped from one vessel to another the temperature rises by stages to 43, 48 and 56 degrees, reaching a final 65 degrees. The spent grains are sparged at 75 degrees. Hops are added in two stages during the copper boil, then the hopped wort is cooled and pumped to the fermentation hall. Sixteen stainless steel vessels hold 350 hectolitres each. The hall is heady with tempting aromas of fruit, with banana dominating, underscored by delicious hints of apple. Fermentation lasts between three and five days at 20 degrees C/68F. Twice a day the yeast is skimmed from the top of the wort, cleaned and then pitched back into the vessels. At the end of primary fermentation the green beer is not filtered and is bottled with a blend of the same top-fermenting yeast and some sugar-rich wort to encourage a second fermentation. The bottles are warm conditioned at 20 degrees for a week, which causes a lively carbonation as fermentation gets under way. The beer is then cold conditioned at eight degrees C/47F for a fortnight to stabilize it.

Schneider Weisse has a complex bouquet of banana, cloves and nutmeg, tart fruit in the mouth and a creamy, fruity finish with hints of bubblegum. Aventinus is bronze-red in colour due to the addition of caramalt. It has a rich spices and chocolate aroma and palate, with more spices, vinous fruit and cloves in the finish. It makes a splendid nightcap or winter warmer.

Schneider may be the flagship wheat beer producer but the biggest brewer of the style is Erdinger. The company in the town of Erding, on the far outskirts of Munich, is based in a modern brewery built in the early 1980s. The original site in the town centre brewed from the mid-1850s and is now a tavern. Erdinger has specialized in wheat beer since the 1930s and now produces two million hectolitres a year.

All the wheat and most of the barley is grown locally by farmers who work to specifications drawn up by the brewery. The wheat is low in protein, producing a soft-tasting beer. Water comes from an underground lake believed to be two million years old.

A double decoction mash is used and Perle and Tettnang hops are added three times, achieving 18 IBUs. Primary fermentation is unusual, taking place in horizontal tanks just 2.8 metres high – the brewers think this produces a cleaner-tasting beer. Breaking with tradition, Erdinger uses a lager yeast for bottle conditioning and the bottles are warm conditioned for a month.

Hefe-Weissbier is 5.3 per cent ABV. It has a relatively restrained aroma for the style, with hints of apples and cloves, more fruit in the mouth, and a gently fruity finish. A filtered version is sold as Kristallklar. A dark Dunkel Weissbier (5.6 per cent ABV) has pleasant chocolate and liquorice notes while Pikantus Bock (7.3 per cent ABV) has spices and chocolate on the aroma and palate.

The most remarkable revival of wheat beer is seen at the Spaten Brewery in Munich. Even though the brewery is the cradle of lager brewing, it now devotes 50 per cent of its capacity to wheat beer production. The wheat beers are sold under the Franziskaner name, the bottle labels showing a cheerful monk holding a mug of beer. The original wheat beer brewery, bought by Josef Sedlmayr and merged with his brother Gabriel's plant, was the oldest in Munich and was next to a Franciscan monastery. The main Spaten wheat beer, **Franziskaner Weissbier** (5.0 per cent ABV) has an ususually high wheat malt content of 75 per cent. The brewer admits this occasionally causes problems during mashing but feels it gives a better flavour to the finished beer. The other brands, Hell, Dunkel, Kristall and Bock, are made more conventionally from a 50:50 blend of German and French barley and wheat malts. A complex hops recipe is made up of Hallertau, Tettnang, Spalt, Perle and Orion varieties. Fermentation takes place in conical fermenters where a "top" yeast sediments to the bottom of the vessels. The beer is then centrifuged to

remove the ale yeast and is re-seeded with a lager culture for bottle conditioning. The main wheat beer has a gentle fruity aroma, tart fruit and spices in the mouth and a light but quenching finish. The **Dunkel** (also 5.0 per cent ABV) is bitter for the style with dark fruit on the palate and finish.

Elsewhere in Munich, Löwenbräu's 5.0 per cent **Löwenweisse** has a strong apples and cloves aroma, hints of banana in the mouth, and a dry and spicy finish. Augustiner's **Weissbier** is 5.2 per cent has a malty aroma and palate and tart, lingering finish. Hacker-Pschorr's **Weisse** (5.5 per cent ABV) is light and undemanding. Höfbräuhaus honours its royal tradition with a crisp, lemon-fruity, tart and marvellously refreshing 5.1 per cent beer.

Outside Munich, Prince Luitpold at Kaltenberg brews a Hell and a Dunkel wheat beer, both 5.5 per cent ABV. The dark is a delight, packed with malt-loaf fruitiness with a slightly sour and quenching finish. In an idyllic setting in the Obberbayern mountains, the Hopf Brewery of Miesbach brews only wheat beer. As the German for hop is Hopfen, the owner, Hans Hopf, has a head start over his competitors in the brand image stakes. The small brewery has had to be substantially extended to cope with demand. Old copper vessels nestle against modern stainless steel ones in the brewhouse,

which produces 50,000 hectolitres a year. The brewing liquor is Alpine water. German and French malts are used, with wheat malt making up 65 per cent of the mash. Hops are Hallertau and Spalt varieties. After primary fermentation the beer is kräusened with brewhouse wort and mixed with a blend of top and bottom yeasts for a second fermentation. The main beer, **Hopf Export** (5.3 per cent ABV; 12 IBUs) has a nostril-widening spicy and peppery aroma underpinned by banana and bubblegum.

In Passau, the Andorfer Brewery's 5.3 per cent **Weissbier** is amber coloured and balances a malty palate with a tart, fruity finish. South-west of Munich, Karg in Murnau has a coppery, yeasty, fruity and tartly uncompromising 5.0 per cent **Weissbier**. In Bayreuth, the Maisel Brewery's 5.2 per cent **Hefe-Weissbier** is a deep reddy-brown, with a delightful apple aroma and palate and a tart, dry finish.

Throughout Bavaria most breweries now have wheat beers in their portfolios. The success and revival of the style, like the cask-conditioned ales of Britain, mark another victory for consumer preference over marketing zeal.

Spaten's Franziskaner now accounts for half the brewery's production

Maisel's Brewery produces a wheat beer with a russet colour and a fruity palate

The Black Forest, one of Germany's most stunning regions, famous for its beer

The aristocratic Fürstenberg produces an aromatic Pilsner and a malty Export

BADEN-WÜRTTEMBERG

The adjacent state to Bavaria is known by a variety of names: Schwaben, Schwabian-Bavaria or, to the outside world, the Black Forest. Swaben was an independent duchy from the tenth to the fourteenth centuries: Schwabia today in Germany means an area famous for its distinctive cuisine and spectacular countryside. It tends to be overshadowed by its better-known Bavarian neighbour but hits back with its own beer festival held at the same time at the Munich Oktoberfest. The Cannstatter Volkfest (the "People's Fest" in the suburb of Cannstatt in Stuttgart) begins at the end of September and runs for two weeks.

Stuttgart's three breweries, Dinkelacker, Stuttgarter Hofbräu and Schwaben Bräu, produce Volkfestbiers broadly in the Munich Märzen style. Local custom determines that these beers are lower in strength – around 4.5 per cent ABV – than the Munich versions but, like their Bavarian cousins, they are amber in colour, rich, malty and satisfying with a good hop character. Almost identical beers are produced for Christmas and the New Year under the name of Weihnachtsbier.

The Stuttgart breweries concentrate on Pilsners – soft, malt-accented, with gentle hop character – all in the classic 4.8 to 5.0 per cent alcohol range.

Dinkelacker is the major brewery in the region and its biggest brand is the oddly-named **CD-Pils**. The CD tag has nothing to do with either Compact Discs or the Corps Diplomatique but comes from the initials of the founder of the brewery, Carl Dinkelacker. The Dinkelacker family has been brewing since the late eighteenth century, built the present city-centre plant in 1888 and still controls the company at a time when most larger breweries are owned by banks or other financial institutions. CD-Pils is mashed and hopped in fine, traditional copper kettles and kräusened during the secondary fermentation. It is hopped four times, the final addition being with Brewers' Gold for aroma as the hopped wort is pumped from the kettle. The finished beer has a malty nose and palate with delicate hop notes in the mouth and a soft finish. Dinkelacker owns the Cluss Brewery in Heilbronn which produces a 5.0 per cent **Cluss Pilsner** and a dark, creamy **Bock Dunkel**.

Schwaben Bräu, in the district of Vaihingen, has an impressive copper brewhouse and vast cellars where the comparatively dry **Meister Pils** is lagered. The Hofbräu, once a royal court brewery but now a public company, is on the edge of Stuttgart and produces malty-sweet beers, the main brand being **Herren Pils**, which translates as Pils for Men, surely Politically Incorrect today.

Fürstenberg from the Black Forest is the best-known of the region's beers as it is widely exported. The beer has noble connections: the Fürstenberg family are aristocrats who have been involved in brewing for more than 500 years. They are renowned patrons of the arts and have a fine collection of paintings in their museum at Donaueschingen, which is also the site of the brewery. **Fürstenberg Pilsener** (5.0 per cent ABV) is decidedly hoppy for the regional style, with an aromatic and malty aroma, a full palate and a dry and bitter finish. **Export** (5.2 per cent ABV) is a deep gold colour with hints of fruit in a big malty body and crisp, dry finish.

In the north of the region, Eichbaum of Mannheim dates from 1697 when Jean de Chaîne founded a brewery called Zum Aichbaum in the Stammhaus tavern: the brewery moved to its present site in 1850 but the tavern has survived as a main outlet for the brewery. At one stage Mannheim had 40 or more breweries but only Eichbaum has survived. It brews both a cloudy and filtered wheat beer (5.3 per cent ABV) with a spicy and fruity palate and an **Apostulator Doppelbock** (7.5 per cent ABV), using caramalt and dark malt. The main product is a 4.6 per cent **Ureich Pils**: Ur means Original and Eich means Oak, the oak tree, Eichbaum, being the brewery's symbol. It is hopped with Hallertau and Tettnang varieties. The beer has malt and citric fruit from the hops on the aroma, a malty-hoppy palate and a dry finish with delicate hop notes. A 5.3 per cent **Export**, in the Dortmund style, has a more rounded and malty character.

DORTMUNDER EXPORT

Dortmund, the great steel and mining city on the Ruhr, is a brewing conundrum. It produces more beer than any other city in Germany or Europe yet it is absurdly shy about its main style of beer, Export, and prefers today to emphasize its Pilsners. The reasons are to do with the decline of heavy industry and its attendant blue-collar working class who were the main consumers of the rounded and malty Exports.

Dortmund has had a brewing tradition since the thirteenth century. It specialized in dark wheat beers until the oldest brewery in the city, Kronen (Crown) switched to bottom-fermentation. When the large Dortmunder Union Brewery began to make lager beers in the 1870s they achieved such renown that they were sold to all parts of Germany and Europe, acquiring the name of Export as a result. Belgian and Dutch brewers were sufficiently impressed by the Dortmund beers to produce specialities they call simply "Dort".

The two giants of Dortmunder brewing are Dortmunder Union and Dortmunder Actien. The giant letter "U" – 17 metres or 55 feet high – blazes out at night from the 1920s functional building that would remind Londoners forcibly of the Thames-side Battersea Power Station. Union in Germany has nothing to do with labour unions or the fermentation system of far-off Burton-on-Trent but refers to a merger, in this case the spectacular bringing together of a dozen breweries under one roof in 1873. Actien indicates a company going public and making its shares available on the stock exchange. Dortmunder Actien, founded by the Fischer family in 1868, went public in 1872, which may have been the springboard for the mergers that formed the rival Union group.

Dortmunder Actien's **DAB Export** is 5.0 per cent ABV with a sweet malt aroma, a full malty body and bitter-sweet finish with a late flourish of hops. It also makes a **Meister Pils**, a full-bodied 5.0 per cent **Original Premium** and, with a nod in the direction of Bavaria, a **Maibock** and a **Termanator Doppelbock**.

The rival **DUB Export** – malty, light-bodied, delicately hopped – is now difficult to find and the brewery concentrates on its 5.0 per cent **Siegel Pils**, hopped with Hallertau varieties (30 IBUs) and lagered for six to eight weeks.

The smaller, family-owned Dortmunder Kronen claims to be the oldest brewery in the region of Westphalia. It traces its roots to a brewery-cum-tavern called the Krone in 1430. It was bought by Johann Wenker in 1729 and it passed to his son-in-laws, whose family name was Brand. The Brand family still runs the business now based, fittingly, in a district of Dortmund called Kronenburg – the brow or crown of a hill. The brewery was bombed in the Second World War and has been extensively rebuilt and modernized. Its **Export** is the most malt-accented of the city's beers, with a rich body and a big, bitter-sweet finish. Sadly, Kronen is so shy about Export that it releases no information about it, preferring to concentrate on its 5.0 per cent **Pils**, hopped with Hallertau (32 IBUs) with a delicate malt and hops aroma, light palate and a lingering bitter-sweet finish, and its 5.3 per cent **Classic** (26 IBUs) with a rich malt nose, rounded malt and a hop balance on the palate and long bitter-sweet finish. Only Classic is available in the brewery museum. Export, the great Dortmunder style, proud beer of a power-house of a city, is no longer considered worthy of being even an artefact.

MÜNSTER

In Münster, the delightful old university city of Westphalia, Pinkus Müller produces a fascinating variety of highly individualistic beers using organic malt and hops. Pinkus Müller is well-known throughout Germany even though it is no more than a beer tavern, making around 10,000 hectolitres a year. The tavern has four dining rooms, specializing in local cuisine. Founder Pinkus Müller started in business producing beer, bread and chocolate and the company has been on the same site since 1816.

Pinkus Müller in Munster is famous internationally for its organic brews. The Dortmunder brewers (top) are now shy of promoting their splendid Export beers

Henninger of Frankfurt is a major producer with two Pilsners in its portfolio

Henninger Alsterwasser ... a beer for those hazy days of summer

NO ONE OUTSIDE COLOGNE CAN CALL A BEER KÖLSCH. IN 1985 COLOGNE BREWERS AND THE GOVERNMENT SIGNED A CONVENTION PROTECTING THE STYLE. LIKE A FRENCH WINE, KÖLSCH NOW HAS AN APPELLATION CONTRÔLLÉE. THE CONVENTION WAS DRAWN UP ON PARCHMENT AND EACH BREWERY APPENDED ITS SEAL.

The best-known brand today is **Pinkus Münster Alt**. Alt means "old" and is a major beer style in Düsseldorf. The Pinkus brand is not a true Alt in the Düsseldorf style as 40 per cent of the grist is composed of wheat malt, the remainder being Bioland organic Pilsner. Organic hops come from the Hallertau, the mash is single-decoction and the brew is kräusened during secondary fermentation, which lasts for four months. A top-fermenting yeast is used and a lactic culture is allowed to breed in the lagering tanks, imparting a deliberate hint of sourness to the finished beer. It is 5.1 per cent ABV, with a rich, slightly vinous aroma, malt and tart fruit in the mouth, and a long and fruity finish with slight acidity.

The brewery does not claim the beer is a wheat one and could not legally do so, as less than 50 per cent of the mash comes from wheat. It underscores the point by producing a **Hefe Weizen** (5.2 per cent ABV) with 60 per cent wheat malt. It is conditioned for one month and has a light fruit aroma, delicate malt and fruit in the mouth, and a dry and fruity finish. Pinkus Müller makes two bottom-fermenting beers, a hoppy and dry **Pils** and a stunning **Special** (5.2 per cent ABV), lagered for three months and producing a full malty aroma and palate with hops developing in the dry, quenching finish.

One of the specialities of the tavern is a syrup made from fresh fruit – strawberries or peaches in summer, oranges in winter – which is added to the Alt to cut the beer's acidity.

FRANKFURT AND HESSE

A cynic might say that it is because Germany's biggest brewing group, Binding, is based in Frankfurt that this area of the country produces the least interesting beers. Certainly Frankfurt and its environs has no distinctive beer style and Binding, which also owns DAB in Dortmund and the Berlin Kindl Brewery and makes in total 2.5 million hectolitres a year, is best known abroad for its Clausthaler low-alcohol lager. Its main brand for the Frankfurt market is broadly in the style of a Dortmunder Export. **Export Privat** has some hops on the nose, a firm, malty body and some delicate fruit in the dry finish.

The second Frankfurt brewery, Henninger, is no slouch in the production stakes, making around 1.75 million hectolitres a year. Its main products are a smooth and undemanding **Kaiser Pilsner**, brewed principally for the international export market, and a slightly stronger and marginally hoppier **Christian Henninger Pilsener**, which oddly spells the indication of style with an additional "e".

COLOGNE AND KÖLSCH

The golden, top-fermenting ales of Cologne (Köln in German) are so highly regarded that the style is protected by federal law.

Brewing has been rooted in the culture and way of life of Cologne, capital of the Rhineland, since Roman times. The name Cologne stems from "colonial" and it was an impor-

tant city of the Roman Empire. Monasteries dominated the production of beer for centuries and gave way to commercial brewers and tavern owners. The modern Kölsch beers are pale but would have been darker in previous centuries when all malt was brown. But they remain top-fermenting, a member of the ale family. The determination of brewers in Cologne, along with their kin in nearby Düsseldorf, to stick to the old tradition may be the result of temperature as well as temperament – cool summers do not demand a chilled beer – and the city's proximity to the Low Countries. The region has long had close links with what is now Belgium and was influenced by the beers enjoyed by such bibulous luminaries as Duke Jan Primus (Gambrinus). Cologne's Guild of Brewers dates from 1396 and has been in the van of protecting the city's beer culture. Today the city and its surroundings have some 20 or so breweries dedicated to brewing Kölsch. Cologne has more breweries than any other major city in Germany or the world. Kölsch came under great pressure at the turn of the century to switch to lager brewing but the offer was refused: one brewer has even removed Pilsner from his portfolio.

The language of the style can be confusing. Kölsch beers look like lagers. They are often called "Wiess", a local spelling of white, but they are not wheat beers even though some brewers use a proportion of wheat malt in the mash. A typical Kölsch is around 5.0 per cent ABV with a malty aroma and some gentle fruitiness. It will be soft due to the local water and there will a delicate, perfumy hop character. Bittering units will be in the high 20s but extreme bitterness is avoided. Hallertau and Tettnang hop varieties are preferred. The Kölsch yeast is a greedy strain, busily turning most of the malt sugars into alcohol, with a dry beer as the result.

The biggest producer of Kölsch today is the Küppers Brewery, founded just 20 years ago. It has built market share through clever promotions that have not pleased some traditionalists. **Küppers Kölsch** is soft, easy-drinking and undemanding. An unfiltered version call **Wiess** is more fruity, yeasty and distinctive.

The best-known and most highly-regarded of the Cologne brewers is P. J. Fruh's **Cölner Hofbräu**. The beer used to be brewed in a tavern on the Am Hof in the city centre but the house brewery became too small to meet demand and new plant has been built a short distance away. **Früh Echt Kölsch**, all malt without wheat, is wonderfully drinkable, with delicate fruit on the aroma, and hops from Hallertau and Tettnang in the finish. Gaffel in the Old Town district has been brewing since 1302 and produces a beer of considerable pedigree: intriguingly nutty for a pale beer and a dry finish. The Heller brewpub in Roon Strasse offers a malty-sweet **Kölsch**

and an unfiltered, fruitier and slightly tart version called **Ur-Wiess**. The Malzmühle (malt mill) brewpub on Heumarkt – Haymarket – uses some wheat malt in the mash and produces a rounded, malt-accented beer with a hint of spice and some delicate hop character from Hallertau. Päffgen in Frisen Strasse has a distinctive floral hop bouquet and a hoppy finish: by far the hoppiest of the style. Sion in the Old Town has a floral hop bouquet from the use of the Hersbrucker variety. It is part of the delight of drinking Kölsch beers that most of the producers are small and many operate from taverns. Discovering the beer makes for a splendid pub crawl.

DÜSSELDORF ALT

Alt means old but the young have taken it to their hearts. Düsseldorf is another great industrial city that was once at the heart of the mining industry. The copper-coloured, top-fermenting beers of the region again have a link with the malty, refreshing milds of industrial England, brewed to refresh people after a shift at the coal-face or the furnace. But unlike English mild or Dortmunder Export, the Alts of Düsseldorf have not declined in step with heavy industry but have found a new audience among white-collar employees, the young in particular. As with Cologne, there is a Low Countries connection: Düsseldorf is close to the Low Countries, in partic-

ular the tongue of the Netherlands that includes Maastricht, and the influence of Dutch brewers has seeped across the border.

Alt beers superficially are the closest to English ale, but the similarities should not be over-stressed. Decoction mashing is used by some brewers and all the beers are cold-conditioned for several weeks, though at higher temperatures than for lager beers, around 8 degrees C/47F. Hop bitterness will range from the mid-30s IBU to 50. Open fermenters for primary fermentation are used by some of the smaller producers, many of them based in characterful city brewpubs where the beer accompanies vast platefuls of local cuisine. Typically, an Alt will be around 4.5 per cent alcohol

The fortunes of Alt brewing have waxed and waned. Two of the biggest producers, Hannen and Schlösser, lost market share as a result of mergers: Hannen is owned by Carlsberg of Denmark, Schlösser by DUB of Dortmund. The major brewer is now the family-owned independent Diebels in the hamlet of Issum a few miles from the city. The brewery was founded in 1878 by Josef Diebels and has been in the family for four generations. It produces more than one and half million hectolitres a year and doubled production between 1990 and 1991.

Diebels **Alt** has a gravity of 1045 degrees and is 4.8 per cent ABV, which means it is well attenuated. The beer has an appealing burnished copper

P. J. Früh's tavern in Cologne offers a fine example of the city's unique beer style

THE ALT BREWERS OF DÜSSELDORF SOFTEN THE LOCAL WATER WITH CALCIUM HYDROXIDE – "LIME MILK" – FOR THEIR BREWING LIQUOR, SHOWING THAT THE *REINHEITSGEBOT*'S CONTROL OF INGREDIENTS DOES NOT EXTEND TO WATER TREATMENT.

Diebels of Düsseldorf is the market leader with its fruity, top-fermenting "old" beer

A functional, modern façade at Diebels leads into a handsome brewhouse

Bitburger in the Rhineland was an early devotee of Pilsner beer

THE SIMON FAMILY, WHICH OWNS THE BITBURGER BREWERY, SHORTENED PILSNER TO PILS AND HAS WON INTERNATIONAL FAME FOR ITS BEER WITH A PRODUCT KNOWN SIMPLY AS "BIT" AND THE SLOGAN "BITTE EIN BIT" – "A BIT PLEASE".

colour with a peppery hop aroma balanced by rich malt. It is bitter in the mouth with a dry and nutty finish and a hint of orange fruit. Ninety eight per cent of the grist is pale Pils malt. The remaining two per cent is provided by roasted malt, more a Scottish practice than a German one. (Other Alt brewers prefer to use Vienna or black malt for colour and flavour.) Hops are Northern Brewer for bitterness and Perle for aroma, producing 32 to 33 IBUs.

Diebels' modern Steinecker brewhouse has tiled walls decorated by a mosaic showing the old brewery at the turn of the century. Four mash kettles feed four wort kettles, where the hops are put in in one addition. A decoction mashing regime is used. The 50 year-old yeast culture is a top-fermenting strain but is cropped from the foot of conical vessels. As with Guinness in Dublin, primary fermentation is rapid and lasts for just two days. The green beer then has a short "diactyl rest", which purges toffee-like flavours, and is stored in tanks for between 10 days in summer and three weeks in winter.

The best way to taste Altbier is to visit the taverns of the Alt Stadt, the cobbled and gas-lit Old Town of Düsseldorf. Im Füchschen, the Little Fox, at 28 Ratinger Strasse, is a cavernous building with tiled walls, red-tiled floors and wooden bench seats. The house beer is tapped from casks on the bar and is served by its own natural pressure, free from applied gas. The beer is maltier than Diebels with a toasty

flavour and a sweet, fruity finish that becomes dry. In common with all Altbiers it is served in a short, stubby glass that is immediately replaced by another as the drinker downs it. Alts are a good companion for local dishes. Im Füchschen's speciality is a huge pickled knuckle of pork.

Zum Uerige offers salted pig's trotter with its Alt. The tavern is at 1 Berger Strasse and the name means the Place of the Cranky Fellow, though the present-day staff are helpful, attentive and friendly, and happy to discuss their beer in English as well as German. The beer is brewed in copper kettles and fermenters viewed from the main bar, part of a warren of rooms. The Alt, dry hopped and made with a dash of roasted malt, is fruity, aromatic and hoppy. Zum Schlüssel, the Key, at 43-47 Bolker Strasse, birthplace of the poet Heinrich Heine, also has its brewhouse on display at the back of the bar. The Alt has a delightful aromatic hop perfume, it is bitter-sweet in the mouth and has a dry finish.

RHINELAND PILSNERS

The Rhineland's love-affair with Pilsner beers shows the impact which the Bohemian style had in the nineteenth century. For this vast and remote region of Germany is a considerable distance from Pilsen and, before the arrival of the railway, beer

and its raw materials moved slowly by water transport. Yet the brewers of the Rhineland switched to bottom-fermenting Pils with a fervour matched only in the far north around Hamburg. Several of the leading companies brew just one beer. Their dedication to the style and rigorous attention to the quality of materials and uniformity of production baulks at the notion of such Bavarian largesse as Dunkels, Bocks and Weizens.

Bitburger is a good case in point. It is brewed in the small town of Bitburg in the Eifel Lake district, close to the historic city of Trier, birthplace of Karl Marx. The company was established in 1817 as a humble farmhouse brewery and made top-fermenting beers. But by 1884 it was producing Pilsner, using ice from the lakes to lager the beer. Its fortunes were boosted when a rail line was built to supply the Prussian army with cannon from the steelworks of Saarbrücken. The Simon family, which still owns the company, began to export its "Pils" to Northern Germany. Today it is one of the most widely exported German beers.

Bitburger's offices, original brewery and "brewery tap" tavern are in the centre of the small town. The superb copper brewhouse is still used but the main production has been switched to a state-of-the-art 1980s plant on a greenfield site on the edge of town. Wort is pumped by underground pipes between the two brewhouses. Enormous care is given to the selection of the finest raw materials: spring barleys – Alexis, Arena and Steiner – and Hersbrücker, Hüller, Perle and Tettnang hops. The beer has three hop additions in the kettle, is 4.6 per cent ABV with 37 to 38 IBUs. It is lagered for three months and is not pasteurized, which helps the delicate balance of malt and hops flavours. Beer for export is sterile filtered.

The Rhineland Pilsners are hoppier than those from the south but less dry and bitter than the interpretation of the style in the far north. Bitburger has a rich malt aroma underscored by floral hops, soft malt in the mouth and a long, complex finish with both bitterness and light citric fruit from the hops, balanced by sweet malt.

The biggest-selling Pilsner in Germany comes from the Warsteiner Brewery. The town of Warstein is in an area of woods and lakes to the east of the Rhine and the Ruhr. The ultra-modern brewery is coy about its ingredients, saying nothing more than "barley malt and Hallertau hops". **Warsteiner Premium** is 4.8 per cent ABV and is lagered for two months. It has a light malt and hops bouquet, rounded and bitter-sweet in the mouth, and a delicate dry finish with some citric notes from the hops, finally becoming dry.

Krombacher Pils from Kreuztal-Krombach uses Hallertau and Tettnang hops. The beer is 4.8 per cent with 24

to 26 IBUs. It has a comparatively brief lagering of just one month. The aroma is soft and malty, with delicate malt and hops in the mouth, and a dry finish with good hop notes. Brauerei Felsenkeller Herford produces yet another fine example of the style, well-attenuated (1046 degrees original gravity but brewed out to 4.8 or 4.9 per cent ABV). It is brewed from premium Pilsner pale malt and 60 per cent Hallertau Northern Brewer hops for bitterness and 40 per cent Perle and Tettnang for aroma. The hops produce 32 units of bitterness. The beer has a rich honeyed malt aroma, rounded malt and hops in the mouth, and a long, dry delicate malty finish balanced by some citric fruit from the hops. Herford also brews a malty Export, a pale Maibock and a dark and fruity Doppelbock.

HAMBURG AND THE NORTH

Hamburg and Bremen have had a major influence on German beer and its impact abroad. They are major ports and for centuries have exported German beer to other countries. In common with all ports, they are cosmopolitan, polyglot places, open to many influences. They were at the heart of the great fifteenth-century trading group of cities known as the Hanseatic League. Other countries' beers came into their ports and had an impact on local styles. In particular, hops from Bavaria and Bohemia came up the Elbe, encouraging the Prussians to use the plant in their own brews.

The love affair with the hop married well with a later infatuation with the beers from Pilsen. Pilsner Urquell from Pilsen was given an award in a brewers' competition in Hamburg in 1863. The Prussian interpretation of the style is dry and intensely bitter, almost austere, a reflection of the time when beers were heavily hopped to help them withstand long sea journeys.

The best-known of the region's brewers is Holsten of Hamburg, a major exporter, some of whose beers in other countries are brewed under licence.

In its home market, Holsten and its subsidiaries produce more than one million hectolitres of beer a year. Its biggest brand is **Edel**, a 5.0 per cent beer with a good malty/hoppy palate and bitter finish: the name means "noble". The 4.8 per cent **Pilsener** is dry in the finish after a hop-accented start and firm palate. A 5.6 per cent **Export**, with a nod in the direction of Dortmund, has a rounded malty character underscored by rich hops. There is also a seasonal Bock called **Ur-Bock** (7.0 per cent ABV). Its brewery in Lüneburg produces a hoppy and dry **Moravia Pils** (38 IBUs), stressing the influence of beers and malt from the Czech lands.

The name of Hamburg's other leading brewer, Bavaria St Pauli, also emphasizes the deep admiration the Prussians feel for the brewers of the south. It was common in the nineteenth century for northern brewers to append either Bavarian or Bohemian imagery to their

Holsten was another early convert to Pils

An old print of a Jever beer wagon loaded with their exceptionally hoppy beer

THE BEERS OF EINBECK WERE GIVEN GREAT CREDIBILITY WHEN THEY WERE DRUNK BY MARTIN LUTHER. THE LEADER OF THE PROTESTANT REFORMATION WAS GIVEN A GIFT OF EINBECK BEER FOR HIS WEDDING AND HE DRANK IT TO SUSTAIN HIM DURING THE DIET (CONFERENCE) OF WORMS IN 1521, WHEN HE WAS EXCOMMUNICATED FROM THE CHURCH FOR HERESY.

Pilsner from Einbeck, known as the "Beer City" of Lower Saxony

company name as lager-brewing developed in those regions. The present company is the result of a merger in 1922 of two separate companies, Bavaria and St Pauli: St Pauli is a district of Hamburg. To confuse the issue further, its products are produced under the label of Astra. They include **Astra Urtyp**, lightly hopped, and **Astra Pilsener** with a splendidly aromatic hop bouquet and palate. It also brews a seasonal **Urbock**.

Its most remarkable beer comes from its Jever subsidiary in the resort town of the same name in German Friesland. Friesland or Frisia, the setting for Erskine Childers' famous spy novel *The Riddle of the Sands*, was once a tiny independent state, a buffer between Germany, the Netherlands and Denmark. The Frisians like bitter drinks and the Jever Brewery, founded in the 1840s, meets the demand with **Jever Pils** which registers 44 IBUs. It is 4.9 per cent ABV, brewed from two-row barley with Hallertau and Tettnang hops. It is lagered for an impressive 90 days. The brewery uses an infusion rather than a decoction mash. The beer has a massive hop bouquet from Tettnang hops, a malty, hoppy and yeasty palate, and a stunningly dry, bitter and hoppy finish with some honey notes from the malt. Jever Pils is exported widely. The brewery also makes for the local market a rounded, malty **Export** and a **Maibock**.

Bremen also has a brewery named in honour of St Paul. It has the full and curious title of St Pauli Girl. The company claims it doesn't know where the Girl came from but uses the image of a young woman carrying foaming jugs of beer. The harbour town formed the first brewers' guild in Germany in 1489 and once had a substantial number of brewing companies. Today the three main breweries share a modern brewing factory and are linked through a complex financial structure. The best-known, as a result of its vigorous export policy, is **Beck's**. The 5.0 per cent beer belongs to no clearly defined style, has a light, malty aroma, a bland palate with some hints of hop from Hallertau varieties, and a short finish. As television commercials testify, Beck's has an impressive, traditional copper brewhouse where anchors in stained-glass windows stress the importance of exporting to the company. **St Pauli Girl** is crisp and clean but hard to distinguish from Beck's. Haake-Beck, in the same complex, makes far more distinguished and hop-accented **Edel-Pils** and **Pils**. An unfiltered version of the Pils is sold as **Kräusen-Pils** in Bremen taverns. The brewery also produces a Berlin-type wheat beer called **Bremer Weisse** (2.75 per cent ABV), quenching and refreshing, fermented with the aid of a lactic culture to give a deliberate sourness. It has a tart and fruity aroma and palate. Locals underscore the fruitiness by adding a dash of raspberry syrup.

LOWER SAXONY AND BOCK

Whatever the Bavarians may think, the origins of strong Bock beers almost certainly lie in the town of Einbeck. Beer has been brewed in the small town near Brunswick and Hanover since at least 1351. It calls itself "Beer City" and marks the fact with three beer casks on its boundary, even though only one brewery survives there today.

Einbeck's beers were sold as far afield as Amsterdam and Stockholm and were brewed strong to help them withstand long journeys by road and water. The early brews would have been dark and top-fermenting, probably made from a blend of barley and wheat malts. Such was their fame that they were referred to by the truncated "Beck", which became "Bock" in the Bavarian accent. At a time when most brewing was undertaken in monasteries or castles, the burghers of Einbeck permitted the production of beer for commercial sale. It was done on a contract basis: citizens would buy malt and hops, which they dried in their lofts. A licensed brewmaster, with a publicly-owned brew kettle, would visit their homes and help them make beer which they then sold. Einbeck, despite its small population, became a powerhouse of modern brewing during the life of the Hanseatic League between the thirteenth and fourteenth centuries.

A commercial brewery was built in Einbeck in 1794 and has been rebuilt on several occasions. The present modern brewery, Einbecker Brauhaus, carries the legend: "Ohne Einbeck gäb's kein Bockbier" – Without Einbeck there would be no Bock beer. Three versions of Bock are produced, all with alcoholic strengths of 6.9 per cent ABV and all quite reasonably labelled **Ur-Bock** – Original Bock. Soft water comes from deep springs, malt from the Brunswick area and hops – Northern Brewer, Perle and Hersbruck – from Bavaria. The beers are hoppier and drier than a Bavarian Bock on the sound historic grounds that the original Einbeck beers would have been heavily hopped to help them withstand long journeys. But the main characteristic of the beers is a rich, rounded maltiness that avoids an overbearing, cloying sweetness. The pale **Hell**, with 38 IBUs, has an appealing malt aroma and palate and a late burst of hops in the finish. The **Dunkel** or dark beer has the same bitterness rating. The aroma and palate are dominated by rich malt with hints of dark fruit and coffee, and again the hops make a late entrance in the dry and complex (malt, fruit, hops) finish. A **Maibock**, on sale between March and mid-May, has 36 IBUs, is crisp, quenching and refreshing, an ideal way to celebrate the arrival of spring. It is lagered for six weeks. The Hell and Dunkel have eight to 10 weeks' maturation.

In Brunswick the Feldschlössen Brewery brews a 4.9 per cent **Pilsner** (and even

spells the word in the correct Czech manner). It also produces two top-fermenting beers, a **Brunswiek Alt** and the Disney-sounding **Duckstein**, a tawny, fruity ale matured over beech-wood chips, with a bitter and tart finish. In the days when there were two Germanys divided by a wall, the East also had a Feldschlössen Brewery. Today both plants are owned by Holsten.

The origins of Hanover's 114-year-old Lindener Aktien Bräuerei lie in a civic brewery run by a brewers' guild: the beers are labelled Gilde to record the historic detail. The founder of the guild was called Cord Broyhan or Broyan and the brewery produces a **Broyan Alt** in his honour. This top-fermenting ale is 5.25 per cent ABV and has a copper colour, rich malt aroma and delicate hop finish. It has several bottom-fermenting beers including a **Pilsner** and a stronger **Edel-Pils**.

BERLIN WHEAT BEERS

When Napoleon's troops reached Berlin they described the local wheat beers as the "Champagne of the North". It was a fitting and perceptive description, for the Pinot and Chardonnay grapes of the Champagne region produce such a tart wine that it only becomes drinkable after a long, slow process in which a secondary fermentation in the bottle involves some lactic activity and finally becomes spritzy and sparkling. Berliner Weisse beers are so tart and lactic that drinkers add a dash

of woodruff or other syrups to the beer to cut the acidity. The style is traditionally low in alcohol, around 3.0 per cent ABV, is extremely pale in colour, has a light fruitiness and little hop aroma. The origins of the style are unknown but one theory is that the fleeing Huguenots picked up the skill of brewing sour beer as they migrated north from France through Flanders. At its height Berliner Weisse beer was brewed by no fewer than 700 producers in the Berlin area. Now there are just two.

The lactic cultures that work with a conventional top-fermenting yeast to produce Berliner Weisse were isolated early in the twentieth century by scientists who founded Berlin's renowned university research and brewing school, the Versuchs und Lehranstadt für Brauerei or VLB for short. The culture is named *lactobacillus delbrücki* after Professor Max Delbrück, the leading research scientist. The Berliner Kindl Brauerei is the bigger of the two remaining producers. Its well water is softened. The proportion of wheat malt is around 30 per cent and the finished alcohol is 2.5 per cent. Bitterness units register a modest 10 from the use of Northern Brewer. After mashing and boiling, the *lactobacillus* is added first to start

Einbeck begat Bock... strong lagers are now brewed throughout Germany but the Saxon city is the original home of the style

THE BERLINER KINDL BREWERY HAD TO REBUILD ITS PLANT AFTER THE WAR AS ITS COPPER VESSELS HAD BEEN CONFISCATED BY THE RUSSIAN ARMY. TO ITS CREDIT, KINDL DESIGNED ITS NEW BREWHOUSE IN CLASSIC BAUHAUS STYLE AND STILL USES COPPER.

Well known producers of Pilsner, the Bitburger family remains dedicated to the art of brewing Black Beer

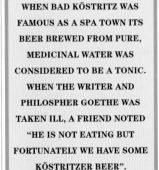

acidification, followed by a top-fermenting brewer's yeast. Fermentation lasts for a week followed by several days of cold conditioning. The beer is then filtered, bottled with a top yeast and kräusened with partially fermented wort.

The Schultheis Brewery blends equal amounts of wheat and barley malts in the mash to produce a 3.0 per cent beer. Hallertau hops produce four to eight IBUs. Top-fermenting yeast and *lactobacilli* are blended together with wort that is between three and six months old to encourage a lively fermentation, which lasts for three to four days. The beer is warm conditioned for three to six months. It is then kräusened and *lactobacillus* added for bottling. The finished beer is complex, fruity, sour and quenching, more assertive than the Kindl version. Unlike Bavarian wheat beers, the Berliner Weisse style is not enjoying a revival and is in serious decline.

BLACK BEER OF THURINGIA

When the wall between East and West Germany came down, West German companies rushed to buy up breweries in the East, many of them rundown and in urgent need of an injection of capital. Many old East German beers were lacking distinction, mainly because the old regime did not adhere to the *Reinheitsgebot*. They exported malt and hops for "hard currency" and were prepared to allow all manner of cheap adjuncts to be used in brewing.

Many breweries have closed. Others have been swallowed by such giants as Holsten. Bitburger alone was motivated by affection as much as commercial enthusiasm. The present chairman of Bitburger, Dr Axel Simon, a descendant of the founder, remembered **Köstritzer Schwarzbier** from his youth and thinks he may have drunk it even before the family's Pilsner. Bad Köstritz was a spa town (Bad means bath) near the great cities of Weimar and Erfurt in Thuringia but had disappeared into obscurity along with its beer behind the wall.

But Black Beer from the region is a style in its own right and may even have inspired the black beers of Japan. It is a style different to the dark but not quite black Dunkel beers of Munich and Franconia and it is likely that the beers were top-fermented much later than in Bavaria. Certainly under the old Communist regime, Köstritzer Schwarzbier varied between being top- and bottom-fermented and was even exported to the West at one stage as "stout".

When Dr Simon arrived he found a superb red-brick Victorian brewery built in 1907 covered in scaffolding. It had fallen into disuse. Brewing was carried out in an ugly modern brewhouse with East European vessels that looked fittingly like army tanks. A weird tangle of pipework led to wort and yeast being trapped in joins, creating yeast infections. Bitburger could have closed the place and moved production to the Rhineland but Dr Simon was determined to make the black beer of Köstritz a Thuringian speciality again.

Black beer, rather like stout in Britain and Ireland, was recommended for nursing mothers: Dr Simon's mother drank it when she was breast-feeding him. It eased rheumatism though, unlike Mackeson, did not claim to stop drinkers farting. Older drinkers still like to beat sugar and egg into the beer: the brewery used to make a sweetened version of the beer but this is now prohibited by the *Reinheitsgebot*, which has been restored to the Eastern lands.

Bitburger has pumped millions of marks into the brewery to restore it. When the sweet version of **Köstritzer Schwarzbier** was dropped, the brewery concentrated on a 3.5 per cent ABV beer brewed with 50 per cent pale malt from the Erfurt area, 43 per cent Munich and the rest roasted malt, the last two from Franconia. Hüller hops for bitterness and Hallertau Mittelfrüh for aroma created 35 units of bitterness. Local spring water is softened for brewing liquor.

Since then Bitburger has dramatically upped the alcohol level to 4.6 per cent. The beer is bigger and dryer but still has an aroma of dark fruit/malt loaf and bitter chocolate, a creamy palate and a long, complex finish with more dark, bitter roasted malt, coffee and chocolate, underpinned by hops. It is a minor classic but perhaps, in the rush to make an acceptable beer for the whole of a united Germany, some of the traditional if quaint Thuringian originality has been lost.

SELECTED GERMAN
BREWERS

Altstadthof,
18 Berg Strasse, 8500
Nürnberg (Nuremberg).

Augustiner Brauerei,
Neuhauserstrasse 16, 8000
Munich 1.

Bavaria-St Pauli Brauerei AG,
Hopfenstrasse 15, Hamburg 4.

**Bayerische Staatsbrauerei
Weihenstephan,**
Postfach 1155, Freising,
Munich.

Berliner Kindl Brauerei AG,
Rollbergstr. 26-80, Berlin 44.

Bitburger Brauerei Theo Simon,
Postfach 189, 5520
Bitburg/Eifel.

Brauerei Inselkammer Aying,
1 Zornedinger Strasse, 8011
Aying.

**Brauerei Beck GMBH &
CO/Haake-Beck/St Pauli Girl,**
Am Deich 18/19, Bremen 1.

Brauerei Binding AG,
Darmstädster Landstrasse
185, Frankfurt 70.

Brauerei Felsenkeller Herford,
Postfach 1351, Herford.

**Diebels, Privatbrauerei Diebels
GMBH,**
Braueurei-Diebels Strasse 1,
Issum 1, Düsseldorf.

Dinkelacker Brauerei AG,
Tübinger Strasse 46, Postfach
101152, Stuttgart 1.

Dortmunder Actien Brauerei,
Steigerstrasse 20, Postfach
105012, Dortmund 1.

Dortmunder Kronen GMBH,
Märkische Strasse 85,
Dortmund 1.

Dortmunder Union Brauerei,
Brau und Brunnen, 2
Rheinische Strasse, 4600
Dortmund 1.

Eichbaum-Brauereien AG,
Käfertaler Strasse 170,
Mannheim 1.

Einbecker Brauhaus,
4-7 Papen Strasse, 3352
Einbeck.

**EKU Erste Kulmbacher Actien
Brauerei AG,**
EKU-strasse 1, Kulmbach.

Erdinger Weissbräu,
1-20 Franz Brombach Strasse,
8058 Erding.

**Fürstlich Fürstenbergische
Brauerei KG,**
Postfach 1249,
Donaueschingen.

**Gaffel, Privat Brauerei Gaffel-
Becker,**
41 Eigelstein, 5000 Köln
(Cologne).

Gilde Brauerei AG,
Hildesheimer Strasse 132,
Hanover 1.

Hacker-Pschorr Bräu GMBH,
Schwanthalerstrasse 113,
8000 Munich 2.

Heller-Trum Schlenkerla,
6 Dominikaner Strasse, 8600
Bamberg.

Heller, Brauhaus Heller,
33 Roon Strasse, 5000 Köln
(Cologne).

Henninger-Bräu,
Hainer Weg 37-53,
Frankfurt/Main 70.

Holsten Brauerei AG,
Holstenstrasse 224, 22765
Hamburg.

**Jever, Friesisches Bräuhaus zu
Jever,**
17 Elisabethufer, 2942 Jever.

Kaisderdom Privatbrauerei,
Breitäckertasse 9, Bamberg
14.

Köstritzer Schwarzbierbrauerei,
Heinrich Schütz Strasse, Bad
Köstritz, 6514 Thüringen.

Krombacher Brauerei,
Hagener Strasse 261,
Kreuztal-Krombach.

**Kulmbacher Mönchshof-Bräu
GMBH,**
Hofer Strasse 20, Kulmbach.

Küppers Kölsch Brauerei,
145-155 Alteburger Strasse,
5000 Köln
(Cologne).

Löwenbräu AG,
Nymphenburger Strasse 4,
Munich 2.

Maisel,
Hindenburger Strasse 9,
Bayreuth.

Malzmühle, Brauerei Schwarz,
6 Heumarkt, 5000 Köln
(Cologne).

P. J. Früh Cölner Hofbräu,
12-14 Am Hof, 5000 Köln
(Cologne).

Päffgen, Gebrüder Päffgen,
Obergarige Hausbrauerei, 64-6
Friesen Strasse, 5000 Köln
(Cologne).

Paulaner-Salvator-Thomasbräu,
Hochstrasse 75, Munich 95.

Pinkus Müller,
4-10 Kreuz Strasse, 4400
Münster.

Reichelbräu AG,
Lichtenfelser Strasse 9,
Postfach 1860, Kulmbach.

Schlossbrauerei Kaltenberg,
Augsburger Strasse 41,
Fürstenfeldbruck, Bayern.

G. Schneider & Sohn,
1-5 Emil Ott Strasse, 8420
Kelheim.

Schultheiss-Brauerei,
28-48 Methfessel Strasse,
Kreuzberg, 1000 Berlin 61.

Schwaben Bräu,
Hauptstrasse 26, Stuttgart 80.

**Gabriel Sedlmayr Spaten-
Franziskaner-Bräu KGA,**
Marsstrasse 46-48, Munich 2.

**Staatliches Hofbräuhaus in
München,**
Hofbräuallee 1, Munich 82.

Warsteiner Brauerei,
Wilhelmstrasse 5, Warstein 1.

**Zum Eurige Obergarige
Hausbrauerei,**
1 Berger Strasse, Düsseldorf.

ENGLAND

Banbury
Hook Norton
Birmingham
Bass Mitchells & Butlers
Brierley Hill
Daniel Botham
Vine (Bull & Bladder)
Burton-on-Trent
Bass
Burton Bridge
Ind Coope
Burton
Marston, Thompson & Evershed
Bury St Edmunds
Greene King
Derby
Lloyds Country Beers
Devizes
Wadworth
Dorchester
Eldridge Pope
Dudley
Holden's
Edenbridge
Larkins
Faversham
Shepherd Neame
Hartlepool
Castle Eden
Henley on Thames
W.H. Brakspear
Hertford
McMullen
Horsham
King & Barnes
Ipswich
Tolly Cobbold
Keighley
Timothy Taylor
Leeds
Joshua Tetley
Whitelocks
Lewes
Harvey
London
Fuller, Smith & Turner
Young
Recommended pubs: see Gazetteer
Manchester
Boddington
Joseph Holt
Hydes Anvil
J W Lees
Peveril of the Peak
Newcastle upon Tyne
Newcastle
Oakham
Ruddles
Ripon
Black Sheep
T. and R. Theakston
Southwold
Adnams
South Woodham Ferrers
Crouch Vale
St Albans
Ye Olde Fighting Cocks
Farriers Arms
St Austell
St Austell
Stockport
Frederic Robinson
Sunderland
Vaux
Tadcaster
Samuel Smith
Trowbridge
Ushers of Trowbridge
Walsall
Bass Highgate
Wolverhampton
Banks's
York
Black Swan

SCOTLAND

Alloa
Maclay
Biggar
Broughton
Dollar
Harviestoun
Dunbar
Belhaven
Edinburgh
Caledonian
McEwan & Younger
Bow Bar
Café Royal
Glasgow
Babbity Bowster
Innerleithen
Traquair House
Orkney Islands
Orkney
Tomintoul
Tomintoul

WALES

Cardiff
S A Brain & Co
Welsh Brewers
Denbigh
Bragdy Dyffryn
Clwyd
Llanelli
Crown Buckley
Felinfoel
Wrexham
Plessey
Wrexham Lager

ENGLAND

MOST VISITORS TO ENGLAND KNOW THREE THINGS ABOUT THE COUNTRY BEFORE THEY ARRIVE: THE NATIVES ARE TRANSPORTED IN RED BUSES AND BLACK TAXIS, THEY ARE RULED BY THE QUEEN, AND THEY DRINK A WARM BEER CALLED BITTER. BUSES AND TAXIS COME IN A MULTITUDE OF COLOURS THESE DAYS, THE MONARCHY HAS ITS PROBLEMS, WHILE THERE IS OFTEN MORE TO TEMPT VISITORS TO PUBS THAN BITTER ALE. BITTER IS A TWENTIETH-CENTURY DEVELOPMENT AND MANY BREWERS AND DISCRIMINATING DRINKERS ARE REDISCOVERING ALES FROM EARLIER TIMES.

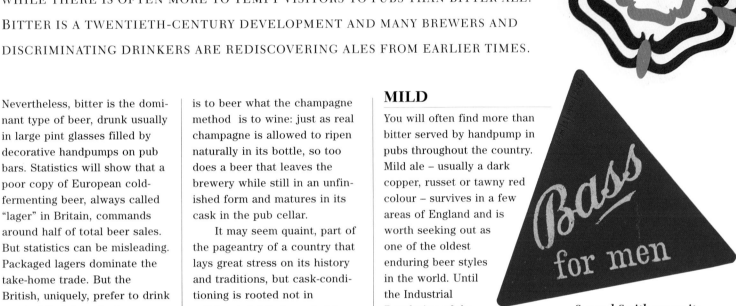

Nevertheless, bitter is the dominant type of beer, drunk usually in large pint glasses filled by decorative handpumps on pub bars. Statistics will show that a poor copy of European cold-fermenting beer, always called "lager" in Britain, commands around half of total beer sales. But statistics can be misleading. Packaged lagers dominate the take-home trade. But the British, uniquely, prefer to drink most of their beer in the cheerful surroundings of the public house. More than 70 per cent of British beer is drunk in draught form. Ale of all types – mild, bitter, porter, stout, strong and seasonal beers – is the preferred tipple of pubgoers.

The English are returning to their ale-drinking roots. With Ireland included, the British Isles is the only major centre of population in the world where the people have stayed loyal to beers brewed by warm fermentation. In England in particular drinkers show a growing and marked preference for cask-conditioned ale, a style much admired in other countries but rarely copied. Cask-conditioning is to beer what the champagne method is to wine: just as real champagne is allowed to ripen naturally in its bottle, so too does a beer that leaves the brewery while still in an unfinished form and matures in its cask in the pub cellar.

It may seem quaint, part of the pageantry of a country that lays great stress on its history and traditions, but cask-conditioning is rooted not in soft-headed folksiness but in good business practice. In the nineteenth century, when Britain's imperial grandeur had reached its zenith, British brewers had vast markets to supply at home and abroad and saw no need to switch to the new methods of lagering beer. At the turn of that century brewers began to build substantial "tied estates" of pubs which they supplied directly with their products. As they owned the premises, the brewers were able to train bar staff in the arcane rituals of tapping and venting casks of ale maturing in pub cellars whose contents had been neither filtered nor pasteurized in the brewery.

MILD

You will often find more than bitter served by handpump in pubs throughout the country. Mild ale – usually a dark copper, russet or tawny red colour – survives in a few areas of England and is worth seeking out as one of the oldest enduring beer styles in the world. Until the Industrial Revolution of the eighteenth and nineteenth centuries and the use of coke in kilning malt, all beer was brown in colour as malt was cured over wood fires. Brown beer was the type of beer drunk in every country until the arrival of pale malts. Mild or brown beer was an important constituent of the first porters and stouts in the eighteenth century in England. They were made by blending two or three different beers, one of which was brown. Until the twentieth century, most beers were stored and matured for long periods in wooden vats. But in the nineteenth century, brewers started to produce a special version of

Samuel Smith wears its Yorkshire heart on its sleeve with the use of the region's historic White Rose emblem. Bass's Red Triangle logo was once Politically Incorrect but now appeals to both genders of drinkers

brown beer called mild. To avoid the harsh tastes of immature beer, mild was brewed using a blend of pale, brown and black or chocolate malts as well as brewing sugar. The hop rate was also reduced: the term mild has nothing to do with alcoholic strength but with the fact that fewer hops are used than in pale ales and porters.

Mild became popular with drinkers who preferred the malty flavour of the ale to the more bitter and sometimes astringent and even acidic character of well-matured beers. Mild appealed to workers engaged in heavy manual labour and, as it was cheaper than other beers, to those on low incomes.

Mild – called brown ale when it is bottled – remained the most popular beer in England until after the Second World War. But the decline of heavy industry and changing tastes that saw a switch to pale-coloured alcoholic drinks of all types, sent mild into an almost terminal spin. It survives today in a few areas of heavy industry. The greatest mild-drinking region is the Black Country based on the great Midlands city of Wolverhampton, though the name Black Country comes not from the beer but from the factory chimneys and mines that once dominated the area.

Banks's Ale is the great Black Country mild

The grip of mild can best be seen at Banks's, England's biggest regional brewer, part of Wolverhampton and Dudley Breweries, which produces half a million barrels a year. Banks's Ale accounts for 60 per cent of production, outselling bitter. In a superb brew-house of burnished copper vessels, mild ale (3.5 per cent ABV) is made from Maris Otter malt, caramel for colour, and with whole Worcester Fuggles and East Kent Goldings hops. The ale has 40 units of colour and 25 bitterness units. The tawny-red beer is wonderfully drinkable with a pronounced port-wine character from the caramel, a gentle but persistent hop presence and light fruit in the finish. It's what they call "empty glass ale" in the Black Country: as soon as one pint is finished you feel the need for a refill.

There are some fine milds to be found in and around the Black Country town of Dudley. Batham's Brewery stands along-side the Vine pub in Brierley Hill, its façade carrying a quotation from Shakespeare's *Two Gentlemen of Verona*: "Blessings of Your Heart, You Brew Good Ale". Daniel Batham started to brew in 1881 when he lost his job as a miner and today Tim and Matthew Batham are the

> A TYPICAL VICTORIAN BLACK COUNTRY MILD HAS BEEN RECREATED AT THE BEACON HOTEL IN SEDGLEY IN A TINY BREWHOUSE. SARAH HUGHES' DARK RUBY MILD – NAMED AFTER THE FORMER OWNER OF THE HOTEL – IS 6.0 PER CENT ABV AND IS PACKED WITH DARK MALT FLAVOURS AND BLACKCURRANT FRUIT.

fifth generation to run the brewery and the handful of pubs. Bathams produces 6,000 barrels a year. Most of that is now bitter but sales of mild are picking up again. The 3.6 per cent mild is made from Maris Otter barley, caramel for colour, and Herefordshire Northdown and East Kent Goldings hops. More Goldings are added in the cask, giving the ale considerable bitterness for the style. A couple of miles away, Holden's Brewery in Woodsetton also began life as a brewpub. Edwin Holden, grandson of the founders, brews 9,000 barrels a year for his small estate of pubs. Like Bathams, Holdens began as a dark mild brewer but also produces bitter today. **Black Country Mild** (3.6 per cent ABV) is made from Maris Otter malt with a complex blend of amber, crystal and black malts for colour. Hops are Fuggles specially grown in Worcestershire.

Bass, Britain's biggest brewing group, owns the Highgate Brewery in Walsall, a Victorian plant which is dedicated to the production of **Highgate Dark**, a chocolatey and liquorice 3.25 per cent mild brewed from pale, crystal and black malts with Fuggles and Goldings hops and some maltose syrup and caramel.

MILD ALE BREWERS
Banks's (Wolverhampton & Dudley Breweries),
Bath Road, Wolverhampton
WV1 4NY.
Bass Highgate Brewery,
Sandymount Road, Walsall
WS1 3AP.
Daniel Batham & Son,
Delph Brewery, Delph Road,
Brierley Hill DY5 2TN.
Holden's Brewery,
George Street, Woodsetton,
Dudley DY1 4LN.

PALE ALE AND BITTER

While there are a few pockets of mild in other parts of England – Manchester has a good choice with **Holt's Mild** (3.2 per cent ABV), **Hyde's Anvil Mild** (3.5 per cent ABV) and **Lees' GB Mild** (3.5 per cent ABV) – bitter leads the field. Bitter is a twentieth-century development of the pale ales brewed primarily for the colonial trade in the previous century. Those pale ales, India Pale Ale in particular, were brewed to both a high alcohol content and hopping rate in order to withstand long sea voyages of three months or more. At the turn of the century, as brewers began to buy their own outlets, they wanted beers that would be ready to be served within days of arriving in the pub instead of having to mature for months.

"Running beers" were the result, made possible by carefully-cultured yeast strains that enabled beers to "drop bright" quickly in cask. New varieties of hops were high in acids and tannins, which meant that fewer had to be used to create the required level of bitterness. Whereas the original pale ales were light in colour, the new running beers tended to be copper-hued due to the use of crystal malt. During the kilning process, the starches in the malt are caramelized. Although crystal malt is added to pale malt in the mash tun, it is not necessary to have its starches converted during the mashing process, however.

"Running beers" was brewers' terminology. They were dubbed "bitter" as a result of their tangy hoppiness by drinkers who in so doing invented a name for a style. The term is applied only to draught beers – bottled versions are known as light ale or pale ale. The most remarkable aspect of running beers or bitter was that they continued to be conditioned in the cask. English brewers remained faithful to a form of technology rejected by the rest of the world as lager-brewing took hold. The running beers of the early twentieth

century were the forerunners of the "real ales" of the 1990s.

With the exception of a handful of specialist breweries – such as Bass's Highgate plant – every brewery in England produces at least one bitter. Usually there are two, a lower-strength "supping" bitter of around 3.6 per cent ABV, and a stronger best bitter of 4.0 per cent or more. Some produce three or four. Crouch Vale, a well-regarded micro in Essex, brews an **IPA** (3.5 per cent ABV), **Best Bitter** (4.0 per cent), **Millennium Gold** (4.2 per cent ABV), and **Strong Anglian Special** (5.0 per cent). The giant of the region, Greene King, produces **IPA** (3.6 per cent ABV), **Rayment's Special Bitter** (4.3 per cent ABV), and **Abbot Ale** (5.0 per cent ABV). In neither case does the low-strength "IPA" reflect the true style. In London the revered independent Fuller's brews **Chiswick Bitter** (3.5 per cent ABV), **London Pride** (4.1 per cent ABV), and a redoubtable 5.5 per cent **Extra Special Bitter**, as fruity as a street market.

Is there a true descendant of the nineteenth-century pale ales that spawned modern bitter? Fittingly you have to go to Burton-on-Trent in the Midlands, where pale ale was fashioned, to find it. Marston, Thompson and Evershed started

Keep tight hold on your mitre... Greene King's strong ale has enormous hop appeal. Crouch Vale (left), an Essex micro, brews a clutch of pale ales

Clash of traditions in Burton... Marston's puts its faith in its union room fermenters

... while mighty Bass has scrapped its unions and now uses modern methods of fermentation

THE TERM "UNIONS" USED AT MARSTON'S HAS NOTHING TO DO WITH TRADE UNIONS. THE OAK CASKS ARE LINKED BY BARM TROUGHS AND PIPES AND ARE SAID TO BE "HELD IN UNION".

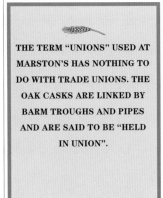

Marston's Pedigree ... a classic Burton pale ale, still fermented in traditional union casks

brewing in Burton in 1834 and moved to the present site, the Albion Brewery, in 1898. Although Marston's is classified as a regional brewer, its **Pedigree Bitter** (4.5 per cent ABV) has national distribution and is second only to **Draught Bass** in "premium" (strong) bitter sales. Pedigree uses no dark malts. In common with the first pale ales, it is brewed from only pale malt (83 per cent) and glucose sugar (17 per cent). It is hopped with Fuggles and Goldings which create 26 units of bitterness, on the low side for the style. The character of Pedigree – at once subtle yet robust, aromatic as well as malty and lightly fruity – is due to the singular fashion in which it is fermented. Marston's is the last brewer in England, and the only one of Burton's much-reduced clutch of breweries, to use the "union room" method of fermentation. The system was developed in Burton in the nineteenth century and rapidly spread to the rest of the country in order to cleanse fermenting beer of yeast. Pale ale production coincided with the arrival of mass-produced glass – now drinkers could see their beer and they clamoured for clarity. The union system removed yeast from beer efficiently and effectively. It was based on the medieval method of brewing where the ale fermented in large wooden casks and frothed up and ran into buckets beneath the casks,

allowing the yeast to be collected and re-used, but the union system turned the medieval method on its head. Troughs are placed above large oak casks, each one holding 144 gallons, with pipes fitted into the bung holes of the casks. The fermenting wort rises up the pipes and drips into the troughs, which are slightly inclined. The liquid runs back into the casks while the yeast settles in the troughs. The end result is a well-attenuated and crystal clear beer.

The Marston's yeast voraciously turns malt and glucose sugars into alcohol. As a result of the high levels of gypsum in the local well water, Pedigree has a renowned sulphury aroma, known locally as the "Burton snatch". Only Pedigree is brewed in the union sets although the same yeast strain is used for the company's other brands of ale.

Union sets are expensive to run and maintain. Brewers abandoned them as new and simpler methods of yeast cleansing were developed. Marston's remained faithful to them to such an extent that an additional fermenting hall with brand-new unions was built at enormous cost in the early 1990s. The company believes that the taste and character

of its beers would change for the worse if the yeast was asked to work in conventional vessels. Marston's also produces a hoppy **Bitter** (3.8 per cent ABV), **Merrie Monk**, a strong mild which is Pedigree with caramel added, and **Owd Rodger** (7.6 per cent ABV), a ripe and fruity barley wine.

There are other fine examples of bitter ales brewed in Burton. Britain's biggest brewer, Bass, produces the biggest-selling premium cask ale in the country: **Draught Bass** (4.4 per cent ABV). Until the early 1980s, Draught Bass was also brewed in union room fermenters. The group thought the system was too capital and labour intensive and the beer is now fermented in conventional open vessels. It has lost some of its subtle balance of flavours and aromas as a result. But it is still a superb beer with a malt and creamy toffee aroma, a hint of sulphur from the water, pronounced malt in the mouth balanced by gentle hop bitterness from Challenger and Northdown varieties (26 IBUs) and a long finish in which malt dominates but with some light hop and a delectable hint of apple fruit. Apple is also present in Marston's Pedigree and is a hallmark of the Burton style.

Bass also brews the bottle-conditioned **Worthington White Shield**, another ale that can claim to be a direct descendant of the original India Pale Ales. William Worthington was a member of the great Burton brewing breed whose company merged with Bass in the 1920s. The beer was brewed at Burton until the 1990s when production switched to Mitchells and Butlers' plant in Birmingham, a subsidiary of the group. White Shield (5.6 per cent ABV, 40 IBUs) has an enticing aroma of spices, peppery hops (Challenger and Northdown), light fruit and sulphur. There are malt, hops and spices in the mouth, with a deep nutty finish, plenty of hop character and a hint of apple fruit. It is brewed from a blend of Halcyon and Pipkin pale malt with a touch of black malt for colour. At the end of the brewing process the beer is filtered and then primed with sugar to encourage a second fermentation in the bottle and re-seeded with a special yeast strain. Although it is an ale culture, the yeast sinks to the bottom of the bottle as though it were a lager strain, and slowly turns the remaining sugars into alcohol. The beer is warm-conditioned for three weeks before it leaves the brewery. It can then be drunk but true White Shield devotees prefer to keep the beer for a longer time. After a year to 18 months the beer takes on a more rounded and fruity character. It is a difficult beer to pour: glass and bottle have to be held almost horizontal and then the pourer slowly raises the elbow of the arm holding

the bottle to allow the beer to enter the glass. As soon as the sediment begins to move towards the neck of the bottle, pouring must stop to ensure a clear glass of ale, though the sediment will do no harm.

The Ind Coope Brewery in Burton, part of the Carlsberg-Tetley group, produces **Ind Coope Burton Ale**, a draught version of the renowned **Double Diamond** bottled pale ale. Burton Ale undergoes such a volcanic second fermentation in cask that while it is declared at 4.8 per cent ABV it can reach 5.1 or 5.2 per cent by the time it reaches the drinker's glass. Ind Coope jettisoned its union room fermenters long before Burton Ale was developed in the late 1970s and the beer is made in conventional modern vessels. It is brewed from pale and chocolate malts with liquid brewing sugar, English hop pellets with Styrian Goldings added for aroma in the cask.

The Burton Bridge microbrewery, based behind the Bridge Inn, produces a fruity/hoppy **Bridge Bitter** (4.2 per cent ABV), using Pipkin pale malt and 5.0 per cent crystal, with Challenger and Target whole hops in the copper and Styrian Goldings for dry hopping in cask.

The importance of yeast in brewing can be seen in the ales brewed by Lloyds Country Beers at the John Thompson Inn in Ingleby, Derbyshire. The brewer uses yeast bought from Burton every week, giving his ales a hint of Burton sulphuriness. The main brew is **Derby Bitter** (4.1 per cent ABV), with a hoppy and fruity aroma, rich

malt in the mouth, and well-balanced finish packed with hops and fruit.

Two other fermentation systems that date back to the eighteenth and nineteenth centuries are the Yorkshire square and the dropping system. The Yorkshire square method is still widely used in both that region and adjacent counties. The only truly traditional stone squares are found in Samuel Smith's Brewery in Tadcaster, North Yorkshire, a company founded in 1758 and the oldest in the region. The square was invented to cope with the particular problems of the yeast strains used in Yorkshire. Yorkshire yeasts are highly "flocculent". This means the cells clump together, separate from the wort and refuse to turn sugars into alcohol unless they are regularly roused by agitating and aerating the wort. A simple answer would be to use a different, less flocculent strain of yeast, but Yorkshire brewers are jealous of the rounded, malty character of

The Ind Coope brewery in Burton is now part of the giant Carlsberg-Tetley group. Its Burton Ale is a noted strong pale ale, a draught version of the famous bottled Double Diamond

Samuel Smith's bitters are staunchly traditional, fermented in Yorkshire "squares", and with rich malty and nutty flavours. The brewery has phased out all brewing sugars in its beers

their beers. In order to encourage the yeast to work effectively, the two-storey square fermenter was developed. The top chamber is known as the "barm deck", barm being a dialect word for yeast. The bottom chamber is filled with wort and yeast. Fermentation forces liquid and yeast through a manhole, where the yeast is trapped by a raised flange while the wort runs back into the bottom chamber via pipes. Every couple of hours wort is pumped to the top chamber to aerate it and mix yeast back into the liquid. When fermentation is complete the manhole is closed, the green beer is left to condition in the bottom storey while the yeast is collected from the top.

Yorkshire beers are not only full bodied as a result of unfermented sugars but also have the famous "thick, creamy head", the result of high levels of carbonation created during fermentation. Samuel Smith's beers – **Old Brewery Bitter** (3.8 per cent ABV) and **Museum Ale** (5.2 per cent ABV) – are classics of the style: rich, malty and nutty but underpinned by good Fuggles and Goldings hop character.

The top-selling standard bitter in the country, **Tetley Bitter** (3.6 per cent ABV), is brewed in modern stainless steel Yorkshire squares in Leeds. It is a highly complex beer with an aromatic, citric lemon aroma from Northdown hops – the beer is dry hopped in cask – a malty, creamy palate, and a long, dry finish packed with more fine hop flavour.

Yorkshire, the largest region of England, has many fine breweries, and great stress is placed on tradition. When Paul Theakston opened his brewery in Masham in 1992 he was insistent that he would ferment in Yorkshire squares and managed to buy some, ironically from a brewery in Nottinghamshire. His **Black Sheep Bitter** (3.8 per cent ABV) has a powerful Fuggles hop aroma, with more peppery hops in the mouth and a long bitter finish. **Special Strong Bitter** (4.4 per cent ABV) is highly complex, with malt, hops, cobnuts and orange fruit on the aroma, a bitter-sweet palate and big hoppy and fruity finish.

Paul Theakston left his family company when it was taken over by the giant Scottish and Newcastle group in the 1980s. Theakston's Brewery and Black Sheep brew cheek-by-jowl in Masham, the former famous for its pale **Best Bitter** (3.8 per cent ABV; 24 IBUs) with a delicate fruit and hops aroma and palate and the famous strong ale, **Old Peculier** (see Special Ales).

In Keighley, Timothy

Samuel Smith's Museum Ale is fermented in traditional stone "Yorkshire Squares" – roofed fermenting vessels made of solid blocks of slate, producing a beer particularly full bodied in character.
The Old Brewery at Tadcaster is the only one still using the Yorkshire Stone Square system of fermentation; so the beer is fermented in what is a living museum.
Samuel Smith's is a small independent brewery.

Taylor's brewery has won a cupboardful of prizes from the Campaign for Real Ale for its magnificent **Landlord Bitter**. The 4.3 per cent ABV beer is brewed only from Golden Promise malt, with Worcestershire Fuggles for bitterness and Kent Goldings and Styrians for aroma.

A rudimentary but highly effective method of cleansing beer of yeast is the dropping system. This is still in operation at Brakspear's Brewery in Henley-on-Thames. When fermentation is under way in open vessels, the wort is dropped one floor to a second bank of vessels, leaving behind spent hops and dead yeast cells as well as yeast in suspension. The wort is roused and aerated and a fresh head quickly forms on the wort. **Bitter** (3.6 per cent ABV) and **Special** (4.0 per cent) are brewed with Maris Otter pale and crystal malts with a touch of black malt for colour. Hops are Fuggles and Goldings. The Bitter, with 38 units of bitterness, has a pronounced citric aroma from the hops, a full malt and floral hop flavour, and a delicate dry finish with continuing firm hop presence.

Also in the Thames Valley, Hook Norton Brewery in the Oxfordshire village of the same name, is a fine example of a traditional Victorian "tower" brewery in which all the stages of the brewing process flow logically from floor to floor: mashing at the top, boiling in the middle, fermentation and racking at the bottom. **Hook Norton Best Bitter** (3.3 per cent ABV), despite its modest

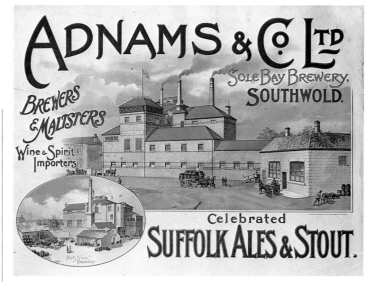

strength, has a fine hop character from Challenger, Fuggles and Goldings varieties, balanced by rich malt and some fruit in the finish. **Old Hooky** (4.3 per cent ABV) is richly fruity with hints of raisins in the finish.

Most bitters are produced in conventional fermenting vessels where the yeast is skimmed off by vacuums, which suck the yeast head from the wort, or by "parachutes", metal funnels placed apex-down on top of the wort so that yeast can collect inside the funnel. Traditional brewers prefer open fermenters, made from wood, iron, stainless steel or lined with polyproplyne, so they can rouse the wort by hand. But good beer can equally be made in modern brewhouses. Charles Wells of Bedford, for example, uses all the trappings of high tech, including mash kettles, lauter tuns and closed conical fermenters, but its bitters are highly regarded. **Bombardier** (4.2 per cent ABV), made from pale and cystal malts with Challenger and Goldings hops – 34 units of bitterness – has a complex malt, hops and fruit character that makes it popular in Germany, Italy and Spain as well as in Wells' own pubs.

THE CHARLES WELLS FAMILY BREWERY BEDFORDSHIRE, Est. 1876.

Further east, in the grain basket of East Anglia, Adnams of Southwold in Suffolk, Greene King in historic Bury St Edmunds, and Tolly Cobbold in Ipswich, brew bitters rich in malt but balanced by generous hopping. Both **Adnams Bitter** (3.8 per cent ABV) and **Tolly Bitter** (3.6 per cent ABV) are pungent with Goldings hops and orange fruit while Greene King's **Abbot Ale** (5.0 per cent ABV) is packed with marmalade fruit in the mouth balanced by an intense hop bitterness (36 units). McMullen of Hertford has a superb brew-house with wooden, high-sided fermenters. Its two bitters, **AK** and **Country**, are well-attenuated ales in which most of the brewing sugars turn to alcohol. AK (3.8 per cent ABV; 22 IBUs) is hoppy and fruity with hints of orange peel on the aroma, while Country (4.6 per cent ABV; 30 IBUs) has a massive hops and fruit appeal.

England's smallest county, Rutland, surrounded by the larger Leicestershire, has the prize-winning Ruddles Brewery, now owned by the Grolsch lager brewery of the Netherlands. **Best Bitter** (3.8 per cent ABV) is a quenching balance of malt, hops and light fruit while

County (4.9 per cent ABV) is packed with hops and fruit due to the blend of Bramling Cross, Challenger, Fuggles and Goldings varieties.

In London, Young's of Wandsworth produces a standard bitter – always known by its Cockney nickname of "Ordinary" – and a Special Bitter that are uncompromising in their tart hoppiness. **Ordinary Bitter** (3.7 per cent ABV) is extremely pale (14 units of colour), brewed only from Maris Otter barley with a little torrefied barley and brewing sugar. Hops are Fuggles and Goldings, which create 32 to 34 IBUs. **Special Bitter** (4.8 per cent ABV; 32 IBUs) has a peppery hop aroma balanced by

East Anglia, the major English barley-growing region, produces beers with great depth of flavour. Adnams (above) brews complex, fruity ales in a superb seaside setting

YOUNG'S BREWERY IN LONDON IS OPEN TO VISITORS WHO CAN SEE STABLES WHERE DRAY HORSES ARE KEPT AND WHO STILL DELIVER BEER TO PUBS CLOSE TO THE BREWERY. THE SITE ALSO HAS DUCKS, GEESE AND A RAM, THE BREWERY MASCOT.

*Making an entrance...
Shepherd Neame, in the
heart of the Kent hop fields,
embellishes its Faversham
head office with a hop motif*

rich citric fruit, ripe malt in the mouth and a big finish packed with fruit and hops. Target hops are added to Fuggles and Goldings and the beer is dry hopped in cask.

South of London in the heart of the Kent hop fields, Shepherd Neame of Faversham is the oldest surviving brewery in England, dating from 1698. It brews two bitters and a strong ale, all bursting with a complex blend of Omega, Goldings, Target and Zenith hops. **Master Brew Bitter** (3.8 per cent ABV) and **Master Brew Best Bitter** (4.0 per cent ABV) have tangy, hoppy and citric-fruit aromas, bitter-sweet palates and massive hop finishes. **Spitfire Ale** (4.7 per cent ABV), available in bottle-conditioned form as well

as on draught, is ripe and fruity, balanced by great depth of hop bitterness.

The family-owned King and Barnes Brewery in Horsham, Sussex, brews a range of highly distinctive ales with an appealing new-mown grass aroma from the house yeast. **Sussex Bitter** (3.5 per cent ABV; 31.5 IBUs) has a complex grist of pale, crystal and chocolate malts, with flaked maize and invert sugar. The hops are Challenger and Goldings. The copper-coloured **Broadwood** (4.0 per cent ABV; 37 IBUs) has a more malty note to the aroma and palate and rich fruit in the finish. The darker **Festive**, which is bottle as well as cask-conditioned, is 4.8 per cent ABV with 41.5 IBUs.

In the West Country, the superb red-brick Victorian brewery of Eldridge Pope of Dorchester produces four bitters: a 3.3 per cent **Dorchester Bitter**, a 3.8 per cent **Best Bitter**, **Thomas Hardy Country Bitter** (4.2 per cent ABV, bottle-conditioned as well as draught) and the renowned **Royal Oak** (5.0 per cent ABV). The beers have great depth, with floral hops from Challenger and Northdown varieties, rich malt from Pipkin pale

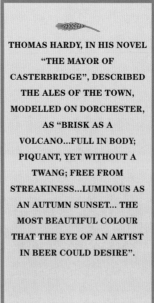

THOMAS HARDY, IN HIS NOVEL "THE MAYOR OF CASTERBRIDGE", DESCRIBED THE ALES OF THE TOWN, MODELLED ON DORCHESTER, AS "BRISK AS A VOLCANO...FULL IN BODY; PIQUANT, YET WITHOUT A TWANG; FREE FROM STREAKINESS...LUMINOUS AS AN AUTUMN SUNSET... THE MOST BEAUTIFUL COLOUR THAT THE EYE OF AN ARTIST IN BEER COULD DESIRE".

and crystal, and a delicate hint of banana fruit from the yeast.

In Devizes, Wadworth's imposing red-brick brewery produces a clutch of bitters of which the best-known is the 4.3 per cent **6X**, an ale that takes its name from the medieval habit of branding casks with Xs to indicate strength. 6X is brewed from Pipkin pale malt, crystal malt and brewing sugar, and hopped with Fuggles and Goldings (22 IBUs).

In the far west, St Austell Brewery in the town of the same name brews a 3.8 per cent **Tinners Bitter** with a delicate aroma of hops and buttercups, with light fruit and hops on the palate and the finish. The powerful five per cent **HSD** is nicknamed "High Speed Diesel" by locals, though officially it stands for Hicks Special Draught, named in honour of the brewery's founder. In the North-west of England, a vast region that takes in the beauty of the Lake District to such great cities as Liverpool and Manchester, there are many fine bitters to enjoy. Manchester is a Mecca for ale lovers. From Boddingtons, with its tart and quenching pale **Bitter** (3.8 per cent ABV), to Hydes' malty/fruity **Bitter** (3.8 per cent ABV; 28 IBUs) and Lees' 4.0 per cent **Bitter** (27 IBUs) and strong **Moonraker** (7.5 per cent ABV; 30 IBUs) with a pronounced orange ester, there is a splendid choice. But the finest pale ale in the city is the uncompromisingly and shock-ingly hoppy **Holt's Bitter** (4.0 per cent; 40 IBUs). Holts is an old-fashioned, traditionalist family firm that refuses to advertise or even to provide its beers outside a small radius around the brewery. It still supplies its beers in 54-gallon hogsheads to some of its larger pubs. The complex bitter is brewed from Halcyon, Pipkin and Triumph pale malts, with a touch of black malt, flaked maize and invert sugar. Hops are Goldings and Northdown.

Down the road from Manchester, Frederic Robinson in Stockport brews a 4.2 per cent **Best Bitter** that strikes a brilliant balance between malt and hops, with pungent Goldings and tart fruit on the aroma, malt, hops and citric fruit in the mouth, and a long, dry and bitter finish. **Old Tom** (8.5 per cent ABV) boasts a picture of a tom cat on the label but the feline does not affect the taste of this powerful vinous, darkly fruity and deeply bitter beer.

PALE ALE AND BITTER BREWERS

Adnams & Co,
Sole Bay Brewery, East Green, Southwold IP18 6JW.

Bass Brewers,
137 High Street,
Burton-on-Trent DE14 1JZ.

Bass Mitchells and Butlers,
Cape Hill Brewery, PO Box 27,
Birmingham B616 0PQ.

Black Sheep Brewery,
Wellgarth, Masham, nr Ripon
HG4 4EN.

Boddington,
Whitbread Beer Co, PO Box 23, Strangeways, Manchester
M60 3WB.

Burton Bridge Brewery,
24 Bridge Street,
Burton-on-Trent DE14 1SY.

W. H. Brakspear & Sons,
The Brewery, New Street,
Henley-on-Thames RG9 2BU.

Crouch Vale Brewery,
12 Redhills Road, South
Woodham Ferrers CM3 5UP.

Eldridge Pope & Co,
Dorchester Brewery, Weymouth Avenue, Dorchester DT1 1QT.

Fuller, Smith & Turner,
Griffin Brewery, Chiswick Lane
South, London W4 2QB.

Greene King,
Westgate Brewery,
Bury St Edmunds IP33 1QT.

Joseph Holt,
Derby Brewery, Empire Street, Cheetham, Manchester
M3 1JD.

Hook Norton Brewery Co,
Brewery Lane, Hook Norton,
Banbury OX15 5NY.

Hydes Anvil Brewery,
46 Moss Lane West,
Manchester M15 5PH.

Ind Coope Burton Brewery,
107 Station Road,
Burton-on-Trent DE14 1BZ.

King & Barnes,
18 Bishopric, Horsham
RH12 1QP.

J. W. Lees & Co,
Greengate Brewery, Middleton Junction, Manchester M24 2AX.

Lloyds Country Beers,
John Thompson Inn, Ingleby
DE7 1NW.

Marston, Thompson & Evershed,
PO Box 26, Shobnall Road,
Burton-on-Trent DE14 2BW.

McMullen & Sons,
The Hertford Brewery, 26 Old
Cross, Hertford SG14 1RD.

Frederic Robinson,
Unicorn Brewery, Stockport
SK1 1JJ.

Ruddles Brewery,
Langham, Oakham, Rutland
LE15 7JD.

St Austell Brewery Co,
63 Trevarthian Road,
St Austell PL25 4BY.

Shepherd Neame,
17 Court Street, Faversham
ME13 7AX.

Samuel Smith,
The Old Brewery, High Street,
Tadcaster LS24 9SB.

Timothy Taylor & Co,
Knowle Spring Brewery,
Keighley BD21 1AW.

Joshua Tetley & Son,
PO Box 142, The Brewery,
Hunslet Road, Leeds LS1 1QG.

T. & R. Theakston,
The Brewery, Masham,
nr Ripon HG4 4DX.

Tolly Cobbold,
Cliff Road,
Ipswich IP3 0AZ.

Wadworth & Co,
Northgate
Brewery, Devizes
SN10 1JW.

Young & Co,
Ram Brewery,
High Street,
Wandsworth,
London
SW18 4JD.

Boddingtons – one of the first "widget" beers in a can ... they call it draught, but it is actually filtered and pasteurized

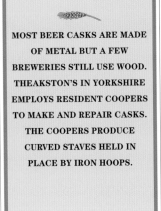

Gale's of Hampshire's Prize Old Ale comes in a stoppered and sealed bottle, while Thomas Hardy's Ale (right) improves if it is laid down for several years

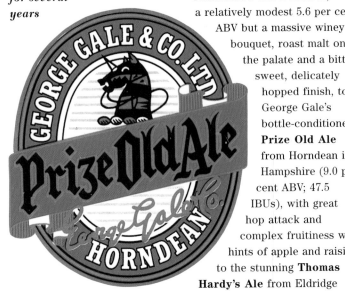

SPECIAL ALES

Brewers are adding to the pleasures of ale drinking in England with a surge of new beers, many of them seasonal. Summer ales, light but well-hopped and refreshing, have been launched in recent years. Several are now producing harvest ales made from the first malt and hops of the new season, making them the Beaujolais Nouveaux of the beer world. John Willy Lees of Manchester was the first in the field with its **Harvest Ale** (11.5 per cent ABV; 34 IBUs), brewed from 100 per cent Maris Otter pale malt and East Kent Goldings whole hops.

The winter months are enlivened by a growing number of old ales and barley wines. Old ale in previous centuries was a beer aged for up to a year in oak vats. It is now brewed conventionally but there is a wide range of aromas and flavours to enjoy. Some old ales are now brewed all the year round. Classics of the style include the world-famous Theakston's **Old Peculier**, with a relatively modest 5.6 per cent ABV but a massive winey bouquet, roast malt on the palate and a bitter-sweet, delicately hopped finish, to George Gale's bottle-conditioned **Prize Old Ale** from Horndean in Hampshire (9.0 per cent ABV; 47.5 IBUs), with great hop attack and complex fruitiness with hints of apple and raisin, to the stunning **Thomas Hardy's Ale** from Eldridge

Pope. Hardy's Ale is bottle-conditioned and reaches 12 per cent alcohol. It is brewed from 100 per cent Pipkin pale malt and its tawny colour comes from three months' maturation and some caramelization of the sugars during the copper boil. It is a rich, winey yet intensely bitter ale with 75 units of bitterness. It will improve with age and some older vintages have remarkable flavours of liquorice, old leather and fresh tobacco. It is brewed in honour of West Country author Thomas Hardy who praised the ales of "Casterbridge" (Dorchester) in his novels.

Barley wine traditionally was the strongest ale in a brewery. There are two superb examples of the style in London. Fuller's **Golden Pride** (9.0 per cent ABV) is matured for three months in untreated wooden hogsheads in the approved eighteenth- and nineteenth-century fashion. It has an appealing sherry colour, a smooth, rich, Cognac-tinted palate with noticeable hop attack in the finish. Young's **Old Nick** is darker (75-80 colour units; 50-55 IBUs) with nutty crystal malt notes, bitter-sweet fruit and a typically powerful Young's hop presence.

SELECTED ADDRESS
George Gale & Co,
The Brewery, Horndean, Portsmouth PO8 0DA.

PORTER

The revival of cask-conditioned ale has encouraged brewers to widen their portfolios and dig deep into history and recipe books. Porter, the beer style that created the modern commercial brewing industry, is now back in fashion, along with several interpretations of its strongest version, stout. Among the many fascinating examples of porters on sale are two available in bottle-conditioned as well as draught versions: **Harvey's of Lewes** (4.8 per cent ABV) and **Burton Bridge** (4.5 per cent ABV). The latter is dark brown with tawny hints, probably close to the colour of an early porter before roasted malts were used. Whitbread, a towering presence in the history of porter brewing, invited three of its breweries in Castle Eden (near Durham), Cheltenham and Sheffield to brew porters to an 1850s' recipe from its London plant. A panel of beer writers tasted them blindfold and unanimously chose the Castle Eden version. Brewed from pale, brown, chocolate and black malts, with English Goldings in the copper and dry hopped with Styrian Goldings, **Castle Eden Porter** (4.5 per cent ABV) has 290 units of colour and 36 units of bitterness. The tiny Larkins Brewery of Chiddingstone is based on a Kent hop farm and its **Porter** (5.5 per cent ABV), with 59 bitterness units, is packed with piny, resiny Fuggles and Goldings character and a bitter-sweet palate and finish dominated by dark fruit and hops. The strength, bitterness and residual sweetness makes it as close to the original style as it is possible to get.

PORTER BREWERS
Burton Bridge Brewery,
23 Bridge Street, Burton-on-Trent DE14 1SY.
Castle Eden Brewery,
PO Box 13, Castle Eden, Hartlepool TS27 4SX.
Harvey & Son,
Bridge Wharf Brewery, 6 Cliffe High Street, Lewes BN7 2AH.
Larkins Brewery,
Larkins Farm, Chiddingstone, Edenbridge TN8 7BB.

BROWN ALES

Most brown ales are bottled versions of mild. The 3.0 per cent **Manns Brown Ale** is one of the last reminders of a malty-sweet London mild, even though it is now brewed by Ushers of Trowbridge in Wiltshire. Manns was a large brewing company in East London that became part of the Grand Metropolitan-Watney group. Manns Brown is a lightly-hopped and gently fruity beer, available only in bottle.

In the North-east of England brown ale has deep roots in a region once famous for its shipbuilding and mining industries. Brown ales there are far more robust than southern mild. They tend to be reddish in colour, more in keeping with the red beers of Flanders than a darker mild. The best-known

version is **Newcastle Brown Ale** from Newcastle Breweries, the Geordie end of the Scottish and Newcastle group. Brown ales were developed as the North-east's rival to the pale ales of the East Midlands and Newcastle Brown Ale was the result of the pioneering work of the splendidly named Colonel Porter in the 1920s. The beer is complex, a blend of two beers: a dark brown beer that is not sold commercially and a 3.0 per cent Newcastle Amber. The blended beer is 4.7 per cent ABV with 24 IBUs. The recipe is made up of pale ale and crystal malts, brewing sugar and syrup and a touch of caramel. A complex blend of Hallertau, Northdown, Northern Brewer and Target hops are used, primarily for bitterness. Newcastle Brown Ale is the biggest-selling bottled ale in Britain and is exported to 40 countries. It is sold in draught form in the United States and has become a cult beer in Russia.

In nearby Sunderland, another former shipbuilding city, the Vaux Brewery produces 4.2 per cent **Double Maxim**, a characterful contribution to the brown ale portfolio. Vaux, a name with possible French origins but rendered as "Vorks" in the throaty local dialect, brewed a **Maxim** ale to celebrate the safe return to Wearside of Captain Ernest Vaux, who had used a maxim gun to great effect in the Boer War. A stronger version, called Double Maxim, was produced in 1938 and remained a bottled speciality until the 1980s when the local branches of the

© The Newcastle Breweries Limited, 1930

Campaign for Real Ale urged the brewery to produce a cask-conditioned version. They did so, and it is made from a blend of pale malts with Challenger, Fuggles and Target hops.

Awa' the lads... period poster for a Geordie classic, Britain's biggest-selling bottled ale and now a great favourite in both the US and Russia

BROWN ALE BREWERS
Newcastle Breweries,
Tyne Brewery, Gallowgate, Newcastle upon Tyne NE99 1RA.
Vaux Breweries,
The Brewery, Sunderland SR1 3AN.
Ushers of Trowbridge,
Directors House, 68 Fore Street, Trowbridge BA14 8JF.

"MILK" STOUT

Milk stout was a late Victorian speciality, a beer designed to be sweeter, lower in alcohol, less gassy and with claimed food value. The best-known example of the breed is **Mackeson Stout**, brewed by a company in Hythe in Kent that had produced ales since the reign of Charles II. The "milk" came from lactose or milk sugar, a by-product of cheese making. Lactose cannot be fermented by brewer's yeast and it is this that gives the finished stout body and sweetness.

Milk stouts achieved massive sales and were popular with people who disliked the roasty, astringent and heavily hopped nature of a dry Irish stout. Mackeson's label claimed that "each pint contains the energizing carbohydrates of 10 ounces of pure dairy milk" and a promotional pamphlet said the stout was ideal for invalids, nursing mothers and even helped those who suffered from stomach disorders, including flatulence. In the aftermath of the Second World War, with severe shortages of food in Britain, the government instructed all sweet stout producers to remove the word "milk" from labels and advertising on the grounds that it was misleading and gave the impression that such beers actually contained milk. Mackeson even had to stop using the image of a milk churn on its label, though it has since been restored.

In spite of these restrictions, Mackeson's sales soared to such an extent that in the 1960s it accounted for an astonishing 60 per cent of the sales of Whitbread, which had bought the Kent brewery. It is now a minority beer but is still a sizeable brand for Whitbread. Although it begins with an original gravity of 1042, the finished alcohol is just 3.0 per cent as the lactose, which accounts for around 9.0 per cent of the grist, does not ferment. The rest of the recipe is made up of pale and chocolate malts and caramel. "Sweet stout" is a misnomer and does the beer little credit, as it has a respectable 26 IBUs. It has a rich aroma of dark, chocolatey malt and delicate hops, with a hint in the mouth of those old-fashioned sweets known as "milk drops". The finish starts sweet but becomes dry. An export version with 5.0 per cent alcohol and 34 IBUs is firmer, fruitier and more rounded. It is possible that Whitbread may introduce it to the home market.

MILK STOUT BREWER
Whitbread Beer Co,
Salmesbury, Nr Preston, Lancashire.

MACKESON'S MILK STOUT

MACKESON
& CO LIMITED
HYTHE
BREWERY
KENT.
REG? TRADE MARK
MILK STOUT

THE ORIGINAL MILK STOUT

Mackeson has now been able to put the milk churn back on its label

SCOTLAND

THE HISTORY, THE CULTURE AND EVEN THE CLIMATE HAVE DETERMINED THE COURSE OF SCOTTISH BREWING. THE END RESULT IS A STYLE RADICALLY DIFFERENT TO THAT OF THE BIGGER COUNTRY TO THE SOUTH.

Commercial brewing was slower to develop north of the border. Ale production was confined to the home and the farm, and it faced competition from home-grown whisky and imported French wine. The Napoleonic Wars cut off the supplies of wine from Bordeaux and from around 1730 commercial brewers sprang up to meet both local supply and a demand from Scots who had emigrated to the West Indies and North America. The term "export" for a strong and malty brew developed into a generic style and even today one of the major brands in Scotland is **McEwan's Export**.

The new entrepreneurial Scots brewers grew at astonishing speed. Companies such as Younger and McEwan not only became powerful forces in Scotland but exported considerable quantities of ale to North America, India and Australasia while Scotch Ale sent to Northeast England via the new railway system out-sold local brews. The brewing industry was mainly confined to the Lowlands, where the finest malting barley grows, and Alloa, Edinburgh and Glasgow became major brewing centres. Although pale malt provides the bulk of the grist in Scottish brewing, amber, brown, black and chocolate versions are widely used even in what are nominally called "pale" ales, while roasted barley and oats add further distinctive tart and creamy flavours.

The cold climate determined the particular nature of Scottish beer. Hops cannot grow in Scotland and as they are expensive to import they are used more sparingly, with a short time in the copper to avoid boiling off the aroma and bitterness. And before temperature control was introduced, fermentation was naturally cooler than in England, around 10 degrees C/50F. The yeast works more slowly and fermentation lasts for around three weeks, followed by a long conditioning period. Slow, cool fermentation, allied to the large number of Scots who worked abroad and acquired a taste for lager, help explain the enthusiasm to embrace the new style of brewing in Scotland. Tennent's Wellpark Brewery in Glasgow started to brew lager as early as 1885. The rush to merge in the 1960s and 1970s, creating the Scottish duopoly of Scottish and Newcastle, and Tennent-Caledonian (a subsidiary of Bass), was driven by the demands of the lager market and the heavy costs of investing in new brewing plant.

Far more than in England, Scottish ale seemed destined for the scrapheap. But due to a long rearguard action by CAMRA and the enthusiasm of a small but growing number of specialist ale brewers, cask beer is starting to revive to such an extent that the busiest bars in Aberdeen, Edinburgh and Glasgow are those that offer real ale. The revival has also seen a welcome reappearance of the names given to Scottish styles, such as "light", meaning a lightly-hopped ale, "heavy" for a standard bitter ale, "export" for a stronger ale, and "wee heavy" for a powerful beer akin to an old ale. Many revivalist ales are also branded with the term shilling, as in 60, 70, 80 and 90 shilling ales, based on a nineteenth-century method of

McEwan's Export recalls when rich and dark Scottish ales were widely exported

IN ITS HEYDAY EDINBURGH HAD 16 BREWERIES, INCLUDING SOME ON THE ROYAL MILE. IT WAS THE BREWERY CHIMNEYS, EMITTING THE FUMES OF MALT AND BOILING HOPS, THAT GAVE THE CITY ITS NICKNAME OF "AULD REEKIE".

Coppers at "Caley" – as it is known – Edinburgh's Caledonian Brewery

invoicing based on strength. This means that a light may be called Sixty Shilling and so on up the strength table to Ninety Shilling for a wee heavy.

The pacesetter in the Scottish ale revival has been the Caledonian Brewery in Edinburgh. Bought by a handful of enthusiasts in 1987 when its previous owners closed the plant, Caledonian struggled to survive but won through on the sheer quality of its ales and its commitment to traditional methods and ingredients. The brewery uses open-fired coppers that encourage a good rolling boil, according to the brewer, who says his ales are properly boiled with hops and not stewed. While the bitterness units of most Scottish ales rarely exceed 30, Caledonian's are noticeably hoppy due to the generous use of Fuggles and Goldings that give the ales a delectable aroma and palate of citric fruit. The 4.9 per cent ABV **Merman XXX**, a recreation of a genuine Scottish nineteenth-century "export", has between 48 and 50 bitterness units. With pale, crystal, amber, chocolate and black malts, it is a highly complex beer with hops, fruit and chocolate on the aroma, and a biscuity, fruity and hoppy palate and finish. Other Caledonian ales include a malty/hoppy **Caledonian Eighty Shilling** (4.1 per cent ABV), an organic **Golden Promise** (4.9 per cent ABV; 50 to 52 IBUs), and a magnificent **R&D Deuchar's IPA**, a loving

recreation of the Scottish interpretation of the India Pale Ale style. Deuchar's IPA, 3.9 per cent ABV; 34 to 36 IBUs, is brewed from Golden Promise pale and crystal malts with Fuggles and Goldings whole hops.

Another Scottish brewer that ploughed a lonely ale furrow for years before breaking through to plaudits and success is Belhaven in Dunbar. The brewery, based in old maltings buildings, is in a superb setting on the coast, close to the English border. It brews the whole gamut of traditional Scottish ales, from 60 to 90 shilling. Its **Belhaven**

Eighty Shilling (4.1 per cent ABV; 33 units of colour; 29 of bitterness) is the Scots classic, with a pronounced gooseberry character on the aroma and palate underscored by peppery, resiny Fuggles and Goldings.

Two other breweries in Border country offer fascinating examples of the art. Broughton Brewery is in the town of the same name where novelist John Buchan was born – it names its major product, **Greenmantle Ale**, after one of his Richard Hannay adventures. It also brews a strong **Old Jock** (6.7 per cent ABV; 32 IBUs) and a traditional **Broughton Oatmeal Stout** (3.8 per cent ABV; 28

Caledonian's organic beer Golden Promise, made from chemical-free malt and hops

IBUs) in which the oats give a pleasing creamy sweetness to balance the slight astringency of roasted barley.

Traquair House near Peebles is a restored medieval brewery, based in the oldest inhabited stately home in Scotland. **Traquair House Ale**, 7.0 per cent ABV, 35 IBUs, is brewed from pale malt and a touch of black, with East Kent Goldings specially grown for the house.

The old independent company of Maclays is based in the famous brewing town of Alloa. In common with Broughton, it has brought back a traditional stout using oats. **Maclays Oatmalt Stout** (4.5 per cent ABV; 35 IBUs) has hops and dark grain on the aroma, subtle malty sweetness in the mouth, and a long bitter-sweet finish with a hint of chocolate from dark malt. Maclays has a wide portfolio, including 60, 70 and 80 shilling ales, a porter and a superbly quenching **Maclays Summer Ale** (3.6 per cent ABV) with great hop character (50 IBUs). Maclay's beers are all far more hoppy than the Scottish norm.

The most northerly brewery in the British Isles is run by an Englishman, Roger White, on Orkney. The Orkney Brewery, based in an old school house, produces **Raven Ale** (3.8 per cent ABV), **Dragonhead Stout** (4.1 per cent ABV), **Dark**

Island (4.7 per cent ABV) and **Skullsplitter** (8.5 per cent ABV). The beers are rich and complex, fruity with good hop balance.

The origins of Scottish – or rather Pictish – brewing have been captured in the remarkable **Fraoch**, an ale that uses heather as well as barley malt in its make-up. Heather was widely used centuries ago to augument the poor quality of the barley grown in the Highlands. Bruce Williams, who runs a home-brew shop in Glasgow, discovered a woman living on the Western Isles who was able to translate a recipe for heather ale from Gaelic. Fraoch is brewed for him at Maclays and uses ale malt, carapils, wheat malt, ginger root and 12 litres of heather. Hops are used primarily for their preservative quality and did not feature in the original recipe. Part of the heather is added to the copper, the remainder in the hop back, where it acts as a filter for the hopped wort. Fraoch comes in two versions, a 4.0 per cent ABV draught and a 5.0 per cent ABV bottled. It has a crisp heather aroma with a hint of liquorice, a dry herbal palate, and a fruity and minty finish.

SCOTTISH BREWERS

Belhaven Brewery Co,
Dunbar, East Lothian EH42 1RS.

Broughton Brewery,
Broughton, Biggar, Lanarkshire ML12 6HQ.

Caledonian Brewing Co,
Slateford Road, Edinburgh EH11 1PH.

Maclay & Co,
Thistle Brewery, Clackmannanshire FK10 1ED.

McEwan and Younger,
Scottish & Newcastle Breweries, Fountain Brewery, Edinburgh EH3 9YY.

Orkney Brewery,
Quoyloo, Sandwick, Orkney KW16 3LT.

Traquair House Brewery,
Traquair House, Innerleithen, Peebles-shire EH44 6PW.

Belhaven brews in splendid old maltings near the English border. Inset, Broughton's beers have a touch of magic while Orkney (left) recalls the days of rampaging Vikings and their powerful ales

> THE MAIN BEAR GATES AT TRAQUAIR HOUSE ARE LOCKED AND WILL REMAIN SO UNTIL A MEMBER OF THE STUART CLAN RETURNS TO THE THRONE OF THE UNITED KINGDOM.

WALES

The course of brewing in Wales has been determined by the power of the Noncomformist church and the temperance movement. The influence of both has waned but Welsh beers remain remarkably low in alcohol, a reflection of the time when brewers and their products kept a low profile.

Felinfoel of Llanelli flies the Welsh brewing flag proudly with Double Dragon strong bitter. But low-gravity and undemanding beers are still the most popular in Wales

Low-gravity beers, pale ales and dark milds, of around 3.0 per cent ABV, suited the tastes of industrial workers when South Wales was a powerhouse of mines and steelworks. In spite of the decline of heavy industry, the two biggest-selling beers in the principality, both filtered and pasteurized, are **Allbright** (3.3 per cent ABV)

from Bass's Welsh Brewers, and Whitbread's **Welsh Bitter** (3.2 per cent ABV).

The cask-conditioned flag has been waved most vigorously by Brains of Cardiff. Its **Red Dragon Dark** (3.5 per cent ABV) is a classic mild ale with a fine chocolate aroma, malty in the mouth, and a light and refreshing finish. Two breweries in Llanelli, Buckley's and Felinfoel, also produce dark milds of 3.4 per cent ABV. All three breweries produce light bitters but drinkers' preferences are switching to stronger ales. **Brain's SA** – nicknamed "Skull Attack" – is 4.2 per cent ABV, malty and fruity. Felinfoel's

Brain's of Cardiff (right) produces its classic Dark Mild in a Victorian brewery

Double Dragon is 5.0 per cent ABV, fruity, slightly vinous and lightly hopped with 25 IBUs. Buckley introduced **Reverend James Original** in the 1990s, a spicy, hoppy and fruity ale of 4.5 per cent ABV.

Brewing in North Wales, for long dominated by the Wrexham Lager Company (**Wrexham Lager**, 3.6 per cent ABV), is now seeing a small flowering of micros, with the Plassey Brewery near Wrexham and Bragdy Dyffryn Clywd in Denbigh which both produce hoppy and distinctive ales.

WELSH BREWERS

Bragdy Dyffryn Clwyd,
Old Butter Market, Denbigh, Clywd.

S. A. Brain & Co,
The Old Brewery, St Mary Street, PO Box 53, Cardiff CF1 1SP.

Crown Buckley,
The Brewery, Gilbert Road, Llanelli SA15 3PP.

Felinfoel Brewery Co,
Farmer's Row, Felinfoel, Llanelli SA14 8LB.

Plassey Brewery,
Eyton, Wrexham LL1 0SP.

Welsh Brewers,
Crawshay Street, Cardiff CF1 1TR,

Wrexham Lager Brewery,
5 Central Road, Wrexham Ll13 7SS

IRELAND

*I*RELAND VIES WITH THE CZECH REPUBLIC FOR THE HONOUR OF BEING THE WORLD'S SMALLEST NATION TO IMPOSE A MAJOR BEER STYLE ON THE CONSCIOUSNESS OF DRINKERS EVERYWHERE. BOHEMIA PRODUCED PILSNER BUT FEW OF THE BEERS OUTSIDE OF PILSEN HAVE MORE THAN A PASSING RESEMBLANCE TO THE ORIGINAL. BUT ASK FOR "A GUINNESS" AND YOU WILL GET THE REAL THING. IN IRELAND ITSELF THERE IS NO NEED EVEN TO MENTION THE BRAND NAME: "A GLASS OF STOUT" WILL SUFFICE. THE ONLY EXCEPTION TO THE RULE OCCURS IN THE CITY OF CORK AND ITS ENVIRONS WHERE TWO OTHER BREWERS, BEAMISH AND MURPHY, ALSO BREW STOUT AND WHERE DRINKERS HAVE TO BE MORE EXPLICIT.

Stout is rooted in the Irish way of life to such a degree that Guinness uses the harp, the national symbol, as the company logo. Just like the people, you cannot hurry a glass of stout. Pouring a pint is an art form. Drinkers must wait patiently as the barperson allows it to settle into black body and white head and then tops it up to ensure that you receive a full measure.

Ale is also brewed in Ireland but it commands a relatively small share of the market. Lager has made some inroads but consumption of stout increased in the late 1980s and 1990s, with clever advertising and presentation winning young people to the joys of the black stuff.

Dry Irish Stout – the dryness a result of the use of roasted barley and generous hopping – is a style in its own right. But the origins of porter and stout lie in London, not Dublin. Before porter became a major style in the early eighteenth century and found its way across the Irish sea, Ireland produced sweet and unhopped ales in the Celtic tradition, a tradition that goes back 5,000 years. St Patrick, the priest who brought Christianity to the island, employed a brewer and for centuries the production of ale was controlled by the church. As a result of the damp climate, it is difficult to grow hops in Ireland and the English found to their astonishment that as late as the eighteenth century Irish ales were unhopped. There is even a suggestion that the first ale brewed by the young Arthur Guinness contained no hops.

The English had become used to heavily hopped, intensely bitter ales. Irish ale did not suit them. English brewers – and Scottish brewers in the north – exported ale to Ireland in vast quantities. As Ireland was ruled from London,

> IRISH STOUT IS OFTEN MIXED WITH OTHER DRINKS. A BLACK VELVET IS STOUT BLENDED WITH CHAMPAGNE: IF THE STOUT IS BOTTLE-CONDITIONED, BLACK VELVET SHOULD PLEASE BOTH BEER AS WELL AS WINE CONNOISSEURS. A BLACK AND TAN IS BROWN ALE MIXED WITH STOUT AND TAKES ITS NAME FROM THE STYLE OF BELTED UNIFORM WORN BY TROOPS WHO FOUGHT THE IRISH REVOLUTIONARIES IN THE 1920S.

The Dublin head office of Guinness where the Irish style of dry stout was founded

it suited both British politicians and brewers to inhibit the growth of an indigenous Irish brewing industry.

GUINNESS

The history of Irish brewing is inextricably linked to Arthur Guinness. He used £100 left to him by a benefactor to open a small brewery in County Kildare in 1756. Three years later he moved to Dublin and took a lease on a disused brewery in St James's Gate at an annual rent of £45. He brewed ale but in 1799 he decided to challenge the English brewers' domination of the Irish market by switching production to porter with the aid of a brewer hired from London. His business expanded rapidly and he used canals and the new railway system to sell porter nationally. Guinness produced two beers, **X** and **XX**. The XX was later renamed **Extra Porter Stout** while a third beer, **Foreign Extra Porter Stout**, was developed for export to the British colonies. Eventually the term "porter" was dropped and the beers became known simply as stout.

Arthur Guinness's son, also called Arthur, not only expanded the business rapidly at home and abroad but was responsible for developing the generic style of dry stout. Until the 1880s, British and Irish brewers paid tax not on the strength of their beers but on malt. In order to avoid paying any unnecessary imposts to the London government, Arthur Guinness II experimented with using some unmalted – and therefore untaxed – roasted barley in his grist. The barley added colour and a roasted, slightly charred character to the stout, making it far more bitter and dry than a London porter. Arthur II also produced the recipe for Foreign Export Stout, which, in common with English Pale Ales, was high in alcohol and massively hopped to withstand long sea journeys. When Arthur II handed over control of the company to Benjamin Guinness, Benjamin built up substantial sales in Belgium – where a taste for strong stout remains undiminished today – and North America. A third of Ireland's population had already emigrated to America following the famine of the 1840s. By the turn of the century Guinness was the biggest brewer in Europe and by the end of the First World War was the biggest in the world, a remarkable achievement for a company based on an island with a population of five million. Its fortunes were boosted by a decision of the British government in the First World War to ban the use of dark, highly-kilned malts in order to save energy. As a result, porter and stout brewing went into steep decline in Britain, leaving the market clear for the Irish.

There are now 19 different versions of Guinness brewed in both draught and packaged versions. The classic Dublin brews use malt, unmalted roasted barley, flaked barley and a blend of English and American hops. Water comes from the Wicklow Mountains and is treated with gypsum to harden it. Arthur Guinness's original yeast is still used though it has been cultured down from some five strains to one. It is a remarkable type of yeast, highly flocculent, and working at a warm temperature of 25 degrees C/77F. Fermentation is rapid, lasting just two days, with the yeast remaining in suspension. It is removed by centrifuge. The magnificent bottle-conditioned **Guinness Original** (4.1 per cent ABV; 43 to 47 IBUs) is produced by blending wort with the fermented beer to create a second fermentation in the bottle. **Irish Draught Guinness** has the same

> GUINNESS BUILT A BREWERY ON LONG ISLAND IN THE UNITED STATES IN 1947 BUT CLOSED IT JUST SEVEN YEARS LATER. IRISH AMERICANS DIDN'T TAKE TO THE LONG ISLAND STOUT AND DEMANDED THAT THE REAL STUFF SHOULD BE IMPORTED FROM DUBLIN.

strength and IBUs as the bottled beer. **Export Draught** for Europe is 5.0 per cent ABV, 45 to 53 IBUs, has a pronounced hop aroma, dark and bitter malt in the mouth and a dry finish. Guinness exported to North America has the same IBUs as the European version but is higher in alcohol and has some fruit on the aroma and a characteristic hoppy finish.

Bottled Guinness brewed in Dublin for Belgium is 8.0 per cent ABV, IBUs around 50 and has ripe dark fruit on the aroma, great depth of hop, burnt raisins in the mouth and a long, bitter-sweet finish. But bottled **Foreign Extra Stout** puts even this remarkable beer in the shade. **FES**, as it is called, is a powerful link to the time of the first Arthur Guinness. Fresh stout is blended with beer that has been stored for between one and three months in unlined oak vats where it is attacked by wild *Brettanomyces* yeast – a beer known as "stale" in the eighteenth century. As a result, the finished beer (7.5 per cent ABV; 60+ IBUs), brewed from pale malt, 25 per cent flaked barley and 10 per cent roasted barley, has a magnificent unmistakable hint of sour fruit on the aroma that comes from the wild yeast fermentation.

The toucan has been used in several Guinness advertising campaigns

Go home to a Guinness.

Murphy's – one of the major stout brewers, now part of Heineken

Macardle's and Smithwick's – ale brewers owned by Guinness

(Opposite) Smithwick's of Kilkenny has the remains of an ancient abbey in its grounds

CORK

The stout tradition is also carried on with great fervour by the two Cork breweries of Beamish and Murphy. Beamish and Crawford were Scottish Protestants who came south, bought an ale brewery on the banks of the River Lee and were brewing porter by 1792. The company's single X porter disappeared in the 1960s and it concentrates on just one version of stout. The company is now owned by Foster's, the Australian lager giant, which gives the stout a presence in Britain through Foster's Courage subsidiary. **Beamish Stout** (4.3 per cent ABV; 38 to 44 IBUs) is brewed from pale and dark malts, malted wheat, roasted barley and wheat syrup, and is hopped with Irish, German and Styrian varieties.

Murphy's Lady's Well Brewery across town from Beamish is on the site of a religious shrine that once supplied water for the brewery. James, William, Jerome and Frances Murphy, devout Catholics, built their brewery in 1856 and, in common with their rivals, produced porter as well as stout. Murphy's is now part of Heineken, which gives the stout a presence in Europe, in Britain through the Whitbread group – which brews it under licence – and in the United States. **Murphy's Stout** is 4.3 per cent ABV with 35 to 36 IBUs, and is brewed from pale and chocolate malts and roasted barley, with Target hops.

IRISH ALES AND LAGERS

Stout accounts for 55 per cent of the Irish beer market. Ale has a 19 per cent share and the rest is lager. **Harp** (3.6 per cent ABV) is the dominant lager brand, owned by Guinness and brewed in Dundalk. It was one of the first major lager brands to build a large market share throughout the British Isles and is typical of the bland and heavily-carbonated lager beers developed in the 1960s and 1970s. Guinness also brews Harp in London and it is produced under licence by several other British breweries. **Harp Export** (4.5 per cent ABV) is claimed to meet the demands of the German Purity Law, which means no cereal adjuncts or sugars can be used in the brewing process. The Dublin giant also owns the country's three ale brewers, Cherry's of Waterford, Macardle's of Dundalk and Smithwick's of Kilkenny.

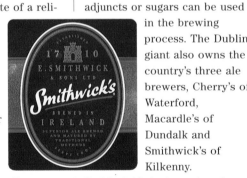

Smithwick's is the major ale producer, based on a site built by John Smithwick in 1710 in the ruins of a Franciscan abbey. The tower and nave of the abbey survive, surrounded by the modern brewery. **Smithwick's Draught** – sold as **Kilkenny Ale** outside Ireland – is firmly in the Celtic tradition, with roasted barley alongside pale malt and maltose syrup. A

complex blend of Challenger, Golding, Northdown and Target is used and is added in three stages during the copper boil. It is 3.5 per cent ABV with 22 IBUs and has a creamy, malty, lightly fruity aroma with some dark fruit in the mouth and a bitter-sweet finish. Stronger versions are brewed for export, including a 5.2 per cent ABV for Germany. A fruity 5.0 per cent **Smithwick's Barley Wine** is brewed by Macardle's. The **Cherry's** and **Macardle's** draught ales are almost identical to Smithwick's.

NORTHERN IRELAND

In Northern Ireland stout from the republic is the main brand. Bass has a brewery in Belfast producing keg bitters. The only cask-conditioned ale on the island comes from a tiny micro, Hilden, near Belfast, which produces a malty/fruity 3.8 per cent ABV **Hilden Ale**, a 3.9 per cent ABV porter and a 4.0 per cent ABV hoppy **Special**.

IRISH BREWERS
Beamish & Crawford,
South Main Street, Cork.
Arthur Guinness & Son,
St James's Gate, Dublin 8.
Hilden Brewery,
Hilden House, Grand Street, Hilden, Lisburn, Co Antrim.
Murphy,
Lady's Well Brewery, Leitrim Street, Cork.
E. Smithwick & Sons,
St Francis Abbey Brewery, Kilkenny.

LUXEMBOURG

THE GRAND DUCHY OF LUXEMBOURG, WITH ITS SMALL POPULATION OF 350,000, IS WEDGED BETWEEN BELGIUM, FRANCE AND GERMANY. ITS INFLUENCE IS GERMANIC, IT BREWS MAINLY PILSNER TYPE BEERS BUT THE COUNTRY DOES NOT ADHERE TO THE *REINHEITSGEBOT*. THERE IS OFTEN A HIGH PROPORTION OF CEREAL ADJUNCTS IN ITS BEERS.

The Henri Funck beers are brewed by the large Brasserie Réunies group. They are typical of the Grand Duchy's lagers, malty but without great hop character

In Luxembourg city, Brasserie Réunies de Luxembourg brews under the names of Mousel, Clausen and Henri Funck. **Mousel Premium Pils** is 4.8 per cent ABV, brewed from 90 per cent pale malt and 10 per cent rice, and hopped with Hallertau and Saaz varieties (28.5 IBUs). It is lagered for five weeks, has a rich malt aroma with some delicate hops, is light and quenching in the mouth, and has some hop character in the finish.

Henri Funck Lager Beer is brewed with an identical specification as the Mousel Pils. A 5.5 per cent ABV **Altmunster** is in the Dortmunder Export style, with a firm body and a good malty characteristic.

The Brasserie Nationale in Bascharage brews **Bofferding** (4.8 per cent ABV) from pale malt and corn (maize), with Hallertau Northern Brewer and selected aroma hops (25 IBUs). It is lagered for a month. It is a refreshing but rather thin beer with some light hops and malt on the aroma, a medium body, and a short, bitter-sweet finish.

Diekirch, from the town of the same name, has an all-malt **Pils** with slightly more character than its rivals. Two tiny breweries, Simon at Wiltz, and Battin in Esch-sur-Alzette, produce occasional **Bocks** along with their **Pils**.

LUXEMBOURG BREWERS
Brasserie Nationale SA (Bofferding),
2 Boulevard John F. Kennedy, L-4930 Bascharage.
Brasserie Réunies de Luxembourg Mousel et Clausen SA,
BP 371, L-2013 Luxembourg-Clausen.

THE NETHERLANDS

*H*OLLAND, AS MOST OF THE WORLD INSISTS ON CALLING THE NETHERLANDS, IS SO CLOSELY IDENTIFIED WITH HEINEKEN THAT CASUAL OBSERVERS COULD BE FORGIVEN FOR THINKING THE DUTCH DRINK NOTHING ELSE. BUT PROMPTED BY THE CROSS-BORDER INTEREST IN BELGIAN SPECIALITY BEERS, THE DUTCH MARKET IS BEGINNING TO CHANGE. A NUMBER OF MICROBREWERS HAVE APPEARED, PRODUCING PILSNERS WITH RATHER MORE CHARACTER THAN THE BRAND LEADERS. SOME MICROS ARE ALSO BREWING FASCINATING VERSIONS OF ALES, SOME BASED ON OLD AND LONG-FORGOTTEN DUTCH STYLES. THEY HAVE PROMPTED THE BEER GIANTS TO WIDEN THEIR PORFOLIOS TO BREW BROWN, DARK AND BOCK BEERS.

But the speciality beers are pebbles on the Dutch beach, and most of the beach is owned and controlled by Heineken. It not only accounts for well over half of the beer brewed and sold in the Netherlands but is a giant on the world market. As the Netherlands has a small population of around 14 million, all the leading brewers have turned to other markets to boost production and sales. Heineken produces more than 40 million hectolitres of beer a year from both its Dutch breweries and some 100 plants world-wide.

This powerful position is a long way removed from the origins of the Dutch company, though the origins were far from humble. In 1863 Gerard Adriaan Heineken bought De Hooiberg (the Haystack), the largest brewery in Amsterdam with records going back to 1592. Such was his success that within a few years he built a second brewery and opened a third plant in Rotterdam in 1873.

In the Netherlands, Heineken had a curious on-off love affair for years with its great rival Amstel. In 1941 the two companies took over another leading Dutch brewery, Van Vollenhoven, and jointly managed it. But it was not until 1968 that Heineken and Amstel formerly merged. Amstel was founded in 1870 by C.A. de Peters and J. H. van Marwijk Kooy. The awe in which brewers held Munich beer can be seen in the original title of their company: "Beiersch Bierbrouwerij de Amstel" – the Bavarian Beer Brewery the Amstel. Amstel is the name of the river that flows through Amsterdam.

The merger in 1968 was prompted by the incursion into the Netherlands the previous year by the large British group Allied Breweries, which had bought the second biggest Dutch brewery, Oranjeboom in Rotterdam. Heineken and Amstel were worried that Allied and other overseas brewers would snap up other Dutch companies and sought strength through merger. The view was heightened when Allied later acquired the Drie Hoefijzers (Three Horseshoes) brewery in Breda. But Allied had mixed fortunes in the Netherlands. It attempted to foist its undistinguished Skol lager brand on a largely unimpressed Dutch audience.

DUTCH PILSNER

Heineken today has its headquarters in Amsterdam but no longer brews there. The old Haystack site is now a restaurant and hotel. The second brewery built by the founding Heineken near Museum Square is a visitors' centre with views of superb copper vessels and video shows depicting the history of the company.

Heineken Pilsner is 5.0 per cent ABV and, in keeping with all its pale lagers, has between 20 and 25 bitterness units. This enormously successful beer is something of a hybrid, a half-way house between a true Pilsner and the light-bodied international style.

Wind in its sails... Heineken used a potent Dutch symbol to boost its international image

A 1950s Amstel promotion to give its beer appeal in the African market

THE CALVINISTS OF GELDERLAND HAVE A REPUTATION FOR BEING CAREFUL WITH MONEY. WHEN GROLSCHE ATTEMPTED TO PHASE OUT THE STOPPERED BOTTLE IN THE 1950S, LOCALS VOICED THEIR OPPOSITION AND THE BREWERY DROPPED ITS PLANS. AS IT IS POSSIBLE TO RE-SEAL A GROLSCH BOTTLE, DRINKERS DID NOT NEED TO CONSUME A WHOLE BOTTLE AT A TIME AND COULD SAVE SOME FOR THE NEXT DAY.

It has a delicate hop and malt aroma, a clean palate and a refreshing finish with some hop notes. **Amstel Bier** is also 5.0 per cent ABV, has a deeper golden colour and a fraction more hop character. These two beers are the ones by which the group is best known internationally. For its home market, Heineken also produces beers of considerably greater character. Amstel 1870 is also 5.0 per cent ABV but has a decidedly more hoppy edge while **Amstel Gold** (7.0 per cent ABV) is rich and fruity, balanced by great hop character.

The best Pilsners within the Heineken group come from the Brand Brewery, bought in 1989. It is the oldest brewery in the Netherlands, dating from the early fourteenth century, in the village of Wijlre, close to Maastricht – the present brewing site dates from 1743. In the 1970s Brand became the official supplier of beer to the Queen of the Netherlands and now calls itself the Royal Brand Brewery. Its **Brand Pils** is sold in North America in a white ceramic bottle and is called "Royal Brand Beer". It is the standard 5.0 per cent ABV and is brewed from 90 per cent pale malt made from two-row summer barley and 10 per cent maize grits. Hops are German Northern Brewer, Perle and Hersbrucker, achieving 26 to 28 IBUs. The beer is lagered for 42 days. It has a perfumy hop aroma, is malty and hoppy in the mouth followed by a firm, hoppy finish. **Brand-UP** is a

premium 5.5 per cent Pilsner, not a soft drink despite the title (UP stands for "Urtyp Pilsner" – Original Pilsner). It is all-malt, uses Hersbrucker, Spalt and Tettnang hops and has an impressive 36 to 38 IBUs. It is lagered for up to 56 days.

The Brand beers are distinguished by their long lagering periods and the company's refusal to pasteurize them. The head brewer declares: "Pasteurization serves to lengthen the shelf-life of a beer but only marginally and at enormous costs to the taste and aroma of the beer".

The most characterful Pilsner in the Netherlands comes from the small St Christoffel Brewery in Roermond in Dutch Limburg. It is owned by Leo Brand, a member of the Brand family. He built his brewery in 1986 after studying brewing at Weihenstephan in Munich and then working in the German brewing industry. His brewery is named after the patron saint of Roermond, once a major coal-mining area, and is distinguished by a fine domed and brick-clad copper kettle which he found in a barn. Leo Brand's main product is **Christoffel Bier**, 5.1 per cent ABV, made only from barley malt, with Hallertau and Hersbrucker hops. It has 45 IBUs, a massive hop-resin aroma, a tingle of hops on the tongue and a big dry and bitter finish. The beer is not pasteurized and Mr Brand tells critics who claim his beer

is too bitter with the riposte: "I am not brewing to please everyone!" The beer is also known as Blond and sub-titled Dubbel Hop to underscore the hoppy intent. He has introduced a "double malt" **Robertus** (6.0 per cent ABV) with a tinge of red in the colour from darker, Munich-type malt: the name comes from Robyn, the Dutch for Robin Redbreast. It is rich and malty with a dry finish.

The name of the company is Grolsche, the name of the beer is Grolsch and both derive from the ancient town of Grolle, now named Groenlo. Grolsche has a second brewery in nearby Enschede and both are in the region of Gelderland. Grolsche is a major Dutch brewer – the country's largest independent – with considerable overseas presence, sold in 40 countries and now brewed under licence in Britain by Bass. It is famous for the old-fashioned "swing-top" stoppered bottle that has become its international symbol.

Grolsch is called **Grolsch Pilsener** at home and **Grolsch Premium Lager** abroad. It is 5.0 per cent ABV, brewed from a complex blend of spring barley malts from Belgium, England, France, Germany and the Netherlands with a small proportion of maize (corn). Hops are Hallertau and Saaz, with aroma hops added at the end of the copper boil. The beer is lagered for 10 weeks and has 27 IBUs. It is not pasteurized, even for export.

Alfa is a small independent

brewery in Limburg dating from 1870. Its **Edel (Noble) Pils** is 5.0 per cent ABV, an all-malt brew made from French and Dutch malts, with Hallertau, Saaz and Tettnang hops. It is lagered for two months but with just 19 IBUs it has only a light hop character.

Oranjeboom of Breda, now in the hands of Interbrew of Belgium, has a light interpretation of the Pilsner style (5.0 per cent ABV) and a drier version called **Oranjeboom Klassiek**. The range of beers is liable to change under new ownership but any improvement in beer character is less likely, given Interbrew's **Dommelsch Pilsener** (5.0 per cent ABV), another light beer from a plant in Dommelen.

The village of Gulpen near Maastricht is home to a highly-regarded independent, Gulpener, established in 1825. Its regular 5.0 per cent ABV **Gulpener Pilsener** is pleasant but unexciting. But the **Gulpener X-pert** premium Pils of the same strength is superb, an all-malt brew bursting with Tettnang hop aroma and flavour with 35 IBUs.

BROWN & DARK BEERS

A few breweries produce dark lagers that bear some resemblance to the Dunkel beers of Munich and Bavaria. They are usually called Oud Bruin – Old Brown – and are around 3.5 per cent ABV, lightly hopped, smooth and easy drinking. Heineken has an everyday brown lager and a stronger, 4.9 per cent ABV **Heineken Special Dark** in some export markets. A new micro, Zeeuwse-Vlaamse in Flemish Zeeland, has a strong 6.0 per cent ABV **Zeeuwse-Vlaamse Bruine** while Gulpen and Grolsche have Oud Bruins in their ranges.

The Düsseldorf influence can be seen in a handful of Alt or Old ales. Arcense has a 5.0 per cent ABV **Altforster Alt**, amber-coloured, with a malty, slightly roasty aroma, thin palate and dry finish. (The same brewery has a top-fermenting Kölsch-type beer called **Stoom** – Steam – **Beer**, also 5.0 per cent ABV, using a blend of barley and wheat malts, Northern Brewer and Hersbruck hops – 22 IBUs – with fruity and peppery hop aromas and flavours.) Grolsche introduced an Alt in the late 1980s called **Amber** (5.0 per cent ABV) with a malty aroma but growing hop character in the big palate and long dry finish. De Leeuw – the Lion – Brewery in Valkenberg, near Maastricht has **Venloosch Alt** (4.5 per cent ABV) with plenty of dark and roasted malt character. The Us Heit – "Our Father" – micro in Dutch Friesland, founded in a cow shed in 1985, has a 6.0 per cent ABV **Buorren Bier**, copper-coloured, fruity and dry: not strictly an Alt but it fits most easily into the category. The energetic Budels Brewery has a 5.5 per cent ABV **Budels Alt** with massive peppery hops on the aroma, dark chocolate and malt in the mouth, and a deep, dry and intensely bitter finish with some fruit and toffee.

DUTCH "DORTS"

The proximity of Dortmund to the Netherlands created great interest in the rounded, malty beers of the great German city. The style has been shortened to the simple expostulatory "Dort" in the Netherlands. Gulpener has a 6.5 per cent ABV **Gulpener Dort**, brewed from pale malt, maize and caramel – hardly *Reinheitsgebot*! – with Hallertau hops. It has 20 IBUs and is lagered for 10 weeks.

Alfa's **Super-Dortmunder** has a redoubtable 7.0 per cent ABV. The beer is ripe and fruity with a clean but sweet finish. De Ridder in Maastricht is owned by Heineken but is given considerable independence. With Dortmund close at hand, this handsome brewery overlooking the river Maas – the Meuse in France and the Mosel in Germany – makes a Dort called **Maltezer** (6.5 per cent ABV) a name that for British drinkers conjures up the image of small chocolate-covered sweets but which is a fruity lager, smooth from the malt and with good hop character in the long finish. De Leeuw produces **Super Leeuw** (5.9 per cent ABV), rich and malty, becoming dry in the finish.

BOCKS

The major revivalist beer style in the Netherlands is Bock or Bok. As in Germany, the word means billy-goat and the potent animal features on several labels. For years Bok meant a dark and sweet beer which had little connection with the well-crafted German versions. From the late 1980s Bok has undergone a transformation. Bok beers come in many colours; some are top-fermented, others are lagered. Strengths vary to accommodate Dubbel Boks and Meiboks.

ORANJEBOOM – THE ORANGE TREE BREWERY – DATES FROM 1538 AND TAKES IT NAME FROM ITS CONNECTION WITH THE DUTCH ROYAL HOUSE OF ORANGE THAT LED THE FIGHT FOR INDEPENDENCE FROM THE SPANISH AND WHICH, THROUGH WILLIAM OF ORANGE, ALSO OCCUPIED THE BRITISH THRONE.

Gulpener of Maastricht brews an impressive range of beers including a Dortmunder-style Export and an old ale fermented with wild yeast

AMERICAN SERVICEMEN WHO TOOK PART IN THE SECOND WORLD WAR REMEMBER BRAND BEER WITH AFFECTION AS IT WAS SUPPLIED TO THE FORCES THAT LIBERATED THE NETHERLANDS FROM THE NAZIS.

Nico Derks of St Martinus has delved into the history books to recreate old beer styles in his tiny Groningen brewery. Right, La Trappe, brewed by the monks of Koningshoeven

THE KONINGSHOEVEN TRAPPIST BREWERY WAS BOUGHT BY STELLA ARTOIS AFTER THE SECOND WORLD WAR WHEN THE BELGIAN GROUP WANTED A BASE IN THE NETHERLANDS. IT INSTALLED A LAGER BREWERY AND PRODUCED A "TRAPPIST PILS" THAT PROVED A FAILURE.

Brand has an impressive **Imperator**, which should be a double with such a name but is brewed all year round and is a single Bock of great quality. It is all-malt, using pale, chocolate and Munich malts with Hallertau, Hersbrucker and Perle hops (6.5 per cent ABV; 22 IBUs). A 7.5 per cent ABV **Brand Dubbelbock** is a winter beer with a tempting port-wine colour, fruity and malty. The spring **Brand Meibock** (7.0 per cent ABV) has a spicy aroma, a citric fruit palate and more spice in the finish.

The Drie Ringen Brewery in Amersfoort makes a 6.6 per cent ABV top-fermenting **Drie Ringen Bokbier**, amber-coloured, packed with ripe fruit and gentle hops and a 6.5 per cent ABV **Drie Ringen Meibok**. Interbrew's Dommelsch subsidiary produces a 6.5 per cent ABV **Dommelsch Bokbier**, dry with light fruit. Its **Dominator** suggests it should be a double but is lower in alcohol (6.0 per cent ABV) than the Bok and is fruity in the mouth. Drie Horne in Kaatsheuvel brews a 7.0 per cent ABV **Drie Horne Bokbier** that is top fermenting and conditioned in the bottle with a dry, fruity and peppery hop character.

A taste of an old-fashioned Dutch Bok comes from arch-traditionalist Grolsche. It is 6.5 per cent ABV, dark, sweet and potable. Its **Grolsche Mei Bok** (6.0 per cent ABV) is amber coloured and much drier, with a good balance of fruit and hops. Heineken has an **Amstel Bock** (7.0 per cent ABV), dark, malty and chewy. Its **Heineken**

Tarewebok, also 7.0 per cent ABV, has 17 per cent wheat in its grist and is smooth and fruity with chocolate notes from dark malt. The Lindeboom (Linden Tree) independent in Neer, Limburg, has two Boks: a 6.5 per cent ABV **Lindeboom Bockbier**, dark, dry and bitter, and **Lindeboom Meibock** (7.0 per cent ABV), amber-coloured, bitter-sweet and fruity. Maasland, a micro in Oss, brews top-fermenting, bottle-conditioned beers of great character and integrity. Its 7.5 per cent ABV **Maasland MeiBockbier** bursts with dark fruit, malt and resiny hops. A 6.5 per cent **Maasland SummerBock** is amber coloured, hopped with Hallertau and German Brewers' Gold, rich, spicy and chocolatey. The St Martinus micro in Groningen brews a top-fermenting Bok called **Bommen Berend** (6.5 per cent ABV), brewed with pale, crystal, amber and Munich malts and hopped with Northern Brewer and Perle. It has an aroma of fruit gums and hops, with hops and dark fruit in the mouth, and a vinous, bitter finish. It is named after Bommen Berend, an unpopular German bishop from Münster who ruled the area in the seventeenth century until he was kicked out by the Dutch.

ALES

Dutch ale was once as rare as a lofty hill in the Netherlands. But brewers are losing their fear of top-fermentation and are recre-ating ales of quality and char-acter.

For decades the ale flag was flown by the country's single surviving Trappist brewery near Tilburg. The abbey is called Koningshoeven, a name meaning "King's Garden" – the land was a gift to the monks from royalty.

The brewery has had a chequered history since the end of the Second World War. It was bought by Stella Artois but the monks then raised the money to buy the brewery back from Stella. They had, with great prescience, held on to their brewing equipment and their top-fermenting yeast strain.

Today their beers, all labelled La Trappe, are made from pale, Munich and other coloured malts, with Hallertau and English Goldings hops. **La Trappe Dubbel** (6.5 per cent ABV) has a tawny appearance with a superb Muscat aroma and palate underscored by peppery hops. The 8.0 per cent ABV bronze-coloured **La Trappe Tripel** has a big Goldings aroma and a spicy palate and finish. **La Trappe Quadrupel** (10.0 per cent ABV) is an annual autumn vintage, reddish in colour with a smooth palate that belies the rich alcohol. In 1995 the abbey launched a new pale **La Trappe Enkel** (Single), at 5.5 per cent ABV, dry, quenching and hoppy.

In Amsterdam ale brewing has been put firmly on the map by the 't IJ brewpub. It was opened in 1984 by songwriter Kaspar Peterson in an old pub bath house beneath a windmill. The name of the brew-pub is an elaborate pun. The IJ is the name of the waterway that fronts Amsterdam harbour. The pronunciation of IJ – "ay" – is virtually identical to the Dutch for egg, which explains the ostrich and an egg on the pub sign. In the sign's background, a windmill standing in a desert suggests that Amsterdam was a beer desert until Kaspar Peterson started to brew.

't IJ brews 10 beers but they are not all available at the same time. **Natte**, meaning "wet", is a 6.5 per cent ABV brown ale in the style of a Belgian dubbel. **Zatte** (8.0 per cent ABV) means "drunk" and is in the tripel style, pale, with a spicy, hoppy character. **Columbus's Egg** (9.0 per cent ABV), is cloudy bronze in colour with a deep winey aroma, citric fruit in the mouth and more fruit in the finish. **Struis**, also 9.0 per cent ABV, is the Dutch for ostrich and is spicy, fruity and dry. The brewery also produces an autumn Bok, beers for New Year and the spring, an English-style bitter and Vlo, "flea beer".

A second enterprising brewpub in Amsterdam was opened in 1992 by two brothers, Albert and Casper Hoffman. While 't IJ is a plain and utilitarian bar, the Brouwhuis Maximiliaan is smart and comfortable, based in a former convent near the city's infamous Red Light district. The beers, unfiltered and unpasteurized, include a Belgian-style Abbey ale, **Kloosterbier** (7.5 per cent ABV), a Cologne-style Kölsch, a 7.5 per cent ABV Tripel, a

Winter Warmer and a spring Märzen. The Hoffmans have worked with a Canadian, Derek Walsh, now based in the Netherlands, to brew a recreation of a London porter (4.5 per cent ABV), ruby red in colour with a dark malt, hops and spices aroma, a spicy and bitter palate, and bitter chocolate on the finish.

St Martinus in Groningen brews the 8.8 per cent ABV **Cluyn**, a recreation of a fourteenth-century ale (*see* Chapter 7: The History of Beer), a Bok (*see* above) and a **Noorder Blond**, a 5.5 per cent ABV bottle-conditioned ale made from a blend of barley and wheat malts in the ratio of 80 per cent barley and 20 per cent wheat. It is hopped with Tettnang. It has an enticing aroma of bubblegum and lemon jelly and a tart and refreshing palate. The micro also produces a 7.5 per cent ABV spiced beer using coriander, woodruff, aniseed and cloves. Owner Nico Derks brews occasional beers, including a mistletoe ale at Christmas and one for Valentine's Day.

Drie Ringen's Hopfenbier (5.0 per cent ABV) has, as the name suggests, a powerful hop character to offset rich and fruity maltiness. 't Kuipertje (the Little Kettle) in Herwijnen brews a similarly fruity/hoppy pale ale called **Lingewal Vriendenbier** and a strong and ripely fruity **Nicks** (7.0 per cent ABV). Maasland's **D'n Schele Os** means the Dizzy Bull (7.5 per cent ABV) with a label showing a cross-eyed bull suffering over-consumption of this strong pale ale made from

barley malt, rye, wheat, spices and hops with a marvellously rich, complex spicy, hoppy and fruity palate and finish. An Easter Bunny beer, **Paasbier** (6.5 per cent ABV) is also spicy, spritzy from hops and with delicious chocolate notes from the use of dark malt. Budels produces **Parel** (6.0 per cent ABV) a golden ale with great hop character, malt and vanilla in the mouth and a bitter-sweet finish. Its **Capucijn** (6.5 per cent ABV) is an Abbey-style beer, deep brown, with a nutty aroma and some resiny hops, sultana fruit in the mouth and bitter-sweet finish.

Even Heineken is experimenting with an ale. It refuses to allow top-fermenting yeasts to come anywhere near its Dutch breweries and is test-marketing **Kylian** (6.5 per cent ABV), brewed by its French subsidiary Pelforth, in Lille. It is the same beer as George Killian's Irish Red Ale, sold on the French market and is smoothy but tart with a gentle hop character. (Killian's brewery was in Enniscorthy but closed in 1956.)

WHEAT BEERS

De Ridder (the Knight) in Maastricht has a wheat beer as its main product. **Wieckse Witte** (5.0 per cent ABV) is packed with tart, lemon and spices characteristics and is deliciously refreshing. Wiecske comes from the same Saxon root as the English wick and means a settlement. The brewery is in an area of Maastricht known as the Wieckse.

The Raaf Bierbrouwerij (Raven Brewery) started life as

Doctored ale... the brewhouse at St Martinus uses former X-ray equipment from a local hospital for its mash tun and copper

*On the right hand of God...
De Ridder Brewery on the
banks of the Maas is next to
the local church, which
silently blesses its wheat beer*

a farmhouse, brewery and maltings at Heumen near Nijmegen
in the 1700s, closed in the 1920s
and re-opened in 1984. It was
bought by Allied Breweries'
Oranjeboom subsidiary, which
busily promoted its spicy and
tart **Raaf Witbier** (5.0 per cent
ABV). Raaf also brewed a
dubbel, a tripel and a Bok but
Allied closed the brewery and
the future of the beers is now in
the hands of Interbrew. Whether
Witbier survives will depend on
whether Interbrew sees it as a
threat to its heavily-marketed
Hoegaarden wheat beer. Arcen
has **Arcener Tarwe** (5.0 per
cent ABV), brewed from a 50:50
blend of barley and wheat
malts, and Hallertau Northern
Brewer and Hersbruck hops. It
has 17 IBUs and uses a Bavarian
wheat beer yeast culture. There
is a delicious aroma of cidery
apples, with more tart fruit in
the mouth and a bitter-sweet
finish. De Drie Horne has a
powerful 7.0 per cent ABV **De
Drie Horne Wit**, darker than is
usual, sweet and fruity. **De
Leeuw's Witbier** (4.8 per cent
ABV) is packed with spices and
tart fruit.

OLD ALE

Gulpener has recreated a long-
lost speciality of the Limburg
area with its **Mestreechs Aajt**
(old dialect for Maastricht Old).
It is fermented by wild yeasts,
based on a style last seen in the
1930s. The wort (made from
pale malt and brewing sugar,
hopped with Hallertau: 10 IBUs)
is exposed to the atmosphere
until it is attacked by
Brettanomyces yeast and *lactobacilli*. The wort is then stored
in unlined wooden casks for a

year or more while a secondary
fermentation takes place. It is
then blended with the brewery's
dark lager. This complex and
fascinating beer (3.5 per cent
ABV) has a sweet and sour
aroma with hints of cherry fruit,
sour in the mouth with a dry
and bitter finish.

STOUT

Arcener Stout (6.5 per cent
ABV) is genuinely top-
fermenting, brewed from pale,
chocolate, Munich and coloured
malts, with Hallertau Northern
Brewer and Hersbruck hops (27
IBUs). It has rich malt and
chocolate aromas, coffee and
chocolate in the mouth and a
dry and bitter finish.
**Heineken's Van Vollenhoven
Stout** (6.0 per cent ABV) is
bottom-fermented. The name
comes from the Amsterdam
brewery founded in 1733 and
closed after it was bought by
Heineken and Amstel. Its
complexity and fruitiness would
increase if Heineken took the
plunge and converted it to a
true ale, fermented with a top-
working yeast.

DUTCH BREWERS

Adbij Koningshoeven,
Trappistenbierbrouwerij de
Schaapskooi, Eindhovensweg
3, 5056 RP Berkel-Eschot.

Alfa Bierbrouwerij,
Thull 15-19, 6365 AC Schinnen.

**Amersfoort De Drie Ringen
Bierbrouwerij,**
Kleine Spui 18, 3811 BE
Amersfoort.

Arcense Bierbrouwerij BV,
Kruisweg 44, 5944 EN Arcen.

**Koninklijke Brand Bierbrouwerij
BV,**
Brouwerijstraat 2, Postbus 1,

6300 AA Wijlre.

Brouwhuis Maximiliaan,
Kloveniersburgwal 6-8,
Amsterdam.

Budelse Brouwerij,
Nieuwstraat 9, 6021 HP Budel.

Dommelsche Bierbrouwerij,
Brouwerijplein 84, 5551 AE
Dommelen.

De Drie Horne Bierbrouwerij,
Berndijksestraat 63, 5171 BB
Kaatsheuvel.

Grolsche Bierbrouwerij,
Eibergseweg 10, 7141 CE
Groenlo/Fazanstraat 2, 7523
EA Enschede.

Gulpener Bierbrouwerij,
Rijksweg 16, 6271 AE Gulpen.

Heineken Nederland NV,
Postbus 28, 1000 Amsterdam.

't IJ Brouwerij,
Funenkade 7, 1018 AL
Amsterdam.

't Kuipertje,
Waaldijk 127, 4171 CC
Herwijnen.

De Leeuw Bierbrouwerij,
Pater Beatrixsingel 2, 6301 VL
Valkenberg an den Geul.

De Lindeboom Bierbrouwerij BV,
Engelmanstraat 52-54, 6086
BD Neer.

Maaslandbrouwerij,
Kantsingel 14, 5349 AJ Oss.

**Oranjeboom Verenigde
Bierbrouwerij Breda-Rotterdam,**
Ceresstraat 13, 4811 CA
Breda.

De Ridder Brouwerij BV
Oeverwal 3-9, 6221 EN
Maastricht.

St Christoffel Bierbrouwerij,
Bredeweg 14, 6042 GG
Roermond.

Stadsbrouwerij St Martinus,
Oude Kijk in 't Jatstraat 16,
Groningen.

US Heit Bierbrouwerij,
Buorren 25, 8624 TL
Uitwellingerga.

SCANDINAVIA

ISTORY IS HARD TO HIDE. WHILE THE SCANDINAVIANS ATTEMPT TO CONTROL DRINKING BY HEAVY TAXATION, AND RESTRICTIONS ON STRENGTH AND AVAILABILITY, THE IMAGE OF ROISTERING VIKINGS DOWNING FOAMING TANKARDS OF BEER CONTAINS A GERM OF TRUTH. BEER HAS A LONG, DEEP-ROOTED HISTORY IN THESE LANDS OF THE FAR NORTH. HOME-BREWING AND DISTILLING ARE MAJOR CRAFT INDUSTRIES IN RURAL COMMUNITIES WHILE THE FINNS STILL MAKE SAHTI, A RYE, OATS AND BARLEY BEER FLAVOURED WITH JUNIPER. SAHTI AND SIMILAR HOME-BREWED BEERS GO BACK FOR AROUND A THOUSAND YEARS. THE VIKINGS BREWED A BARLEY-BASED BEER THEY CALLED AUL AND HANDED DOWN, VIA THE FINNISH OLUT, THE SWEDISH ÖL AND THE DANISH OL, THE UNIVERSAL TERM ALE FOR A TOP-FERMENTING BEER. TODAY THERE ARE A FEW DARK BEERS, BOTH TOP AND BOTTOM FERMENTING, BUT SCANDINAVIA IS FIRMLY IN THE LAGER CAMP WHERE ITS MAINSTREAM BEERS ARE CONCERNED.

Old and new in Copenhagen… a brash new office block and a strikingly ornate minaret are both faces of the giant Carlsberg group

DENMARK

Denmark is a country with a population of five million. In common with Heineken of The Netherlands and Stella Artois of Belgium, the largest Danish brewing group has had to turn itself into an international giant to achieve success. For many beer drinkers, Carlsberg is as quintessentially Danish as Hans Christian Andersen and his Little Mermaid.

The great brewing dynasty was founded by Christian Jacobsen, a farmer with brewing skills who arrived in Copenhagen from Jutland in 1801. Within 10 years he had saved sufficient money to rent his own brewery where he made wheat beers. He quickly decided that science and technology had to become the allies of modern brewing. When his son, Jacob Christian Jacobsen, heard of the experiments in lager brewing going on in Bavaria he made the long and arduous coach journey to Munich and went to work with Gabriel Sedlmayr at the Spaten Brewery.

Jacobsen was fired with enthusiasm for the new beer and determined to brew it in Denmark. When he reached home he made a beer in his mother's wash-tub using the Munich yeast and then turned to making lager beer commercially.

His first lager beers were, like those in Munich, dark brown in colour and were well received. He inherited money on his mother's death and built a new brewery outside Copenhagen. It was on a hill – berg in Danish – and Jacobsen named it after his son, Carl. From that simple conjunction of words a legend was born.

The first beers from the new brewery appeared in 1847. They were a great success. Within a decade or two, Jacobsen built a second brewery alongside the old one. It was dubbed "New Carlsberg" and was run by his son, Carl. It was not so much a brewery as an architect's dream, gleaming

Carlsberg's rich and powerful Elephant is a Danish-style Bock

Special Brew inspired a style of strong lagers in Britain known as "headbanger beers"

PURE BOTTOM-FERMENTING, SINGLE-STRAIN LAGER YEASTS FIRST CULTURED BY EMIL HANSEN WERE OFFICIALLY DUBBED *SACCHAROMYCES CARLBERGENSIS* IN THE BREWERY'S HONOUR.

copper vessels set amid cool tiling and bronze sculptures, all fronted by the world-famous elephant gates modelled on the Minerva Square obelisk in Rome.

In 1875 Jacobsen created the Carlsberg Laboratories that carried out research in brewing technique. He hired a young scientist, Emil Hansen, who isolated the first pure single-cell yeast culture, one of the major breakthroughs in brewing practice. Both the Old Carlsberg brewery and the rival Tuborg plant had been experiencing problems with their beers. Hansen proved that the cause in both cases was multi-strain yeasts which contained bad strains as well as good. By isolating the good strains he was able to allow them to produce beers of consistent quality.

Carlsberg and Tuborg merged in 1970 to form United Breweries, although Tuborg has retained its own brewery in Copenhagen and is left to market its own products. The group exports to more than 130 countries and brews under licence in several more.

Overseas Carlsberg and Tuborg are both identified by pale, clean, quenching but undemanding versions of the Pilsner style. At home they have a wider portfolio. The main Carlsberg brand is a 4.7 per cent **Carlsberg Pilsner** that is often referred to as Hof from the Danish for "Court". It is a well-balanced and refreshing beer with a malty edge, but

lacking great hop character. **Let** – "Light" – **Pilsner** is a mere 2.8 per cent ABV and is typical of the thin lagers produced throughout Scandinavia to deter over-consumption of strong alcohol. At the other end of the scale, the 5.8 per cent **Carlsberg Black Gold** is a big, buttery-malty beer of considerable character.

Tuborg was founded in 1873. The brewery launched a pale lager in 1875, the result of research in Germany by head brewer Hans Bekkevold. Its main pale beers today are in the same strength range as Carlsberg's. The best-selling beer is **Tuborg Green**, which takes its name from the colour of the label, similar to Carlsberg Hof but with a shade more hop character. **Tuborg Gold Label**, at the top of the range, has a good balance of malt and hops. **Tuborg Classic**, 4.8 per cent ABV, was brewed to commemorate 100 years of brewing, and has a deep golden colour.

Both companies produce characterful dark beers. Carlsberg has a bottom-fermenting beer called **Gammel** ("old"), **Porter and Imperial Stout** – all on one label. It is not a mistake, for the early stouts were called porter stouts and one constituent element of them was a well-aged old or "stale" beer. It is an impressive 7.7 per cent ABV with rich dark

fruit, bitter coffee and scorched vanilla notes. Tuborg's porter is similar with a creamy palate and dry finish, dominated by burnt malt and dark fruit. Carlsberg recalls its origins with **Gamle**, a Munich-style dark lager (4.2 per cent ABV), smooth and chocolatey, and Tuborg has a similar beer called **Tuborg Red Label**. Seasonal beers include two for Easter, Carlsberg and Tuborg **Paskebryg** (7.8 per cent ABV), red-gold in colour, and similarly coloured Christmas beers, **Julebryg** (5.5 per cent ABV).

Several Danish brewers produce beers they call Bock in the German style. Carlsberg makes no such claim for its **Elephant** but this rich, malty-sweet, dangerously drinkable beer falls into the category. Named after the brewery's elephant gates, it is 7.5 per cent ABV and is made from pale malt and brewing sugar, with Hallertau hops (38 IBUs). Carlsberg does not declare the lagering period for the beer but its smoothness implies considerably more time than that given to its **Carlsberg Special Brew** (8.9 per cent ABV), widely exported and brewed under licence. Like an ageing boxer, the beer punches its weight, but is short on style and easily falls flat on its face. It is heavy and syrupy.

United Breweries controls around 80 per cent of the Danish beer market and owns two subsidiaries, **Wiibroe** and **Neptun**. Wiibroe was founded in 1840 at Elsinor, scene of Shakespeare's *Hamlet*, and even brewed a beer under the Hamlet name. It now makes a light lager (3.6 per cent ABV) but concentrates on low-alcohol products. Its one beer of note is an **Imperial Stout** (6.5 per cent ABV), similar to Carlsberg's. Neptun does not brew in the conventional sense: Carlsberg supplies it with wort which it turns into beer.

The second biggest Danish group is Ceres, in the old university town of Aarhus in Jutland. Its brands include those from another Jutland brewery, Thor. United Breweries also has a small stake in the company. Ceres has a splendid, bottom-fermenting dark beer called **Ceres Porter** and "Stowt" – a phonetic spelling to help Danish consumers – with the subsidiary tag of Gammel Jysk, which means "old Jutland". It is 7.7 per cent ABV, brewed with Munich as well as pale malt, and is delightfully spicy, slightly oily and darkly fruity with hints of liquorice. Ceres also brews a golden lager called **Red Eric**, in honour of the Viking who discovered Greenland and brewed beer there to celebrate. The group has a strong lager of 7.7 per cent ABV, **Dansk Dortmunder**, with a strong nod across the border to the home of German Export, which is also sold as **Ceres Special Brew Export Lager** and has a malt and pear drops aroma, a creamy/malty palate and a long, bitter-sweet finish. It makes a rich, sweetish **Ceres Christmas Beer** (5.8 per cent ABV). With a name like Thor, Ceres's partner has to

brew a strong lager – it is called **Buur**, an old Danish dialect word for beer (7.6 per cent ABV).

Albani, based on the island of Odense, has cashed in on the success of Carlsberg's Elephant with a 6.9 per cent **Giraf**, sweet and yeasty. The strongly independent Faxe achieved cult status in the 1970s with its **Faxe Fad**, a "draught" beer in a bottle, meaning the beer was not pasteurized. It too has a strong lager in the Export style which it sold in Britain in cans under the risible title of **The Great Dane**. Its 5.0 per cent mainstream Pils has a delicate malt, hops and vanilla aroma, a firm-bodied, malty palate and a gently hoppy finish.

NORWAY

Taxation on beer is steep in Norway. In a blinkered approach to drinking problems, the government increased taxes on beer in the 1980s more steeply than on wine and spirits. It is impossible to find beers of more than around 4.5 per cent ABV, which tends to reinforce the production of Pilsner-style lagers. Stronger beers are made mainly for export or can only be sold in highly-regulated shops, not bars.

The country's brewers persevere, despite the prohibitionist attitudes of politicians and bureaucrats. As well as pale lagers, there are some Bocks, summer beers, Christmas beers and Munich Dunkels, rendered respectively in Norwegian as Bokkol, Summerol, Jule Ol, and Bayerol. Beers in the Dortmunder Export style are known as "Gold

Beer". The country has its own version of the German Purity Law, which means the beers are all-malt, clean, rounded and quenching. Brewers tend to fully attenuate their beers, leaving them dry and crisp.

In Oslo, the major brewing group of Ringnes brews some dry, rounded, malt-accented beers. **Frydenlund** has tart, hoppy offerings. Close to Oslo, the Aass Brewery in Drammen dates from 1834 and is still independent and family-owned. Aass means a summit and is pronounced "orss". The brewery produces a conventional but high quality **Aass Pilsner**, a 6.0 per cent Christmas beer and a rich, malty, firm-bodied Amber of the same strength. Its 6.1 per cent **Aass Bokkol** is dark, rich and creamy, with a slightly tart finish, and is matured for between five and six months.

Mack of Tromsø is 300 kilometres inside the Arctic Circle and is the most northerly brewery in the world. Its **Artic Lager** (4.5 per cent ABV) is pale gold with a pronounced vanilla/toffee aroma, hoppy in the mouth and with a tart, refreshing finish. It also brews a stronger (6.0 per cent ABV) Gold, a dark and tasty Bayer and a rich Bokkol.

The Tromso Brewery is the world's most northerly, its beers malty and warming

WHEN DENMARK JOINED THE EUROPEAN UNION, CERES HAD TO REMOVE THE COLOURING AGENT FROM ITS RED ERIC BEER THAT GAVE IT A PINK TINGE. IT CONTRAVENED THE EU'S REGULATIONS ON PERMITTED ADDITIVES IN DRINKS. OVERNIGHT, THE MIGHTY VIKING'S BEER TURNED PALE.

Aass brews a clutch of well-matured, complex and fine-tasting beers

Bla ("blue" in Swedish) is the mainstream lager of the country's brewing giant

PRIPPS' ROYAL BEER – THE PRIDE OF THE BREWERY – COMES IN A BOTTLE DESIGNED BY PRINCE SIGVARD BERNADOTTE OF SWEDEN, WHICH EXPLAINS THE REGAL NAME.

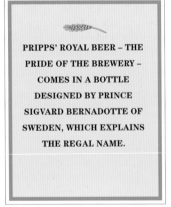

Sprendrup, a Swedish independent, brews rich and refreshing lagers

SWEDEN

The Swedes are troubled more than their neighbours by anxieties over the pleasures and problems of consuming alcohol. As a result beer is taxed to the hilt, to such an extent that scores of smaller breweries have been driven out of business. Beer sold in pubs and bars cannot exceed 3.6 per cent ABV. Stronger beers can only be bought in state shops and restaurants at daunting prices. Confusingly for the consumer, and especially for visitors, beers of the same name are produced in both Class II and Class III strengths, 3.6 and 5–5.6. As in all countries that have attempted to suppress alcohol, production has been concentrated into fewer and fewer hands until there are only three breweries of size left.

The biggest by far is Pripps, founded in Gothenburg in 1828 by Albrecht Pripps. It merged with Stockholm Breweries in 1964 but retained the old family name. The company is nationalized but the government is keen to sell it off. Volvo, the state car company, has a stake in Pripps. Its mainstream lager is called **Pripps' Bla**, which is not a critical noise but means blue. It is a sweetish, malt-accented beer with a buttery palate and some light citric fruit in the finish. It is called **Pripps' Fatöl** when sold in draught form. Pripps brews several light lagers under different labels. The most characterful is **Royal**, an all-malt Pilsner bursting with Hallertau hops on the aroma and finish. Pripps'

most interesting beers are the darker ones: a malty Munich dark called **Black & Brown**, a warm, rounded, nutty Christmas beer **Julöl**, and a coppery, hoppy **Dart**. But the stand-out beer is **Carnegie Porter**. This intriguing beer dates back to 1836 when a young Scottish brewer named David Carnegie opened a brewery in Gothenburg, one of many Scots who sought work in Scandinavia and the Baltic states. Although interest in the beer has waned over the years, Pripps, to its credit, never turned its collective back on the brand. Even though the group has closed the specialist brewery that produced it, it is still properly top-fermented in the main brewery near Stockholm. Interest has risen in recent years and Pripps is giving it some promotion. It has launched a vintage-dated version every year that has six months' maturation in the brewery and is then bottle-matured for the same period. Although the beer is then filtered and pasteurized, it does improve slightly over time, developing what the brewers call a "port-like" note. The 3.5 per cent version is pleasant but the 5.6 one, restored in 1985 after years of abandonment, is superb with a dark malt aroma reminiscent of Dundee cake – appropriate given the origins of the founder – a cappuccino coffee palate and a finish that becomes dry with more dark malt and hops developing. It won a gold medal at Brewex, the international brewing exhibition held in 1992 in England's Burton-on-Trent, for the best

foreign stout in the show: the award was given by British judges – quite an accolade.

Spendrup in the Stockholm suburbs, with splendid views over a tree-fringed lake, is the result of a merger between several old-established companies in an attempt to survive both the prohibitionist tendencies of the government and the might of Pripps. From a handsome and traditional brewhouse it produces a malty, flavoursome **Spendrup Premium** and a **Spendrup Old Gold** of quite outstanding quality. Old Gold, in its 5.0 per cent form, has a rich malt and vanilla aroma, a quenching citric fruit palate and an intensely dry and bitter finish. It is a world-class lager beer.

Falken Breweries of Falkenberg is owned by the world giant agribusiness Unilever. The brewery was founded in 1896 by a spring of natural pure water and has never moved from the spot. It uses the Anglicized spelling of Falcon for its beers which include a **Bayerskt Munich Dark** and a sweetish Julöl Christmas beer. Warby, which has fine breweries with burnished copper vessels at Varby and Solleftea, is a co-operative owned by Swedish retail shops. Its beers are rounded and full-bodied. The small Till company is famous for a pale lager with good hops and fruit notes called Sailor.

FINLAND

The Finns are a fiercely independent people who have, to their chagrin, been ruled at various times by the Swedes and the Russians. In spite of a

long period of prohibition that lasted from the turn of the century until 1932, the country has a proud brewing record that labours under the same restrictions as its Scandinavian neighbours. Beers are available in four classes and only the weakest Class I versions can be advertised.

The oldest brewery in Finland was built by a Russian, Nikolai Sinebrychoff, in 1819 to produce porter and other top-fermenting beers. By 1853 it had switched to bottom-fermentation.

After the Second World War Koff Porter, one of the brewery's original beers, was reintroduced. The brewers were keen to make it in the true top-fermenting fashion but they didn't possess an ale yeast. They claim they saved the yeast from a bottle of Dublin-brewed Guinness and made a culture which is still going strong today. **Koff Porter** is made only in the strongest Finnish bracket at 7.2 per cent and is the most powerful beer produced in the country. It is made from four malts and is hopped with German Northern Brewer and Hersbruck varieties (50 IBUs). It is conditioned in the brewery for six weeks and is then pasteurized. In common with Pripps of Sweden's Carnegie Porter, the brewery is now producing a vintage version in a fine club-shaped bottle.

Sinebrychoff – the Finns shorten it to Koff for convenience and to mark a long-nurtured distrust of the Russians – brews a strong lager named in honour of the founder Nikolai, a reddish **Jouloulot Christmas beer** of around 5.0

per cent ABV and a copper-coloured ale type beer called **Cheers**, which is bottom-fermented. A 6.8 per cent **Extra Strong Export Lager** – perfumy, sweetly malty – is sold only for export and on ferries to Sweden. It is aimed at the Carlsberg Elephant market.

Hartwall has three breweries, including one in the major city of Turku and another in remote Lapland. **Lapin Kulta** is 5.3 per cent ABV, is brewed from pale malt and some unmalted cereals and hopped with Hallertau and Saaz varieties. Brewing liquor comes from a fjord. The beer is lagered for an impressive six months and has a smooth malty aroma, bitter-sweet malt and hops in the mouth and some light citric fruit in the finish. Hartwall produces other lagers under the Aura and Karjala labels. Its most interesting brew is a **Weizen Fest** wheat beer, the only one in Finland, made to a recipe devized by Sigl of Austria and using an Austrian yeast.

The small Olvi Brewery produces a Bavarian Märzen style beer called **Vaakuna** (5.5 per cent ABV) with a big malty aroma and palate.

Great interest has been aroused in recent years by the revival of sahti, the traditional rustic beer style of Finland. The basic cereal used in sahti is rye, which gives the finished drink a tart and spicy character. Oats are also used, as is barley malt for its enzymes and husk. Hops are used sparingly, mainly for their antiseptic qualities: the main seasoning comes from juniper berries. **Sahti** was made for centuries as part of the natural

way of rural life, using saunas to kiln the grains. The mash is filtered through juniper twigs and then fermented, often using the household's bread yeast.

Perhaps as part of the worldwide revival of traditional brews, several small commercial breweries in Finland are now making sahti, though they tend to use more barley malt and less rye as a result of problems of mashing with the dark, huskless grain. The Lammin Sahti Brewery is the best known and sells the beer in a container like a wine box. It is around 8.0 per cent alcohol, has a hazy copper colour and a winey, spicy, aromatic "nose" and palate.

ICELAND

Iceland has just one brewery for its small population of 200,000. Tongue in cheek, the company is called **Polar Beer** and brews a good Pilsner-style of the same name (5.3 per cent ABV) and a low-gravity brew rather oddly called Märzen.

SCANDINAVIAN BREWERS
Carlsberg Brewery,
100 Vesterfaelledvej DK 1799, Copenhagen.
P. Lauritz Aass,
PO Box 1107, Drammen, Norway 3001.
Oy Hartwall AB,
PO Box 31, SF-00391 Helsinki.

Making Finns Koff... the Sinebrychoff Brewery was built by a Russian and the name is shortened to "Koff" as a result of a long-standing distrust of the Finns' "big bear" neighbour

HARTWALL'S LAPIN KULTA FROM LAPLAND DROPS THE "LAPIN" EOR THE EXPORT MARKET IN CASE PEOPLE ACQUAINTED WITH FRENCH THINK IT HAS SOME CONNECTION WITH RABBITS.

SOUTHERN EUROPE

ITALY

The Italians have discovered beer. Or rather young Italians, concerned with "la bella figura" – life style – have decided that beer is the drink of the moment. They leave wine to their fuddy-duddy parents. In Milan and Rome there are bars and even replicas of English pubs specializing in beer. British brewers have responded by exporting enthusiastically to Italy. Other overseas brewers have moved into the Italian market by acquisition as well as exports. Kronenbourg-BSN of France has a stake in the biggest Italian brewing group, Peroni. Labatts of Interbrew owns Peroni's main rival, Moretti. Wünster, founded in the nineteenth century by a Bavarian aristocrat, Heinrich von Wünster, is also part of the Belgian Interbrew group, while Poretti belongs to Carlsberg.

Anton Dreher, the great Viennese brewer, opened a brewery in Northern Italy in the 1860s. Today a brewery bearing his name is owned by the omnipresent Heineken. While the ghost of Dreher would be less than impressed by the thinnish lagers brewed in his name he might be amused by McFarland, an attempt at a Celtic "Red Ale", which attempts to cash in on Italian interest in Scotland and its malt whiskies but which unintentionally pays homage to Dreher's "Vienna red" style. **McFarland** (5.5 per cent ABV) is bottom-fermented and lacks the rounded and fruity character it seeks to emulate but the company deserves some praise for effort.

Poretti of Varese, to the north of Milan, has also brought some much-needed variety and innovation to the Italian beer market with its **Splügen Fumée**, a multi-lingual beer using smoked malt from Franconia in Bavaria – Splügen is the name of a mountain pass. The beer has a light but evident hint of smokiness on aroma and palate. Poretti also brews a rich, slightly fruity and vinous strong lager called **Splügen Red** (7.0 per cent ABV) and a German-style Bock of 6.0 per cent.

The most characterful beers are brewed by Moretti, due as much to the labels of the beers as to the contents of the glass. The brewery is famous for its image of a man in a fedora hat and large drooping moustache sipping a glass of beer. Moretti was founded in Udine to the north of Venice in 1859 when the region of Friuli was still annexed to the Austro-Hungarian empire. The Austrian connection lingers on in **La Rossa** – the Red – an all-malt beer of 7.5 per cent and 24 IBUs, made from pale malt and 10 per cent darker Munich malt. **La Bruna** (6.25 per cent ABV) is in the style of a Munich Dunkel, malty, smooth, with hints of roasted grain and chocolate. Moretti also has in **Sans Souci** (4.5 per cent ABV) an interpretation of the German Export style, with a firm malty body and a perfumy hop aroma. The company's main brand, **Birra Friulana**, is marketed as an "Italian Pilsner" – at least the spelling is correct

THE BRITISH CARLSBERG-TETLEY GROUP HAS UPRATED ITS FAMOUS DOUBLE DIAMOND PALE ALE TO TRIPLE DIAMOND TO CATER FOR THE DEMAND IN ITALY FOR STRONG, RICH-TASTING BEERS.

The moustached image of Moretti gives the brewery's beers rather more gravitas than they deserve

– made from pale malt and 30 per cent maize (corn). A restaurant next to the brewery's offices sells in the winter an unfiltered and more aggressively hopped version of the beer called **Integrale** – whole.

Market leader Peroni's main brand is **Nastro Azzuro** – Blue Riband. Brewed from Alexis and Prisma pale malts, with 20 per cent maize, and hopped with Saaz, it is 5.3 per cent ABV and is lagered for 10 weeks. Peroni also brews a similar beer called **Raffo**, named after one of many breweries it has acquired. The company was founded in 1846 in Vigevano and soon moved to Rome. It has plants strategically placed throughout the country and in the 1960s it opened three state-of-the-art breweries in Bari, Rome and Padua.

In the Italian region of South Tyrol and close to the Austrian border, the Forst (Forest) Brewery has not only labels but even its address – Lagundo/Algund – in both Italian and German. **Forst Pils** (4.8 per cent ABV) is brewed from pale malt and maize and hopped with Hallertau (30 IBUs). Forst also produces a 5.0 per cent **Forst Kronen** in the Export style and a 6.5 per cent **Forst Sixtus** made from pale, chocolate and crystal malts that – as the name implies – is in the Trappist/Abbey tradition.

Nastro Azzurro is the Blue Ribbon of Italian brewing, a sweetish interpretation of the Pils style, and Peroni's market leader

ITALIAN BREWERS
Birra Forst SPA/Brauerei Forst AG,
Via val Venosata 8, 1-39022 Lagundo.
Birra Moretti SPA,
Viale Venezia 9, 33100 Udine.
Birra Peroni Industriale SPA,
GA Guattini 6/A, 00161 Rome.

MORETTI'S IMAGE OF THE MAN WITH THE GOLDEN MOUSTACHE WAS CAPTURED ON FILM IN A CAFÉ IN 1942 BY A MEMBER OF THE RULING FAMILY, MANAZZI MORETTI. THE BAFFO D'ORO – GOLDEN MOUSTACHE – IS NOW BOTH THE COMPANY TRADE MARK AND THE NAME OF A 5.0 PER CENT, ALL-MALT BEER.

SPAIN AND PORTUGAL

Spain has a long association with beer. When the Romans marched through the Iberian peninsula they were impressed by local intoxicants made from soaked grain. Flemish and German members of the court of Charles V set up the first commercial Spanish breweries. The Spanish beer market was closed to outside influence during the long Franco dictatorship but now brewing groups from other countries have arrived in force to exploit the growing interest in beer among both Spaniards and the vast number of tourists.

The only major independent is Damm of Barcelona. It was founded in 1876 by Augusto R. Damm, who had learned his brewing skills in Alsace. It panders to the hordes of Germans who pour into Spain every summer with Voll-Damm, a 5.5 per cent lager more in the Dortmunder Export style despite the Franconian term "Voll", which is similar to a Munich Helles. Most of the Spanish brewers make an Extra or an Especial of around 5.0 per cent with a malty rounded character similar to a Dortmunder. Coruña's **Especial Rivera** and **Estrella Extra** are good examples, as are **Ambar Export** from Zaragoza and **Keler 18** from San Sebastian. Damm's other main claim to fame is a low-alcohol beer brewed for the 1992 Barcelona Olympics with the intriguing name of **Sin**.

El Aguila – the Eagle – has had its seven breweries whittled down to four by Heineken. Its **Aguila Reserva Extra** is a powerful 6.5 per cent ABV with 28 IBUs. **Adlerbrau** is an interpretation of a Munich Dunkel, brewed from pale and caramalts with some corn grits. Northern Brewer and Brewers' Gold produce 28 IBUs. It has an estery, fruity aroma, quenching malt in the mouth and a smooth finish with hints of dark chocolate.

Aguila's everyday beer is **Aguila Pilsener** (4.5 per cent ABV), brewed from pale malt and corn grits with Northern Brewer and Brewers' Gold hops, which are Spanish varieties of German hops. The beer has 23 IBUs and is conditioned for three weeks.

San Miguel's Premium Lager (5.4 per cent ABV, 24 IBUs) is made from pale malt, with Hallertau Northern Brewer and Perle varieties plus Styrian Goldings. Selecta XV, also 5.4 per cent, has a fruity and hoppy aroma, with rich malt and hops in the mouth, and a long finish with good hop character.

Mahou Lager, with its Kronenbourg influence, is 4.7 per cent ABV and has a pronounced malt and toffee aroma, sweet malt in the mouth and a full finish that becomes dry with some late hops developing.

In general Spanish beers suffer from short conditioning periods, which means they lack the finesse of a Northern European lager and often have yeasty, estery and grainy textures.

Two major brewing groups dominate Portugal and, while the influence is yet again Northern European, the quality is high. Brewing records go back to the seventeenth century and there have been French, German and Danish influences since the eighteenth. But, in common with its Iberian neighbour, Portugal was shut off from the outside world during the long years of the Salazar dictatorship.

Central de Cerjevas of Lisbon brews under the Sagres label. **Sagres pale lager** is rich and malty with good hop character on the palate and finish while a brown version in the Munich Dunkel style is smooth and chocolatey. The company has also launched a top-fermenting beer known incongruously as Bohemia, which with its fruity and hoppy character is more akin to Belgium than the home of

golden Pilsners. When Portugal joined the European Union, Sagres launched **Sagres Europa**, a firm-bodied, malt-accented, 5.4 per cent Dortmunder-style lager.

Unicer in Oporto was nationalized until 1991, since when it has gone into partnership with Carlsberg of Denmark. Its everyday lager, broadly in the international Pils style, is malty and quenching. A 5.8 per cent **Unicer Superbock** is yet another curious interpretation of practices further north.

GREECE

The Greek brewing industry has been virtually wiped out as a result of opening its door to foreign groups. The only Greek brewery of any size or influence, Fix, went out of business in 1984. It was owned by the Greek Minister of Defence and when his political fortunes waned his brewery followed him into extinction.

The market is now dominated by Heineken, which brews both Heineken and Amstel locally. Henninger Hellas was created by the German Henninger group but has been bought by Kronenbourg-BSN, which plans to concentrate on Kronenbourg. Löwenbräu has

built a brewery under the name of Löwenbräu Hellas to promote a Greek version of the Munich beers.

In the north of the country, **Aegean** produces a 5.0 per cent lager with a sweet malty aroma, pronounced toffee on the palate and a bitter-sweet finish.

To English speakers, the term "Hellas" has a certain poignancy when surveying Greek beer. The country had its own Purity Law, which meant the beers were all malt but this has been abandoned under pressure from foreign brewers. It is a pity there is so little of ethnic interest.

MALTA

Malta has long been independent but a benign British influence hovers over the beers of the George Cross island. The Farson's Brewery produces lagers under the Cisk name but is best known for its ales. These include a well-hopped **Hop Leaf** pale ale (1040 degrees – the brewery still endearingly declares strength by original gravity), a stronger **Brewer's Choice** (1050), fruity and hoppy, a mild **Blue Label** (1039) and a genuine **Milk Stout** (1045; 3.4 ABV), brewed with lactose (milk sugar) to give a

rounded, creamy, slightly sweet palate and a surprisingly dry finish with hints of dark fruit and chocolate. The malts are pale, mild and crystal with some caramel and have a respectable 30 IBUs. The stout is called **Lacto** and carries the claim "Milk Stout with Vitamin B for Extra Energy" – the island has yet to meet Environmental Health Officers. Malta is a beery time warp and Southern Europe could do with a few more of them.

IMPORTANT ADDRESS
Simonds, Farsons Cisk
The Brewery, Mriehel,
Malta GC.

British-influenced Farson's of Malta produces a a mild, a pale ale and even a milk stout

SWITZERLAND

NOT SURPRISINGLY, IT IS THE GERMAN REGION OR CANTON OF SWITZERLAND THAT HAS THE BEST BEER TRADITIONS. IT WAS IN THIS CANTON THAT AN IRISH BENEDICTINE MONK CALLED ST GALL BUILT AN ABBEY IN THE SEVENTH CENTURY, WHICH OVER TIME DEVELOPED SEVERAL BREWHOUSES. ST GALL, WHO BROUGHT LEARNING AND CHRISTIANITY FROM IRELAND TO EUROPE, IS CONSIDERED TO BE THE FOUNDER OF SWISS BREWING AND THE TOWN WHERE HIS ABBEY STOOD IS NAMED ST GALLEN IN HIS HONOUR.

*Swiss guard...
Feldschlössen's castle-like brewery began life as a chemicals factory. The brewhouse, with its copper vessels, is equally impressive*

In modern times the Swiss government has attempted to stop monopolies in brewing appearing by restricting breweries to their cantons of origin. But the system fell apart in the early 1990s when the leading Swiss brewer Feldschlössen signed a trading agreement with Kronenbourg-BSN of France and then merged with the Cardinal group. The Swiss market is now wide open and the result is likely to be a rapid fall in the number of 30 breweries.

FELDSCHLÖSSEN

The most remarkable aspect of the Feldschlössen beers is the brewery, whose name means "Castle in the Field". It is a former chemicals factory near Basel, set in rolling and verdant grounds, designed, as the name indicates, like a castle. The magnificent interior has a stained glass window that incorporates a picture of the founder Théophil Roninger who had worked in German breweries before launching his own in 1874. The brewhouse is a symphony of burnished copper set on marble floors, the plaster ceiling supported by marble pillars. After all this inspirational architecture, the beers are rather less than dramatic. The 5.2 per cent **Hopfenperle** has some light fruitiness on the aroma along with a delicate hop presence, is lightly malty in the mouth, and with a finish that becomes dry with tart hoppiness. A version of the beer using darker malts is called **Dunkleperle** while the castellated brewery is commemorated by a stronger, maltier **Castello**.

HÜRLIMANN

Hürlimann of Zürich is the country's most energetic exporter and is best-known for the world's strongest beer, **Samichlaus** – Santa Claus. The 14.0 per cent beer was made possible by the brewery's long association with the cultivation of pure yeast strains. Hürlimann was founded in 1865 by Albert Hürlimann – his father had started a brewery in the family's name in 1836 but had gone out of business. The move to cold fermentation for lager beers demanded a more scientific knowledge of the workings of yeast and Hürlimann became a world leader in developing specific strains that would work at the fermenting and conditioning temperatures required for different types of beer. The major problem with producing strong beers is that the yeast is eventually overwhelmed by the alcohol it produces: the yeast "goes to sleep", brewers say. Hürlimann tackled this problem and produced a strain of yeast that could ferment beer to a high level of alcohol. In 1979 it used the yeast to brew a strong Christmas beer as an experiment. The interest created by the beer encouraged the brewery to make it every year and in 1982 it was given the accolade of the strongest beer in the world by *The Guinness Book of Records*, much to the chagrin, no doubt, of EKU in Germany.

Strong does not necessarily equate with quality and some powerful lagers in other countries – known vulgarly as "headbangers" in Britain – are thick, sweet and cloying. Samichlaus avoids this by its long maturation. It is brewed every year on December 6, when the Swiss celebrate St Nicholas, and not released until the same date the following year. Although Hürlimann is a little coy about giving too much information about the beer, it is thought the beer is roused from time to time by pumping it from one vessel to another, rather like the British "dropping" system. This is to ensure the yeast doesn't go to sleep on the job. The reddish-brown beer has a blend of pale and darker

malts and is hopped with Hallertau, Hersbrucker and Styrian hops (30 IBUs). It has a complex aroma of port wine, dried fruit, malt and peppery hops. The palate has coffee, bitter chocolate, nuts and malt while the finish is reminiscent of Rémy Martin cognac.

The Swiss are punctilious about brand names and no beer can be called a Pilsner for fear of upsetting the Czechs. Hürlimann's main beer is simply called **Hürlimann Lager** and is 4.7 per cent ABV. It has a hoppy aroma, a medium body and a short finish. Its subsidiary company Löwenbräu (no relation to the Munich brewery of the same name) also has a bluntly named **Löwenbräu Lager** of 4.8 per cent ABV, brewed only from pale malt and with Hallertau and Hersbrucker hops (21 IBUs). It has a malty nose and body, with some light hops in the finish. **Sternbräu** at 5.5 per cent ABV and 28 IBUs is a richer and more distinctive beer in the Export style, firm bodied, malty and with a good Saaz hop character. A 5.4 per cent Dunkel is called **Hexenbräu** – Witches' Brew – and is rich and chocolatey while **Drei-Königs Bier** is a 6.5 per cent strong pale beer with great malt character. It is named after the coat of arms of a district of Zürich.

Cardinal in Fribourg has a 4.9 per cent Helles or pale lager that carries the brewery name and **Anker**, a dark and top-fermenting beer in the German Alt tradition (5.8 per cent ABV). Cardinal was founded in 1788 and was substantially rebuilt in 1877 when it was bought by the

renowned watchmaker Paul-Alcide Blancpain, who may have some connection with the French Blancpain who settled in England and became Whitebread or Whitbread. The brewery's strong **Rheingold** (6.3 per cent ABV) is malty and perfumy, firm bodied and with a big and complex malt-and-hops finish.

Calanda of Chur, Frauenfeld in the town of the same name, and the Ueli Brewery in Basel all produce wheat beers in the Bavarian style. Ueli is a micro based in the Fischerstübe beer restaurant at Rheingasse 4, founded in 1974 by Hans Nidecker with the help of a member of the German Binding brewing family. Ueli means jester but the beers are serious without being pompous: a delicate, clean, refreshing lager, a 3.5 per cent **Dunkel** with heavy malt and toffee notes, a tart, aromatic, spicy 4.0 per cent **Weizenbier** and a pale **Reverenz**, also 4.0 per cent. The restaurant specializes in dishes cooked with beer.

IMPORTANT ADDRESS
Brauerei Hürlimann AG, PO Box 654, 8027 Zürich.

Samichlaus is the world's strongest beer at 14 per cent ABV. It is lagered for a year

Hürlimann's lagers are the product of pioneering work on yeast cultivation

Beers from the Americas

THE FIRST BEERS IN BOTH NORTH AND LATIN AMERICA WERE NATIVE BREWS USING THE CEREALS FROM THE FIELDS AND PLANTS FROM THE GROUND OR THE JUNGLES. IN NORTH AMERICA ENGLISH SETTLERS BROUGHT AN ALE CULTURE WITH THEM WHILE THE SECOND WAVE OF IMMIGRANTS FROM CENTRAL EUROPE RAPIDLY SPREAD THE LAGER MESSAGE. AS A RESULT OF PROHIBITION AND THE GREAT DEPRESSION, A HANDFUL OF AMERICAN BREWERS DOMINATED THE MARKET WITH THIN VERSIONS OF THE LAGER STYLE BUT NOW A BEER RENAISSANCE LED BY SMALL CRAFT BREWERS IS PRODUCING ALES AND LAGERS OF GREAT QUALITY. IN LATIN AMERICA, SPANISH, GERMAN AND EVEN AUSTRIAN INFLUENCES HAVE DEVELOPED SOME GOOD EXAMPLES OF THE PILSNER AND VIENNA STYLES, AS WELL AS SOME BLAND INTERNATIONAL BRANDS. THE CARIBBEAN'S BEERS RANGE FROM THIN LAGERS TO HIGH-QUALITY, PILS-STYLE AND – AS A LEGACY FROM COLONIAL TIMES – SOME FINE DRY AND SWEET STOUTS.

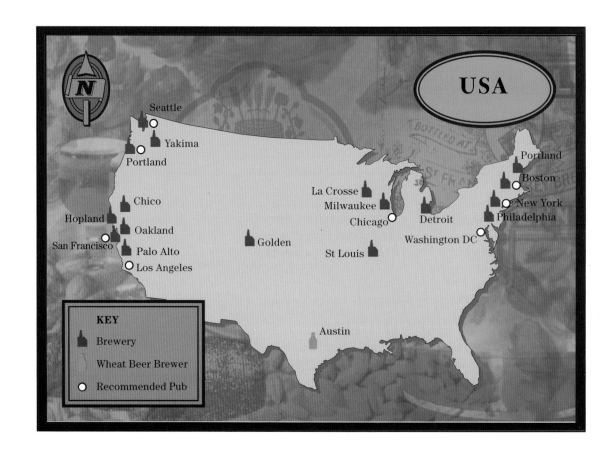

USA

Seattle
Yakima
Portland
Chico
Hopland
Oakland
San Francisco
Palo Alto
Los Angeles
Golden
La Crosse
Milwaukee
Chicago
St Louis
Detroit
Washington DC
Portland
Boston
New York
Philadelphia
Austin

KEY
Brewery
Wheat Beer Brewer
Recommended Pub

UNITED STATES

THE UNITED STATES IS A CONUNDRUM. IT IS A BREWING COLOSSUS, THE WORLD'S BIGGEST PRODUCER. BUT THAT STATISTIC REFLECTS ONLY THE SIZE OF THE COUNTRY, FOR THE AMERICANS ARE MODERATE CONSUMERS, WELL DOWN THE LIST OF DRINKING NATIONS AND NOT EVEN IN THE TOP TEN. IT IS ALSO A COUNTRY WHERE MARKETING ZEAL HAS TRIUMPHED OVER TRADITION, WHERE CRAFTSMANSHIP PLAYS SECOND FIDDLE TO THE NEED TO FLOOD BARS AND TAVERNS WITH MASS VOLUME BEERS MADE TO IDENTIKIT RECIPES FROM THE CANADIAN TO THE MEXICAN BORDERS.

In a country that lauds the free market, brewing has been concentrated to an astonishing degree, with more than 90 per cent of all beer sales controlled by just a handful of producers, the biggest of which accounts for nearly half the beer brewed.

Yet the conundrum is a deeply complex one. Most beer lovers who inhabit or have occasion to visit the United States complain that the mainstream lagers found there are bland and watery. But the dedication to quality of the producers of these beers cannot be gainsaid. The beers are often produced in breathtakingly beautiful plants, using the finest ingredients, which are then used so sparingly that the end products are almost devoid of malt or hop character. It may be the awesome size of the country that dictates to the people who run the breweries that beers cannot be too memorable in order to appeal to the lowest common denominator. There is little room for diversification

when, in the case of Anheuser-Busch, biggest of the giants, you are making more than 90 million barrels of beer a year, most of it in the shape of just one brand, Budweiser.

American beer is locked into a culture and economy that had to grow, compress, rush and cut corners in order to catch up with the rest of the industrialized world. And now, as the world's single super-power, it can build only on what it knows. Nowhere is that more true than in the brewing industry. Other great brewing nations – Britain at first, then Ireland, Germany, Bohemia and the Netherlands – brought their styles and the ability to make them to the New World. But Americans applauded when Henry Ford declared history to be "bunk" and those pioneering styles have been ignored, denied and subsumed by mass-produced and massively promoted pale lagers that were once from the Bavarian and Bohemian moulds but have long

lost any authenticity or credibility. There is a cynical saying in the brewing industry that "people drink the advertising". It is as true of the perpetrators as it is of the recipients. If you call your main product "the

More than just Bud... there is now a wide and growing choice of ales and lagers in the US as the shelves of this store testify

Cracking a keg – but not for pleasure. Government officials poured beer down the drain during Prohibition

Samuel Adams of Boston is one of the most successful of the new wave of craft brewers

King of Beers", you had better believe it or the whole corporate structure falls apart like castles built of sand.

Yet a counter-culture is developing. It has to be searched for, teased out, but it is worth the effort. For alongside the everyday beers, there is now a remarkable surge of small breweries dedicated to the consumer, not the production chart. Beers rich in choice and heritage are available, some based on long-forgotten but indigenous styles, others that look to Europe for their inspiration. There is a pleasing irony in the fact that while many European brewers now ape the American giants by neutering their beers of flavour, the new wave of American craft brewers are rediscovering the joys of the barley corn and the hop flower. If you fancy a rich Märzen, a ripe Bock, a roasty stout, a chocolatey porter, or an India Pale Ale so hoppy your eyeballs pop, then the United States is now the place to drink. It is a counter-culture that points to a country at ease with itself. Conformity in beer drinking was a by-product of an immigrant nation in which people did not wish to over-stress their Dutch, German or Italian roots and ate and drank "all-American" products. Now that pasta and Pilsner are no longer seen as a threat to the American way of life a thousand beers can flourish.

The beer produced by all the small companies amounts to between 1 and 2 per cent of the total. The percentage will double but will not threaten the hegemony of the giants. That is not the aim of the operation.

Unlike Britain, where more than 70 per cent of all beer is sold on draught in pubs, the American craft brewers are not attempting, *faute de mieux*, to muscle in on the big producers' markets. In a country where packaged beer for home consumption is the dominant type, the small producers are offering a specialist product unashamedly aimed at those prepared to pay a dollar more for a beer than those who pack the supermarket trolleys high with **Bud** or **Miller Lite**.

Prohibition is another facet of the American beer conundrum. Although the right to manufacture and sell alcohol was restored in 1933 after 13 years of illegality, the shadow of that frightening period – in which bootleg liquor was in the hands of the Mob – hung over the brewing industry for many decades. Only the biggest brewers survived Prohibition, able to make a living from soft drinks, yeast production and ice cream. Thousands gave up the ghost and more followed during the Depression of the 1930s. Brooklyn, once the greatest brewing borough in the whole country thanks to its Dutch settlers, lost all its producers. With a mass market to themselves, the giants went for the hard sell and the soft option of national brands. The country lost much of its regional diversity and traditional beer styles.

In particular, it lost its ales.

Brewing existed in North America before the first settlers. The Indians and Mexicans made porridge-type beers, quickly made and spiced with herbs and plants. When the British arrived on the East Coast they began to brew in order to keep their communities healthy as well as happy. Brewers from the old country were cajoled into joining the settlers in the New World. They brought with them ale yeasts while farmers grew barley and other cereals and began to nurture a hop industry. As in Europe, beer-making moved out of the home and the hearth and into specialist factories. The first commercial brewery was set up in New Amsterdam (now New York City) in 1623. Ale, porter and stock ale – a strong, long-matured beer similar to old or stale in England – were the staple products of the first brewers. George Washington brewed his own ale at Mount Vernon. Thomas Jefferson was a brewer and his recipe at Monticello has been preserved. Another of the great American revolutionaries, Samuel Adams in Boston, was a significant brewer. He is now immortalized by a modern craft brewery bearing his name.

From 1840 the beer scene changed dramatically and fundamentally. The second wave of

> GEORGE WASHINGTON WAS A LOVER OF LONDON PORTER AND HAD IT IMPORTED UNTIL IT BECAME POLITICALLY INCORRECT TO BE SEEN DRINKING AN ENGLISH BEER.

immigrants, a vast army of central Europeans forsaking despotism, unemployment and the drudgery of semi-feudal rural life, brought with them the skills and the thirst to make the new cold-fermented beers perfected in Munich, Pilsen and Vienna. Lager-brewing established itself rapidly and the Germanic influence can be seen in such famous names as Anheuser-Busch, Pabst, Heileman, Schlitz and Stroh. Samuel Adams in Boston may commemorate a great American patriot but the owner is Jim Koch, descendant of German immigrant brewers, though to avoid bringing a blush to American cheeks he delicately pronounces it "Cook".

The original British settlers were no match for the Central Europeans. Determined to stamp their mark on the New World, they grasped all the technologies made possible by the Industrial Revolution to produce beer in enormous quantities. They used the railroad to speed their products outside their home bases and they made a Faustian pact with the new service industries of marketing and advertising to tell the American people that their beers were the best, the greatest, the kings. By the turn of the twentieth century, there were 4,000 American breweries. Before the marketing men took over with their mission to turn beer into a commodity, those breweries served cities, towns and neighbourhoods with a vast range of styles.

The twin attacks of Prohibition and the mass-market mentality caused such havoc that by the 1980s there were just six national giants and 20 independent regional brewers left. It has been the enthusiasm of the craft brewers that has restored choice and style – in every sense of the word – to the American beer scene. As Charles Finkel of the Pike Place Brewery in Seattle says: "It is not a beer revolution, it is a renaissance. We're going back beyond Prohibition and the second wave of immigrants with their lager culture to the Founding Fathers. Americans are going back to their roots."

> PIKE PLACE BREWERY IN SEATTLE IS BASED ON THE SITE OF A FORMER BROTHEL. FAR FROM HIDING THIS SHADY PAST, THE BREWERY CELEBRATES THE HOUSE OF ILL REPUTE WITH A BARLEY WINE CALLED OLD BAWDY.

THE GIANTS

No study of world beer is complete without looking at the remarkable Anheuser-Busch empire that brews the biggest beer brand ever known. Its origins lie in St Louis, Missouri, literally and physically Middle America. With the birth of the railroad, a far-sighted brewer in St Louis could send beer across the Rockies to the West Coast, down the Mississippi to the South, up to the Great Lakes and Chicago in the North, and to the burgeoning cities of the East. It was the genius of Adolphus Busch to seize these opportunities. On a vaster scale, he followed in Arthur Guinness's and William Bass's footsteps by building national brands while others were content to stay loyal to their localities.

The first brewery to bear the name of Anheuser-Busch was bought from George Schneider who had built a "hole in the ground" plant called the Bavarian Brewery in 1852. The South German influence was obvious and extended as far as Schneider bearing the same Christian and surname as the founder of the famous wheat beer brewery in Kelheim south of Munich. But the German-American Schneider was a business failure and his small neighbourhood concern was bought and sold three times before being acquired in 1860 by Eberhard Anheuser.

Anheuser was born in 1805 in Kreuznach in the German Rhineland. He emigrated to the United States in 1843 and settled first in Cincinnati and then in St Louis. He had trained as a soap manufacturer and became first general manager and then partner in a soap business called Schaffer, Anheuser & Co. When he died in 1880 at the age of 75 his brewing business had become one of the biggest in the country. Among the many tributes to him was a lengthy obituary in a German language paper produced for German-Americans, *Anzeiger des Westens*.

In 1861 Adolphus Busch married Lilly Anheuser,

a successful wholesaling company. Five years after joining Anheuser, Busch bought out the half-share in the brewery owned by William D'Oench – who retired back to Stuttgart – and became a full partner in the company. In 1879 the "Bavarian" tag was dropped from the company's name, which became Anheuser-Busch Brewing. When Anheuser died, Busch became president and the company has remained in the family ever since. The current president is August Busch III. In common with many dynastic American corporate giants, Anheuser-Busch has had its share of family squabbles and scandals but they have not inhibited growth. Today A-B has plants in Newark, New Jersey; Los Angeles; Tampa, Florida; Houston, Texas; Columbus, Ohio; Jacksonville, Florida; Merrimack, New Hampshire; Williamsburg, Virginia; Fairfield, California; Baldwinsville, New York State; Fort Collins, Colorado; and Cartersville, Georgia.

Busch had a flair for marketing. He grasped the opportunities for selling beer outside its city of origin, using the new means of transport at his disposal. Ice-making and refrigerators made not only bottom-fermentation possible on a commercial scale but enabled beer to be transported in refrigerated trucks on rail and road. Busch also recognized that commercial success would come from producing a type of beer acceptable to the great

bulk of Americans, not just those of German origin used to the dark and heavy Bavarian style. Encouraged by Anheuser, Busch travelled widely in Europe in the late 1860s and early 1870s, concentrating on Bavaria and Bohemia. He studied the brewing process in Pilsen closely but knew that Pilsen-style beers were already being brewed extensively else-where in Europe and in parts of the United States, especially in Michigan and Wisconsin. He wanted something different and he found it in Budweis. This small town in Southern Bohemia (České Budějovice today) was a brewing legend. For centuries the quality of its beers – called generically, in the German style, Budweisers – had made them popular among the Bohemian court to the extent that they were known as the "beer of kings". The marketing appeal of such a fine title was not lost on Busch. He enjoyed, too, the style of beer, maltier and less aggressively hopped than Pilsners, and with a deli-cate hint of apple fruit. While he was in Europe, Busch became acquainted with the work of Louis Pasteur on yeast propagation and the heat-treat-ment called "pasteurization" that prevented beer from being attacked by bugs, giving it longer shelf life. Busch's experi-ences coalesced into a determination to make a pale, golden lager with a soft and appealing palate, pasteurized to withstand long journeys throughout the United States. It is not known whether he took any Budweis yeast back with him but he did introduce

Adolphus Busch (inset) toured Central Europe to get the inspiration for the beer brand that transformed American brewing. The success of Budweiser forced other big brewers to turn increasingly to bland versions of lager beer

daughter of Eberhard. Three years later he joined his father-in-law at the Anheuser Bavarian Brewery. Busch was born in 1839 in Kastel near Mainz in the Hesse region of Germany, the son of an innkeeper and landowner. He arrived in the US in 1857 and reached St Louis via New Orleans and the Mississippi. He worked on the riverfront as a clerk and gradually worked his way in business until he owned

European two-row barley to his adopted country, a variety that produces a sweeter beer than the native six-row. He also picked up – probably in Franconia, northern Bavaria – the German habit of maturing and clarifying beer over a bed of beechwood chips. Adopted by Busch, the method was to become an important (though largely irrelevant) element of the Budweiser myth.

Back in St Louis, Busch put his plans into action. He called in Carl Conrad, a St Louis wine merchant and restaurateur, to help him develop a beer that, in his own words "would be acceptable to all tastes – a beer lighter in colour and with a more delicate taste than Pilsner beer". After, it is claimed, much thought Busch chose Budweiser as the name for his new "national beer" because it had a slightly Germanic sound yet was easily pronounceable by native Americans. Busch also claimed that, as no other American brewer was using the title, he could not be accused of passing-off or copying an existing brand. Budweiser was launched in 1876. It was not an overnight success. Until the turn of the century, A-B's leading beer was called simply **St Louis Lager Beer**. It also had a second beer with the extravagant name of **Anheuser-Busch St Louis White Label Pilsener Exquisite**. If the company's own description is anything to go by ("It combines

all the virtues of the European Pilsener – the excellent aroma of hops; the strengthening, pure taste of malt; the clear Rhine Wine color; the small-beaded, creamy, white-as-snow foam which covers the last drop left in the glass") it must have been quite a beer.

But gradually sales of Budweiser climbed in step with the growth of the company. In 1870 A-B was brewing a modest 18,000 barrels a year. By 1901 it had passed the million mark. Budweiser was now the flagship and had been joined in 1896 – at first only on draught – by a "super premium" lager called **Michelob**, which also took its name from a Bohemian town (it is pronounced with a hard "ch": Mikelob). A-B had gone national and such local and regional specialities as a Munchener, an Erlanger (Märzen), a Bock and an Old Burgundy barley wine fell by the wayside.

By the 1890s Budweiser was being promoted as the "King of Beers" and the "Original Budweiser". The first claim is effective but, on closer examination, devoid of meaning: who crowned it? And by no stretch of the imagination could it claim to be original, for the beers beloved of the Bohemian court were called Budweiser and the old Samson Brewery in České Budějovice had also used the term. When the Budweiser Budvar brewery was formed in České Budějovice in 1896 and attempted to enter the

American market early in the twentieth century, A-B blocked the move with a law suit, the first of many between the two companies.

The A-B catalogue for 1889, with a charming naivety, described Budweiser as a "pale and innocuous beverage". The company claims the recipe has never changed in the beer's long history. That is remarkable, for few beers have never been "tweaked", to use a brewer's expression. New varieties of malt and hops appear in every generation and brewers are always experimenting to improve the aroma, flavour and colour of their beers. If the A-B claim is true, this means that from the outset the company used substantial amounts of rice as an adjunct to barley malt. Rice is listed before barley on the label and it is thought to constitute around 40 per cent of the grist. All the large American brewers use substantial amounts of unmalted adjuncts, usually corn (maize) rather than rice. This is because the high level of enzymes in native six-row barley can convert the starches in unmalted grains – which have no "diastatic power" – as well as in the malt. In the case of rice, it is cooked to break down the cell walls and then added to the mash, where the malt enzymes add its sugars to the wort. Rice is a useful adjunct if the aim is an exceptionally pale beer with a light flavour.

Budweiser is brewed from a blend of two-row and six-row pale malts and rice. The hops are both US and European varieties in the form of whole flowers. A single decoction mash is used and the beer is lagered for a maximum of a month – 21 days is usual. The beer has a starting gravity of 1044 degrees and a finished alcohol by volume of 4.8 per cent: it is well attenuated. In spite of the careful choice of hops and their skilful blending, the units of bitterness are just 12 (it is thought this figure may have been lowered to around 10 IBUs since the data was revealed). With such a low malt content, too high a hop rate would overpower the flavour. During maturation strips of beechwood, about a foot long and a couple of inches wide, are placed in the conditioning tanks where they attract yeast particles. During lagering, the beer is

Michelob, another Anheuser-Busch brand with a Bohemian resonance and a shade more character than Budweiser

kräusened by adding a portion of partially-fermented wort to encourage a second fermentation. The finished beer has no discernible aroma, a light, clean, quenching palate and a short finish. The brewery calls the finish "fast", which says it all. Even these characteristics are masked by the house rule that the beer must be served at 42 degrees Fahrenheit (6 Celsius). When the beer warms up there is the faintest of hints of apple fruit, suggesting that old man Busch may have emulated Jacobsen of Carlsberg by bringing some yeast back from Budweis under his hat.

The premium **Michelob** (4.8 per cent ABV; 10 IBUs) has a similar specification to Budweiser's but a lower rice ratio. As a result it has a pleasant malt aroma and palate and a smooth finish with a hint of hop. Both beers are also brewed in Light (low calorie) and Dry versions to fit the fashionable sector of the market. Dry beers are attenuated fully to ensure that as little flavour as possible remains. Do the people who make them go home in the evening and declare: "I had a swell day at the brewery: I made a totally tasteless beer"? **Michelob Dry** has a starting gravity of 1041 degrees but is brewed out to 4.8 per cent ABV. As the company's own tasting charts state, the beer has "no aftertaste". On the credit side,

A-B introduced in the 1980s **Michelob Classic Dark** (4.7 per cent ABV; 10 IBUs), with some roasted malt added to the pale malts and rice. It has some pleasant malty character with hints of dark fruit in the finish. **King Cobra Malt Liquor**, another 1980s launch, belongs to the style of American beers that are high in alcohol and aimed at the urban poor in search of a cheap buzz. They are often brewed with substantial amounts of brewing sugar to cut production costs and help boost the alcohol. A-B's contribution is 5.9 per cent ABV, with 11 IBUs. It is brewed from pale and crystal malts and maize with US hop varieties and is malty and syrupy with a full-bodied palate and a sticky finish. Busch (4.7 per cent ABV; 10 IBUs) is a survivor from the early days of the company but is now a disappointingly thin brew, with a slight sweetness of palate and a grainy aroma.

At the quality end of the production line, A-B experimented with both a Märzen and a Pilsner (the latter with just 9 IBUs) but they have been discontinued. The group has entered the fast-growing, but probably short-lived, "ice beer" market. Of greater interest is the introduction of **Elk Mountain Amber**, an ale that takes its name from the group's own hop fields. It may well be the first ale ever

What does a brewery do when it can't make beer? Prohibition in the United States was fuelled by a powerful temperance movement that found an ally in the government during the First World War, which masked its own anti-alcohol beliefs behind a call to preserve grain supplies for animals and domestic use. While Prohibition – the Volstead Act – did not take complete effect until January 1920, 36 states had already declared for partial or total prohibition since 1916. Anheuser-Busch prepared for the inevitable clamp-down by developing a non-alcoholic barley drink called **Bevo**, which was an enormous success, plus a malt tonic drink, **Malt Nutrine**. Other ventures into alcohol-free or low-alcohol drinks (beers of 2.7 per cent alcohol or less were permitted) included **Buschtee, Caffo, Ginger Ale, Root Beer** and **Grape Bouquet**. In 1920 **Budweiser Near Beer** [sic] was launched to keep the brand in the public eye. A-B also went into ice-cream production in a big way, converting several of its breweries solely to ice cream. By 1926 ice-cream production reached one million gallons a year. The group became a major supplier of yeast to the baking industry, again using the Budweiser name. A-B also set up a vehicle manufacturing division and diversified into refrigerated cabinets to back up the ice-cream business.

brewed in the history of the company and is an attempt to guard its flank from the growing power of the craft brewers and their "specialty" beers.

The second biggest brewing group in the US, Miller of Milwaukee, had a far slower rise to fortune than Anheuser-Busch. It was founded in 1855 as Charles Best's Plank Road Brewery and was bought by Frederic Miller, who built it into one of the region's biggest breweries. In 1965 it was in eleventh place in the pecking order. In 1969 it became part of the giant Philip Morris cigarette group, which began aggressively to build the brewing division's market share. For years the brewery's flagship brand had been **Miller High Life** (4.67 per cent ABV; 3.65 per cent by weight), a pale lager that predated Prohibition. Under Morris's tutelage, Miller launched **Miller Lite** (4.18 per cent ABV; 3.30 per cent by weight), one of the first low-calorie beers. Fully brewed out to turn the maximum amount of sugar into alcohol, light beers appealed to Americans concerned with health and expanding waistbands. Miller Lite was an enormous success though this "fine Pilsner beer brewed from the finest ingredients" had to undergo some rapid changes in the 1980s when Miller was charged by the Center for Science in the Public Interest of using a foam enhancer, propylene glycol alginate,

chill-proofing the beer with papain, using amyloglucosidase to speed up starch conversion and preserving the finished beer with potassium metabisulphite. Miller said it had stopped using all chemical aids in the beer. The shock waves caused other large brewers to take greater care in the ingredients they used.

Miller improved its image in the late 1980s with **Miller Genuine Draft** (4.67 per cent ABV; 3.65 per cent by weight), a dark golden beer that, despite the name, came only in bottled form. It used the new Japanese system of cold filtering rather than pasteurizing beer to enhance aroma and flavour. In the 1990s Miller surprised the brewing industry by launching a series of Miller Reserve beers brewed from 100 per cent barley malt. Two, **Amber Ale** and **Velvet Stout** (both 5.10 per cent ABV; 4.00 per cent by weight), use imported English ale yeasts and are good beers by any standards. Amber Ale has a rich, perfumy hop aroma, rich dark malt in the mouth and a long bitter-sweet finish that becomes dry with good hop notes. Velvet Stout is more of a porter, with a chocolate malt aroma, creamy dark malt in the mouth and a finish that develops a dry malt-and-hops character. America's craft brewers may well think these beers are the sincerest form of flattery.

Miller, which now brews some 40 million barrels a year,

has bought the old Jacbob Leinenkugel Brewery of Chippewa Falls, Wisconsin. It was created in 1867 by Leinenkugel and his partner John Miller, no relation to the Milwaukee Millers. It has added some new products, including a **Red Lager** and a **Genuine Bock** to its standard brews.

Adolph Coors of Golden, Colorado, is the third biggest US brewer. As a result of its isolated base high in the Rockies it is often dismissed as the Mr Nobody of American brewing but it runs the single biggest brewing plant in the country, producing some 20 million barrels a year. The site was chosen by Adolph Coors in 1873 because of its easy access to the fine spring waters from the Rockies: the company makes great play of the quality of its water. Locked in its mountain fastness, Coors is as famous for its corporate and political conservatism – it fought long and hard against union recognition – as it is for its beer.

The Golden Brewery is superb, packed with burnished copper vessels. As with Anheuser-Busch, enormous care is taken in choosing the finest

Miller built its brands aggressively but fell foul of the consumer protection lobby with Miller Lite. It is building bridges with its new Special Reserve beers that have quality and integrity

WHEN MILLER BREWING WAS CHARGED WITH USING CHEMICALS IN MILLER LITE, ONE JOURNALIST COMMENTED THAT HE OFTEN COMPARED AMERICAN BEER TO THE BY-PRODUCT OF THE HORSE BUT HE NOW WISHED TO APOLOGIZE TO THE HORSE.

Joseph Schlitz founded a brewing empire that was once the biggest in the US and fell from grace with "flaky" beer

Stroh, which took over Schlitz, has added some more characterful brands such as Augsburger Golden (right)

ingredients. Coors owns its own barley fields and hop gardens. Its beers are a blend of pale malted barley and cereal adjuncts (refined starch) and whole hops. The finished results have the minimum of taste and character. Drinkers could be forgiven for thinking the Rocky Mountain spring water was the most memorable flavour. For years the brewery produced just one brand called **Coors** (5.0 per cent ABV) with the tag line "banquet beer". It has now branched out with a low-calorie **Coors Light** (4.2 per cent ABV) – nicknamed the "Silver Bullet" as a result of the aluminium can in which it comes – and a super premium **Coors Gold. Herman Joseph's Original Draft** has a fraction more body; a Winterfest beer brewed for Thanksgiving has a slight spicy aroma and palate from dark malt and is broadly in the old Vienna Red tradition; while George Killian's is yet another version of the long-dead Irish ale from Wexford now reincarnated in France and the Netherlands as well as in the US. In 1987 Coors opened a second brewery in the Shenandoah Valley near Elton, Virginia. The group makes much of the fact that, in the wake of the Miller Lite furore, it brews without preservatives or additives. It does not pasteurize its beers, preferring to sterile-filter them. Coors survived Prohibition by making **Coors Golden Malted Milk**, which may have had a shade more barley character than its modern beers.

Stroh of Detroit became the fourth biggest American brewing group by taking over one of the most famous names in beer – Schlitz. The fall of Schlitz, once America's biggest brewing concern with the slogan "the beer that made Milwaukee famous", is testimony to the fact that you can fool some of the drinkers some of the time but not all the drinkers all of the time. Schlitz was founded in 1849 by August Krug who sold the Milwaukee plant in 1858 to his son-in-law Joseph Schlitz. Schlitz died the following year during a boating holiday in his native Germany but his name lived on and his brewery grew until it rivalled Anheuser-Busch in size. Disaster struck Schlitz in the 1970s. The national brewers launched a price war to gain market share and Schlitz attempted to undercut its rivals by reducing the barley and hop content of its brews, saving 50 cents on each barrel brewed. In order to give the beers shelf-life and a foaming head, Schlitz replaced a silica-gel containing enzymes with a stabilizer called Chillgarde. Unfortunately for Schlitz, Chillgarde reacted with another ingredient called Kelcoloid (propylene glycol alginate) causing tiny flakes of protein to coagulate in the beer. When drinkers complained about Schlitz's "flaky beer", the company removed the Kelcoloid, a foam stabilizer. As a result the beers, lacking natural malt proteins to give a good natural head, went, according to one wholesaler, "as flat as apple cider". Schlitz's sales nose-dived and in 1982 the company was only saved from extinction when it was bought by Stroh. The Schlitz brands linger on but Stroh concentrates on its own brews.

Stroh was founded in 1850 by Bernard Stroh whose family came from Kirn in the German Rhineland and included at least one innkeeper. Bernard started to brew "Bohemian" beer in the Pilsner style and adopted the European fashion of heating the brew kettles in America by direct flame. This method encourages what brewers call "a good rolling boil" to extract the best aromas and flavours from the hops. It also causes a slight carameliza-tion of the malt sugars which leaves a slight but distinctive port-wine note to the beer, evident in the "super premium" **Signature** (4.84 per cent ABV; 3.78 per cent by weight). Stroh has moved in recent years into more characterful beers that recall its roots. Using the Augsburger title, it produces **Augsburger Golden** (4.93 per cent ABV; 3.85 per cent by weight), with some hop notes on the aroma and finish, and **Weiss**, a wheat beer with some fruitiness but lacking the true Bavarian spici-ness. Under the Schlitz name, **Erlanger** is a firm-bodied beer that promises the flavour of a Bavarian Märzen but fails to deliver.

Pabst, another Germanic giant of Milwaukee, was the biggest brewery in the United States at the turn of the century but its fortunes have declined, though it remains one of the six national giants. It was founded in 1844 by Jacob Best from Rheinhessen who joined forces with Captain Frederick Pabst from Leipzig. (Best also founded the Plank Road Brewery which subsequently became Miller.) Pabst's fortune was made by its **Blue Ribbon** beer (4.56 per cent ABV; 3.65 per cent by weight), which became the mass drink of the industrial working class – fortuitously known as "blue collar" workers. The decline of industry was matched by the falling sales of Blue Ribbon. Pabst became entangled in mergers and takeovers. It bought Olympia Brewing of Tumwater, with a pale lager called **Olympia** (4.56 per cent ABV; 3.65 per cent by weight) and known as "Oly", which itself had acquired Hamm's Brewery in St Paul, Minnesota. Finally, and in the way of those that go down·the takeover trail, Pabst itself was bought by the California million-aire Paul Kalmanovitz, who already owned the Falstaff, General and Pearl Breweries.

The last of the national giants, Heileman, was founded in 1858 by Gottlieb Heileman and John Gund in La Crosse, Wisconsin. It remained a sizeable regional company until it bought other breweries in the 1960s. It now owns Blitz of Oregon, Henry Weinhard, Rainier of Seattle, and Lone Star, the famous beer of Texas. The mainstream beers are typical of the light lager style. The flagship **Old Style** (4.84 per cent ABV; 3.80 per cent by weight) is more post- than pre-Prohibition, with a strong corn syrup character. Even the ales in its portfolio are now thin and disappointing. Rainier's was nick-named the **Green Death** (5.50 per cent by weight) from its emerald-coloured label and reputed alcoholic kick but its hops and malt attributes are now muted. On the credit side, Heileman has brought back the old Blatz name in Milwaukee, building a new small plant under the name of a company that was one of the national giants until the post-war years. Among the interesting beers brewed by Blatz are a **Kulmbacher Imperial** (4.33 per cent ABV; 3.40 per cent by weight) and **Milwaukee Weiss**, a Bavarian-style wheat beer.

THE REVIVALISTS

Good beer, like a good man, is no longer so hard to find. In San Francisco it may be a struggle to get a Budweiser but the local beer, **Anchor Steam**, is on tap in dozens of bars. The impact of the micros is now considerable. They have set up their own distribution networks and as a result their beers are now widely available. Their presence and their availability have been enhanced by the work of the American Homebrewers' Association which fostered an interest in good beer and encour-aged a generation of keen homebrewers to turn their skills into commercial ventures. The AHA's related organization, the Association of Brewers, organizes the annual Great American Beer Festival, a showcase for the work of the micros. Some of the leading American craft brewers are now sufficiently big to shrug off the "micro" tag. They brew more beer than many British and German companies and are major producers by any standard.

Two men have played a pivotal role in the revival of craft brewing in the United States. They come from different stock. One was the scion of a rich family of German origin, an amiable man who used his wealth to save a brewery and revive the country's only indige-nous beer style. The other is a gruff, bluff man of Scottish-Canadian stock who brews ales

By luck rather than design, the Pabst group now owns Ballantine, once the greatest top-fermenting ale brewed in the US. Peter Ballantine arrived in the United States from Ayr, Scotland, in 1830 and started to brew in Albany, New York State. He brewed an Ale, an India Pale Ale and a Christmas beer called Burton. The beers were originally matured in oak vessels. Ballantine's beers survived Prohibition, one of the few ales to do so, and have enjoyed a peripatetic existence ever since. They have been brewed in Newark, New Jersey, at the Narragansett Brewery on Rhode Island, and then at the Falstaff Brewery in Fort Wayne, Indiana. They are now brewed by Pabst in Milwaukee, an unlikely setting for British pale ales. In its Rhode Island days, Ballantine's IPA was around 7.0 per cent ABV with a hefty 60 IBUs in the true India Pale Ale tradition. By the time this beer-on-wheels reached Indiana (and it must have been tempting to rename it Indiana Pale Ale), the strength had declined to around 5.5 per cent and the bitterness had been decreased to 40 IBUs. The Pabst version has some hop character but this historic ale is now a shadow of its former self. Pabst has added another top-fermenting ale called Old Tankard, with some malty/fruity character.

BY THE MID-1990S THERE WERE 500 CRAFT BREWERIES IN THE UNITED STATES. THE NUMBER IS EXPECTED TO DOUBLE BY THE TURN OF THE CENTURY.

Heileman's Old Style is quite the opposite, a modern, light-tasting beer. For the genuine old style, drinkers have turned to the revivalist Anchor Steam (left)

*The Anchor Brewery in its
nineteenth-century heyday,
refreshing an army of gold
prospectors*

*Fritz Maytag swapped the
family wash tub for the mash
kettle when he bought the
Anchor Brewery*

SAN FRANCISCO STEAM
BEERS HAD SUCH LIVELY
SECOND FERMENTATIONS IN
CASK THAT WHEN THE CASKS
WERE TAPPED IN LOCAL BARS
THEY GAVE OFF A HISS OF
ESCAPING GAS THAT WAS
SAID TO SOUND LIKE STEAM.

with a devotion to style in a remote town in the hop fields of Washington State. Their impact has been nationwide, encouraging a generation of beer lovers to invest in mash tuns, brew kettles and fermenters, and produce ales and lagers of often startling quality.

The first man is Fritz Maytag, a member of the powerful washing-machine dynasty. He was a student at Stanford University and enjoyed a local speciality called Steam Beer. One day in 1965 he went into his favourite bar, asked for a glass of Steam and was told it would be his last as the Anchor Steam Brewery was about to close. So Maytag cashed in his chips in the family firm and bought the brewery. There are some cynics who scoff at any suggestion that Maytag was playing out a part in the American Dream, but he stood to lose every penny of his fortune by taking over a failed business which produced a beer that only a handful of people wanted to drink.

Steam Beer is a San Francisco speciality that dates from the California Gold Rush of the 1890s. When the gold diggers poured into the small town with a largely Mexican, wine-drinking population, they demanded beer – and they wanted the cold, refreshing

lager beers they had enjoyed on the East Coast. The few ale brewers in San Francisco had neither ice nor mountainous caves in which to store beers. The one ingredient they could get was lager yeast and they used it to brew a beer but still using ale temperatures. They developed special shallow vessels, a cross between a fermenter and a cool ship, that exposed more of the beer to the atmosphere, causing it to cool quickly.

Fritz Maytag inherited a clapped-out brewery with just one employee – it was so broke it was using baker's yeast to ferment its beer. It took 10 years for Maytag to turn Anchor Steam into a profitable concern. He has now moved from its former run-down site under a freeway to an Art Deco building in Mariposa Street that was once the headquarters of a coffee-roasting company. As well as turning Anchor into a successful brewery, Maytag has toured the world in order to immerse himself in the history and practice of brewing. In particular, a visit to some of Britain's finest producers of cask-conditioned ales encouraged him to branch out from his flagship beer into ale brewing where he has adopted with fervour the English habit of "dry hopping" – adding hops to the finished casks to give beer improved aroma. His new brewery is magnificent, packed with gleaming copper vessels built to his specification by a German firm.

After mashing and boiling, **Anchor Steam Beer** is fermented separately from the ales to avoid any cross-fertiliza-

tion of yeast strains. Fermentation takes place in open vessels just 2 feet deep, using lager yeast but at a warm temperature of 16-21 degrees C/60-70F. The beer has a finished strength of 5.0 per cent ABV, 4.0 per cent by weight using the American system. The grist is a blend of pale and crystal malts and no brewing sugars are used. Hops are Northern Brewer, added three times in the kettle. Following fermentation, the green beer is warm-conditioned for three weeks and is then kräusened by adding some partially-fermented wort to encourage a second fermentation. The beer is bronze-coloured and highly complex, with a rich malty-nutty aroma, malt and light fruit in the mouth, and a finish in which the hops slowly dominate. It has 30 to 35 units of bitterness. While it is clean and quenching like a lager, it also has a decidedly ale-like fruitiness.

The other beers are fermented in conventional vessels that are 6 feet deep. **Liberty Ale**, launched in 1975, was inspired by Maytag's tour of British brewers even though it commemorates the ride by Paul Revere from Boston to Lexington to warn the American revolutionaries that the British army was marching to arrest them. His ride signalled the beginning of the American Revolution. Liberty Ale is a world classic, 6.0 per cent ABV, 4.8 by weight, brewed from pale malt and hopped with American Cascades. American hop varieties, like the grapes of California, are big, bold and

assertive, adding a citric fruitiness to beer that often borders
on a grapefruit note. In the case
of Liberty Ale, Cascades are
added to the kettle and the
maturation tank, giving the beer
an intense lemon-citric aroma
and palate and a dry and hoppy
finish.

The remaining Anchor
beers include **Porter** (5.0 per
cent by weight, 6.0 by volume)
with a smooth coffee character,
a refreshing **Wheat Beer** with
delicate apple notes, made with
70 per cent wheat, **Old
Foghorn** barley wine (7.0 per
cent by weight, 8.75 per cent
ABV), winey and intensely bitter
with 85 IBUs, and **Our Special
Ale**, brewed every year for the
Thanksgiving and Christmas
periods. It is brewed with a
different specification each year
and always includes a secret
spice, which in the past has
included cloves, coriander,
cinnamon and nutmeg.

Some of Fritz Maytag's
disciples are now criticizing his
conservatism which causes him
to pasteurize both his bottled
and draught beers. Some craft
brewers are now offering
draught beer in cask-conditioned form and are producing
bottle-conditioned packaged
versions. Maytag counters these
arguments by saying bluntly
that he does not trust retailers
to stock and serve his beers
sufficiently well to allow him to
make them in a naturally-
conditioned form. Fritz Maytag
is not a man to be either left
behind or overtaken, and it is
likely that he will adapt to the
changing demands of American
beer lovers. Whatever the
outcome, nothing should detract

from his enormous contribution
to the revival of American beer.

From his redoubt in the
Yakima Valley, surrounded by
the Cascade Mountains, Bert
Grant makes clear his allegiance. His Oldsmobile carries a
registration plate with the
words REAL ALE. His wife,
Sherry, has a Porsche bearing
the legend ALE WIFE. They are
tough and committed practi-
tioners of the brewers' art in a
region that still has a powerful
feel of the old frontier about it
and where visitors
are asked to hand
in their guns before
entering hotels. Bert
Grant was born in
Scotland but left for
Canada at the age of
two. He became an
analytical chemist
for Canadian
Breweries, which became
Carling O'Keefe. When the
company started a headlong
slide towards oblivion he
crossed the border and worked
for Stroh in Detroit for four
years before moving to Yakima
to rebuild a hop-processing
plant in the heart of the
American hop fields. He started
to brew at home and his efforts
were appreciated by friends.
When production reached 500
barrels a year, he decided to go
commercial. His first brewpub
was in the former Yakima Opera
House. He has moved to a
greenfield site on the edge of
town where he has the capacity
to make 25,000 barrels a year.
He also has a brewpub in the
old railroad station where his
ales are cask-conditioned,
though the bulk of his production is filtered as bars do not

understand the
concept of sedi-
mented beers.
Bert Grant is a
stickler for style.
His **Scottish Ale**, which he
describes as "the best beer in
the world", has an amber colour
and nutty roastiness from dark
crystal malt but is perhaps a
shade too hoppy to be
genuinely Scottish. The hoppiness is accounted for by
Cascades in the kettle and
Willamettes (a Fuggle deriva-
tive) used for dry hopping. The
5.6 ABV (4.5 by weight) beer
has 45 IBUs. It has a rich
sultana fruitiness balanced by a
pungent hoppiness, with more
dark fruit in the mouth and a
fruity and bitter finish. Grant's
Celtic Ale is also too generously hopped to emulate a soft
Irish beer. Grant's **India Pale
Ale**, complete with a label
showing British soldiers in front
of the Taj Mahal, is closer to
style. It bursts with hop character, has 50 IBUs and is 4.5 per

*Kilts in the Cascades…
Sherry and Bert Grant are
proud of their Scottish Ale
and dress up for the occasion.
Left, Grant's IPA, with a deep
hoppy character, is close to
the genuine style*

Tale of a tub... Pete Slosberg needs to cool off after brewing up another wicked batch of beer

PETE SLOSBERG FIRST BREWED HIS WICKED ALE AND LAGER AT THE PALO ALTO BREWERY IN CALIFORNIA. WHEN THE BREWERY WENT INTO RECEIVERSHIP, SLOSBERG SPENT A FRANTIC WEEKEND REMOVING HIS STOCKS OF BEER FROM THE BREWERY BEFORE THEY WERE IMPOUNDED BY THE LOCAL SHERIFF.

cent ABV. Other Grant beers include a wheat beer, pungent with lemon and bubblegum, a chocolatey **Porter** with a pronounced hint of peat smoke from imported Scottish malt, and a 7.0 per cent ABV **Imperial Stout** with a resounding 100 IBUs. It is packed with aromas and flavours of liquorice, fresh leather, coffee and apple fruit. Bert Grant's ales are sold in 27 states of the US, as far south as Florida. His dedication to fine beer has been the inspiration behind the brewing resurgence in the North-west United States.

WEST COAST BREWERIES

The Sierra Nevada Brewing Company in the university town of Chico, northern California, was one of the first of the new wave of specialist craft brew-

eries. It was founded in 1981 by Ken Grossman and Paul Camusi. Grossman made the leap from home-brewing to commercial production and concentrated at first on ales for the simple reason that he lacked conditioning tanks for lager. A new brewhouse was installed in 1987 and in 1993 production exceeded 70,000 barrels. Sierra Nevada is growing by 50 per cent a year. The flagship beer is bottled **Pale Ale** (4.2 per cent by weight, 5.3 per cent ABV); in draught form it is called **Sierra Nevada** and is a shade darker and a fraction less strong. It has won four gold medals at the Great American Beer Festival. It has a spicy, citric Cascade hop aroma, malty on the palate and with a dry and hoppy finish. Sierra Nevada also brews a coffeeish **Porter**, a 6.0 per cent ABV **Stout** with a roasted malt character, and the renowned **Big Foot Barley Wine**, at 12.5 per cent ABV one of the strongest beers brewed in the United States. It has a vast aroma of hops and dark malt, massive alcohol and hops in the mouth and a shatteringly rich and warming finish. The hops are Nugget for bitterness, with a late addition of Cascade for aroma, and Cascade and Centennial for more aroma during conditioning. Sierra Nevada does not filter in bottle or keg. All the bottled beers are naturally conditioned, the ales filtered, re-seeded with yeast, primed with sugar and matured for several weeks before leaving

the brewery. The brewery also produces lagers of exceptional quality.

Pete Slosberg is another Californian home-brewer who went the whole hog. His beers – **Pete's Wicked Ale** and **Wicked Lager** – have upset some traditionalists on the grounds that they don't sound serious beers but Slosberg is now one of the most successful small brewers in the US. Wicked Ale (5.0 per cent ABV) has won the Great American Beer Festival's gold medal in the brown ale category. It is copper coloured with a distinctive chocolate and slightly winey palate. It is brewed from pale, crystal and black malts and is hopped with Cascades. The beers are now brewed under contract in St Paul, Minnesota.

Mendocino Brewing has the ideal address: Hopland, about 90 miles north of San Francisco. It is based in an old saloon in Mendocino County and was founded by Michael Laybourn, Norman Franks and John Scahill in 1982 who planted hops amid the vines of the area. It was California's first brewpub since Prohibition. The beers are named after birds of the area and include **Peregrine Pale Ale**, hoppy and fruity, **Blue Heron Pale Ale**, full-bodied and with great hop character, a copper-coloured **Red Tail Ale** (4.4 by weight, 5.5 ABV) with nutty crystal malt character and a superb hop aroma and finish from Cascade and Cluster varieties, and the stand-out **Black**

Hawk Stout, as smooth and dangerously drinkable as a chocolate liqueur.

San Andreas is based in Hollister near the famous San Andreas Fault. The brewery survived the 1989 earthquake but now tempts fate with beers named **Earthquake Pale Ale** (dry and hoppy), **Earthquake Porter, Survivor Stout** and **Seismic Ale**.

Across the bay from San Francisco in Oakland, Pacific Coast offers a fine range of English-style ales: a dark **Mariners' Mild**, a hoppy **Gray Whale Ale**, a rich, firm-bodied and malty **Blue Whale Ale**, and a dry and tart **Killer Whale Stout**.

THE NORTH-WEST

Portland, Oregon, is one of the major revivalist brewing centres in the United States. The success of the Portland Brewing Company moved it from its delightful, Irish-style bar with attached brewhouse in the city centre to a greenfield site in 1995 in a custom-built, Germanic-style brewery. The new plant has a capacity of 70,000 barrels a year and vessels that match Anchor in San Francisco for beauty. One of the founders, Fred Bowman, was a keen home-brewer who recreated an English strong ale called **Bishop's Tipple** from Salisbury, fell in love with brewing and found partners to go commercial. **Portland Ale** (5.0 per cent ABV) is made from pale malt only and has a big citric fruit aroma from Cascade hops, tart fruit in the mouth and a quenching finish. **McTarnahan's Ale** is a degree

stronger and is named after a major shareholder in the brewery. It is made from pale and crystal malts and is hopped with Cascades. It has a rich, nutty aroma, dark sultana fruit on the palate and a bitter-sweet finish. A **Porter** made with English black malt has a dark chocolate and coffee character and a big hoppy finish, while a **Stout** has a dark, almost burnt malt aroma, with coffee and chocolate in the mouth and a smooth, creamy finish.

The BridgePort Brewing Company is based in Portland's oldest warehouse, a handsome building smothered in climbing ivy. The brewery was opened in the early 1980s by the Italian-American wine-making Ponzi family who became fascinated by the possibilities of quality beer production. The stainless-steel brewhouse produces a cask-conditioned ale in the English style called **Coho**, 4.4 per cent ABV. The hops are English Goldings and Nugget and the beer is dry-hopped in cask. It has a lilting citric aroma from the hops, more bitter hops in the mouth and a dry and bitter finish. Other beers include a peppery-hoppy **Bridgeport Ale**, a **Blue Heron Ale** named after Portland's emblem, made from pale, crystal, black and chocolate malts with a hoppy aroma, soft malt in the mouth and a tart and quenching finish, and a rich **Stout** packed with dark malt and fruit, with a hoppy finish.

In Seattle the Redhook Brewery is the major craft brewery in the North-west. It was launched in 1982 by Gordon Bowker and Paul

Shipman. Their success led to a move in 1988 to a converted "trolley barn" (tramshed) in the old Swedish Fremont district of the city. In 1994 it built a new brewery on the edge of the city. Before the move, Redhook produced 90,000 barrels a year. Its range includes a spicy **Wheat Hook**, a piny and orange-fruity **Extra Special Bitter** hopped with Tettnang and Willamettes, and a **Blachook Porter** made from black malt and roasted barley, and three hop varieties. It has a bitter chocolate and coffee aroma and a dark fruit finish, more of a stout than a porter.

In 1994 Redhook rocked the brewing industry when it agreed to sell 15 per cent of its shares to Anheuser-Busch. A-B said it would use its know-how and marketing muscle to sell Redhook beers nationally. By 1995 the A-B stake had grown to 25 per cent and Redhook announced it planned to build a new, 30-million-dollar plant in Portsmouth, New Hampshire, opening up the East Coast to its products. The arrival of A-B is seen by some microbrewers as a sinister threat, by others as a

BridgePort of Portland is based in an old, ivy-covered warehouse. Its beers include a cask-conditioned Coho

Redhook is a major West Coast craft brewery, originally based in the old Swedish area of Seattle

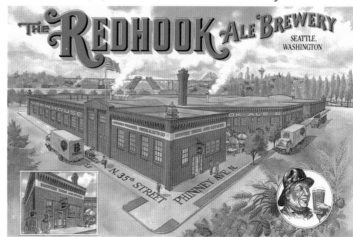

Steve Hindy and Tom Potter restored Brooklyn's once proud brewing tradition with their Lager and Brown Ale. They have now added a stout and an India Pale Ale

The stern face of Samuel Adams, brewer and patriot, adorns the labels of Jim Koch's beautifully crafted but controversial brews

boost for the image of craft brewing. Writing in the New Jersey-based *Ale Street News* in April 1995, industry analyst Mort Hochstein observed: "When elephants march, ants get trampled".

The Seattle-based Pike Place Brewery is owned by Charles Finkel, a man as dedicated to beer style as Bert Grant. As well as the tiny brewery, Finkel owns a brewery museum and a store selling both beer books and home-brew supplies. His ales include **Pale Ale, East India Pale Ale** and **Porter**. The Pale Ale (4.5 by weight, 5.5 ABV) uses imported Maris Otter malt from Norfolk, England, 20 per cent crystal malt and is hopped with East Kent Goldings. It is a rich amber colour, has a peppery hop aroma, a biscuity palate and hops and dark fruit in the finish. East India Pale Ale (6.0 per cent by weight, 7.0 ABV) is brewed with pale, carapils and Munich malts and is hopped with Chinook, British Columbian and Goldings hops. It is tawny gold in colour, has a massive grapefruit aroma from the Chinooks, more tart fruit in the mouth and a powerful hoppy finish. **Porter** (5.0 per cent by weight, 6.0 ABV) has a rich coffee and chocolate aroma and palate from pale, crystal, chocolate and black malts, and dark winey fruit in a bitter finish.

EAST COAST

The Brooklyn brewing tradition has been revived by former journalist and keen home-brewer Steve Hindy and banker Tom Potter. When they planned their production they sought the advice of veteran brewer Bill Moeller, who was keen to recreate a pre-Prohibition Brooklyn recipe. **Brooklyn Lager** (4.5 per cent by weight, 5.5 ABV) is a revelation, an indication of how rich and full-bodied American lager beers must have been before Prohibition, the Depression and the rise of the national giants suppressed aroma and flavour. It is almost ale-like in character, is brewed with crystal as well as pale malt and is dry-hopped. It has a rich malt, hops and cobnuts aroma, ripe malt in the mouth and a long finish full of malt and hops character. **Brooklyn Brown** is a a top-fermenting ale (4.8 per cent by weight, 6.0 ABV) made from pale, crystal, chocolate and black malts and hopped with Cascade and Northern Brewer. It is dry-hopped. Chocolate and coffee dominate the aroma and palate and the finish is dry, hoppy and chocolatey. Both beers have won awards from the Great American Beer Festival. They have been contract-brewed by F X Matt of Utica but Hindy and Potter were planning to open their own brewery in Brooklyn in 1996. Garrett Oliver, former brewmaster at the Manhattan Brewery, joined them in 1994 and plans to add a

stout and an India Pale Ale.

The Boston Brewing Company is now the biggest craft brewery in the United States thanks to the tireless work of its founder, Jim Koch. His beers are better known by the Samuel Adams name, as the stern face of the American patriot, revolutionary and brewer glare out from the labels. Jim Koch is the descendant of Bavarian brewers who brought their skills to the United States but who were forced out of business during a bout of merger mania in the mid-1950s.

Jim Koch, Harvard-educated, gave up a business career to restore his family's traditions by selling beer in 1985. **Samuel Adams Boston Lager**, sold door-to-door by Koch, was an almost instant success. The beer was contract-brewed, a point stressed by critics of Koch's aggressive marketing style. To answer the critics, Koch built a small brewery, using equipment designed by Peter Austin in England (known as the "father" of the British microbrewing industry) on the site of the former Haffenreffer Brewery in Boston's Jamaica Plain.

Although several of his beers are still contract-brewed, the Boston plant is responsible for Samuel Adams Boston Ale, based on the old English style known as Stock Ale, a well-matured beer that was used for blending with younger ales. **Boston Ale** (5.0 per cent ABV) has an appealing amber colour, a big peppery-resiny aroma from Fuggles and Saaz hops – the ale is hopped three times during the boil and again during conditioning – is tart and fruity in the mouth with a big malt-and-hops finish. Koch also produces a chocolatey **Cream Stout**, a spicy **Wheat** and even a **Cranberry "Lambic"**, though no wild yeasts are involved. In 1994 Koch produced a **Triple Bock** that reached a staggering 17.5 per cent ABV, making it the strongest beer in the world. Whether it will knock Hürlimann of Switzerland from its perch in the *Guinness Book of Records* with its Samichlaus remains to be seen, as the brewers' yeast used by Koch gave up at around 12 per cent and fermentation was finished with a Champagne culture.

A superb pale ale is brewed by the Geary Brewing Company in Portland, Maine. Peter Austin was again involved in designing the equipment for David Geary, who produced his first ale in 1986. Geary learnt his brewing skills in England, which explains the character of his Pale Ale, made from pale, crystal and chocolate malts imported from Britain. The hops are American varieties. **Pale Ale** is 3.6 per cent by weight, 4.5 ABV and has a fine hop aroma and palate with a rich but restrained fruitiness in the finish. Geary also produces a stronger winter beer, **Hampshire Special Ale**, its label showing boats frozen in Maine. It is 5.6 per cent by weight, 7.0 ABV and is rich, warming, spicy, fruity and hoppy.

In Philadelphia, the Dock Street brewpub panders to the city's roots with some stunning beers in the Central European tradition: two Pils, Bohemian and German, a malty Dunkel, a vinous Bock, and a spicy Hefe-Weisse. Appealing to a wider audience, Dock Street also brews an English-style bitter and IPA, an Irish Red Ale and a smooth, chocolatey stout. It is renowned for its winter **Barley Wine** (9.5 per cent by weight, 11.8 ABV) which is fermented with an English ale yeast and finished with a Champagne culture. Hops in the kettle are English Fuggles and German Perle and Tettnang and dry-hopping uses Fuggles and Northern Brewer. The beer has 60 IBUs, a spicy aroma, smooth and creamy on the palate, and a lively, fruity/spicy/hoppy finish.

UNITED STATES BREWERS

Anchor Brewing Co,
1705 Mariposa Street, San Francisco, CA 94107.

Anheuser-Busch Inc,
1 Busch Place, St Louis, MO 63118-1852.

Boston Beer Company,
30 Germania Street, Boston, MA 02130.

Brooklyn Brewery,
118 North 11th Street, Brooklyn, NY 11211.

Celis Brewery,
2431 Forbes Drive, Austin, TX 78754.

Adolph Coors Company,
East of Town, Golden, CO 80401.

Dock Street Brewery and Restaurant,
2 Logan Square, Philadelphia, PA 19103.

D. L. Geary Brewing Company,
38 Evergreen Drive, Portland, ME 04103.

Pierre Celis, the man who recreated the Belgian wheat beer tradition with Hoegaarden, moved to Austin in Texas when he was bought out by Interbrew. He now brews Celis White, which closely resembles his spicy original, a perfumy Golden, a top-fermenting Bock and an aromatic Grand Cru that faithfully replicates the Hoegaarden version thought it is less strong – 4.0 per cent by weight, 5.0 ABV – to comply with Texan law.

Celis stunned other craft brewers early in 1995 by selling a 51 per cent controlling share in his company to Miller of Milwaukee. Celis will remain in charge of brewing while Miller will market his beers nationwide.

Grant's Yakima Brewing and Malting Company,
1803 Presson Place, Yakima, WA 98902.

G. Heileman Brewing Co Inc,
100 Harborview Plaza, PO Box 459, La Crosse, WI 54601-4051.

Mendocino Brewing Company,
13351 Highway 101, Hopland, CA 95449.

Miller Brewing Company,
3939 W Highland Blvd, Milwaukee, WI 53208-2816.

Pabst Brewing Company,
917 W Jumeau Ave, PO Box 766, Milwaukee, WI 53233-1428.

Pacific Coast Brewery,
906n Washington Street, Oakland, CA 94607.

Pete's Wicked Brewing Company,
514 High Street, Palo Alto, CA 94301.

Pike Place Brewery,
1432 Western Avenue, Seattle, WA 622-1880.

Portland Brewing Company,
1339 Northwest Flanders Street, Portland, OR 97209.

Redhook Brewery,
3400 Phinney Avenue North, Seattle, WA 98103.

Stroh Brewery Company,
100 River Place, Detroit, MI 48207-4224.

Sierra Nevada Brewing Company,
1075 East 20th Street, Chico, CA 95928.

THE OLDEST BREWERY IN THE US IS YEUNGLING OF POTTSVILLE, PENNSYLVANIA, FOUNDED BY GERMANS FROM STUTTGART. IT USED THE AMERICAN EAGLE ON ITS LABELS. ANHEUSER-BUSCH ALSO USES THE EAGLE EMBLEM AND TOOK YEUNGLING TO COURT IN A BID TO STOP THE SMALL BREWERY USING THE BIRD. BUT THE A-B CASE WAS THROWN OUT.

Dock Street brews Central European-style beers for descendants of Germans in Philadelphia as well as English and Irish ales

CANADA

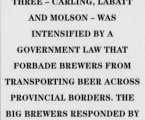

Going up... a Molson beer truck in Toronto. With Labatt, it dominates the Canadian market and has pioneered such developments as "dry beer"

THE DOMINATION OF THE BIG THREE – CARLING, LABATT AND MOLSON – WAS INTENSIFIED BY A GOVERNMENT LAW THAT FORBADE BREWERS FROM TRANSPORTING BEER ACROSS PROVINCIAL BORDERS. THE BIG BREWERS RESPONDED BY BUILDING BREWERIES IN EVERY PROVINCE. THE SMALLER COMPANIES DIDN'T HAVE THE CAPITAL TO MATCH THEM AND LANGUISHED AS A RESULT.

*C*ANADIANS UNDERSTANDABLY BRIDLE WHEN EUROPEANS THINK OF THEIR COUNTRY AS AN APPENDAGE OF THE UNITED STATES. BUT THERE ARE STRIKING SIMILARITIES IN THE DEVELOPMENT OF THE BEER MARKET, WITH A SUBSTANTIAL AMOUNT OF CROSS-BORDER TRADING AND LINK-UPS. LABATT FOR EXAMPLE NOW OWNS THE MAJOR US BRAND ROLLING ROCK AND THE INTRODUCTION IN THE 1990S OF "ICE BEER" WAS SPEARHEADED BY CANADIAN BREWERS AND TAKEN UP BY THE GIANTS IN THE UNITED STATES.

The shape of Canadian brewing, in common with its neighbour, was determined in large measure by Prohibition, which ran for longer, throughout the First World War and until 1932. The result was an industry dominated by a few giants. The big three all started as ale brewers but, encouraged by what they saw in the US, have concentrated on lagers in the 5.0 per cent ABV bracket. Six-row barley enables them to use substantial levels of adjuncts, usually corn. With low bitterness rates of around 10 IBUs, mainstream lagers tend to be sweet, creamy, undemanding and underhopped. The domination of the giants was intensified in 1989 when Molson and Carling merged, giving the new group around 50 per cent of the market. Foster's of Australia, the previous owner of Carling, now has a substantial stake in Molson and Miller of Milwaukee also has a minority shareholding.

The beer scene is changing slowly but for the better. Micros are emerging and there are now some characterful ales. But brewpubs are illegal in many provinces and the new genera-tion of entrepreneurial brewers has had to fight a guerrilla war to establish their outlets.

Molson is the oldest brewery in Canada and the whole of North America. Its origins date from the nineteenth century when John Molson emigrated from Lincolnshire in England, clutching a copy of John Richardson's *Theoretical Hints on the Improved Practice of Brewing*. In 1786 he opened a brewery in Montreal and the company he founded is still controlled by his descendants. Carling O'Keefe dates from a merger in the nine-teenth century between the breweries founded by Sir Thomas Carling in 1840 and Eugene O'Keefe in 1862. Today Molson brews in Ontario, Vancouver, Edmonton, Winnipeg, Prince Albert, Regina, and St John's, Newfoundland. Its main brands are 5.0 per cent light-tasting beers, **Golden** and **Export**, plus the ubiquitous **Carling Black Label**, also 5.0 per cent and firmer-bodied. It produces specialist beers for some regional markets, including a 6.25 top-fermenting **Brador**, rich and fruity, and **Royal** and **Imperial Stouts**. In 1993 Molson declared it was no longer using preservatives in its products and launched "Molson Signature", specialist all-malt beers, including a smooth, fruity **Cream Ale** with a hint of hop, and a malty/nutty **Amber Lager. Molson's Ice**, also introduced in 1993 to counter the pioneering Labatt's version, has a slightly skunky, perfumy aroma but no discernible palate or finish. Labatt dates back to a small brewery built in 1828 in London, Ontario by an innkeeper named George Balkwill. He sold the business to William and George Snell in 1828 who in turn sold it to Samuel

Eccles and John Labatt in 1847. Labatt became the sole owner in 1853.

In June 1995 Labatt was bought by Interbrew of Belgium. As well as Rolling Rock in the US, Labatt also controls Moretti in Italy. Its Canadian beers are thin, with some perfumy aroma from malt and adjuncts. The flagship brand is the bland **Labatt's Blue** (5.0 per cent ABV), which is also produced in a Light version. **Labatt's Classic** is all-malt but light in flavour while **Labatt's 50 Canadian Ale** has some faint malt and hop character. Its **IPA** has nothing in common with the style, while its **Porter** is thin and caramel-tinted. **Ice Beer**, launched with a crescendo of hype in 1993, started the craze for the style. During the brewing process the temperature of the beer is lowered until ice crystals form. These are removed, according to the brewery, to take out proteins and other undesirables. Although the finished beer is high in alcohol, 5.8 per cent ABV in the case of Labatt, most of the flavour has also been removed. Beers brewed in this fashion can only have rounded and pleasing flavours if they are lagered for lengthy periods. In the case of the Canadian and American ice beers, the rapid brewing method adopted leaves

behind some rough esters that give a perfumy, nail-polish aroma and finish.

Moosehead is the largest and longest-surviving independent in Canada. Its remote plants in New Brunswick and Nova Scotia have had a turbulent and roller-coaster history. Its story began with John and Susannah Oland brewing in their backyard in Darmouth, Nova Scotia, in 1867, using old family recipes brought from Britain. Their ales were sufficiently popular for the Olands to win a contract to supply the armed forces. Renamed the Army & Navy Brewery, the company moved to new premises on the waterfront at Dartmouth, Nova Scotia. Three years later John Oland was killed in a horse-riding accident and his widow was forced to sell a controlling interest in the brewery. With the help of an inheritance, she bought back her stake in 1877 and renamed the company S. Oland, Sons & Co. When Susannah died her youngest son George took over control of the brewery, but again they faced tragedy. When two ships collided in Halifax Harbour in 1917, brewmaster Conrad Oland was killed and his brother John injured. The indefatigable family soldiered on. With the help of insurance money from the explosion, George Oland and his

son moved to a new site in St John, New Brunswick. Even though Prohibition was still in operation and beer was restricted to 2.0 per cent ABV, the Olands prospered and returned to Halifax. Their fortunes soared in 1931 when George Oland rechristened his main ale brand with the charismastic name of Moosehead. Such was the success of the brand that the company name was changed in 1947 from New Brunswick to Moosehead. Today Moosehead has breweries in St John, New Brunswick and Dartmouth, Nova Scotia.

Moosehead has had enormous success in the United States but the brewery's beers have paid the price. **Moosehead Pale Ale** has some light hop aroma from the use of Czech Saaz and is dry in the finish but has little ale character while **Canadian Lager** (5.0 per cent ABV) is in the inoffensive but unexciting mainstream.

It is scarcely surprising that ale brewing has taken root in Victoria on Vancouver Island, British Columbia. For this is the most English of Canadian regions, its population packed with ex-patriates. Spinnakers, on the outskirts of the town, was the dream of Paul Hadfield and John Mitchell, both from Vancouver town on the mainland. Mitchell returned home in 1982 from a trip to Britain with samples of 14 English ales. When the two men and their friends tasted them they were fired with enthusiasm to build a small brewery to produce beers along similar lines. They faced major legal obstacles. The city of Victoria at first refused to

Labatt's flagship brand is Blue. The brewery is now a world giant, with subsidiaries in the United States and Italy

The heavily hyped ice beer is aimed at people who prefer their beer devoid of taste

Upper Canada is the old name for Ontario and the beers are full of complex flavours with inspirations from English mild ale and Belgian red

grant a licence for a brewpub but later said it would give planning permission as long as local people supported the idea in a referendum. Ninety-five per cent voted yes. Then permission to both brew and retail beer needed an amendment to Federal law, which was approved just two months before the brewpub was due to open. Spinnakers, with superb views out over the sea, was packed from opening day in May 1984.

The small attached brewhouse, built by an English firm in Manchester, has been expanded twice to meet demand. Paul Hadfield's main brew is **Spinnaker Ale** (4.2 per cent ABV). It is made from pale malt with a dash of crystal and is hopped with Cascades from Yakima and Centennial from Oregon. It has an apple fruit aroma, more tart fruit in the mouth and a light dry finish. **Mount Tolmie**, also 4.2 per cent, uses caramalt, chocolate and crystal blended with pale malt. Mount Hood hops are added in the copper and the beer is dry hopped with Cascade. It has a citric fruit aroma, dark, tart fruit in the mouth and a dry and bitter finish. **Doc Hadfield's Pale**

Ale (4.2 per cent ABV) uses Mount Hood for aroma and bitterness. The ale has a piny aroma with citric fruit in the mouth and a light, dry finish with fruit notes. **Mitchell's ESB**, named in honour of the other founding partner, is 4.6 per cent, copper-coloured, with a grapefruit aroma and palate from Chinook hops and a citric finish, with hints of sultana fruit from crystal and chocolate malts. There is a late addition of Cascade hops.

A 4.9 per cent **India Pale Ale** is hopped with Centennials and is mashed with pale malt only. It has a resiny hop aroma, tart fruit and hops in the mouth and a citric fruit finish. A complex **Porter** (4.9 per cent ABV) uses pale, crystal, choco- late and roasted malt and malted wheat, with Centennial and Hallertau hops. It has a herbal, slightly lactic aroma, and is tart in the mouth. **Empress Stout** is the same strength, with bitter chocolate and hops in the mouth. As a sight for sore British eyes, the beers are served by beer engine and hand- pump. Paul Hadfield has now branched out with a Hefe- Weizen and a lambic.

There are more handpumps on view in Swan's Hotel in the centre of Victoria. The hotel,

restaurant and attached Buckerfields Brewery are owned by Michael Williams from Shropshire in England. He emigrated to Canada and became a sheep farmer. He moved into property, bought an old warehouse in Victoria and turned it into Swans. The brew- house is run by Chris Johnson, a home-brewer who worked in the hotel kitchen and graduated to head brewer. Malt, including pale, crystal, chocolate and roast plus oatmeal, all come from the major English malting company, Bairds. He brews a 5.0 per cent **Bitter** with a nutty, malty aroma with piny hops, dark raisin fruit in the mouth and a dry, bitter finish. The 4.5 per cent **Pandora Pale Gold** has light citric fruit on the aroma, quenching hops in the mouth and a bitter- sweet finish. An impressive 8.0 per cent **Scotch Ale** has big winey fruit and hops on the aroma, raisin and sultana fruit in the mouth and a complex finish with malt, nuts and late hop. **Appleton Brown Ale** (5.0 per cent ABV) is named after the designer of the brewhouse, Frank Appleton. It has pronounced apple fruit and cinnamon aromas, dark fruit in the mouth, and a creamy, bitter-sweet finish. **Rye Weizen** has a four-hour run-off

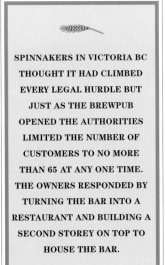

SPINNAKERS IN VICTORIA BC THOUGHT IT HAD CLIMBED EVERY LEGAL HURDLE BUT JUST AS THE BREWPUB OPENED THE AUTHORITIES LIMITED THE NUMBER OF CUSTOMERS TO NO MORE THAN 65 AT ANY ONE TIME. THE OWNERS RESPONDED BY TURNING THE BAR INTO A RESTAURANT AND BUILDING A SECOND STOREY ON TOP TO HOUSE THE BAR.

from the mash tun because of the sticky rye grain. It is 5.7 per cent, has a dark biscuity aroma, a bready, spicy palate and a dry finish with a late burst of fruit. **Oatmeal Stout** (5.4 per cent ABV) has a rich, dark coffee and hops aroma, bitter-sweet malt, chocolate and hops in the mouth, and a tart and bitter finish.

> UNIBROUE'S STRONGEST BEER CARRIES A WARNING AS DIRE AS ALL THE MESSAGES ON LABELS FROM THE SURGEON-GENERAL ABOUT THE DANGERS OF ALCOHOL. THE BEER IS CALLED LA FIN DU MONDE – THE END OF THE WORLD.

Upper Canada Brewing Company in Toronto uses the early settlers' name for the province of Ontario. The sizeable micro was founded in 1985 by Frank Heaps. The 5.0 per cent **Dark Ale** is a cross between a strong English mild with a dash of Belgian red ale sourness. It has an intensely fruity aroma and palate with more tart dark fruit and bitter hops in the finish. A 6.0 per cent **Rebellion Malt Liquor** is fruity and spicy, while **Upper Canada Lager** is malty and firm bodied. A 4.3 per cent **Wheat Beer** has more than 35 per cent wheat malt blended with pale barley malt. Hops are Northern Brewer (18 to 20 IBUs). The beer is filtered and has a tart and fruity aroma and palate with some light spiciness in the finish. **True Bock** is rich, malty and fruity. All the beers are brewed without additives and are not pasteurized.

In the old brewing town of Guelph, the Wellington County Brewery produces an **Arkell Best Bitter** to mark a family connection with the Swindon brewing family of Arkell in Wiltshire, England. The 4.0 per cent cask-conditioned ale has a peppery Goldings hops aroma, malt and fruit in the the mouth and a long, hoppy-fruity finish. The brewery also produces a fruity **Wellington SPA** (4.5 per cent ABV), a hoppy **County Ale** (5.0 per cent ABV), a rich and fruity strong ale called **Iron Duke** (6.5 per cent ABV), and a roasty and chocolatey **Imperial Stout** (8.0 per cent ABV).

The Francophone areas of Canada are also joining the beer revival. Many of the first French settlers came from Normandy and Flanders and have an ale-brewing tradition. Les Brasseurs du Nord in St Jerôme, north of Montreal, brews a dry **Blonde**, a fruity **Rousse** and a smooth, dark **Noire**. La Cervoise in the heart of Montreal has **La Main**, a sweetish amber ale, a golden **Good Dog** ale, and a dry stout called **Obelix**.

Le Cheval Blanc, also in Montreal, has a chocolatey **Ambrée**, an espresso-like **Brune** and a tart **Weissbier**. Unibroue in the Montreal suburb of Chambly brews a bottle-conditioned, aromatic **Blanche de Chambly** and a spicy Belgian-style ale called **Maudite** (8.0 per cent ABV).

CANADIAN BREWERS

Labatt Brewing Co Ltd,
150 Simcoe Street, PO Box 5050, London, ON N6A 4M3.

La Cervoise,
4457 Blvd St Laurent, Montreal, PQ H2W 1Z8.

Le Cheval Blanc,
809 Ontario Street, Montreal, PQ H2L 1P1.

Molson Breweries of Canada Ltd,
3300 Bloor Street W, Suite 3500, Toronto, ON M8X 2X7.

Moosehead Breweries Ltd,
89 Main Street, PO Box 3100, Station B, St John, NB E2M 3H2.

Spinnakers,
309 Catherine Street, Victoria BC V9A 3S8.

Swans Hotel/Buckerfields,
506 Pandora Street, Victoria BC, V8W 1N6.

Upper Canada Brewing Company,
2 Atlantic Avenue, Toronto, Ontario M6K 1X8.

Wellington County Brewery Ltd,
9500 Woodlawn Road W, Guelph, ON N1K 1B8.

Upper Canada's Rebellion is a 6.0 per cent ABV beer with a fruity and spicy aroma and palate

LATIN AMERICA AND THE CARIBBEAN

*L*ATIN AMERICA HAS A FASCINATING AND LONG BREWING TRADITION AND IT IS TRAGIC THAT THE TRADITION HAS LARGELY BEEN SUBMERGED AND SUBORNED IN RECENT YEARS BY MODISH THIN LAGERS FROM MEXICO THAT ARE NEITHER TYPICAL OF THAT COUNTRY NOR THE CONTINENT AS A WHOLE. YUPPIES IN MANHATTAN, LONDON AND BERLIN WHO DRINK **CORONA** AND **SOL** STRAIGHT FROM THE BOTTLE WITH A WEDGE OF LIME STUCK IN THE NECK MAY BE MAKING A STATEMENT ABOUT THEIR LIFESTYLE – RASPBERRY WOULD BE A BETTER FRUIT – BUT ARE DENYING THE QUALITY AND THE HERITAGE OF GOOD LATIN AMERICAN BEER.

Sol briefly became a cult beer in Europe but fickle young drinkers have moved on

Long before Europeans arrived in Latin America the natives were making a variety of beers from the ingredients to hand. The Mayans of Central America brewed from fermented corn stalks while the Aztecs of northern Mexico produced a more advanced beer made from maize that had been allowed to sprout. According to legend, it was the task of specially chosen maidens of the Inca tribe living around Lake Titicaca to chew the cooked maize pulp used in brewing. Only their beauty and the purity of their saliva would start fermentation, it was believed. Even when the Spanish had conquered vast areas of the continent, peasants continued to make *pulque* from the juice of the algave plant. The name comes from a Spanish word meaning "decomposed", as the drink will keep for only a day before going off.

Pulque and other native drinks survive in Latin America. In the remote areas of the Upper Amazon a black beer has been made since at least the fifteenth century. The colour comes from the use of roasted barley and grain that are dark brown in colour. It is flavoured with lupin plants. The American beer writer and anthropologist Alan Eames – nicknamed the "Indiana Jones of Beer" – searched and found the beer in remote areas and encouraged a Brazilian brewery,

> AMAZON DARK BEERS ARE FLAVOURED WITH THE LUPIN PLANT. THE NAME COMES FROM THE LATIN LUPINUS, MEANING WOLFISH, AS LUPINS ARE THOUGHT TO RAVAGE THE SOIL THEY GROW IN. THE WORD COMES FROM THE SAME ROOT AS HUMULUS LUPULUS, THE WOLF PLANT, THE LATIN NAME FOR THE HOP.

Cervejaria Cacador in Brazil, to make it commercially. It is called **Xingu** (5.0 per cent ABV), pronounced shin-gu, the name of a tributary of the Amazon River. It is a modern, conventionally-brewed interpretation of the style, using hops for both flavouring and as a preservative.

Small Spanish breweries – *cervecería* – were established from the sixteenth century but distilled spirits such as mescal and tequila were more popular than beer until the arrival of ice-making machines in the nineteenth century. The first lager beers were known as *sencilla* or *corriente* and were matured for short periods.

Some earlier breweries achieved remarkable success, however. In December 1543 Don Alonso de Herrera from Saville, known as a citizen of "New Spain" (Mexico), built a brewery in Mexico City and launched a beer called **Zerbeza**. It means Desire, the sort of name that modern marketing department of breweries would

pay a lot of money for. Such was the local desire for Zerbeza that Don Alonso had to add 100 additional vats to keep up with demand.

The modern influences in Mexican brewing are Germanic. Some of the first lager breweries were established by Bavarians, Swiss and Alsatians. The country was briefly and incongruously a colony of the Austrian empire, with Archduke Maximilian doubling as Emperor of Mexico. One of the few benefits of the association was the influence of the great Viennese brewer Anton Dreher, who invented the style of dark amber beers that use cara or crystal malts as well as pale malt. The style has virtually vanished from Austria but is alive and well in the former colony.

Today two giants dominate Mexican brewing. In Mexico City, Modelo runs the biggest brewing plant in the country, which rivals all but the top five American groups in size. It is best-known today for **Corona**, the beer that spawned the Mexican lager-and-lime craze.

> THERE ARE MANY FANCIFUL REASONS FOR PUTTING LIME IN MEXICAN BEER, ONE BEING THAT IT KEEPS FLIES AWAY. IN FACT THE HABIT DATES FROM THE 1950S WHEN THE CUAUHTÉMOC BREWERY LAUNCHED TACATE, WHICH WAS SERVED, IN THE MANNER OF TEQUILA, WITH SALT AND FRESH LEMONS.

Like its competitor, **Sol**, **Corona Extra** (4.6 per cent ABV) has been around for decades and was a bottom-of-the-range product made cheaply for poor peasants and industrial workers. It comes in a utilitarian plain glass bottle with an embossed label. It has around 40 per cent rice in its recipe and a low hop rate that creates around 10 to 12 IBUs. Served extremely cold, it is a refreshing drink for those engaged in hard manual labour, which is more than can be said for the well-heeled young Americans on surfing holidays. They took up the beer with enthusiasm and extolled its peasant-cum-worker attributes when they returned to California and Manhattan – a middle-class attitude known as being "prolier than thou". It was the Americans who added lime to the beer, which caused amusement and consternation in Mexico, though sad to say the habit has now been taken up there as well.

A beer with not only pedigree but taste is Modelo's **Negra Modelo** – Black Modelo. It is dark brown rather than black, a cross between a Vienna Red and a Munich Dunkel, 5.3 per cent ABV, 19 IBUs, with a chocolatey aroma with some hop character, sweet dark malt in the mouth and a long finish with a hint of spice, more chocolate and hops, ending with a dry roastiness. Modelo also owns the Yucatán Brewery which produces a similar dark beer called **Negra Leon**. The dark colour of these beers owes only part of its inspiration to

Corona was Modelo's bottom-of-the-range brew but became trendy in the USA and Europe

Modelo's portfolio includes Negra, a cross between German Dunkel and Vienna Red

Vienna. Before modern malting developed, Latin American brewers dried their grain in the sun, giving beers a russet hue as a result.

Modelo has the single largest brewing plant but the group has been overtaken in size by the merger of Moctezuma and Cuauhtémoc. They both belong to a holding company called Valores, which runs seven breweries in Mexico. Moctezuma dates from 1894 when it was built by Henry Manthey, William Hasse, C. von Alten and Adolph Burhard in

Orizaba, Veracruz. Cuauhtémoc, named after an Aztec emperor, took on the name in 1890 when the Casa Calderón Brewery in Monterrey was extended. Moctezuma is best known today for **Sol** (4.6 per cent ABV), a Corona lookalike also produced in a clear glass bottle. It is believed to have an even higher level of adjuncts than Corona. Of far greater interest is **Dos Equis** – Two Crosses – dark lager (4.8 per cent ABV), widely available in foreign markets. It is in the Vienna style, a fraction paler than Negra Modelo, and

with a rich dark fruit and chocolate aroma and palate, with more chocolate and light hops in the finish. **Superior** (4.5 per cent ABV) is a far more interesting pale lager than Sol, with some hop bite.

Cuauhtémoc also has a thin quencher in the Corona/Sol style with the risible name – to outsiders – of **Chihuahau**, which is a Mexican state as well as a small dog. Tecate – once advertised as "the Gulp of Mexico" – is another pale ("clara") beer useful for quenching the thirst, as is **Carta Blanca** ("white label")

Mexican colossus... Modelo's brewery dominates the Mexico City skyline

launched in 1890 in the Pilsner style but now another thin mainstream beer. **Bohemia** is in a different league, an indication of what Mexican brewers can achieve when they turn their gaze away from their neighbour to the north. At 5.4 per cent ABV it has some clout and good hop character – Saaz are used – that complements the rich malt and vanilla aroma and firm malty body.

Mazatlán in Sinaloa state is now owned by Modelo. It opened in 1900 and was established by Jacob Schuehle who also built the original Moctezuma Brewery. **Pacifico Clara** is a light lager while **Pacifico Oscura** is a thin amber beer.

Brazil was invaded by the Portuguese rather than the Spanish but the modern brewing tradition is Germanic. **Brahma**, brewed by Companhia Cervejaria in Rio de Janeiro, is a fine Pilsner-style beer (5.0 per cent ABV) with a rich malt and vanilla aroma, a malty palate and a bitter-sweet finish with late developing hops. The group produces more than 31 million hectolitres a year and, surprisingly, its brands include a top-fermenting, 8.0 per cent ABV **Porter**. Some zealous porter sniffers suggest another possible origin of the beer style's enigmatic name: they say it comes not from London street porters but from Portugal!

In Peru, the similarly-named Compañia Cervecera brews **Peru Gold** with a striking native face mask on the label. The beer is 5.0 per cent ABV, has a rich corn and vanilla aroma, is tart and quenching in the mouth, and has a dry finish with some citric fruit notes from the hops. It also produces **Cuzco Peruvian Beer**. In Venezuela, the Polar brewing company's **Polar Lager** (5.0 per cent ABV) is so remarkably thin that it makes Corona and Sol seem malty and hoppy by comparison. It is nevertheless a major brand, responsible for more than 12 million hectolitres a year. The Cardenal group in the same country has a more distinctive range, including **Nacional "Cerveza Tipo Pilsen"** – Beer Type Pilsen, which indicates the astonishing impact of Pilsen beer and deserves marks for honesty of promotion. A German influence can be seen in the brewery's **Tipo Munich** beer, a malty, burnished gold lager, while **Andes** is more typical of the light beers of the continent.

Cervecería Bieckert in Buenos Aries, Argentina, despite being a former Spanish colony, is also heavily influenced by German and Czech styles. **Cerveza Pilsen** (4.8 per cent ABV) is brewed from pale malt, rice and maize and is hopped with American Cascades. It has 13 IBUs. Pilsen is more of an illusion than an allusion, for the lightly hopped and heavily adjuncted beer is low on aroma, body and flavour. **Especial** (5.0 per cent ABV) has 14 IBUs and the same grist recipe and has a shade more character. The most interesting product is **Africana** (5.5 per cent ABV), a bottom-fermenting beer that is a hybrid Munich Dunkel and Vienna Red. It is brewed from pale, crystal and chocolate malts with rice and maize and is hopped with Cascades (14 IBUs). It has a tempting roasted malt aroma, a smooth chocolate palate and a dry finish with hints of dark fruit, more chocolate and a tart Cascade note.

LATIN AMERICAN BREWERS
Cervecería Bieckert SA, Ponsato 121 Llavallol (1836) Pcia, Buenos Aires, Argentina.
Cervecería Moctezuma, Avenida Alfonso Reyes 2202, Nte, Monterrey NL 64442, Mexico.
Cervecería Modelo, 156 Lago Alberto, Mexico City 11320, Mexico.

Bieckert's Africana Negra from Buenos Aires is a dark lager

THE CARIBBEAN

The islands of the Caribbean have brewed beer for centuries. The quickly made native porridge beers, known by a welter of names in the different islands – *tesguino*, *chicha*, *izquiate*, *sendecho*, *zeydetha* and *zeyrecha*, the last two sounding like derivatives of the Spanish *cerveza* – succumbed to both the imported beers of the British, Spanish and French and to the comfort of locally-made rum. Guinness's **West Indies Porter** had a profound impact in the early nineteenth century. Known today as **Foreign Extra Stout** (7.3 per cent ABV), it is brewed in Spanish Town, the former capital of Jamaica, and by the Carib company in Trinidad.

The main beers today are light lagers but several Caribbean brewers keep a stout in their lockers. There is even a **Prestige Stout** from the unlikely location of Haiti where there is a morbid joke that under the old Duvalier regime all beers were lagered or stored for very long periods. Cuba's main brewery was founded in the last century by two brewers of German extraction, Obermeyer and Liebmann, who went to Havana from Brooklyn. The Nacional Dominicana Brewery in Santo Domingo, Dominican Republic, produces more than two million barrels/2.4 million hectolitres a year and is the biggest brewery in the region. **Bohemia** is the main product, a 5.0 per cent lager that is a rather thin interpretation of the Pilsner style.

The major brewery in the former British West Indies is

Desnoes & Geddes of Kingston, Jamaica. It was founded in 1918 as a soft drinks business by Eugene Desnoes and Thomas Geddes. The families are still in control, with Peter Desnoes and Paul Geddes running the company, though Heineken now has a small shareholding. The flagship brand is **Red Stripe** (4.7 per cent ABV; 14 IBUs), a malty, sweetish rather perfumy beer, the product of a short lagering regime. Its grist is made up of 70 per cent barley malt and 30 per cent corn. In common with many Australian beers, Red Stripe began life as an ale but switched to cold fermentation in the 1930s. Red Stripe is brewed under licence in Britain by Charles Wells and is popular in the West Indian community. The company's **Dragon Stout** (7.0 per cent ABV) is also a lager, with a sweet malt character overlain by chocolate and dark fruit with some hop character. The Jamaicans do not shy away from stressing the alleged aphrodisiac qualities of the beer. Its most famous promotion declared that "Dragon Puts It Back".

On Barbados, the Banks Brewery produces **Banks Beer**, a 4.5 per cent lager made from two-row pale malt and brewing sugar. It is hopped with Yakima Clusters and Styrian Goldings and has 16 IBUs. The beer has a delicate, citric hop aroma, smooth malt in the mouth and a finish that becomes dry with good hop notes. It is lagered for a month. **Carib Lager** from Trinidad is a fully brewed-out beer, dry and quenching in the finish with some hops on the aroma and a firm, malty body.

Jamaican lager for Rude Boys and not so polite girls

PLEASE RETURN BOTTLE 5 CTS. REFUND FOR YOU

IMPORTANT ADDRESSES
Banks (Barbados) Breweries Ltd, PO Box 507C, Wildey, St Michael, Barbados.
Desnoes & Geddes Ltd, 214 Spanish Town Road, PO Box 190, Kingston 11, Jamaica.

Life's a beach… the ideal setting in which to enjoy the delicate aroma of Banks Beer, the pride of Barbados

Beers from the Rest of the World

MODERN BREWING METHODS – FOR BOTH ALE AND LAGER – WERE PART OF THE BAGGAGE OF IMPERIALISM IN THE EIGHTEENTH AND NINETEENTH CENTURIES. BRITISH, FRENCH, DUTCH AND GERMAN SETTLERS BREWED FOR THEMSELVES AND THEIR TROOPS BUT THE TASTE FOR BEER REMAINED AND SPREAD WHEN THE TROOPS AND SOMETIMES THE SETTLERS RETURNED HOME. LAGER IS NOW THE DOMINANT BEER STYLE IN AFRICA, INDIA AND ASIA AND OFTEN OF THE HIGHEST QUALITY. BUT THERE ARE RESIDUAL POCKETS OF ALE BREWING, INCLUDING THE POST-IMPERIAL STOUTS OF SRI LANKA AND A TOP-FERMENTING BEER OR TWO IN JAPAN.

AFRICA AND THE MIDDLE EAST

Africa was the birthplace of brewing. Although no records exist, it is likely that beers similar to those in Ancient Egypt were widespread throughout the vast continent. They exist today in the traditional "porridge beers" in which a mash made of millet, sorghum, cassava flour, palm sap, maize and even banana is allowed to ferment spontaneously with wild yeasts in the atmosphere and in the brewing pots and is then spiced with bitter herbs. In countries still struggling to throw off the last vestiges of colonialism and create modern societies, porridge beers are an important part of the diet of poor people, containing vitamin C and several important B vitamins. The beers have many different names such as chibuku in Central Africa and dolo in West Africa.

The survival of these traditional beers is important, for conventional modern brewing is expensive as barley and hops do not grow in most parts of Africa and have to be imported. The Kenya government is attempting to create barley and hop industries in the cooler altitudes: so far the barley grown can only be used as an unmalted adjunct in brewing as its quality is not sufficiently high for malting. Hops are also grown in South Africa. European brewing groups with interests in Africa have been reluctant to experiment with beers made from local cereals, though the Nigerian government decided in the mid-1980s that 25 per cent of local grain should be used in brewing. Nigeria has the biggest number of breweries in Africa, around 30. The main brewing group, Nigerian Breweries, is jointly owned by Heineken and the United Africa Company and they made it plain to the government that if it pressed ahead with plans to make all breweries use only local cereals then some beers would be withdrawn from the market. They consider that cereals such as sorghum do not contain sufficient starch to convert into fermentable sugar.

SOUTHERN AFRICA

Modern brewing in Africa came as part of the baggage of colonialism. British, French, Dutch and Germans needed to refresh themselves and they set up rudimentary breweries, often on farms, that blossomed into substantial commercial plants once the newcomers had set down firm roots. Southern Africa, in particular, became a melting pot of brewers. In 1820 the Mariendahl Brewery was set up at Newlands; the Germans arrived in Natal in the 1840s and began brewing; the British opened a brewery in Durban; and in 1862 a Norwegian named Anders Ohlsson bought the Mariendahl Brewery. Ohlsson opened a second brewery and rapidly became a brewing giant on the Cape, eliminating most of the competition and establishing his Lion Beer as the principal brand.

The gold rush in the Transvaal created an enormous demand for beer. Ohlsson now faced serious competition from the British. The leading British-owned brewery was Castle and Castle Beer soon vied with Lion as the main brand in the region. Castle, owned by Frederick Mead, merged with smaller companies to form South African Breweries. SAB expanded from the traditional heartland of beer-drinking in Johannesburg, Durban and Cape Town to Port Elizabeth and Salisbury, Rhodesia (now Harare, the capital of Zimbabwe). After many years of talks and stand-offs, SAB and Ohlsson finally merged in 1956,

making the enlarged SAB the biggest brewing group in the whole of Africa.

SAB experimented with lager-brewing as early as 1896. Today **Lion Lager** and **Castle Lager** (5.0 per cent ABV) dominate the market from the Zambesi to the Cape. Anders Ohlsson's memory is recalled in **Ohlsson's Lager**, also 5.0 per cent. In the 1980s a micro-brewery started to produce an all-malt lager at Kynsa in Cape Province and tested occasional cask-conditioned ales and stouts. A second micro called Our Brewery opened in Johannesburg, brewing an unpasteurized ale.

During the years of apartheid, blacks were not encouraged to drink conventional beer. They were confined to insultingly-named "kaffir bars" where the only beer was a porridge-type called "kaffir beer". The end of race discrimination and rising expectations among the black population are likely to cause a demand for modern beer. The demise of porridge beer in South Africa and Zimbabwe will be a mixed blessing, marking the end of years of oppression but also the loss of a link with brewing's past.

KENYA

The most characterful Pilsner-style beer in the whole of Africa comes ironically from a brewery in Kenya founded by British settlers, including a gold prospector. East African Breweries – now Kenya Breweries – imported both

equipment and a brewer from the old country: the brewer came from the famous brewing town of Burtonwood, near Warrington. Hops were imported from Kent and the main products were ale and stout. Lager brewing was developed in the 1930s. White Cap and Tusker rapidly became admired lager beers, not only winning prizes at international competitions – including two gold medals and one silver at the World Beer Competition in 1968 – but gaining even more chutzpah from the fact that Ernest Hemingway pronounced them his favourite beers when he was hunting in Kenya.

Tusker Premium Lager is a well-attenuated beer, with a starting gravity of 1044 degrees but reaching 4.8 per cent ABV. It is brewed from 90 per cent barley malt and 10 per cent cane sugar and is hopped with imported Hallertau and Styrian

(Above) Ernest Hemingway claimed that Kenya's beers were his favourite. (Left) Castle is the dominant brand of South Africa. Perhaps the new multi-racial society will spawn more interesting brews. (Opposite left) Heineken is well established in many parts of Africa, including Nigeria

TUSKER'S NAME COMES FROM AN INCIDENT WHEN ONE OF THE FOUNDERS OF THE KENYAN BREWERY WAS KILLED BY AN ELEPHANT. THE BROTHER OF THE FOUNDER NAMED THE BEER IN HIS HONOUR – RATHER ODD AS THE ELEPHANT WAS THE AGGRESSOR, NOT THE VICTIM.

hops. A regular, everyday version of **Tusker** and the more fruity **White Cap** are around 4.0 per cent ABV. Pilsner Lager is almost identical to Tusker Premium. Kenya Breweries has subsidiaries in Uganda and Tanzania and supplies the Zimbabwe market.

NIGERIA

Nigerian Breweries built its reputation on the quality of Star Lager, brewed to mark the opening of the first of the group's plants in Lagos in 1949. Additional breweries were built in Aba, Kaduna and Ibadan to quench the thirst of the Nigerians, the greatest beer drinkers in Africa. The influence of Heineken is clear to see in **Gulder**, also 5.0 per cent but with a shade more hop character than Star. Gulder has become the flagship brand, with a gentle malt and citric hops aroma, tart and refreshing in the mouth and a finish that starts malty and becomes dry with good hop character. The company also produces a 7.0 per cent **Legend Stout**, roasty and chocolatey, brewed to meet the enormous demand for stout in Nigeria and to counter the challenge of Guinness.

Guinness has three breweries in Nigeria producing an 8.0 per cent version of the stout. These breweries make a beer using conventional pale malt. Guinness sends out from Dublin a concentrate made by making dark stout and removing the water. The concentrate (the recipe of which is a closely-guarded secret) is blended with the pale beer to make **Nigerian Guinness**.

Golden Guinea Breweries in Umuahia is another leading Nigerian company. It started life as the Independence Brewery in 1962 and came under state control. It receives support today from Holsten of Hamburg, which advises on raw materials and technical processes. **Golden Guinea Lager** is 5.0 per cent with a good balance of malt and hops on the aroma and palate. The brewery also produces **Eagle Stout**.

FRANCOPHONE AFRICA

The biggest non-African brewery group operating on the continent is the French BGI – Brasseries et Glacières Internationales. Founded in Tonkin, Indochina, in the nineteenth century, BGI has been active in all the countries that were French colonies in Africa and Asia. It is best known for its **33 Export** lager but also brews for the African market such brands as Beaufort, Castel, Flag, Gazelle and Regag. It has a powerful presence in Benin (main brand **La Béninoise**), Cameroon, Central African Republic (**Mocaf** and **Mocaf Blonde**), Gabon, Niger (**Bière Niger**), Ivory Coast, Mali,

Tunisia and Zaire. The main producer in Zaire, formerly the Belgian Congo, is the Belgian giant Interbrew, best known for Stella Artois. It brews under the name of Brasimba and produces two lager beers, **Simba** and **Tembo**. In the finest Belgian tradition, the first brewery in the Belgian Congo was founded by Jesuits in 1902 at Ki-Santu.

In the Republic of the Congo, the SCBK Brewery at Pointe Noire near Brazzaville brews **Ngok**, local dialect for Le Choc – crocodile. One of the most highly-regarded lagers in Francophone Africa, **Mamba**, is brewed in Abidjan, capital of the Ivory Coast by Solibra, owned by Interbrew. The brewery also produces a strong Bock lager and a tawny Brune, the latter with a faint hint of an Abbey-style beer from Belgium.

The island of Madagascar's Star Brewery has three plants devoted to just one lager brand called **Three Horses Beer**. The smaller island of Réunion has a lager with the enticing name of **Bourbon**, which takes its name from the town where the brewery is based and has no whisky connections. Mauritius, for a small island, has had impressive success with the lager beers produced by the Mauritius Brewery. **Phoenix** (4.5 per cent ABV) won a gold medal at the International Brewers Exhibition (Brewex) in 1983 and a gold at Monde Sélection in 1989. Stella Lager – no connection with Stella Artois – has also won two golds. **Blue Marlin** (5.6 per cent ABV) was introduced in 1989 and won a Monde Sélection gold three years later.

NORTH AFRICA AND THE MIDDLE EAST

The surge of Islamic fundamentalism in North Africa and the Middle East makes the future of brewing in the region uncertain. All the Iranian breweries have closed since the ayatollahs came to power. The fate of Iraq's state-controlled breweries, producing **Ferida, Golden Lager** and **Jawhara** beers, is unknown. Egypt has a state-controlled brewery in Cairo producing **Pyramid** lager. Arab Breweries in Amman, Jordan, brews **Petra** lager.

Tempo Beer Industries in Israel dominates the market through five brewing plants. Its flagship brand is **Maccabee** (4.9 per cent ABV) with a pronounced malt aroma, bitter-sweet malt and hops in the mouth, and a dry finish with some hops and vanilla notes. Tempo also produces **Gold Star** and **Malt Star** lagers.

The major brewing group in Turkey, Anadolu Industri, brews **Efes Pilsen** (5.0 per cent ABV) with a tangy malt and hops aroma, rich malt in the mouth, and a long bitter-sweet finish that becomes dry and hoppy. The beer is exported widely throughout the Middle East, Africa and Europe. A smaller company, Türk Tuborg, is a subsidiary of the Danish Carlsberg/Tuborg group and brews Tuborg under licence. The island of Cyprus has **Keo Beer**, a 4.5 per cent lager, with a good balance of malt and hops on the aroma, some vanilla notes and hops on the palate, and a bitter-sweet finish.

AFRICAN AND MIDDLE EASTERN BREWERS

Anadolu Industri,
Ankara, Turkey.

Arab Breweries,
Prince Muhammad Street, Amman, Jordan.

Brasimba,
Avenue du Flambeau 912, Kinshasa, Zaire.

Brasseries et Glacières Internationales,
Algiers, Algeria.

Golden Guinea Breweries,
5 Route de Coyah, Conakry, Guinea.

Kenya Breweries,
Thika Road, Ruaraka, Nairobi, Kenya.

Mauritius Brewery,
Phoenix, Mauritius.

Nigerian Breweries,
PO Box 496, Aba, Nigeria.

SCBK Brewery,
Kronenberg, Point Noire, Brazzaville, Republic of Congo.

Solibra,
Abidjan, Ivory Coast.

South African Breweries,
Sandton 2146, South Africa.

Star Brewery,
Antananarivo, Madagascar.

Tempo Beer Industries,
Tel Aviv, Israel.

Tempo is the major brewing group in Israel. The modern mechanized plant produces the flagship brand Maccabee

AUSTRALIA

OSTER'S LAGER IS ONE OF THE WORLD'S BIGGEST BEER BRANDS YET IT TAKES ITS NAME FROM TWO NEW YORK BROTHERS WHO LIVED IN AUSTRALIA FOR LITTLE MORE THAN A YEAR. THEY CHANGED AUSTRALIAN BREWING DUE NOT TO A DEVOTION TO GOOD BEER BUT AS A RESULT OF OWNING A REFRIGERATION PLANT. THE BROTHERS SET UP THE FOSTER BREWING COMPANY IN MELBOURNE IN 1887, SOLD IT THE FOLLOWING YEAR AND RETURNED TO TOTAL OBSCURITY IN THE UNITED STATES.

JOHN BOSTON, THE FIRST COMMERCIAL BREWER IN AUSTRALIA, HAD NEITHER BARLEY NOR HOPS TO HAND. HE USED CORN FOR HIS MALT AND FOR FLAVOURING TURNED TO THE LEAVES AND STALKS OF THE CAPE GOOSEBERRY.

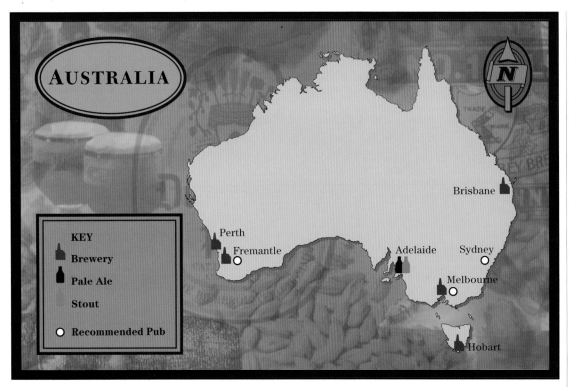

AUSTRALIA

KEY
Brewery
Pale Ale
Stout
Recommended Pub

Perth · Fremantle
Brisbane
Adelaide · Sydney
Melbourne
Hobart

any type. Today lager beers dominate the country but, confusingly, many of them are still called "bitter", perhaps to pander to older Australians who still think of Britain as "home". Even the ubiquitous **Castlemaine XXXX** is called Bitter Ale in its country of origin.

In common with other countries, Australia has been the victim of a spate of takeovers, mergers and closures. To the intense annoyance of proud Australians, half of their brewing industry is now in the hands of the New Zealand Lion Nathan group. The collapse of the Bond Corporation allowed Lion Nathan to buy up Castlemaine, Toohey's and Swan. It then moved on to acquire Hahn of Sydney and South Australian of Adelaide.

The other half of Australian brewing is in the hands of Foster's, formerly Carlton and United Breweries. The worldwide fame of Foster's can be seen by its owner's decision to subsume both CUB and even the overall holding company, Elders IXL, into the name of the beer

But the Foster brothers determined the future of Australian brewing. The first settlers from Britain took with them an ale culture, but ale was not best suited to the searing heat of the vast continent. The reality was that, before refrigeration, the high temperatures made it difficult to brew a consistent beer of

brand. Aided by the international success of the film *Crocodile Dundee*, whose star Paul Hogan had also advertised Foster's Lager, the brand is now one of the world's leaders.

Foster's and Lion Nathan have encouraged a wide choice of brands to remain, no doubt to appease those drinkers who have always been loyal to the likes of Tooth, Toohey, Emu and Swan. But there is little to choose between any of the mainstream lagers. They are all served ice cold and, when the temperature in the glass rises, tend to be sweet and lightly hopped: cane sugar is widely used as an adjunct in Australian lager brewing, usually in the ration of 70 per cent malt to 30 per cent sugar. Units of bitterness range from 14 to 22 while lagering is extremely brief, lasting between one and two weeks. British drinkers, used to the versions of Foster's and XXXX brewed in their country, would be surprised to find that the originals are more robust, both being around 5.0 per cent ABV, the standard strength for everyday Australian beers.

Both Castlemaine Perkins and Foster's became truly national groups in the 1980s when they muscled in to the biggest Australian beer market in New South Wales. By this time, Castlemaine Perkins had merged with Swan of Western Australia. Continuing the Irish link, Castlemaine bought Toohey's of Sydney, a brewery that had once primarily served the Catholic community, while the rival Tooth brewery, of English Anglican stock, served the Protestant one.

WESTERN AUSTRALIA

Two birds dominate brewing in this enormous but sparsely-populated state: the black swan, the state symbol, and the emu, indigenous to Western Australia. The Swan Brewery started brewing in Perth in 1857. The rival Emu Brewery began life as the Stanley Brewing Company, run by a William Mumme, a name similar to both a French Champagne and a type of beer once brewed centuries ago in the Brunswick area of Germany. In 1908 Stanley became Emu. After decades of tough and raucous competition, the two birds merged in 1928. Swan, now based in a new brewery in Canning Vale and part of the Lion Nathan group, has on paper a wide range of products but with scarcely perceptible differences between them. The Emu name is kept alive with **Emu Export** (4.9 per cent ABV), almost identical to Swan Lager. **Emu Bitter** (4.6 per cent ABV, with 26 IBUs) is the most bitter of the brewery's products, with hop varieties from Victoria and Tasmania. **Emu Draft** is not draught at all but a 3.7 per cent packaged beer, lightly hopped but with more body from the use of crystal malt.

Among the main Swan brands, **Export Lager** (4.8 per cent ABV) has marginally more body and hop character than the 4.9 per cent **Swan Lager. Swan Gold** sounds like a premium product but is a modest 3.5 per cent ABV aimed at the low-calorie market. The roasty/chocolatey and well-hopped **Swan Stout** (6.8 per cent ABV) is brewed for Swan by Cooper's of Adelaide and is a rare top-fermented genuine ale.

The Matilda Bay Brewing Company was set up by a former Swan brewer, Philip Sexton. He built a pub brewery in the Sail and Anchor hotel in Fremantle in 1984 and then added a micro-brewery in Nedlands called Matilda Bay. In 1988, with four million dollars of investment from Foster's, a new custom-built brewery was set up in Perth, using a redundant all-copper brewhouse from de Clerck in Northern France.

Sexton's main beer is **RedBack**, named after a local spider, and is the first-known wheat beer to be brewed in Australia. RedBack is made from 65 per cent malted wheat, grown in the Avon Valley. The rest of the grist is two-row barley malt and the hops are Saaz and Hersbrucker. The 4.8 per cent ABV beer is available in both bottle-conditioned and filtered draught versions. It has a lightly spicy and fruity aroma and palate. **Dogbolter** started life as a strong ale but is now fermented with a bottom yeast culture. A Pils has, by Australian standards, a robust 40 IBUs. The Sail and Anchor brewpub specializes in handpumped, top-fermenting beers (*see* Australian pubs on pages 189–90). Matilda Bay has added a brewpub called

Despite Castlemain's fire-breathing promotion, its Gold is a modest 3.5 per cent ABV

BEFORE FLEXIBLE LICENSING LAWS ARRIVED IN AUSTRALIA THE COUNTRY WAS INFAMOUS FOR ITS "SIX O'CLOCK SWILL" WHEN DRINKERS THREW BACK AS MANY GLASSES OF BEER AS POSSIBLE BEFORE "HOTELS", AS BARS ARE KNOWN, WERE FORCED TO CLOSE.

At drink two birds... Swan and Emu (left) merged their nests in 1928

*Bearded in the brewery...
Thomas Cooper turned a
sideline into a brewing
dynasty. His ales were once
laughed at but are now
Australian classics*

RedBack in Melbourne which brews a spicy, fruity **Hefe-Weizen** in the Bavarian fashion, and a **Pils** with a Munich-style rounded maltiness.

SOUTH AUSTRALIA

The South Australian Brewing Company in Thebarton, Adelaide, was a major independent until it was bought by Lion Nathan. The modern brewery is high-tech and produces only bottom-fermenting beers, even though they include a stout. The company grew by a succession of mergers, dating from 1888 when the Kent Town Brewery, the West End Brewery and a wine and spirits merchant joined forces. Later acquisitions included the Broken Hill Brewery – whose beers were popular with the tough breed of miners in the area – Waverley, Port Augusta and, in 1938, the biggest coup in the shape of a merger with the larger Southwark Brewery. The new Thebarton plant is called the Southwark Brewery as a mark of respect for the dear-departed.

South Australian brands also pay homage to former breweries. **West End Premium** (5.0 per cent ABV), named after the company's old site, is dry in the finish; Pride of Ringwood and Hersbrucker Hallertau hops create 25 IBUs. **Southwark Premium** (5.5 per cent ABV) has a good balance of malt and perfumy hop, with 22 IBUs. **Old Australia Stout** (7.4 per cent ABV) is a dark lager but with an abundance of roast and chocolate character. It is brewed from pale malt, roasted barley and cane sugar, with Pride of Ringwood hops. IBUs are 37. **Broken Hill Lager** (4.8 per cent

ABV; 22 IBUs) also has some roasted barley in its make-up. It is one of the most characterful of the mainstream Australian lagers, with a good hop aroma (Ringwood), a rounded palate and a quenching, bitter-sweet finish.

Port Dock is a brewpub in Port Adelaide producing a golden **Lighthouse Ale**, a malty **Black Diamond Bitter** and a fruity 6.0 per cent **Old Preacher**.

COOPER'S OF ADELAIDE

The swing to lager brewing threatened the total eclipse of ale in Australia. One company went on producing ales, to the derision of the rest of the industry, but today Cooper's ales of Adelaide are now not only cult beers throughout Australia but are recognized as classics of the style worldwide.

Thomas Cooper emigrated from Yorkshire in 1852. His wife was the daughter of an innkeeper and she used the skills of brewing she had picked up from her father to make beer at home. Thomas worked first as a shoemaker and then as a dairyman in their new country before setting up as a commercial brewer. When his first wife died Thomas remarried and produced an impressive 16 children.

The Cooper family still runs the company. Against all the advice of marketing experts, they have remained faithful to ale and didn't add a lager to their portfolio until 1969. The 5.8 per cent bottle-conditioned and draught **Sparkling Ale** throws a heavy sediment after six weeks' conditioning in the brewery. The title

"sparkling" causes some amusement as the beer tends to be cloudy in the glass. It is brewed from pale and crystal malts with cane sugar making up around 18 per cent of the recipe. Hops are Pride of Ringwood pellets, with 26 bitterness units. Primary fermentation used to be in open wooden vessels made of local jarrah hardwood. The beer was cleansed of yeast by dropping it from the fermenters into 108-gallon "puncheons". Cooper's has now switched to primary fermentation in conical vessels. The beer is centrifuged and given a dosage of fermenting wort and sugar to encourage a second fermentation in bottle and keg. Sparkling Ale is intensely fruity, with apple and banana dominating, a peppery hop aroma, citric fruit from the hops in the mouth, and a quenching finish with more hops and fruit.

Cooper's Stout (6.8 per cent ABV) is also a sedimented beer. Roasted malt is added to pale and crystal. It has an oily, coffeeish aroma and palate. A lower strength version of Sparkling Ale has been introduced (4.5 per cent ABV, 26 IBUs) with delectable apple fruit on the aroma and palate, and good hop character. **Cooper's Dark** (4.5 per cent ABV) is made from pale, crystal and roast malt and has a fruity and chocolate character. It is based on a famous Welsh beer, Brain's Dark from Cardiff, discovered by a member of the Cooper family when he was visiting Britain.

The success of Cooper's has prompted others to emulate the sparkling ale style, which is believed to have been developed early in the twentieth century to counter the threat of lager. The Lion Brewing micro in Adelaide opened in 1992 to make a 5.0 per cent **Sparkling Bitter Ale**, packed with hop aroma and with a bitter finish.

NEW SOUTH WALES

The biggest beer-drinking state is home to Tooth's and Toohey's of Sydney, now in the hands of Foster's and Castlemaine/Lion Nathan. The Tooth plant is known as the Kent Brewery in honour of founder John Tooth's home in Kent in South-east England, the principal hop-growing region of the old country. The symbol is no longer used, but Tooth's used to inscribe its products with the White Horse of Kent, which can still be seen on the hop "pockets" or sacks used back in England. The white horse is derived from the battle flag of two legendary Saxon chiefs who invaded England, Hengist and Horsa, whose names mean Stallion and Horse.

Both Tooth's and Toohey's pay homage to a dark or amber style of beer known in the state as Old Ale. Tooth's version is best known as Old or XXX but it has been renamed **Kent Old Brown** after the brewery. It has a sweetish palate and a lightly fruity aroma, and is top-fermenting. **Sheaf Stout** (5.7 per cent ABV, 35 IBUs) is also a genuine ale with a woody, earthy aroma, coffee on the palate and a dry finish. **Resch's Draught** is a well-balanced lager, more aggressively malty and hoppy than the norm, and is named after a brewery bought by Tooth's in 1929.

Toohey's has continued the

legacy of old ales with the exotically-named **Tall Ships**, a higher strength version of the long-running **Hunter Old** (4.7 per cent ABV), a top-fermenting brown ale with some fruity and roasted barley character. Conventional lagers include **Toohey's Red**, with some late hop in the finish, and **Toohey's Light Bitter** that, despite the British ale connotations, is bottom-fermenting.

Hahn was set up as a micro-brewery in 1988 in Sydney but has been bought by the all-conquering Lion Nathan, which descended on Australia like the All Blacks pack in full flood. **Hahn Premium Lager** is an all-malt beer with plenty of hop aroma and bitterness.

VICTORIA

Melbourne is the home of Foster's/CUB, which also has a second plant at Ballarat. As well as **Foster's Lager** (5.0 per cent ABV), sweetish and with a hint of fruit – the result of a short lagering – the group produces **Carlton Crown Lager**, almost identical to Foster's. **Carlton Draught** is a shade more rounded in flavour and slightly darker in colour. **Victoria Bitter** is a lager with malty dryness in the finish while **Melbourne Bitter** has some hop bitterness. **Abbots Lager** and **Abbots Stout** take their name from the Abbotsford Brewery, the main Melbourne site. The stout is roasty with hints of coffee and chocolate and

is bottom-fermenting. With the exception of the Abbot brews, the hallmark of Foster's is the remarkable similarity of all the beers.

QUEENSLAND

If Elder's dominates Victoria, Queensland is the undisputed home of **Castlemaine XXXX**. What was once a simple cask marking handed down from medieval monks has become, in the hands of modern marketing gurus, a secular synonym for "Stuff you, Jack". Queensland drinkers couldn't give a XXXX for any other beer, according to the advertising, and at night the four letters blaze out from the Castlemaine Brewery like a neon-lit, two-fingered salute.

The Brisbane version of XXXX, still sold as **Bitter Ale**, uses whole hops rather than pellets, an unusual practice in modern Australia. The 4.8 per cent lager does have a hint more hoppiness than its main rivals but like them is malty sweet. **Gold Lager** is 3.5 per cent and even more malt-accented. **Malt 75** (4.8 per cent ABV) is an additive-free lager, drier than XXXX. The most characterful beer from the brewery is **Carbine Stout**, named after a famous racehorse. It is the last surviving stout from a brewery that once made several. At 5.1 per cent ABV, it is now bottom-fermenting with a roasty palate and a dry finish.

Powers was set up near

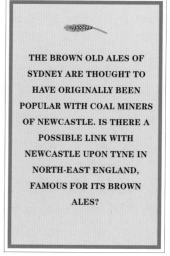

Despite the name, Toohey's Red is a conventional lager, not Belgian-inspired

THE BROWN OLD ALES OF SYDNEY ARE THOUGHT TO HAVE ORIGINALLY BEEN POPULAR WITH COAL MINERS OF NEWCASTLE. IS THERE A POSSIBLE LINK WITH NEWCASTLE UPON TYNE IN NORTH-EAST ENGLAND, FAMOUS FOR ITS BROWN ALES?

The magnificent frontage of the Cascade Brewery in Hobart, designed while the owner was in jail

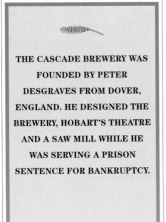

THE CASCADE BREWERY WAS FOUNDED BY PETER DESGRAVES FROM DOVER, ENGLAND. HE DESIGNED THE BREWERY, HOBART'S THEATRE AND A SAW MILL WHILE HE WAS SERVING A PRISON SENTENCE FOR BANKRUPTCY.

Brisbane in 1987 to bring some much-needed choice to the region. Busily promoted, especially at major sports events, Power's success annoyed the giants and it succumbed to the blandishments of Foster's. Whether **Power's Big Red**, a more flavourful lager than most, will keep its distinctive character under new ownership remains to be seen.

TASMANIA

The island of Tasmania is one of the major barley-growing areas of Australia and, with Victoria, supplies most of the continent's hops – Pride of Ringwood is the leading hop variety grown. With a famous English independent brewery called Ringwood based in Hampshire it would be pleasing, if fanciful, to believe that the hop strain first came from the old country. As Hampshire is not known as a hop-growing area there is little to support the notion, though Tasmanians claim that cuttings from

Hampshire were smuggled on to the island in breach of the quarantine laws. If the story is true, the hop has found its way home again, for the organic version – free from pesticides and fertilizers – is used by a handful of British brewers producing organic beers.

With the pick of the barley and hop crops to hand, it is not surprising that Tasmania's two breweries produce some of the tastiest beers in the country.

The Cascade Brewery in Hobart is the oldest continuously working Australian brewery. The superb plant, looking like a cross between a traditional English brewery and a Yorkshire woollen mill, started to produce ale and porter in 1832. It drew both its brewing liquor and its inspiration from the pure waters flooding down from the Cascade Mountains. In 1922 it merged with Tasmania's other brewery, Boag's of Launceston – both breweries still operate – and in 1927 switched to lager brewing when it installed a new plant from Switzerland.

Cascade Premium Lager is a well-attenuated beer (original gravity 1044–1048 but with 5.2 per cent ABV) and is noticeably full-bodied with a crisp finish and some citric hop notes. In spite of their names, **Cascade Draught, Cascade Bitter** and **Cascade Stout** are all bottom-fermenting. The stout has plenty of roasted malt and chocolate character.

Boag's, at the other end of the island, traces its origins to 1927 but there have been some interruptions in brewing over the years. Cascade has left it to

brew in the fashion the managers prefer: Boag's uses the traditional European double-decoction mashing system that uses several mash kettles, while Cascade has a hybrid ale-and-lager step-infusion system in which the temperature of the mash is raised within one vessel. **Boag's Draught** is a lager, again well attenuated, from a gravity of 1040 degrees to 4.7 per cent ABV. It has a perfumy hop aroma and a dry finish. **Boag's Lager** (5.4 per cent ABV) has 27 IBUs, hoppy by Australian standards. **Boag's Stout** is less characterful than Cascade's, though.

AUSTRALIAN BREWERS
Cascade Brewery Co,
156 Collins Street, Hobart TAS 7000.
Castlemaine Perkins (Lion Nathan),
11 Finchley Street, Milton QLD 4064.
Cooper's Brewery Ltd,
9 Statenborough Street, Leabrook, Adelaide SA 5068.
Foster's/Carlton and United Breweries Ltd,
1 Bouverie Street, Carlton VIC 3053.
Matilda Bay Brewing Co Ltd,
130 Stirling Highway, North Fremantle WA 6161.
Power Brewing Co Ltd (Foster's),
Pacific Highway, Yatala QLD 4207.
South Australian Brewing Co Ltd (Lion Nathan),
107 Port Road, Thebarton SA 5031.
Swan Brewery Co Ltd (Lion Nathan),
25 Baile Road, Canning Vale WA 6155.

NEW ZEALAND

*M*ODERNIZATION HAS BEEN A RECURRENT THEME IN NEW ZEALAND BREWING SINCE THE TURN OF THE TWENTIETH CENTURY. THE CAPTAIN COOK BREWERY IN AUCKLAND MADE MUCH OF THE FACT THAT AS EARLY AS 1907 ITS ALES AND STOUTS WERE FILTERED, PASTEURIZED AND ARTIFICIALLY CARBONATED. TODAY THE TWO GROUPS THAT DOMINATE KIWI BREWING, LION NATHAN (FORMERLY NEW ZEALAND BREWERIES) AND DOMINION PRODUCE SWEET, MALTY, LIGHTLY HOPPED AND UNDEMANDING LAGERS.

Steinlager is the hoppiest and best-known of Kiwi lagers. It's hard to break the mould: even a CAMRA-inspired micro in Nelson (left) has had to concentrate on lager to survive

As New Zealand is a more conservative society than Australia and is less ambivalent about its links with Britain, it might be expected that a revival of traditional brewing would have taken root in the islands, but even the micros that sprang up in the 1980s and 1990s have had to bow to prevailing attitudes. When former All Blacks rugby player Terry McCashin opened his Mac's micro in Nelson in 1982 he was encouraged by a visit to Britain and the success there of the Campaign for Real Ale. But today, under the screw from consumers, he concentrates on lager. Mac's Lager is generously hopped by local standards, his Real Ale uses a lager yeast and is pasteurized in the bottle while his best-selling product is an everyday sweetish lager.

Lion Nathan has had great success at home and abroad with its **Steinlager**, a 4.8 per cent beer with 22 IBUs. It has the greatest hop character of any of the mainstream New Zealand beers. **Rheineck** (3.8 per cent ABV) is sweet and undemanding, **Leopard DeLuxe** has some light fruit but little hop, while **Lion Red** (3.7 per cent ABV) is malty and amber coloured. **Lion Brown** is easily the most interesting of the group's beers. Although it is fermented with a lager yeast, the temperature is kept high, leaving considerable estery fruitiness in the finished beer.

Dominion Breweries has a **Double Brown** in the same style. Its mainstream lagers, **DB Draught** and **DB Export**, are malty but **Kiwi Lager** has some good hop aroma.

Harrington's is a new micro based in Victorian brewing buildings in Christchurch. It produces – bravely for New Zealand – a sweetish **Harrington's Wheat Beer** and a **Harrington's Dark** with coffee notes. Another wheat beer, WeissBier, can be found in the Loaded Hog brewpub in Christchurch. The pub also offers an interpretation of an English brown ale called **Hog's Head Dark**. In Auckland the pioneering Shakespeare brewpub has a lager with good hop bitterness, a malty **Red Ale** and an English-style bitter called **Falstaff**.

NEW ZEALAND BREWERS

Dominion Breweries,
80 Greys Avenue,
Auckland.

Lion Nathan,
54–65 Shortland Street,
Auckland.

Mac's Micro,
Stoke, Nr Nelson.

THE CAPTAIN COOK BREWERY IN AUCKLAND WAS NAMED IN HONOUR OF THE GREAT ENGLISH SEAFARER WHO BREWED A RUDIMENTARY ALE WHEN HE ARRIVED IN NEW ZEALAND IN 1773 TO CLEAR HIS CREW OF SCURVY. HE USED SPRUCE, TEA PLANTS AND MOLASSES.

JAPAN AND THE FAR EAST

*J*APAN HAS COME A LONG WAY IN A SHORT TIME IN BREWING TERMS. BEER WAS INTRODUCED, ALMOST BY ACCIDENT, BY THE AMERICANS IN 1853. THE UNITED STATES WAS KEEN TO DEVELOP TRADE WITH JAPAN BUT PLACED A KNUCKLEDUSTER INSIDE THE VELVET GLOVE BY SENDING THE US NAVY UNDER COMMODORE MATTHEW PERRY TO NEGOTIATE A TREATY. A JAPANESE WHO WENT ON BOARD ONE OF PERRY'S SHIPS WAS OFFERED A BEER. INTRIGUED, HE FOUND A HANDBOOK ON BREWING – WRITTEN IN DUTCH – AND MANAGED TO MAKE BEER FOR HOME CONSUMPTION.

JAPAN AND THE FAR EAST	Kuala Lumpar
Bangalore	Asia Pacific Breweries
Mohan Meakin	**Qingdao**
United Breweries	Tsingtao
Beijing	**Seoul**
Mon-Lei	OB Brewery
Colombo	**Singapore**
McCallum's	Asia Pacific Breweries
Guilin	**Shanghai**
Wei Mei	Shanghai Lager
Ho Chi Minh City	Swan Lager
My Tho/BGI	**Tokyo**
Hong Kong	Asahi Breweries
Hong Kong Brewery	Kirin Brewery Co
Hyderabad	Sapporo Breweries
Vinedale Breweries	Suntory Brewery
Kandy	*Beer Bar Brussels*
Ceylon Brewery	*Rising Sun*
UKD Silva	

Following the Meiji reforms of 1868, when Emperor Mutsuhito (above) encouraged Westernization and industrialization, efforts were made to create indigenous commercial breweries. Again the Americans gave a hand and a brewery was established in Yokohama by Wiegand and Copeland. Eventually the brewery became wholly-owned by Japanese and was named Kirin after a mythical creature, half dragon and half horse.

BLACK BEER

The black beer influence may come from the Franconia region

of Bavaria but the dark lagers there are brown rather than black. Schwarzbier is now confined to Saxony and the opaque, bottom-fermenting beer from Köstritz may be the historic link with Japan's black beers.

Kirin and Sapporo, the oldest of Japan's breweries, produce the most interesting versions of the style. **Sapporo Black Beer** is the classic. At 5.0 per cent ABV, it is brewed from pale, crystal, Munich and chocolate malts with a small amount of rice.

Kirin Black Beer, also 5.0 per cent, has a pronounced roasted coffee and liquorice palate after a gentle, grainy start. The finish is light and quenching with some gentle hop character. **Asahi Black** (5.0 per cent ABV) is less dark, with a hint of red/brown in the colour. It is by far the sweetest of the Japanese black beers and many drinkers blend it with lager to balance the caramel character. **Suntory's Black Beer** (5.0 per cent ABV; 23 IBUs) is jet black and opaque. All the black beers are minority brands, sold on draught or packaged for specialist bars or restaurants. The brewers deserve credit for maintaining a style that in most modern brewing climates would have been consigned to the grave decades ago.

PILSNERS AND LAGERS

Kirin Lager is the most distinctive of the Japanese mainstream Pilsners, lagered, it is claimed, for an impressive two months. At 4.9 per cent ABV and 27.5 IBUs from Hallertau and Saaz hops, it is full-bodied and rich-

tasting and is firmly in the Pilsner mould. A stronger lager (6.5 per cent ABV) stresses the German influence with the remarkable name of **Mein Bräu** – My Brew. More recent beers include a hoppy **Spring Valley**, an all-malt **Heartland, Ichiba** made from the first malt of the season, and the confusingly named **Golden Bitter**, which is bottom-fermenting and has a fine, resiny hop character.

Sapporo's most impressive brand is **Yebisu**, a fragrant malty/hoppy beer broadly in the Dortmunder Export style and hopped with Hallertau Mittelfruh and Hersbruck. It is 5.0 per cent ABV and has an enticing golden colour. It takes its name from a Shinto god. Other lagers include 4.5 per cent **Sapporo Draft Beer** (which comes in bottles and cans) and has a grainy aroma, malt in the mouth and a dry finish with some hop notes; and a German-influenced **Edel-Pils** with a delightful hop aroma.

Suntory's state of the art breweries can be programmed to produce almost any type of beer. In general Suntory's range is mild and light-tasting, dry in the finish but with only delicate hoppiness. **Suntory's Malt's**, as the name suggests, is on the malty side while **Suntory's Light's** (4.5 per cent ABV), aimed at the calorie-conscious, may be "a healthy delight" but has little else to recommend it. **Dynamic Draft** is fermented with a Canadian yeast.

Asahi's Super Dry is brewed out or fully-attenuated to turn all the malt sugars to alcohol. It launched a brief craze for dry beers in several

countries, the United States in particular, but the decline was almost as rapid as the rise: it seems that beer drinkers, contrary to the views of marketing departments, do like taste and flavour. Asahi also produces **Asahi Z**, another well-attenuated beer, and a more flavoursome **Asahi Gold**.

JAPANESE SPECIALITIES

As well as black beers, the Japanese big four have some other surprises in their lockers. Kirin brews a superb 8.0 per cent ABV **Kirin Stout**, a complex bitter-sweet, bottom-fermenting beer with delicious dark toffee notes. A micro-brewery set up in Kyoto produces a German-style, top-fermenting **Kyoto Alt**, copper coloured and with a delectable nuttiness from crystal malt.

Sapporo and Asahi also brew stouts. Sapporo's is called **Yebisu Stout** and is soft and mellow while **Asahi's Stout** is big-bodied, full of dark bitter-sweet fruits. Suntory has experimented with a Bavarian **Weizen** wheat beer, beautifully made and with a delicious apple-and-clove quenching palate.

JAPANESE BREWERS
Asahi Breweries,
23-1 Azumabashi 1-chome, Sumida-ku, Tokyo 130.
Kirin Brewery Co,
26-1 Jingumae 6-chome, Shibuya-ku, Tokyo 150.
Sapporo Breweries,
7-10-1 Ginza, Chuo-ku, Tokyo 104.
Suntory Brewery,
1-2-3 Motoakasaka, Minato-ku, Tokyo 107.

Sapporo Draft Beer is now available outside Japan

ASAHI STOUT IS TOP-FERMENTING AND ALSO USES A *BRETTANOMYCES* YEAST CULTURE TO GIVE A HINT OF LACTIC SOURNESS. THIS IS A THROW-BACK TO THE BRITISH METHODS OF THE EIGHTEENTH CENTURY WHEN PORTERS AND STOUTS WERE DELIBERATELY AGED OR "STALED" IN OAK VATS.

Asahi led the craze for dry, tasteless beers, but it also brews a Japanese black beer

Shanghai Swan Lager... one of the few enigmatic Chinese beers to escape to the West

A MICROBREWERY IN CHANGSHA IN HUNAN PROVINCE IN CHINA WAS BUILT BY PETER AUSTIN OF ENGLAND. AUSTIN IS CALLED "THE FATHER OF THE MICROBREWERY REVOLUTION" IN BRITAIN. HE STARTED THE RINGWOOD BREWERY IN HAMPSHIRE, SOLD EQUIPMENT TO OTHER MICROBREWERS, THEN SPREAD HIS WINGS TO FRANCE, THE UNITED STATES AND CHINA.

CHINA

One of the most populous nations on earth remains an enigma, not least where brewing is concerned. For centuries an alcoholic drink was made from rice but it is not clear whether this was beer or wine. Today there are thought to be 100 breweries in the country but the number could be far higher as China slowly opens up to Western influence and technology while living standards rise. But only one beer is well known outside China and it comes from a brewery set up with the aid of German technology in the late nineteenth century.

When the Germans leased the port of Tsingtao on the Shantung peninsula close to Japan and Korea they naturally built a brewery which survives and thrives. The name of the port is now Qingdao in Shandong province but Tsingtao is still used as the name of the extremely pale Pilsner-style lager brewed there and exported widely: it is something of a cult beer in the United States among aficionados of Chinese cuisine.

China now has its own barley and hop industries though supplies and quality are erratic. The 5.2 per cent **Tsingtao**, when it is on form, has a good Pilsner malt and hop attack with some vanilla notes in the finish.

A malty, lightly hopped beer from Shanghai known either as **Shanghai Lager** or **Swan Lager** from the emblem on the neck label has occasionally been seen in the West. It has no connection to the Swan subsidiary of Lion Nathan in Australia, though several Western breweries are establishing partnership arrangements with Chinese breweries. Shanghai also produces a dark lager called **Guangminpai**. The capital, Beijing, has a lager called **Mon-Lei** with a reddish hue as though influenced by Austrian "red" lagers. A similar beer, **Wei Mei**, comes from Guilin.

Across the border in South Korea, the OB Brewery in Seoul produces two lagers, **OB** and **Crown**.

The Hong Kong Brewery has a 5.0 per cent **Sun Lik Beer** with a traditional Chinese dragon adorning the label.

THE REST OF ASIA

German technology built the Boon Rawd Brewery in Thailand and the German influence continues today in the production of the superb **Singha Lager**. The Singha is a mythical lion-like creature and the beer named in its honour is suitably powerful. The rival **Amarit**, in contrast, is a much milder and malty-sweet brew that contains some ale-like fruitiness.

One of the best-known Asian beers is Tiger of Singapore and Kuala Lumpur. It refreshed the British during both the colonial period and the Second World War and was immortalized by the British writer Anthony Burgess in his novel *Time for a Tiger*, a marketing slogan used by the brewery since the late 1940s. **Tiger** (5.1 per cent ABV) and **Anchor** of the same strength are both clean-tasting, quenching light lagers. Tiger has the greater hop character and is now much influenced by the Heineken style. APB also brews a roasty/creamy, bottom fermenting **ABC Stout** with a powerful 8.1 per cent ABV rating. APB has introduced a **Tiger Classic** seasonal beer for the New Year festivities as well as **Raffles Light**, named after Raffles Hotel in Singapore, a legendary watering-hole in colonial times.

APB has joined with the Vietnamese to build a brewery in Ho Chi Minh City (Saigon). The French BGI group was called in by the Vietnamese at the end of the war with the United States to build a brewery at My Tho to revive the **33** brand, which had refreshed the French during the colonial period.

The Bintang Brewery in Indonesia produces beer with a Dutch influence, down to the familiar stubby Dutch bottle. **Bintang** is 5.0 per cent ABV with a grainy aroma, a malty/perfumy palate, and a finish that becomes dry with some light hop notes.

One of the most famous beers in Asia and the Pacific is **San Miguel** of the Philippines. The Filipino company is a giant concern with several breweries as well as interests in food and agriculture. **San Miguel Pale Pilsen** is 5.0 per cent ABV with around 20 IBUs. It is made with 80 per cent malt and is lagered for a month. **Gold Eagle** is similar to San Miguel, a fraction

lower in alcohol and a shade darker in colour. **Cerveza Negra** (Black Beer) is 5.2 per cent ABV with a pleasing roasted malt character. **Red Horse** (6.8 per cent ABV) is a full-bodied, malty lager in the Bock style.

INDIAN SUB-CONTINENT

The British stamped their mark on India with India Pale Ales brewed in Burton-on-Trent for export to the sub-continent. But by the 1880s German lagers swiftly replaced ales as they were more suited to both brewing and consumption in the torrid climate. Even today some lagers have a fruity, ale-like character caused by problems of temperature control. Burma's **Mandalay Beer**, for example, is a notably fruity brew even though it is bottom-fermenting. Napal's **Star Beer** is more in the lager mould with a hoppy intensity.

While some Indian states are strictly prohibitionist, the country's breweries range from the far north in the Simla Hills to Bangalore and Hyderabad in the south. The main brewing groups are Mohan

Meakin and United Breweries. Lager beers tend to be malty and sweetish with only light hop character. The best-known brands are **Cobra** and **Kingfisher**, both widely exported; Kingfisher is brewed under licence in Britain by Shepherd Neame in Kent. Mohan Meakin, founded in 1855, brews a large portfolio of lagers for the home market, including **Baller, Gymkhana, Lion, Krown** and **Golden Eagle**, ranging from 4.0 per cent to 5.0 per cent ABV. In Hyderabad, Vinedale Breweries produces two premium lagers called **Flying Horse** and **Jubilee**, both around 5.0 per cent ABV, and two stouts called **Kingfisher** and **London**.

Stout is a hangover – a pleasant one – from British colonial times, the finest examples of which are found in Sri Lanka. McCallum's Three Coins Brewery in Colombo has a rich, fruity, chocolatey **Sando Stout** (6.0 per cent ABV), named after a Hungarian circus strongman who toured the country. It is bottom-fermenting, along with the all-malt **Three Coins Pilsener**.

The most remarkable stout

is found at the Celyon Brewery in Nuwara Eliya in the tea-planting area and close to the Holy City of Kandy. **Lion Stout** (7.5 per cent) is top-fermenting, using Czech, British and Danish malts, Styrian hops and an English yeast strain, all transported up precarious roads to the brewery 3,500 feet above sea level. It is served in cask-conditioned form by handpump in the Beer Shop in the brewery's home town and in UKD Silva in Kandy.

ASIAN BREWERS
Asia Pacific Breweries,
459 Jalan Ahmad Ibrahim, Singapore.
Bintang Brewery,
Jakarta, Indonesia.
Boon Rawd Brewery,
Bangkok, Thailand.
Ceylon Brewery,
Nuwara Eliya, Kandy, Sri Lanka.
Hong Kong Brewery,
13 Miles Castle Peak Road, Shan Tseng NT, Hong Kong.
McCallum's Brewery,
299 Union Place, Colombo, Sri Lanka.
Mohan Meakin,
Solan Brewery, Himacar, Tredesh, India.
OB Brewery,
Seoul, South Korea.
San Miguel,
40 San Miguel Avenue, Mandaluyong, Manila, Philippines.
United Breweries,
24 Grant Road, Bangalore, India.
Vinedale Breweries,
Hyderabad, Pakistan.

Tiger in the tank... Tiger Beer refreshed drinkers in colonial times

Kingfisher is India's best-known beer, now brewed under licence in England

ANTHONY BURGESS SAYS HE GOT THE TITLE FOR *TIME FOR A TIGER* FROM A SLOGAN ON A BREWERY CLOCK IN SINGAPORE. WHEN THE BREWERY ASKED TO VET HIS MANUSCRIPT, HE ANNOYED THE MANAGEMENT BY INCLUDING A REFERENCE TO CARLSBERG BEER AS WELL.

Sri Lanka's Lion Stout is a cask- and bottle-conditioned beer brewed near Kandy

167

The beers from Papua New Guinea (above and below right) have won many awards

SOUTH PACIFIC

PAPUA NEW GUINEA

The South Pacific Brewery of Port Moresby, Papua New Guinea, was the inspiration of Australians who had gone to the territory to work in the gold fields. Imports of beer were erratic and the quality variable – Allsopp's beer from England was dubbed "Allslopps". In the late 1940s Joe Bourke, a gold prospector, applied for a licence to build a hotel in the town of Wau. Annoyed by the lack of beer from Australia and other countries, he planned a brewery. With other Australians he founded a syndicate which raised £150,000 to launch South Pacific Brewery in Port Moresby, the capital of the islands. They were fortunate to discover Rudolf Meier, a Hungarian who had trained and brewed in Germany.

Production started in 1952 on a small basis. In spite of problems getting supplies of ingredients and often running short of water – the brewery uses rain water collected in tanks – the company prospered. Sales soared in the 1960s when Prohibition was ended for the islanders – until then only settlers had been allowed access to alcohol. Today the company is run largely by Papuans, though Australians are still involved as well.

The brewery made headlines in 1980 when its **Export Lager** won the gold medal in the Brewex international beer competition. It has also won awards in the Monde Sélection competition. Although it faces competition from a San Miguel brewery built by the Filipino giant, South Pacific is the brand leader with a modern plant. In the 1990s it added a stout to its range, a reflection perhaps of the residual support for the style in Australia. **SP Lager** (4.5 per cent ABV) has a perfumy aroma, a malt and vanilla palate and a cornflour finish that becomes dry. The estery character of the beer suggests a brief lagering,

SP Export Lager (5.5 per cent ABV) has a delicate aroma with a faint malt note, a light malt palate and short finish that becomes dry with faint hop notes. It doesn't drink its strength.

Niugini Gold Extra Stout (8.0 per cent ABV) is a deep brown-black in colour and has a rich chocolate and cappuccino coffee aroma, with dark fruit in the mouth and a big finish packed with hops and tart fruit.

IMPORTANT ADDRESS
South Pacific Brewery Ltd, PO Box 6550, Boroko, NCD, Papua New Guinea.

HAWAII

In the spring of 1995, Hawaii got its first microbrewery, the Kona Brewing Company. It was the dream of Spoon and Pops Khalsa, who both grew up in Oregon, US, and became lovers of good beer. When they planned their brewery they called in Ron Gansberg, John Kittredge and John Forbes from the BridgePort micro in Portland, Oregon. Together they planned two ales for the 25-barrel brewery. Brewing liquor is water naturally filtered through the volcanic aquifer. Barley and hops are imported from the US along with BridgePort's top-fermenting yeast strain.

The two beers are **Pacific Golden Ale** (3.5 per cent by weight; 22 IBUs), using a blend of pale and honey malts and hopped with Bullion and Willamette, and **Fire Rock Ale** (4.1 per cent by weight; 40 IBUs), a darker, amber beer using pale and Munich malts and hopped with Cascade, Galena and Mount Hood varieties.

The beers should appeal not only to Hawaiians and Americans but also to the British, for a half acre of the main island is still British territory and the site of an obelisk commemorates the site of the death of Captain Cook. Ships of the Royal Navy regularly visit Hawaii and the crew will now have some good ale to enjoy.

IMPORTANT ADDRESS
Kona Brewing Company, PO Box 181, Kealakekua, HI 96750.

Hawaii's microbrewery is making ales that will please both islanders and visitors

THE BEER BUSINESS

*B*EER IS BREWED THROUGHOUT THE WORLD, FROM THE EQUATOR TO – ALMOST – THE POLES. MOST OF IT IS LAGER BEER AND MORE AND MORE OF PRODUCTION IS FALLING INTO THE HANDS OF A FEW INTERNATIONAL GIANTS. BUT CONSUMERS ARE DEMANDING CHOICE AND VARIETY, AND CRAFT BREWERS IN MANY COUNTRIES ARE RUSHING TO MEET THE DEMAND.

The beer business becomes ever more complex. Both producers and consumers seem to pull in different directions. At one extreme there is growing variety. Inspired by the British experience, ale production – which includes wheat beer – is making a spirited recovery in many countries. It has found a response among drinkers seeking taste and quality. But ale makes up only a fraction of total world beer production. The split is in the region of 93 per cent lager to just seven per cent ale.

And the bulk of lager production goes to "international" brands such as Budweiser and Heineken. Because they have to appeal to a vast, polyglot mass market, such beers are common denominator brews, both unremarkable and inoffensive, avoiding the extremes of either bitterness or sweetness.

The giants of world brewing seek ever greater market share. They do so in different forms: in the case of such leading German brewers as Holsten and Löwenbräu their strategy is one of brewing under licence in other countries. Anheuser-Busch follows a similar path, though in 1995 it leased a large British brewery, the former Watney plant at Mortlake in London, in order to have greater control over the products brewed in Britain. Heineken has several licensing agreements worldwide but it has also followed a more aggressive path of outright acquisition of breweries in such diverse areas as France, Greece and Italy. Guinness, for long content to rely on building breweries in Africa and the Caribbean in order to be in strict control of production and quality, has gone on the takeover trail and is now a major force in Spanish brewing. The Belgian giant Interbrew, owners of Stella Artois and Jupiler lager brands, bought Labatt of Canada in June 1995, which will move it up several places in the table (below). Carlsberg, happy for decades to follow a similar to course to Guinness, has also become more involved in acquisitions. In Britain it has a half share in the large Carlsberg-Tetley group, formed when Allied Breweries decided to sell its brewing interests and concentrate on retailing.

The enormous power and influence of the world's biggest players can be seen in the split between production for home and overseas markets (see table on page 170).

Once a company sells more beer outside its home country the tendency will be to ignore such "old-fashioned" values as tradition, custom, regional variety and diversity and concentrate on what are known as core products: mass volume and high profit international brands.

This tendency can be seen even in Britain where ale, including stout, still commands half the market and comfortably outsells lager in the draught sector. Yet the top ten advertising "spends" in 1993 were primarily for lager.

Although by 1995 cask-conditioned beer – "real ale" – was the only growth sector of a flat beer market, just one cask beer appears in the top

WORLD'S MAJOR BEER-PRODUCING COUNTRIES

		million barrels	million hectolitres
1.	USA	144.9	237.14
2.	Germany	73.4	120.13
3.	China	61.4	100.49
4.	Japan	43.0	70.37
5.	UK	34.1	55.81
6.	Brazil	32.4	53.03
7.	Russia and CIS	30.6	50.08
8.	Mexico	26.0	42.55
9.	Spain	15.9	26.02
10.	Czechoslovakia	14.2*	23.24*

*1992 before separation into two countries

WORLD'S BIGGEST BREWERS
(ANNUAL PRODUCTION)

		million barrels	million hectolitres
1.	Anheuser-Busch	62.35	102.0
2.	Heineken	32.82	53.7
3.	Miller	30.75	50.3
4.	Kirin	21.39	35.0
5.	Carlsberg	21.30	34.0
6.	Brahma	17.12	28.0
7.	Foster's	15.89	26.0
8.	BSN/Kronenbourg	15.28	25.0
9.	Santo Domingo (Columbia)	14.10	23.5
10.	Coors	14.06	23.0
11.	South African	13.99	22.9
12.	Modelo (Mexico)	13.51	22.1
13.	Moctezuma (Mexico)	12.41	20.3
14.	Antarctica	11.68	19.1
15.	Asahi	11.61	19.0
16.	Stroh	11.31	18.5
17.	Interbrew	10.08	16.5
18.	Polar	9.53	15.6
19.	San Miguel	8.55	14.0
20.	Bass	8.37	13.7
21.	Heileman	7.33	12.0
22.	Labatt	7.03	11.5
23.	Guinness	6.97	11.4

Sources: Brewers and Licensed Retailers Association (UK); CAMRA Research Department

TOP 10 DRINKING COUNTRIES
(ANNUAL CONSUMPTION PER HEAD)

		Pints	Litres
1.	Czech Republic	293.5	166.8
2.	Germany	253.8	144.2
3.	Denmark	225.6	128.2
4.	Irish Republic	225.2	128.0
5.	Austria	215.7	122.6
6.	Belgium	197.1*	112.0*
7.	New Zealand	184.4	104.8
8.	United Kingdom	180.0	102.3
9.	Australia	179.5	102.0
10.	Hungary	172.6	98.1

*Includes Grand Duchy of Luxembourg

ANNUAL ADVERTISING SPEND BY BRITISH BREWERS
(£1,000s)

1.	Guinness	8,940
2.	Heineken	6,314
3.	Budweiser	5,094
4.	Carlsberg	5,062
5.	Foster's	4,521
6.	Holsten	3,643
7.	Castlemaine	3,588
8.	Boddington	3,515
9.	Murphy	3,380
10.	Carling	3,339

Sources: Register-MEAL, The Advertising Association, NTC

A merger is announced... executives from Scottish & Newcastle and Courage celebrate their union

ten advertising spends. That is Boddingtons, owned by Whitbread, and the advertising is split between the draught version of the beer and a canned one. Guinness and Murphy are processed stouts, the rest of the list is made up of lagers. Of these, only Carling – despite its Canadian origins – is a British brand, now owned by Bass. The rest are all international brands brewed under licence. The reason is not difficult to divine: cask beer has a short shelf-life – about one week – while pasteurized processed beers have a life of about four months. As a result of both longevity and high pricing, processed beers are far more profitable than cask. Keg ales and stouts are twice as profitable as cask, lager is four times as profitable. Government investigations have found that brewers charge up to ten pence a pint more for lager than for a cask beer of similar strength.

It is the urge for ever greater market share that fuels takeovers, mergers and acquisitions. Even the American giants are not immune. Anheuser-Busch has close to a 50 per cent share of the US beer market yet it has taken a substantial stake in one of the larger craft brewers, Redhook of Seattle. A-B has also bought an 18 per cent stake in Modelo of Mexico. Miller, which is showing an interest in craft brewing, too, has bought out Pierre Celis, brewer of Belgian-style wheat beer, in Texas.

In Europe, BSN, Heineken and Interbrew dominate France, Belgium and Holland. The worry is that when companies of this size start to buy up craft breweries – lambic and gueuze producers in the case of BSN and Interbrew – traditional beers become victims of the mass market mentality. Interbrew has also blurred the distinction between genuine Trappist ales and Abbey ones with its vigorous promotion of such Abbey beers as Leffe. At present only Germany stands aloof from the scramble for market share. It still has around 1,200 breweries, all of them regional, no one

Henninger vigorously promotes its beers but German brewers remain regional with no national giants

single company dominating the market. Whether the Germans can remain immune from international market forces is doubtful in the long term. The same forces are certain to have a detrimental effect on brewing in the old Eastern bloc as can be seen most painfully in the Czech Republic where such a magnificent and innovative beer as Pilsner Urquell has had its brewing methods adapted to meet the perceived needs of the Western market.

In Britain, which once mirrored Germany in the number and diversity of its brewers, brewing is now dominated by a handful of giants constantly elbowing for even greater market share. In the spring of 1995, Scottish and Newcastle (best known under its former separate names of McEwan and Younger) bought the Courage group from its owner, Foster's, for £425 million. This leapfrogged S&N above Bass into the top position in British brewing with a 35 per cent share of the market. It means that, between them, just four enormous groups – Bass, Scottish-Courage, Carlsberg-Tetley, and Whitbread – account for around 85 per cent of all beer brewed in Britain.

DISTRIBUTION OF BEER PRODUCTION BETWEEN HOME AND EXPORT MARKETS (MILLION HLS)		
	Local	Worldwide
Anheuser-Busch	101.9	102.0
Miller	49.5	50.3
Coors	23.0	23.0
Stroh	16.5	18.5
Heileman	11.3	12.0
Heineken	6.9	53.7
Carlsberg	5.3	21.3
Interbrew	10.4	16.5
BSN (France)	10.2	25.0
Holsten	7.0	7.9
Löwenbräu	1.4	2.8
Foster's	8.2	26.0
Labatt	9.6	11.5
Santo Domingo (Columbia)	15.2	23.5
Kirin	34.9	35.1
Asahi	16.9	19.0
Brahma (Brazil)	22.5	28.1
Modelo (Mexico)	21.0	22.1
Moctezuma (Mexico)	20.0	20.3
San Miguel (Philippines)	11.2	14.0
Polar (Venezuela)	14.0	15.6

Sources: Brewers and Licensed Retailers Association (UK)

MARKETING FROTH

There is a certain fevered frenzy in the marketing departments of giant corporations that forces them to think up ever more bizarre departures from the brewing norm. The aim is to attract to beer drinking those groups – young people in general and women in particular – who are not great consumers of the product. The marketing gurus believe that success can be achieved by flashy advertising for products that lack all the attributes that seasoned drinkers love in beer: the malty, fruity, yeasty, hoppy aromas and flavours that make it such a delight. In their place come "lite" beers, dry beers and ice beers, concoctions largely devoid of taste let alone merit. But this type of market is fickle. Young people constantly crave new pleasures, new kicks, new fashion drinks. The brewers struggle to keep one step ahead of the fashion, thinking up weird but far from wonderful new brews. Briefly, coloured lagers and – the reverse of the same duff coinage - colour-less lagers burst upon the scene and quickly disappear. Such practices would be risible and could be ignored save that the quest for blandness and mass acceptability rubs off on to mainstream beers as well.

There is a worldwide complaint that much-loved beers have lost some of their character in recent years. In lagers this may express itself in a reduction in colour to make brands acceptably light on the world market, matched by a less evident hop character. Where ale is concerned, yeasts are genetically engineered to make them "drop bright" quickly so that the length of time for secondary fermentation is reduced to the bare minimum. But without a proper conditioning, ales cannot develop those ripe and fruity/hoppy characteristics that allow them to stand out from the pack. In Britain some of the big ale brewers are producing versions of their products in a pasteurized form served by a mix of nitrogen and carbon dioxide gases. They boast of the beers' "smoothness", a weasel word meaning bland.

BUCKING THE TREND

But all is not doom and gloom. Craft, family and regional brewers survive and prosper. In Britain, where Anheuser-Busch has built market share for Budweiser after a disastrous start by the simple expedient of throwing millions of pounds at the product through advertising and promotion, the rival Czech Budweiser Budvar has crept into the top 100 imported beers without a penny spent on it. With help from CAMRA, which has fought for Budvar's independence, beer lovers have discovered the beer and drunk it with appreciation in ever-increasing volumes. Craft brewers blossom in Britain, adding to choice, and pleasure. The market share of the speciality beers of Belgium, though small, is growing. France has rediscovered a beer culture. A growing number of Dutch people know there is more to beer than standardized lagers. Even in the great lager land of Germany drinkers are turning to ales as well with appreciation. Sweet ice-cold lagers have lost a little of their hegemony in Australia. In the United States,

most encouraging of all, the beer renaissance gathers an unstoppable pace and momentum, 500 craft breweries in 1995, 1,000 expected by the year 2,000, with a variety and abundance of styles that would have beggared belief twenty years ago in a land dominated by Bud and Lite.

As with wine and whisky, the great beers – the noble beers – of both the ale and lager families will appeal only to a minority of drinkers. But such drinkers are the flag-wavers and the proselytizers. The noble beers will survive because people, both brewers and consumers, care sufficiently passionately about them to preserve them for the next generation of connoisseurs to enjoy and cherish.

CONSUMING INTERESTS

CAMRA

The Campaign for Real Ale (CAMRA) is the world's most successful consumer organization. It has transformed the British brewing industry in the interests of drinkers and encouraged a worldwide development of craft brewing that has restored traditional values, quality and choice.

The international appreciation of Belgian ales, the discovery of fine beers in France and the Netherlands, the struggle to maintain the independence of Czech brewers and, above all, the mushrooming of craft brewing in the United States are all the result of the ripple effect of CAMRA's activities in Britain.

The campaign was launched in 1971 as a drinkers' revolt against keg beer. Mergers and takeovers in the 1960s and 1970s had created six giant brewing groups determined to break away from regional beers and concentrate on national brands. Instead of cask-conditioned ales, the nationals plumped for keg – a filtered and pasteurized version of ale that was consistent, had a long shelf life, was highly profitable but lacked the richness and maturity of flavour of cask.

Many drinkers mourned the loss of their regional ales but there was no one to speak for them until CAMRA arrived. It was a mass movement waiting to happen; within a couple of years

Plaque outside the Farriers Arms in St Albans, Herts, recording a historic meeting

THE FIRST BRANCH MEETING OF THE CAMPAIGN FOR REAL ALE WAS HELD HERE 20TH NOV 1972

it had a thousand members and by the late 1970s it had 28,000 members. It organized beer festivals, it staged mock funerals outside breweries that had axed cask beer, and it produced reports detailing the overpricing of keg beers and the poor materials used in their production. It began to publish the annual *Good Beer Guide* listing the best pubs that sold "real ale", as CAMRA dubbed cask beer.

The campaign inspired regional brewers to stick to cask beer and it encouraged the first wave of new "microbrewers", usually homebrewers keen to expand, to add to choice and diversity. Finally the national brewers were forced to concede they had misread the market and began to brew and sell cask ale again.

CAMRA spread its wings. As well as cask beer, it began to take a keen interest in the survival of the British pub and organized annual awards for pub design. A technical committee studied brewing methods and ingredients and set up tasting panels to give accurate assessments of beers for use in the *Good Beer Guide*. It organized an annual award for the best beers in different categories, culminating in the Champion Beer of Britain blind tasting that coincides with the Great British Beer Festival. It is CAMRA's influence and research into old recipes that has led to the renaissance of such forgotten brewing styles as porter, stout, old ales, barley wines and winter ales.

CAMRA in the 1990s began to grow at a startling speed and by mid-1995 was close to 50,000 members. There were a number of reasons for the growth. The campaign was holding an ever-greater number of beer festivals throughout the country, as many as 15 a month. Furthermore, many drinkers were concerned about rising beer prices and brewery profiteering. They had also discovered through a government investigation into the brewing industry that the national groups charged more for their beers than regionals, and manipulated the market in their favour through discounts and loans to pubs. As a result of lobbying by CAMRA, the government introduced a rule forcing the big brewers, who control most of the country's pubs, to take "guest" real ales from other, smaller breweries – at a stroke improving choice for millions of pubgoers.

EBCU

In 1990 three beer organizations set up the European Beer Consumers' Union (EBCU). The founding members were CAMRA, PINT from the Netherlands and OBP from Belgium. PINT – pronounced with a short "i" – stands for Promotie Informatie Traditioneel Bier: Promotion and Information about Traditional Beer. It was founded in 1980 to campaign for traditional beer and pubs in the Netherlands. It produces a bi-monthly magazine and runs beer festivals, including the annual Bokbier (strong beer) festival in Amsterdam in October.

OBP was set up in Belgium in 1984. The full name means Objectieve Bier Proevers or Objective Beertasters. It is primarily concerned with designating beer styles in a punctilious fashion. OBP's best-known member, Peter Crombecq, publishes the annual *Bierjaarboek* with detailed information and tasting notes about every beer brewed in Belgium. The organization campaigns against monopolies and has lobbied the Belgian government to defend the status of lambic and gueuze beers.

EBCU has become an effective lobbying force in Europe and has important contacts in the European Commission and European Parliament. It argues the case for a European-wide agreement on ingredients listings for beers and has won *appellation contrôlée* status for lambic and gueuze. It has widened its influence by recruiting groups in France, Finland, Sweden and Switzerland.

CAMRA CANADA

British CAMRA was the inspiration for its Canadian off-shoot. But unlike the campaign in Britain, CAMRA Canada was unable to save a brewing industry that had become dominated by two giants, Molson (including Carling) and Labatt, which had weakened the country's great ale-brewing tradition in favour of bland lagers and such high-tech products as "ice beer". CAMRA Canada was formed in the early 1980s when both expatriate Britons and native Canadians came together to pool resources and brew good beer at home. This was no easy task as both home-brewing and brewpubs were illegal at the time. The campaign has been successful in getting these bans lifted in most provinces. Brewpubs now flourish on the West Coast thanks to the influence of British

expats and in French-speaking Quebec, which had retained an ale-drinking culture as many of the original settlers came from northern France.

As a result of the vast size of the country, the campaign has effectively split into autonomous regional groups, lobbying for a sliding scale of beer tax to favour craft brewers, easier access into Canada for imported beer, and lifting remaining restrictions on brewpubs and home-brewing.

AMERICAN HOMEBREWERS' ASSOCIATION

With no consumer movement in the United States, the revival of interest in quality beer has come from a mass home-brewers' movement. The AHA has provided a forum for home-brewers to pool ideas and resources. It has also become a publishing powerhouse, beginning with a highly professional magazine *Zymurgy* (from the Greek word for the art and science of brewing) and progressing to a series of books on international beer styles. The AHA has been a genuine catalyst, inspiring many home-brewers to move into commercial brewing. It has turned the definition of beer styles into an art form, defining in minute detail the difference between, for example, a brown porter and a dark porter.

The high-spot of the year is the Great American Beer Festival. Its awards to commercial and home-brewers in a vast number of categories are highly prized. The influence of the AHA can been seen in the fact that two US brewing giants, Anheuser-Busch and Miller, are now producing ales and stouts as they see the beer market beginning to move away from bland lagers.

KEY ADDRESSES

Campaign for Real Ale,
230 Hatfield Road, St Albans AL1 4LW.
Phone: 01727 867201.
EBCU,
care of CAMRA as above.
OBP,
Postbus 32, 2600 Berchem 5, Belgium.
PINT,
Postbus 3757, 1001 AN Amsterdam.
Fax: 020-411 6915.
CAMRA Canada,
10 Ontario Street West, Suite 604, Montreal,
Quebec H2X 1Y6. Fax: 514-844-0102.

GAZETTEER OF PUBS, BARS AND TAVERNS

*B*EER CAN BE ENJOYED AT HOME BUT IT IS A CONVIVIAL DRINK, BEST CONSUMED IN THE COMPANY OF OTHERS IN THE CHEERFUL SURROUNDINGS OF A PUBLIC HOUSE, BAR OR CAFÉ. IT IS IN PUBS AND BARS THAT BEER ON DRAUGHT, WHETHER ALE OR LAGER, IS AT ITS BEST AND FRESHEST, DRAWN FROM THE CELLAR AND LOVINGLY CARED FOR BY EXPERIENCED STAFF. WE OFFER A SELECTION OF SOME OF THE BEST OUTLETS THROUGHOUT THE WORLD FOR ENJOYING BEER IN ALL ITS GLORY.

BELGIUM

BRUSSELS

Falstaff, 17 rue Henri Maus.

More a restaurant than a pub, the Falstaff is famous for its many extraordinary features. Its location ensures a well-heeled clientele – it's right next to the Bourse or Stock Exchange. The decor is an odd mixture of art deco, art nouveau and rococo, characterized by elaborate mirrors and stained glass. The opening hours are unbelievable and better defined by the closing times: the Falstaff shuts at 5 a.m. – and opens again for breakfast two hours later. The full menu, though, is only served between noon and 2 p.m. – but the huge range of Belgian beers, especially Trappist ales, is available virtually round the clock.

A La Morte Subite,

7 rue Montagnes aux Herbes Potagères.

All visitors to Brussels find themselves gawping open-mouthed at the splendours of the Grand' Place. When you've finished gawping, just nip up the Galeries Royale St Hubert arcade for traditional gueuze at the Morte Subite. You won't die – the café is named after a card-game once played there regularly (and the beer Morte Subite is named after the café). The café itself is very basic – just a single long bar, with prices painted up on the mirrors and a few tables and chairs. The range of food is basic, too, more snack than meal. But then, you're only here for the beer.

Moeder Lambic Ixelles,

Boendaalse Steenweg 441, Elsene.

Take a number 95 or 96 bus from outside the Falstaff and get off at the Ixelles Cemetery in the suburb of Elsene, and you find yourself at a café which serves more than 50 Belgian beers on draught alone and a range of bottled beers. For avid beer tourists this is the place to find many of the rarities and oddities for which Belgium is justly famed.

't Spinnekopke, 1 Place du Jardin aux Fleurs.

Just five minutes' walk from the Grand' Place is the Spinnekopke or Little Spider where the speciality is not just drinking beer but cooking with it – owner Jean Rodriguez is an acknowledged authority and author on the subject. The beer-list runs to 70 or so brews, the cooking is excellent and you'd never believe beer was such a versatile ingredient. If all you want is a drink, try the draught faro and lambic from the local Cantillon Brewery.

BRUGES

't Brugs Beertje, Kemelstraat 5.

Is this Belgium's most famous bar? It deserves to be, for although there's nothing special about the setting, the building, or the decor, there's something very special about owner Jan de Bruyne. The evangelist of native styles, de Bruyne has spearheaded the Belgian beer revival of recent years and refuses to give Pils-style lagers house room. He does, however, have room for some 200 proper native ales, and in the back bar, known as the Beer Academie, he holds tutored tastings for parties of acolytes from all over the world.

GHENT

De Hopduvel, Rokerelstraat 10.

Ghent's huge medieval prosperity was founded on textiles, and its architectural heritage is worthy of a city that was once the wealthiest in Northern Europe. De Hopduvel is a stiffish walk from the city centre but the café does not disappoint. A maze of tiny rooms hung with assorted breweriana, the café also has a covered garden at the back and a popular grill upstairs. The list of 120 beers includes a range specially commissioned from the Van Steenberge Brewery.

ANTWERP

Kulminator, Vleminckveld 32.

Although not much of a tourist trap, Antwerp, and especially the Old Town round the cathedral, is extremely attractive and boasts many fine cafés. On the edge of the Old Town is the elegant, candle-lit Kulminator with its staggering list of 500 beers. This is an embarrassment of riches even by Belgian standards, but then the Kulminator has no food and is the unofficial headquarters of Belgium's beer consumers' association, the Objectieve Bier Proevers.

FRANCE

LILLE

Les Brasseurs, Place de la Gare.

Opposite the railway station, this is a large and opulent brewpub, the first of a small chain in northern France. A tiny brewhouse produces a range of top-fermenting ales, including an amber and a wheat beer plus seasonal offerings. The front bar has alcove seats while to the rear a restaurant area offers a range of dishes including the Lille speciality, a thin pizza-style bread with a choice of toppings.

PARIS

A La Pinte du Nord, 38 rue Saint-Quentin.

One minute from Gare du Nord, this small bar specializes in French and Belgian beers, including Pelforth Brune and Leffe Blonde. There is simple food and accommodation as well.

Frog and Rosbif, 116 rue St Denis.

This Parisian brewpub is based on the famous Firkin chain in London. The bar is decked out with old church pews, food includes steak and kidney pudding, Scotch eggs, Cornish pasties and bangers and mash. The microbrewery produces 800 litres a week of Inseine (4.2 per cent ABV) and Parislytic (5.2 per cent ABV) brewed with English malt, hops and yeast.

The Cricketer, rue des Mathurins.

Near the Opéra, this is a traditional English pub – the fixtures and fittings were brought over, lock, stock and barrel, from Ipswich – and offers Adnams of Suffolk's Extra Bitter and Broadside. The walls are awash with fascinating (to a cricket lover) old prints of the game but must cause great head-scratching among the locals.

CZECH REPUBLIC

PRAGUE

U Fleku, 11 Kremencova, New Town.

Named after the proprietors in the eighteenth century, Jakob and Dorota Flekovskymi, U Fleku is the last survivor of Prague's long tradition of brewpubs. The recipe for its black beer is reputed to go back to the late fifteenth century. It has become one of the most popular meeting places in Prague for foreigners, even though it is some way outside the centre, partly because of its size (pub and beer garden together can seat 500), partly because of its heritage, and partly because most of the staff speak German and even a little English. One peculiarity of U Fleku, perhaps because of its tourist-trap status, is that drinks are paid for one by one rather than by running up a tab.

U Kalicha, Na bojisti 12, Nové Mesto, Prague 2.

The Chalice is a shrine to the Good Soldier Schweik (Svejk in Czech) the anti-hero of all anti-heroes, the conscripted militia man who did his best to avoid fighting and dreamed of the girls, the plum brandy and the beer in U Kalicha. There are drawings and extracts from the book decorating the walls of the large tavern. Writer Jaroslav Hasek modelled Schweik on a regular in the pub.

Howzat for a French pub? The Cricketer in Paris is dedicated to the Anglophile's summer game with fine Suffolk ales

U Fleku is Prague's famous brewpub with a strong dark lager. Left, Les Brasseurs offers instant refreshment to train travellers in Lille

U Černého Vola, Loretánské námesti 1, Hradčany, Prague 1.

The Black Ox is in a superb location, across the road from the Loreto church and close to the castle and cathedral. The small tavern has stained glass windows, rustic benches, sausage snacks and the sublime beer from Velké Popovice.

U Zlatého Tygra, 17 Husova.

The Golden Tiger owes much of its present good fortune to the fact that its 13th-century cellars are regarded as ideal for storing beer – and Czechs like their beer properly kept. However it has also gained fame as a gathering place for artists and writers: President Václav Havel was a regular during his spells out of prison, and still has the place opened up after hours occasionally to give official guests a taste of what Czech beer ought to taste like. As a result, the pub is rather too small for its popularity, so a back room is set aside for VIPs. The present building is baroque and was one of the first in Prague to take to the new Pilsner beer which was introduced in the 1840s. It is very typical of Prague pubs, which means it's permanently packed, the air is opaque with tobacco smoke, and the waiters are brusque.

ČESKÉ BUDĚJOVICE

The Old Meat Market, off main square.

This spacious beer hall with a long central corridor and side alcoves has been fashioned from a meat market and the food on offer is still heavy going for herbivores. But the beer is magnificent, fresh from the Budweiser Budvar Brewery down the road and served at great speed by black-suited and white-aproned waiters who run up a tab on the back of a beer mat.

GERMANY

COLOGNE AND DÜSSELDORF

See brewpubs listed in section of Germany in The World A–Z of Beer (see pages 80–82) for Kölsch and Alt beer outlets.

MUNICH

Augustiner Gaststätte, Neuhauserstrasse 16.

The flagship for the smallest of Munich's six breweries, Augustiner, the Gaststätte is an art nouveau gem in the middle of the city's pedestrianized shopping area between Karlsplatz and

Munich's Hofbraühaus – royal court brewery – complete with oompah bands and lederhosen

Marienplatz. As well as a big basic beer hall, the tavern boasts an ornate restaurant and an oval garden. Bavarian dishes such as pork chops in beer sauce are served all day alongside Augustiner Hell, Dunkel and wheat beer on tap, and bottled Maximator Doppelbock in spring and Märzen in the autumn.

Donisl, corner of Marienplatz and Weinstrasse.

This is the bierkeller with everything. It's got history: built in the fourteenth century as a gaol, it eventually became a weinstube and, in the seventeenth century, a bierkeller; in the last days of the Second World War it was flattened by the Allies but has been lovingly recreated. It's got variety: an oompah band serenades (if that's the right word) from a minstrel's gallery, while one of the bars is a noted gay hang-out. It's got a good story: in 1983, when it used to open all night every night, it was the centre of the celebrated Knockout Drop Affair, with staff slipping mickeys into the drinks of the small-hours customers and then rifling their wallets. And it's got beer: Hell, wheat beer and Pilsner from Hacker-Pschorr on tap, with Dunkel in bottle.

Hofbräuhaus, Platzl 9.

The Hofbräuhaus is so much the quintessence of everybody's idea of a Munich beer hall that one suspects that all the stiffish old boys with Tyrolean hats and toothbrush moustaches are actually paid extras. This great cavern of a place has rustic benches, many side alcoves and a large, sunlit garden in spring and summer. There's the obligatory oompah band, and the hefty barmaids moving like icebreakers through the throng, five steins in each hand, plus the association with Adolf Hitler (although no blue plaque, surprisingly) – the Brownshirts met here in the 1930s. The only unpleasantness these days comes from occasional shouting-matches between Australian and New Zealand visitors. The beers are from the Hofbräu, once owned by the Bavarian royal family. And the secret of carrying so many steins, incidentally, is not to fill them more than half-full.

Mathäser Bierstadt, Bayerstrasse 5.

If you hate oompah bands, the whole of Munich is to be avoided but especially the Mathäser Bierstadt, where for a small fee they actually let punters conduct one. This is the biggest of the Munich beer halls and is the Löwenbräu flagship. Its two halls and profusion of smaller rooms can accommodate 5,000 drinkers, and for those who overindulge there is a genuine vomitorium.

Schneider Weisses Bräuhaus, Tal 10.

Bomber Command was here in the Second World War and when the Lancasters left there was no Schneider Brewery left. Rather than rebuild on the site, however, the company decided to relocate to the greenbelt and convert the old Bräuhaus into a beer hall. Schneider had taken over the brewery in the nineteenth century when the traditional cloudy wheat beer was being superseded by Pilsner. Wheat beer is still the speciality although Dunkel and Pilsner are served from the wood during the evening in this large, often crowded tavern a few yards from the Marienplatz. Service is fast and furious, food is simple and basic – wheat beer and white sausage is the staple – and on the way to the toilets you can look at photos showing the results of Allied bomb damage.

Paulaner Bräuhaus, Kapuzinerplatz 5.

This big brewpub with its marble-clad main entrance and gleaming coppers is the home of Pilsner beers in Munich. The style was brought back from Bohemia by two brewing students, Eugen and Ludwig Thomas, who started up the brewery more than 100 years ago. Eventually it was taken over and converted into a beer hall by Paulaner, which started brewing on the site again in 1989. A draught Pilsner is still on the menu, but the unfiltered wheat beer and Hell are the house specialities. The pub also has a restaurant and, curiously, a library.

Forschungsbräustuberl,

Unterhachingstrasse 76, Perlach.

This pub takes five months of every year off. The Jakob family, who have been brewing their Pilsissimus Export and St Jakobus Bock here since 1936, take the whole business very seriously and spend their annual holiday researching and experimenting for other brewers. While the bräu-stuberl is open – from March to October – the two beers are served in earthenware litre jugs, with only cold sausage and cheese on the food menu. This is a place for people who like – and understand – their beer.

Unionsbräu Keller, Einsteinstrasse 42.

Heretical to say that Germany has followed where Britain and America led, but in the field of brew-

THE MUNICH OKTOBERFEST

he Munich Oktoberfest is the world's oldest celebration of beer and, in terms of the amount of beer consumed, is also the biggest festival, though more modern events in Britain and the US offer greater choice. Potential visitors should be aware that, despite its name, the festival ends on the first weekend in October and runs for 16 days from the middle of September. During that time more than 10 million pints of beer will be consumed and the millions of visitors will also despatch 600,000 sausages, 750,000 roast chickens and 65,000 pork knuckles. The Oktoberfest is not exactly gemütlich for vegetarians.

The origins of this lederhosen and lager extravaganza date from 1810 when the Crown Prince Ludwig of Bavaria married Princess Theresa. The locals organized a festival on a meadow just outside the city centre and called it the Theresienwiese – Theresa's Meadow – or the 'Wiese for short. That first festival was "dry" – there was just a horse race and fair – but this is Bavaria and the annual event soon attracted the Munich brewers and the thirsty locals. Once the railway reached Munich, the festival started to attract revellers from all over Germany and Central Europe.

Ten giant canvas beer halls are the centre of the modern festival. Only the Munich brewers are allowed to have a tent and some of them cheat. For example, both Hacker and Pschorr have separate tents even though they have been one company for years and are now owned by Paulaner, which also has its own tent. On the other hand, Crown Prince Luitpold of Kaltenberg has been refused permission to have a tent, even though he has opened a brewpub in the city and brews some of the most interesting beer in the area.

The tents are all similar in style: row after row of benches where drinkers down great mugs of beer. In the centre of each tent is a podium for the inevitable oompah band which in between other ditties plays an interminable number called *Ein Prosit* (A Toast) with which all and sundry join in. On the Saturday of the opening day of the festival a parade of brewers' horse-drawn drays, bands and representatives of every craft in Bavaria winds it way through the city centre. The following day, a shorter parade which is confined to brewers' drays puts on a vivid display at the Theresienweise. It all adds up to a carnival of bibulous pleasure. The only disappointment is the disappearance of the true Oktoberfest beers, the Märzen beers brewed in March and lagered until September. Corner-cutting brewers have switched instead to Oktoberfest beers, pleasant, well-rounded and highly quaffable but a shadow of the traditional beers that made this festival a benchmark for all others to follow.

Beer-lovers planning to visit the festival are advised to book accommodation months in advance as every hotel and guest house in Munich and the suburbs fill to bursting point. The tourist office will book rooms but will accept only written requests: Fremdenverkersamt, Postfach, 8000 Munich 1. Fax: 49-89-239-1313.

Not to be outdone by the Müncheners, the people of Stuttgart also have an Oktoberfest called the Cannstatter Volksfest. It takes place in a suburb of the city called Cannstatt on a meadow known in the local dialect as the Wasen.

The world's greatest beer extravaganza... ten giant tents with beer and – guess what? – oompah bands. Inset, the festival begins with a parade

pubs it is true. This one was established in 1991 by Löwenbräu, which had taken over and closed down the Unionsbräu in 1922. It still serves the Löwenbräu range, but the real stars are the unfiltered Hell from the wood and the traditional seasonal ales brewed and lagered in the cellar. A plus is that all the ingredients are organic. The tiny brewhouse is open to view at the back and, fascinatingly, the wooden fermenters are tilted at an angle in exactly the same manner as the now redundant ones at Pilsner Urquell in Pilsen.

MUNICH BEER GARDENS

Am Nockherberg, Hochstrasse 77.
This is one of the original beer gardens, which sprang up beside the cool caves used for lagering before artificial refrigeration was invented. Here Paulaner beers are served on draught, but customers are welcome to bring their own picnic lunches. During the Starkbierfest in March drinkers spill out of the beerhalls and into the Nockherberg, completely filling its 3,000 seats. The garden also fulfils the need for a public park for the inhabitants of the surrounding flats.

Chinesischer Turm, Englischer Garten Park.
A Chinese Tower in an English garden in a German city may seem unreal enough but what gives it a surreal air is that the 50-foot pagoda around which the 6,500 seats are arranged is also a platform for... you've guessed it, an oompah band. The beers are from Löwenbräu and an added attraction is an antique wooden carousel and organ. In the summer the park is home to the MCC – Munich Cricket Club – whose arcane rituals bemuse the Germans. The club has a special rule that a batsman cannot be given out if his concentration was disturbed by a nude jogger.

Hofbräu Keller, Innere Wienerstrasse 19.
This garden, one of the city's oldest, was attached to the original Hofbräu Brewery until it was demolished in 1990 to make way for a hotel. The old bierkeller, though, is still an integral part of the garden. Hofbräu beers are served, including the full range of seasonal specialities.

The secret of carrying so many foaming jugs of beer is not to fill them too full

GREAT BRITAIN

LONDON

Argyll Arms, 18 Argyll Street, W1.
The Argyll is just off Oxford Street, next door to Oxford Circus tube station and almost opposite the world-famous Palladium music hall. This splendid Victorian pub, with its giant mirrors and maze of little bars, is consequently always packed with tourists and office-workers. The "gents" toilet is a masterwork of mid-Victorian craftsmanship, while a unique survival is the manager's office, sited so that he can see what his patrons are up to in all five bars.

George, 55 Great Portland Street, W1.
The BBC's local, the George was once patronized by the beer-drinking luminaries of the great days of radio – Dylan Thomas, Louis MacNeice, George Orwell. A magnificent Victorian pub with gas mantles, polished panel work and old wine casks, it is familiarly known as the Gluepot. The name was often given to pubs frequented by furniture workers, joiners and cabinet makers and was attached to the George, rather scornfully, by the conductor Sir Henry Wood who used the Queen's Hall next door to rehearse the BBC Symphony Orchestra.

Lamb, 94 Lamb's Conduit Street, WC1.
With London's pubs so beset by fake Victoriana, it's refreshing to find one where the real thing survives, right down to the "snob-screens" above the bar which supposedly prevented Victorian and Edwardian middle-class patrons being recognized from the public bar when they were entertaining ladies other than their wives. Another big plus for the Lamb – once the Bloomsbury Set's local and long a favourite with London University academics – was its stubborn adherence to real ale when all about was keg. The Lamb is a particularly pleasant resort on a hot summer's night as it stands on a pedestrian precinct. It is one of the finest outlets for Young's superb ales.

Princess Louise, 208 High Holborn, WC1.
Long a London landmark with its peerless location, long bar and palatial gents' loo, the Princess Louise was dying on its feet in the 1970s as a Watney house where only Red Barrel keg beer was served and where few ever ventured. But when Watney sold the dingy and dilapidated wreck, it turned into a flourishing and vibrant

Beer and pool downstairs, a spot of culture upstairs. The Old Red Lion is one of London's best theatre pubs

free house, well maintained and awash with a grand selection of the finest ales the kingdom has to offer. The pub has magnificent moulded ceilings, ornate columns, glass screens, imposing mirrors and snug side alcoves.

Cittie of Yorke, 22 High Holborn WC1.
An amazing Victorian recreation of a fifteenth-century gothic Great Hall. The clientele, too, represent a Victorian recreation of a medieval original: they're mainly barristers, clerks and judges from the nearby Law Courts and Inns of Court. Other Victorian survivals include a gantry over the great wine-butts, used until the Second World War by the staff who had to keep the casks topped up, private booths of the sort once common in central London pubs but now a rarity, and the capital's longest bar counter. In keeping with its name, the pub is now owned by Yorkshire brewer Sam Smith's. In winter the bar is always toastingly warm thanks to the heat from open stoves.

Castle, 34 Cowcross Street, EC1.
Blood once mixed with money in this pub on the edge of the City, where Smithfield Market "bummarees" or meat porters in their offal-spattered overalls rubbed shoulders with Savile Row-suited stockbrokers and investment bankers. The bummarees have gone but there are still plenty of City gents. The Castle is the only London pub that is also a pawnbroker. A large mural on the wall, not quite obscured by the out-of-place Wurlitzer juke box, says that George V, strapped for cash

after gambling, "popped" or pawned his watch for £5 in the pub. In more modern times, the "pop shop" side of the business allowed bummarees to spend their wages before they got them.

Old Mitre, Ely Court, Ely Place, Hatton Garden, EC1.
This ranks as one of London's most hidden pubs, for although tourists by the thousand surge past within yards, few find its secluded courtyard entrance. Not that it's ever less than packed, for plenty do know it, not least for its place in the chaotic legal history of a country which has never completely shaken off its medieval cobwebs. The pub was, in the late medieval period, part of the "liberty" of the Bishop of Ely, Cambridgeshire: that is, it had earlier been the Bishop's town house and he still had the licensing of it, so London constables had no jurisdiction there. This situation, once repeated in odd corners of many cities, has now been regularized, so if you have just robbed one of the diamond-merchants of Hatton Garden, do not count on the pursuit stopping at the gates of Ely Place. The courtyard of the pub has the stump of a tree round which Queen Elizabeth I is reputed to have danced.

Old Red Lion, 418 St John Street, EC1.
One of the best-known of London's many theatre pubs, the Old Red Lion is a handsome four-storey, red-brick building, dating from the turn of the century but on a site which has been a tavern for centuries. This small patch of London once contained many interesting pubs: the Angel,

Islington, itself has long gone and is now buried under a Co-op Bank; next to it was an ancient inn called the Peacock; the Crown & Woolpack, derelict for a long time, was a haunt of red revolutionaries and had a bust of Lenin; and the Empress of Russia, insensitively modernized, was long a favourite of both cast and audiences from the Sadler's Wells theatre nearby. The Old Red Lion itself, with its tiny upstairs auditorium, its well-preserved and plush interior, and its good food, thrives. It claims that Tom Paine wrote the first draft of *The Rights of Man* there.

Dirty Dick's, 204 Bishopsgate, EC2.

The original Dirty Dick was an 18th-century London ironmonger called Nathaniel Bentley, whose shop stood on the site. Bentley was tragically transformed into a dirty and ragged recluse after his fiancée died on the eve of their wedding, and he was so grief-stricken, it is said, that he never washed again. The modern Dirty Dick's dates back to about 1870 and has bars in the vaults and on the first floor as well as at ground level. The main bar, until a few years ago, was decorated with ghastly relics such as two mummified cats which were said to have been in Bentley's shop – although why an ironmonger should be selling mummified cats is anyone's guess. All that is gone now in favour of bare bricks and stripped floors, along with ales from Young's of Wandsworth.

Black Friar, 174 Queen Victoria Street, EC4.

London's only no-holds-barred art nouveau pub was designed in 1903 as a celebration in bronze and coloured marble of the Dominican friars whose monastery once stood on the site. It has recently been restored to its full florid glory at a cost of nearly a million pounds. The wedge-shaped building has a welter of designs showing monks carousing. The great marble-topped bar serves a small area with a vast open fireplace while marble alcoves offer some comfortable seating areas. A marvellous and unique pub.

Olde Bell, 95 Fleet Street, EC4.

Not all the journalists have fled Fleet Street; and those remaining (at Reuters and the Press Association) use the Olde Bell as their watering hole. Supposedly designed by Sir Christoper Wren who rebuilt St Paul's Cathedral after the Great Fire of London, the Olde Bell is one of central London's oldest pubs, having been constructed in

1670 to remove the wages from the armies of workers refashioning London after the fire. The pub's size does not match its present popularity, and on hot days drinkers spill out into St Bride's churchyard next door.

Olde Cheshire Cheese, Wine Office Court, 145 Fleet Street, EC4.

Did Dr Samuel Johnson really drink here? He's not actually recorded as having done so, but since he lived next door it's reasonable to assume that he did – and often. The site was once a friary: its well is still visible in the cellar, which has its own oak-beamed, stone-floored bar, and a medieval tunnel running down towards the Thames. The present building is post-Great Fire with many Georgian alterations producing a warren of small rooms with high-backed wooden settles and open fires. An upstairs restaurant serves such traditional English fayre as roast beef, steak and kidney pie, and the sort of "nursery puddings" that still haunt men who survived the rigours of private schools.

Punch Tavern, 99 Fleet Street, EC4.

The Punch was one of the most famous pubs of Fleet Street in the great days of the newspaper industry and either gave its name to or took its name from (accounts vary) the once-great but now defunct satirical magazine, *Punch*. Cartoons from *Punch* are an important component in the decor, as are huge pub mirrors. The interior has been knocked into one but is still divided into small intimate seating areas, and what used to be a separate public bar is now a busy dining area.

Prospect of Whitby, 57 Wapping Wall, E1.

London often disappoints those in search of real antiquity: so little of the original City survived the Great Fire of 1666, and so much of London outside the City is eighteenth, nineteenth or twentieth century. The Prospect of Whitby, however, is an exceptional survival from the early 1500s, complete with low ceilings and stone-flagged floors. A rustic beer garden and riverside terrace complete its charm. The infamous Judge Jeffreys, it is said, would feast in lodgings upstairs while watching the bodies of those he had condemned swinging from the Thames-side gallows. Samuel Pepys, diarist, roisterer, and Secretary to the Navy Board, was another contemporary user of the pub. The name relates to a sail-barge engaged in the coastal trade with the north-east of England, bringing coals from Newcastle.

Flounder and Firkin, 54 Holloway Road, N7.
One of the original Firkin brewpubs, conceived
and designed by maverick entrepreneur David
Bruce in the 1970s and 1980s to bring the fun
back into pub-going. The no-frills decor, since
imitated (badly) by copy-cat "ale-house" chains
such as Slug & Lettuce, shows a lot of plain,
scrubbed timber and a wealth of fascinating old
beer and brewing artefacts on the walls. The tiny
brewery in the cellar, producing such beers as
Whale Ale, is open to public view. The Flounder is
a welcome outpost of civilization in an area dominated by terrible pubs and Arsenal football ground.

Flask Tavern, 14 Flask Walk,
Hampstead High Street, NW3.
One of two famous North London pubs so named,
the Hampstead Flask was pilloried as a low dive
by Samuel Richardson in the eighteenth-century
cautionary novel *Clarissa*, when it was known as
the Thatched House. The rather smarter pub of
today dates from 1874 and has an ornate saloon
and a splendidly unspoilt public bar. The name
dates back to the eighteenth century or before and
relates to the practice of selling local spring water
by the flask to those who had spent all day
walking out from central London.

Crockers, 24 Aberdeen Place, NW8.
Known to all as Crocker's Folly but
properly called the Crown Hotel,
this huge and incredibly ornate
Victorian pub was built in 1892 by a
speculator named Frank Crocker to
serve the new Marylebone railway
station. Alas for poor Crocker, the
railway company went and built
their station a mile away, so the
inhabitants of St John's Wood had
this vast confection of marble, plaster work and
etched glass all to themselves. Today, however,
the incredible architecture along with good food
and an array of real ales have made the pub as
justly popular as Crocker – who leapt to his death
from an upstairs window – hoped it would be.

Anchor, Bankside, SE1.
London's river is perhaps its greatest glory, and
the many pubs that line its banks are the best
places from which to appreciate it. One of the
oldest of them is the Anchor, a maze of little
rooms built in 1750 when the old brothel-and-slum
district Shakespeare knew was largely redevel-

oped. The Anchor, built by a brewer named Thrale
after whom one of the bars is named, was an
instant hit with the literati of the day, and pubgoers from north of the river queued up to rub
shoulders with stars such as Dr Johnson and
Boswell, Oliver Goldsmith, David Garrick and
Edmund Burke. But the Thames is the real star,
and can be watched either from the Chart
Restaurant upstairs or the terrace across the way.

George, 77 Borough High Street, SE1.
Supposedly a true Shakespearean survival, the
George is in fact only a fragment of its original
self, two wings having been demolished to make
way for railway warehouses (now gone). Actually
the courtyard itself is the only bit Shakespeare
would have known: he is said to have performed
in it as a member of a company of strolling
players before fame beckoned. The actual building
he knew, though, was pulled down a century later
and replaced with a galleried coaching inn. But
even if the George is not quite all it pretends to
be, it is still a landmark pub, unique in London as
the last survivor of the great age of coaching inns,
and is a fascinating and lovely place to visit.

Westminster Arms, 7 Storeys Gate, SW1.
If you want to get an honest answer out of your
MP, lie in wait for him here. He's
bound to turn up eventually – they
all drink here and the pub even has
a division bell in the bar – and
without the array of policemen,
ushers, clerks and what-have-you to
protect him, he's at your mercy.
This is parliament's "local" and,
with its cellar bar, its restaurant
and its fine range of beers it's well
worth a visit in its own right.

White Horse, 1 Parsons Green, SW6.
This huge Victorian pub would be (and was) an
unexceptional Bass house were it not for the partnership of tenant Sally Cruikshank and cellarman
Mark Dorber. Between them they turned the pub –
with Bass's blessing – into a more or less permanent beer festival where the brewery's standard
range, kept in immaculate condition, makes room
for guest ales from many regional breweries and
even occasional rarities such as draught wheat
beer. The annual winter festival of old ales is a
must in the diary of every true beer lover. The
fierce insistence on quality that is maintained in

The beer never goes flat in the Flounder... this fun-loving brewpub is one of a small chain

Crockers (left) is an ornate Victorian masterpiece with a tragic history

White Horse, Parsons Green... mecca for beer-lovers and foodies

THE GREAT BRITISH BEER FESTIVAL

The Great British Beer Festival is, according to its organizers, the Campaign for Real Ale, the "biggest pub in the world". CAMRA also believes that GBBF is the world's biggest beer festival as far as choice is concerned. Whereas the Oktoberfest offers just 10 beers, GBBF is a showcase for cask-conditioned ales, with around 300 on offer each year, celebrating the unique British beer style that would have disappeared but for CAMRA.

The festival has been staged since the mid-1970s and has enjoyed a peripatetic existence. It was held in London for several years but the campaign then took it to Brighton, Leeds and Birmingham in order to stress the regional diversity of cask beer. It is now back in London in the Great Hall at Olympia in Kensington and is held during the first week in August.

The cask beers are ranged on gantries that run the length of the hall and are divided into regions of Great Britain in order to underline the fact that real ale is a British not an English phenomenon, with beers from Scotland and Wales as well. Great emphasis is placed on style, with promotions for mild, porter, stout, old ales, barley wines and bottle-conditioned beers as well as pale ale or bitter. British ciders and perries are also on show as the campaign is keen to preserve these fruit-based drinks.

The festival also features beers from other countries in a large section at the rear of the Great Hall. Belgian and German wheat beers, Trappist ales, lambic and gueuze, dark lagers and genuine Pilsners are just some of the styles that can be found. In 1995 the festival, for the first time ever, had cask-conditioned ales from the East Coast of the United States, a significant example of the deep impression CAMRA has made on the American microbrewing movement.

The festival is enormous fun. There is live entertainment, ranging from rock and jazz to classical music, during every session while children have a room with clowns and other attractions. The serious side of the festival is expressed through the Champion Beer of Britain competition, held on the opening day. Beers voted for by both CAMRA members and the general public are tasted blind by panels in categories ranging from mild ale to barley wines. The winners in each category then go forward to a final panel and the beer with the most marks is declared Champion Beer of Britain.

As well as the Great British, CAMRA organizes beer festivals throughout the country, often as many as 15 in a month, stressing regional choice and such seasonal styles as winter ales. Information concerning all CAMRA festivals: 01727 867201; fax 01727 867670.

The biggest pub in the world... cask-conditioned ale in the stunning surroundings of Olympia's Grand Hall

the cellar is also at work in the kitchen: the food is on a much higher plane than pub food anywhere else in the Capital.

Dove, 19 Upper Mall, Hammersmith, W6.
Another riverside pub, the Dove was a very grand retreat, a morning's journey from London when it was built in the reign of Charles II. At the time, the western reach of the Thames was very fashionable – the poet Pope lived in Twickenham, the Duke of Sussex had a house next to the Dove, and *Rule Britannia* was written upstairs by a man with no other claim to fame whatever, James Thomson. Since those early days, the Dove has maintained its appeal – William Morris, Graham Greene and Ernest Hemingway are all associated with the pub. The Dove is one of the oldest Fuller's houses – the brewery brought it in 1796 – and a pint or three of London Pride on the terrace overlooking the Thames is possibly the best way to idle away a summer's afternoon that London has to offer.

ST ALBANS, HERTFORDSHIRE
Ye Olde Fighting Cocks, off George Street and through Abbey gateway.
You can drive down to this old ale-house, though a walk is better, taking in the awesome bulk of St Albans Abbey, dedicated to the first Christian martyr, Alban, whose shrine was built by King Offa and around which the modern cathedral stands. The Fighting Cocks claims to be England's oldest licensed premises though the licence was granted for the "sport" of cock-fighting. The small sunken seating area inside reached via steps was the cock-fighting pit in Stuart times. The pub has a conical roof atop a round building that was known for several centuries as the Round House. The main bar is spacious and comfortable with low beamed ceilings and there is a large and attractive beer garden. The pub is on the edge of Verulam Park with its Roman remains and large lake.

Farriers Arms, Lower Dagnall Street.
A splendid example of an endangered species, a no-frills and unvarnished street-corner "boozer" with two simple bars, magnificent hand-pumped beer from the Hertford brewery McMullen, where darts, dominoes, cribbage and whist are played and pub grub is of the cheap and cheerful sausage-egg-and-chips variety. The locals are friendly and the toilets are in the yard. Outside there is a plaque commemorating the pub – wrongly – as the meeting place of the first

branch of the Campaign for Real Ale, but let's not quibble. Go and marvel before the modernizers ruin it.

LEEDS

Whitelocks, Turks Head Yard, Briggate.

Leeds's handsome city centre has been enjoying a major wash and brush-up in recent years, emerging from its coating of soot as a wonderland for lovers of decorative Victorian architecture. Undoubtedly, the place for a lunch break is Whitelock's, an unspoilt gem with bars arranged in line alongside a long narrow courtyard secluded from the main drag and full of original carved wood, etched and coloured glass, and brasswork. Popular with office workers and the growing number of tourists who are discovering post-industrial Leeds as the ideal centre for touring Yorkshire.

YORK

Black Swan, Peasholm Green.

Before the Industrial Revolution, York was England's second city. What is today the Black Swan started life in the fourteenth century as one of its grandest private houses, the home of the Bowes family, ancestors of the Queen Mother. William Bowes was MP for York four times, sheriff in 1407 and Lord Mayor twice. His son was also Lord Mayor, and his grandson was Lord Mayor of London and Court Jeweller to Elizabeth I. The house probably became an inn in 1715, still equipped with all the refinements of a great house: moulded plaster ceiling and fine Jacobean panelling and doorcase in the front parlour; elegant stairs of about 1700; and, in the upstairs dining room, panelling covered with seventeenth-century chiaroscuro paintwork. Luckily the inn declined in the nineteenth century, and was thus never vandalized by the Victorians; a restoration of 1930 revealed intact many fine original features.

CUMBRIA

Masons Arms, Strawberry Bank, Cartmel Fell.

One of Britain's best-known brewpubs, the Mason's Arms range includes a celebrated damson beer and the pub also makes its own cider. But the in-house brewery is far from being the pub's only attraction: it stocks more than 250 bottled beers from all over the world, many of them imported by the licensee, while the range of home-cooked food is celebrated across a wide area – especially by vegetarians, who are so often badly catered for in pubs. Another bonus is the setting, with its breathtaking views across the Winster Valley. But perhaps its greatest asset is its interior, which is basically that of a seventeenth-century farmhouse with kitchen, parlour, Jacobean panelled saloon and now an upstairs room as well. The celebrated children's writer Arthur Ransome lived just up the lane in a cottage where he wrote some of his *Swallows and Amazons* novels.

MANCHESTER

Peveril of the Peak, 127 Great Bridgwater Street.

This classic urban pub takes its name from a stagecoach which used to ply the cross-Pennine route to the Derbyshire Peak District. The coach itself took its name from a very ancient North Midlands land-owning family: William de Peverel was a natural son of William the Conqueror, who commanded Nottingham Castle from 1068, and subsequent Peverils owned land around Castleton. Sir Walter Scott's novel, *Peveril of the Peak*, came out in 1823. The pub itself is unusual in being triangular in shape and boasts a Victorian tiled exterior with original mahogany and stained glass in the three bars, which are grouped around a central servery and are homely rather than plush.

WEST MIDLANDS

Vine (Bull & Bladder), Delph Road, Brierley Hill, near Dudley.

This famous Black Country pub is also the brewery tap for the small family firm of Batham's, whose mild and bitter it sells. The brewery, which owns another eight pubs in the area, is just behind the Vine, whose nickname stems from the fact that part of the building used to be a slaughter-house and butcher's shop – a combination which may not be obvious but is not uncommon in the Black Country: Sally Perry's brewpub in Upper Gornal is another example. The Vine is a rambling many-roomed pub in a basic style which owes nothing to the rather self-conscious "no frills" style of modern ale-house decor but is simply the way the pub has evolved down the years. You can stand and quaff in the corridor if you prefer, served through a hatch. The pub grub is simple and plentiful and there are regular live jazz concerts in the large back room at weekends.

The Dove in Hammersmith: popular with writers, including Ernest Hemingway

Britain's oldest licensed building... but the licence was for cock-fighting not ale

The Masons Arms in the Lake District serves its own fruit beer and international brews

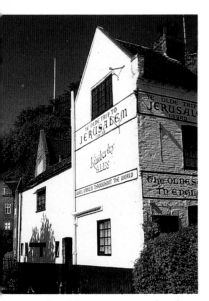

The oldest inn in England, the Olde Trip to Jerusalem refreshed soldiers en route for the Crusades

EAST MIDLANDS

Olde Trip to Jerusalem, Brewhouse Yard, Castle Road, Nottingham.

The current building is a seventeenth-century development of a twelfth-century inn and can claim with some historical justification to be the oldest inn in England. There is also a brewhouse that once served the castle – this even pre-dates the original inn. The upstairs bar of the pub, reached by a winding stone staircase, is carved from sandstone below the castle. The walls, panelled at the bottom, disappear into the Stygian gloom of the rock. Side alcoves have been cut from the sandstone. The downstairs bar is also hewn from the rock face and has old oak settles and barrel tables set on flagstoned floors. Soldiers had their last draft of ale here before setting out to fight in the Crusades, hence the name of this wonderfully atmospheric and unspoilt ale-house.

EDINBURGH

Bow Bar, 80 West Bow, off High Street and Grassmarket.

Once a rarity in Scotland, and still not common enough, are pubs which sell a variety of real ales from different breweries. One such is the Bow Bar, a single-room traditionally-decorated urban classic in the heart of the Old Town where English ales such as Draught Bass and Timothy Taylor's Landlord share the counter with the Caledonian range of Edinburgh-brewed real ales. Often there are as many as 12 real ales at a time – added to which is a fine collection of more than 100 single malt whiskies.

Café Royal, West Register Street.

A design flagship of the late nineteenth century, the Café Royal boasts big Victorian-style chandeliers, marble floors and stairs, a great gantry over the island bar, and incredible Doulton tilework murals portraying such leading lights of science and technology as James Watt, Michael Faraday, George Stephenson, William Caxton and Benjamin Franklin. An air of sophistication is maintained by the selection of morning newspapers and by the fringe productions put on here during the Edinburgh Festival. Scottish and English real ales are complemented by a choice of 40 malt whiskies. There is an acclaimed Oyster Bar that specializes in sea fish.

Neary's in Dublin, adjacent to the Gaiety Theatre, an ornate bar popular with the city's acting fraternity

GLASGOW

Babbity Bowster, 16-18 Blackfriars Street.

A highly individual conversion of a Robert Adam townhouse in the heart of the rejuvenated Merchant City district of Glasgow, the Babbity Bowster takes its name from a folk song and dance, Bab at the Bowster, illustrated at the pub by a ceramic plaque of kilted piper and dancer. It is the only pub in the district with an outdoor drinking area – none of your boulevardiers in "Glasgae" – and until recently was the only pub in the whole of Scotland to serve real cider. Its restaurant has a bias towards Scottish produce, though not to the exclusion of all else, and it serves Maclay's range of real ales, including one specially brewed for it.

IRELAND

DUBLIN

The Brazen Head, 20 Lower Bridge Street.

Built on the site of a tavern dating back to the twelfth century, The Brazen Head claims to be the oldest drinking establishment in Ireland, if not the whole of Europe. The place is steeped in history, and is redolent of the secret meetings of rebels and smugglers. In 1798 it was the meeting place of Oliver Bond and Thomas Reynolds, and in the late nineteenth century it was frequented by Robert Emmett, Wolfe Tone and Daniel O'Connell. Tucked away off an alleyway close to the River Liffey, it is splendidly atmospheric and has been mercifully left alone by modernizers.

Davy Byrnes, 21 Duke Street.

Renowned as Dublin's most literary pub, Davy Byrnes is one of the city's finest bars. Although at times patronized by many great literary figures, such as James Stephens, Liam O'Flaherty and Padraig O'Conner, it is best known for its connections with James Joyce. *Dubliners* has mention of Davy Byrnes, but the Joycean character with which the premises is most associated is Leopold Bloom of *Ulysses*. There is a portrait of the writer by Harry Kernoff on one wall, and other splendid decorations include paintings of Dublin and Bacchanalian murals. The pub is well-known in Dublin for its excellent seafood.

Neary's, 1 Chatham Street.

Neary's is a fine old bar that has long been a favourite haunt of the acting fraternity – the back

door is conveniently situated across an alleyway from the stage door of the Gaiety Theatre.
McDaid's, Harry Street.
To be found down a lane opposite Neary's, this splendid Dublin pub was once the watering-hole of the poet Paddy Kavanagh and the boisterous writer Brendan Behan.

BELFAST

Crown Liquor Saloon, 46 Great Victoria Street.
The Crown is owned by the National Trust and is a Victorian gem, with a long granite-top bar and seating in "donkey boxes" – partitioned private drinking areas separated by carved wood and painted glasswork. The floor is tiled and there is a plethora of mirrors and ornately moulded ceilings. It is said locally that you haven't been to Belfast until you've been to the Crown.

THE NETHERLANDS

AMSTERDAM

In De Wildeman, Nieuwe Zijdskolk.
The Wild Man Inn is well-named since its owner, Henk Eggens, stands at a magnificently-moustached 6 feet 8 inches. Eggens was a leading character in Holland's beer revival during his years as manager of the Gollem Café (see below). Now he has a billet of his own down a side-street just off the pedestrianized Nieuwedijk and close to Centraal Station – and what a find it is. Its 160 beers include 30 from the Netherlands, it sells spirits from the cask, and – unusually for a country addicted to cheroots – it includes a no-smoking bar. Beer specialities are chalked on a board. The Wild Man is rather like Dr Who's famous Tardis: it is small on the outside but surprisingly spacious inside, with a raised area at the rear that allows drinkers to overlook the long bar. Light snacks are also served.
Café Gollem, 4 Raamsteeg.
Gollem was so popular in the 1980s when its management led the Dutch beer revival that habitués are bound to say it's not what it was. But this small café in its little alley still has the biggest beer list in Amsterdam, with 200 choices from around the world. The food is more limited – just bread, cheese and ham – but who really needs more? House specialities include the rarely-sighted sour wheat beers of Berlin.

Maximiliaan, 6-8 Kloveniersburgwal.
Café, restaurant and brewery all in one, Maximiliaan also leads in serious modern interior design. It was opened in 1992, and one remarkable feature is that the brew kettles are not just visible from the bar – they're actually in it. Kölsch and wheat beer are permanent fixtures. One of the other four beers brewed here – Maximator, Max Tripel, Meibok, and Winterbier – will be available as well. Stray too far while hunting for this café and you will find yourself in the city's notorious red light district. A beer at Maximiliaan will help you get over the shock.
't IJ Proeflokaal, 7 Funenkade.
Amsterdam's independent brewery, 't IJ, was founded in 1984 in a converted bathhouse in the city's dockland. Its brewery tap only opens from 3 p.m. until 8 p.m. from Wednesday to Sunday but, with all of the 't IJ beers – Struis, Columbus, Zatte, Bockbier, Natte, Mug Bitter and Plzen – regularly on draught, it's a golden opportunity to sample beers which are all too hard to find elsewhere. To add to the fun, the bar has a collection of 2,000 empty beer bottles from all over the world. Food is limited to drinkers' snacks, but children are welcome and there's a selection of board games to keep them happy. There is a cavernous downstairs room when the ground floor bar gets overcrowded.

ROTTERDAM

Cambrinus, 4 Blaak.
Between the Blaak railway and metro station and the waterfront is Cambrinus. The name is a variant of Gambrinus, itself a nickname for Jan Primus, Duke of Brabant 1251–95, reputed to be capable of downing 144 mugs of beer at a single sitting. But it would take even such a doughty drinker as Jan Primus more than two sittings to taste his way through the beer-list at this café – it stocks some 300. The modern bar has a dining room at the back which takes *cuisine à la bière* seriously; beyond that, a terrace overlooks the old harbour.

The Crown Liquor Saloon in Belfast, featuring wonderfully ornate Victoriana

Big owner, big beer selection in Amsterdam's In De Wildemann

BOCK BEER FESTIVAL

*E*very October, the Dutch beer drinkers' organization PINT runs the Bock Beer Festival in Amsterdam, a two-day extravaganza featuring the strong beers, both top- and bottom-fermenting, of the Netherlands.
Information: 31 2520 22909.

UTRECHT

Jan Primus, 27 Jan van Scorel Straat.
Another tribute to the Prince of Beer is this street-corner café in the unassuming suburb of Wilhelmina Park. There's no music, no gaming machines, and not a lot in the way of food; what there is is a list running to 130 beers and a regular clientele who are genuinely pleased to see strangers and – horror of horrors for the reserved English visitor – are likely to try to engage you in conversation!

UNITED STATES

BOSTON, MASS.

Bull & Finch, 84 Beacon Street.
If you've seen *Cheers* on TV you'll feel at home here for this is the inspiration for the series, more suds than soap. A large central bar is the focus of the roomy, comfortable old saloon where the humour is drier than the beer.

Doyle's, 3484 Washington Street, Jamaica Plain.
Stresses the Irishness of Boston with rooms dedicated to the Kennedys and Michael Collins, the Irish nationalist who negotiated the treaty with Britain in 1921 that created the Free State and sparked a civil war in which he was killed. But all are welcome – even Brits these days – and the style, beer and cuisine are multi-cultural.

MANHATTAN, NEW YORK CITY

American Festival Café, Rockefeller Center, 20 W 50th, Midtown.
Has superb views out over the famous ice-skating rink. From the comfort of the plush surroundings customers can choose from a beer menu built around American craft breweries, including Catamount, Brooklyn, Grants and Yuengling.

Brewsky's, 41 East 7th Street.
A tiny bar with strong Ukrainian associations, sawdust on the floor, a collection of canned beers, photos of old movie stars on the walls, 400 bottled beers and many independent brewers' draught beers.

Fraunce's Tavern, 54 Pearl Street.
This is one of the oldest taverns in the country, dating from 1790 when New York was still under British rule. George Washington said goodbye to his troops from the steps of the tavern. Inside it has the atmosphere of a period London chop house, with lots of wood panelling, settles and long tables. There is usually a beer from at least one independent brewery, often Brooklyn.

Jimmy Armstrong's Bar,
corner of 10th Avenue and West 57th St.
A splendid bar in an otherwise unremarkable part of Manhattan, just before the island falls into the river. The bar, with its comfortable seating, wood and glass partitions and a Double Diamond mirror from Burton-on-Trent in England, offers a wide range of American craft brewers' beer, from Anchor Steam in San Francisco to Brooklyn.

North Star, 93 South Street.
This is a loving recreation of a Victorian London pub in the old harbour area, with tall ships bobbing in the water. Both natives and ex-pats can revel in London pub grub, such as fish and chips and bangers and mash while supping the likes of Fuller's and Young's beers (in keg form). The pub has a nicotined-coloured ceiling to add to the authenticity, glass partitions and alcove seating.

Peculier Pub, 145 Bleecker Street, West Broadway, Greenwich Village.
The in place for students from New York University, where beer connoisseurs know the correct spelling of Peculier in the manner of Theakston's of Yorkshire. The narrow tavern, dominated by a long bar, specializes in Belgian and British ales.

Zip City, 3 West 18th Street.
If you want to know where to get unfiltered Helles, Pilsner, Märzen, Vienna Red, Dunkel, Bock, Doppelbock or Maibock, Zip City is the best place outside of Munich. The large bar, where young Manhattans "stand in line" to get in, is the creation of Kirby Shyer near Union Square Park in the old Flatiron garment district. The brewpub is a converted wrought-iron building from 1895 that once, with delicious irony, housed the National Temperance Society. The brewplant comes from Austria and the food is international. Zip City is a nickname for New York City in Sinclair Lewis's novel *Babbitt*.

BROOKLYN, NEW YORK CITY

Peter's Waterfront Ale House, Atlantic Avenue.
Stunning views of Manhattan from outside. Inside this small, smart tavern is reminiscent of a Scots or Irish bar. Peter the owner has an ironic sense of humour – a sign promises "Honest warm beer,

Peculier spelling but a splendid and eclectic choice of beers in this New York bar

lousy food and an ugly owner". All the threats are unfulfilled: the beer in particular is eclectic and in fine form and includes Fuller's Extra Special Bitter from London, Paulaner Oktoberfest from Munich and a clutch of US microbrewers' products.

Peter Doelger's, Berry Street.

More than 100 years old, it was once owned by Doelger's Manhattan Brewery. It is comfortable and well lived-in, with large plate-glass windows, a cracked tiled floor, a small raised platform for musicians, Polish food – always fish on Fridays – and good beer, including Brooklyn Lager, Warsteiner and Bass Ale. Baseball on TV in the season.

WASHINGTON, DC

Brickskeller, 1523 22nd Street NW.

On the edge of Georgetown, it has the biggest selection of craft brewers' beers in the United States. Regular tutored beer tastings are held there.

CHICAGO, ILL.

Goose Island, 1800 North Clybourn.

Few bars can boast a range of beers as wide as Goose Island's. To his three regulars – Lincoln Park Lager, Golden Goose Pilsner, and Honker's Pale Ale – brewer Gregory Hall adds no fewer than 15 seasonal and special brews inspired by beers as diverse as Irish stout, Weizen and barley wine. The cuisine is just as diverse, with dishes of Mexican, Belgian and German ancestry. The pub itself was once the Turtle Wax factory and now aims for an English pub atmosphere with exposed beams and wooden floors. It is the home of the Chicago Beer Society, which meets here on the first Thursday of every month.

SAN FRANCISCO, CALIF.

San Francisco Brewpub, 155 Columbus Avenue.

Unlike many brewpubs in the US, this is not an imaginative conversion of an old warehouse or a factory or a fire station: it was built as a tavern in 1907 and was originally called the Andromeda Saloon. It later changed its name to the Albatross Tavern and became as colourful as the surrounding Barbary District: Jack Dempsey worked here as a doorman, and Baby-Face Nelson was captured here in 1929. One of its four regular brews, Albatross Lager, recalls its history. Others are Emperor Norton Lager, Gripman's Porter and Serpent Stout, and there are three seasonal beers including

Andromeda Wheatbeer. The decor features stained glass windows, tables made from old sewing machines, and a brass-inlaid mahogany bar.

20 Tank, 316 11th Street.

Just south of the Market District, near Folsom, is a brewpub that's all-American: the glass frontage bears a five-foot neon beer mug and the exposed ductwork is a major feature of the warehouse-style interior. The food is all-American, too, with chilli and nachos high on the menu. Kinnikinick Club Ale and Kinnikinick Old Scout Stout are the best-known beers, but other regulars include Mellow Glow Pale Ale and Moody's High Top Strong Ale, and there are up to seven seasonal and special brews.

MARIN COUNTY, CALIF.

Marin Brewing Co, 1809 Larkspur Landing Circle.

A drive across the bridge or a ferry ride from San Francisco brings you to a large, plush and welcoming restaurant and bar with attached microbrewery owned by Grant Johnson. He supplies the bar with a hoppy pale ale, a roasty stout and two fruit beers, raspberry and blueberry. The food is wide-ranging and imaginative and service is wonderfully attentive and friendly. From the deep seats of bar and restaurant there are magnificent views of the bay and the island that once housed a prison. Grant Johnson, with a nice irony, calls his dark beer Breakout Stout.

DUBLIN, CALIF.

Lyons Brewery

This is a bar, not a micro. Brewing ceased decades ago and there are no known Irish connections in the small town where Judy Ashworth runs a roomy tavern dedicated to quality beers from far and near. The long bar groans with taps for such specialities as Celis White, Pyramid Peach and Lind India Pale Ale. Judy, who is a great enthusiast, will show fellow connoisseurs her tiny but immaculate cool room where beers are stored and will debate the merits of such English ales as Sam Smith's and Greene King.

LOS ANGELES, CALIF.

Gorky's, 536 East 8th Street.

Gorky's bills itself as a café and Russian brewery, and the all-grain, cask-conditioned beers include an Imperial Russian Stout and a "Russian" Red

Ganders don't need to wander from Goose Island, a Chicago brewpub with an impressive range

THE GREAT AMERICAN BEER FESTIVAL

The Great American Beer Festival was clearly inspired by the British festival but has developed into a major showcase not only for beer but for brewing as well. It is run by the Association of Brewers, a subsidiary of the American Homebrewers' Association, which inspired a legion of beer-lovers to forsake bland, cold lagers and rediscover the joys of the grain and the hop. Held every October in Colorado, GABF invites all American brewers, from Anheuser-Busch to the tiniest micro, to participate. The centrepiece of the festival is the judging of beers, broken down punctiliously into dozens of styles. You don't just find porters, for example, but brown porters and dark porters, while stouts come in all colours and ratings, from dry Irish to imperial Russian. The entire style range encompasses light beers at one end of the spectrum to barley wines and Doppelbocks at the other, stressing the enormous variety and diversity of American beer. The winners of each category are awarded gold medals, which are much coveted. Information from: Great American Beer Festival, PO Box 287, Boulder, Colorado 80306; tel 303 447 0816; fax 303 447 2825.

Other beer festivals are beginning to develop in the US. One of the largest on the East Coast is the Under the Brooklyn Bridge Festival, held in mid-September and featuring around 70 American and overseas beers. Information from Brooklyn Brewery, 118 North 11th Street, Brooklyn, New York 11211, tel: 718 486 7422. More information on American beer and beer festivals from the national magazine *All About Beer*, published in Durham, North Carolina, tel: 919 490 0589.

Putting on the style... the Great American Festival is a showcase for beer and the profusion of styles now available

Ale. The menu continues the theme, with Russian pastas a speciality, and the decor is billed as "Bolshevik Modern". Not surprisingly this highly subversive set-up, just in front of the flower market in downtown Los Angeles, attracts students and artists – in fact some of the artists may even have works on show in Gorky's permanent exhibition.

PORTLAND, OREG.
BridgePort Brewpub,
1313 NW Marshall Street. This is the place for clear-sighted drinkers – smoking is banned throughout. Founded in 1984 as Columbia River Brewing, this is Oregon's oldest surviving microbrewery. The pub was opened two years later in this century-old building in the city's Northwest Section. To three regular brews – BridgePort Ale and Blue Heron and Coho Pacific Light Ale – brewer William Lundeen adds four seasonal ales including a stout and a barley wine. The kitchen

specializes in pizzas made with home-made sourdough crusts.

SEATTLE, WASH.
Redhook Brewery & Trolleyman Pub,
3400 Phinney Ave N.
British drinkers might feel familiar with some of the names on brewer Al Triplett's list, with names like Ballard and ESB. They might feel at ease in the pub, too – modern, comfortable, spacious and

friendly, with a big open fire to give a homely atmosphere. Like so many US microbreweries, Redhook is housed in a building with a fascinating past of its own: it was the Fremont Trolley-Car Barn and home to the Seattle Electric Railway, and has national landmark status. Those who like to taste their beer and the home-made pub food that accompanies it will be pleased that the Trolleyman is non-smoking. Redhook is one of America's oldest craft breweries: it was founded in 1982, and the pub was opened in 1988.

On the right track... Redhook's Trolleyman Pub is a showplace for the brewery's fine-tasting ales

CANADA

MONTREAL, QUEBEC

Le Cheval Blanc, 809 Ontario Street.

Le Cheval Blanc has been a pub since 1937, and in the hands of the family of current owner/brewer Jerôme Denys for all that time. Jerôme relaunched it as a brewpub in 1987 and, although a limited menu includes Hungarian sausage and tacos, the beer is the thing. Jerôme's regular brews are an amber ale, a pale ale, Golden Wheat Ale, and a brown ale, but his specials include a maple syrup beer and bottle-conditioned kriek and frambozen.

TORONTO, ONTARIO

Rotterdam, 600 King Street.

A bar for homesick ex-pats, Rotterdam Brewing serves Younger's Tartan, Guinness, Murphy's, Stone's and Smithwick's on draught. But why drink keg beer from the wrong side of the country when you could be drinking cask-conditioned Scotch Ale, Nut Brown Ale, Milk Stout or any one of 18 other ales and lagers produced on the premises? The menu is long, too: calamari, guacamole, nachos, steaks, sausages, pastas, fish, smoked turkey, sandwiches, and falafel are just some of the dishes on offer. The red-brick building which houses the brewpub is a century old, and the decor goes in for street-lamps, stone walls, and marble-topped tables. A slightly disquieting note: look up, and through the glass ceiling you will see several tons of brewery perched right over your head.

VANCOUVER, BRITISH COLUMBIA

Swan's Brewpub, Buckerfield's Brewery, 506 Pandora Street, Victoria.

Located in an 80-year-old seed warehouse in Victoria's Old Town district, Swan's was established in 1989 along the lines of a traditional English local, right down to hanging baskets, plenty of exposed timbers, and a polished oak bar with brass hand pumps. The beers brewed up by Frank Appleton and Chris Johnson include a bitter, a pale, a stout, a brown ale, and a barley wine at Christmas – although the average English pub-goer might be surprised to be offered a "Ragin' Cajun Halibut Burger!"

Spinnakers, 308 Catherine Street.

This is a place that really brews. In fact Jake

Thomas produces no fewer than 20 beers in all sorts of styles – an India Pale Ale and four different stouts rub shoulders with four Weizens, one of them mit hefe, a bock and a dark lager. All beers are unfiltered and cask-conditioned. The building itself dates back to the 1920s and has a ground-floor restaurant and an upstairs taproom. It has been a brewpub since 1984, claiming to be Canada's first. As at Swan's, halibut is a speciality.

AUSTRALIA

MELBOURNE

Redback Brewery Brewpub, 70 Flemington Road, North Melbourne.

A branch of Perth's Matilda Bay Brewery Company, this lively Melbourne pub offers Dogbolter, Brass Monkey stout and Redback beers, with good food and live music every night.

Loaded Dog, 324 St Georges Road, North Fitzroy.

This is a roomy, friendly pub brewery with five house beers and a hundred others. The name comes from a Henry Lawson short story set in mining days in which a retriever named Tommy finds a stick of gunpowder, a yellow mongrel steals it and takes it into a pub which explodes. The story is told on the pub menu and on the walls of the dining room. There is also a model of a beer-swilling dog. Beers on offer include Yellow Mongrel, Ruby Bitter and Thunder Ale.

Limerick Arms, 364 Clarendon Street, South Melbourne.

This is a top jazz pub with live bands seven nights a week. It has 30 imported beers.

SYDNEY

Pumphouse Brewery Brewpub, Little Pier Street, Darling Harbour.

Built on the site of an old water-pumping station that generated the energy to power Sydney's elevators at the turn of the last century, the Pumphouse still features an enormous cast-iron water tank. It has a large beer garden and an attractive balcony.

Lord Nelson Hotel, 19 Kent Street, The Rocks.

The Lord Nelson, at Millers Point, an extension of Sydney's historical Rocks area, is the city's oldest continuous licensed hotel, built in 1841 and named after Horatio Nelson. The handsome sandstone building has been lovingly restored

Victorian grandeur in Sydney... the Hero of Waterloo dates from 1843

The Sail and Anchor in Fremantle (right) was Australia's first brewpub for 50 years

At the Sail and Anchor there is a good range of tasty ales, including a bitter and a stout

and its small brewery produces six house beers all brewed without chemicals or adjuncts and fermented with an English yeast culture. The beers are Old Admiral, Victory Bitter, Quayle Ale, Trafalgar Pale Ale, Three Sheets and Nelson's Blood. The ales all have strong associations with Admiral Nelson save for Quayle Ale, a wheat beer named after a visit by former US Vice-President Dan Quayle. The hotel also produces Two Dogs, an alcoholic lemonade that has become a cult drink in Australia and was launched in Britain in 1995 by Bass.

The Hero of Waterloo Hotel,
81 Lower Fort Street, The Rocks.
The Hero of Waterloo is another impressive sandstone building, this one dating from 1843. It was a favourite drinking place for troops in colonial times and it has retained open, log-burning fires. It is popular with British and Irish visitors today as well as locals, and offers Bass, Guinness and Newcastle Brown Ale. Don't miss the stone cellars and the infamous tunnel linking the hotel to the harbour, used for rum smuggling and the involuntary recruitment of sailors. Young men who got drunk at the bar would be dropped through a trap door into the cellar, dragged along the tunnel and Shanghaied aboard a waiting clipper.

Australian Hotel, 100 Cumberland Street, The Rocks.
The Australian Hotel was built in 1913 and retains not only many original features but a ban on poker machines and pool tables. Its beers are supplied by Scharer's Little Brewery based in the George IV inn in Argyle Street, Picton. The microbrews are chemical and additive free and include a 5.0 per cent lager and a 6.4 per cent dark Burragorang Bock. The hotel has an acclaimed

menu that includes kangaroo fillet, crocodile marinated in herbs, and marinated emu.

FREMANTLE
Sail and Anchor, 64 Station Terrace.
Situated opposite Fremantle market, this pub-brewery was set up in 1984 when the Victorian red-brick Freemason's Hotel was bought and refitted. When the brewery was up and running it became the first new brewery in Australia for more than 50 years. The success of the Sail and Anchor prompted its owners to expand and build the Matilda Brewing Company which has achieved great national success with its two leading brands Redback and Dogbolter. Brewmaster Ken Duncan produces three regular beers for the Sail and Anchor: Seven Seas Real Ale (4.6 per cent ABV), a fruity and hoppy English-style bitter, Brass Monkey Stout (6.0 per cent), a roasty, coffeeish oatmeal stout, and Ironbrew Strong Ale (7.0 per cent), a rich and warming dark ale. The pub is next door to the popular Markets area packed with stalls selling antiques, bric-à-brac and clothes.

NEW ZEALAND
AUCKLAND
Shakespeare Tavern, 62 Albert Street.
Brewpub with Sir Toby Belch's Ginger Beer and King Lear Old Ale.
Nags Head, St Georges Bay Road, Parnell.
Six draught beers in a welcoming atmosphere.

JAPAN
TOKYO
Beer Bar Brussels, 75 Yarai-cho, Kagurazaka.
As you would expect, the Beer Bar Brussels has a good selection of Belgian brews. It is one of a small chain of bars specializing in Belgian beers and offers 80 brands, including Hoegaarden Wit, Chimay, Orval and lambic and gueuze.
Rising Sun near Yotsuya Station.
Irish landlord, international beers and shepherd's pie.
Sapporo
Sapporo Brewery's renowned beer garden is at North 6, East 9, Higashi-ku.

BEER AND FOOD

CHAPTER 5

*F*OR CENTURIES, BEER AND FOOD WERE NATURAL COMPANIONS IN THE HOMES OF RICH AND POOR ALIKE IN GRAIN-PRODUCING AND BREWING NATIONS. IT IS TRAGIC THAT WINE AND ITS ACCOMPANYING WINE SNOBBERY HAVE SHUNTED BEER OFF THE TABLE AND OUT OF THE KITCHEN, FOR BEER CAN BRING OUT BOTH THE RICH AND SUBTLE FLAVOURS OF FOOD EQUALLY AS WELL AS THE JUICE OF THE GRAPE. THIS SECTION OFFERS SOME COMPANIONS FOR MEALS AND RECIPES FOR COOKING WITH BEER. WHERE A PARTICULAR STYLE IS MENTIONED THAT BEER SHOULD ALSO BE DRUNK TO ACCOMPANY THE DISH.

GERMAN BEER SOUP *(serves four)*

1 pint/600ml German lager bier
1 crushed clove
1 small cinnamon stick
1 teaspoon demerara sugar
½ teaspoon lemon juice
1 teaspoon cornflour
2 eggs, separated.

Mix beer, clove, cinnamon, sugar and lemon juice and bring to the boil. Mix cornflour with just one table-spoon of liquid and pour into the soup to thicken. Beat the egg yolks well until frothy and stir into the soup. Beat the egg whites stiffly and drop into boiling water. Poach egg until white and serve floating on top of the soup.

RUDDLE'S STEAK AND KIDNEY PUDDING *(serves four)*

This version of a classic English dish was devised by Rosemary Ruddle, wife of the former owner of Ruddle's Brewery in Oakham, Rutland, England. If Ruddle's County Bitter is not available, any strong (around 5.0 per cent ABV) pale ale will suffice.

Crust
10oz/275g plain flour
1 teaspoon baking powder, pinch of salt
5oz/150g beef suet, shredded
½ pint/300ml water
Filling
1½lb/700g shoulder steak
½lb/225g ox kidney
salt, pepper, flour

1 clove garlic
½ teaspoon basil
½ teaspoon thyme
4 bay leaves
¾ pint/450ml pale ale

To make the crust, sift together the flour, baking powder and salt. Mix in the suet. Add water to make a soft dough. Put aside one third of the paste for the lid of the pudding. Roll out the remaining paste, flour well and fold in half. Continue to roll, pulling gently to form a bag shape and use it to line a greased basin.

For the filling, cut steak into small squares, trimming off gristle and any excess fat. Skin, core and cut up kidney. Mix together and roll in seasoned flour. Place the peeled clove of garlic at the bottom of the basin lined with paste. Layer the meat in it with chopped basil, thyme and bay leaves. Pour in the beer.

Roll out the remaining paste and cover the basin. Wet the edges and press well down. Tie a cloth over and place in a pan of water to boil steadily and gently for about four hours. Top up the pan with hot water from time to time.

CARBONADE FLAMANDE
(serves four)

This classic Belgian dish of beef stewed in beer should use a rich-flavoured Belgian beer if possible. A brown ale, such as Liefman's Goudenband, is ideal.

2lb/900g beef, cubed
4 shallots or 2 onions
2oz/50g butter

Belgo's restaurant in London has increased the appreciation of Belgian food and beer

salt, black pepper, pinch of ground coriander
2 sprigs of thyme
18fl oz – 1¾ pints (0.5 – 1.0 litres) of beer
2 tablespoons flour
1 tablespoon Dijon mustard (optional)

Chop the shallots or onions and fry them in the butter in a casserole. Add the beef and brown for about five minutes. Season with salt, pepper, ground coriander and thyme. Pour in sufficient beer to cover the meat completely and simmer gently for 1½ hours.

Lift out the meat with a slotted spoon and set aside. Run the sauce through a sieve and return it to the pan. Blend the flour with a little of the sauce and add to the pan, adding mustard if preferred. Simmer, stirring, until the flour is cooked, about two minutes. Return the meat to the sauce and heat through. Serve with steamed or boiled potatoes and sweet onions. (This version of the recipe is recommended by Madame Rose Blancquaert, former owner of Liefman's Brewery who now runs De Mouterij restaurant in Oudenaarde: quoted in Michael Jackson's *Beer Companion*.)

MUSSELS WITH BEER AND BACON *(serves four)*

Another classic Belgian dish. For beer use Hoegaarden white beer or a similar style, such as Blanche de Namur or Silly.

4lb/2kg fresh mussels
Half a large onion, diced
2 sticks of celery, chopped
2oz/50g butter
1pt/600ml Hoegaarden Blanche
7oz/200g diced smoked bacon
2 tablespoons chopped parsley

Clean and beard the mussels, lightly sauté the chopped onion and celery in butter. Add the mussels and then the beer, bring to the boil and simmer briskly for about four minutes until the

mussels open. Add the bacon at the end of cooking or it will make the mussels too salty. Sprinkle with chopped parsley and serve with pommes frites and bread to soak up the juices. Recipe from Philippe Blaise of Belgo's restaurant, Chalk Farm, North London.

LAMB BOULANGÈRE *(serves four)*

Use a premium and well-hopped ale. This recipe come from Sue Vesson of the Swan in the Rushes pub in Loughborough, Leicestershire, who uses Bateman's XXXB.

4 chump chops
sauté mixture of celery, onion, carrot, parsley stalks and bay leaves
1pt/600ml Bateman's XXXB
2–3 onions, thinly sliced
1½lb/750g old potatoes, peeled and thinly sliced
fresh chopped rosemary
a little butter

Seal the chump chops in a little hot fat with the sautéd vegetables. Pour on the beer and lightly braise the chops for a few minutes. Strain off the liquor and put chops aside. Sauté the onions very lightly until just soft, then layer with the potatoes to nearly fill a medium roasting dish, ending with a layer of potatoes. Pour over the beer liquor, adding a little stock if necessary to reach just below the top layer. Dot the top with butter and sprinkle with rosemary. Bake in the centre of a medium oven

THE ANNUAL DINNER OF THE BRITISH GUILD OF BEER WRITERS IN 1992 OFFERED THE FOLLOWING DISHES:

Menu

SLICED CANTONESE-STYLE BEEF WITH A SPICY DARK ALE; SESAME SEED ROLLS, NAVARIN OF LAMB COOKED IN BITTER WITH A GARNISH OF TURNED VEGETABLES AND DUMPLINGS MADE WITH LIGHT ALE; SLICED CARROTS GLAZED IN STOUT, CAULIFLOWER AU GRATIN, BOULANGÈRE POTATOES SLICED WITH ONIONS; PORTER CHEDDAR; BLACKBERRY, APPLE AND MILD TURNOVERS WITH DAIRY CREAM; COFFEE WITH FRUIT AND MACKESON CAKE.

THE BEERS THAT ACCOMPANIED THE MEAL WERE: TIMOTHY TAYLOR'S LANDLORD BITTER; WORTHINGTON WHITE SHIELD; BATEMAN'S SALEM PORTER; ROBINSON'S OLD TOM; TIMMERMAN'S CASSIS; ANCHOR BREWERY CHRISTMAS ALE; YOUNG'S WINTER WARMER.

(190°C/375°F/gas mark 5) for about 45 minutes, until the beer is almost absorbed and the potatoes tender. Increase heat slightly (200°C/400°F/gas mark 6), place chops on top of the potatoes and return to oven for 10–15 minutes.

COD STEAKS IN BEER *(serves four)*

As cod is a delicate fish, do not use too overpowering or fruity a beer. A lager, mild or pale ale would be perfect.

1 pint/600ml beer
1 sliced carrot
2 sliced shallots
1 stalk sliced celery
2 sprigs parsley
4 black peppercorns
2 cloves
1 bay leaf
4 cod steaks

Sauce

½oz/15g butter
1oz/25g flour
½ pint/300ml milk
2 tablespoons Parmesan cheese
2oz/50g diced Gruyère
1 egg yolk, beaten
1 tablespoon butter
2 tablespoons double cream, whipped
salt, pepper

Take a deep frying pan large enough for the cod steaks. Pour in the beer and add vegetables, parsley, peppercorns, bay leaf and cloves. Bring just to the boil, then cover and simmer for 20 minutes. Place cod steaks in this liquid and cook on a low heat for 15 minutes. Turn once and when they start to flake, transfer to a shallow baking dish. Keep hot in a low oven or under a grill.

Boil the liquid. Reduce for five minutes and then strain. Set aside to be used in the sauce. Melt butter in a pan. Blend in flour and cook for a couple of minutes or so to make a roux. Add milk gradually and bring to the boil. Stir thoroughly, making a smooth and thick sauce. Do not allow to go lumpy. Stir in the fish liquid and set aside. Add Parmesan, Gruyère and egg yolk. Cook over a low heat. Beat well with a spatula and do not allow to boil. Sauce should become smooth. Stir in butter and whipped cream. Season to taste and pour sauce over cod steaks.

BEER BUBBLE AND SQUEAK

(serves four)

A traditional Cockney dish made more interesting by adding pale ale, either Young's Bitter or Fuller's London Pride.

¾lb/350g Brussels sprouts
¾lb/350g potatoes
pepper and salt
½ teaspoon chopped chives
½ pint/300ml pale ale

Wash, peel and top the sprouts. Peel and slice the potatoes. Cook normally and then mash vegetables together. Add pepper and salt to taste, the chives and the pale ale. Fry the mixture in butter lightly until brown. Reduce the heat and cook gently until a brown crust forms.

CHERRY BEER SORBET *(serves four)*

A Belgian speciality using kriek beer.

5oz/120g sugar
⅓ pint/200ml water
5oz/120g cherry purée
⅓ pint/200ml Kriek

Dissolve sugar in water to make a syrup. Cool then mix in cherry purée and beer, and freeze in an ice-cream maker. Serve decorated with mint leaf.

BEER CAKE

8oz/225g plain flour
3oz/75g butter
3oz/75g soft brown sugar
3oz/75g currants
1 egg
¼pint/150ml mild ale or stout
½ teaspoon bicarbonate of soda

Cream the butter. Rub the sifted flour and soft brown sugar into the butter. Add currants. Beat the egg with beer, dissolve the bicarbonate of soda, add to the mixture and stir well. Placed in a well-greased tin and bake in an oven preheated to 180°C/360°F for one hour.

AT A DINNER HELD BY MARSTON'S OF BURTON-ON-TRENT IN LONDON, 1994, THE MENU WAS AS FOLLOWS:

Menu

SMOKED DUCK SALAD ON A FAN OF LETTUCE SERVED WITH PALE ALE AND LENTIL VINAIGRETTE, ACCOMPANIED BY MARSTON'S INDIA EXPORT PALE ALE.

FILLET OF BEEF STUFFED WITH OXTAIL AND MUSHROOM, SERVED WITH AN ALE AND GAME SAUCE; BRAISED RED CABBAGE, GLAZED CARROTS, PARISIENNE POTATOES, ACCOMPANIED BY MARSTON'S ALBION PORTER.

UNION BAKED APPLE STUFFED WITH FRUITS STEEPED IN MARSTON'S UNION MILD, TOPPED WITH CARAMELIZED NUT SAUCE, ACCOMPANIED BY MARSTON'S UNION MILD.

A SELECTION OF TRADITIONAL CHEESES FROM STAFFORDSHIRE AND DERBYSHIRE, ACCOMPANIED BY MARSTON'S OWD RODGER.

THE CULTURE OF BEER DRINKING

*T*HE PLACES WHERE WE DRINK ARE OFTEN STEEPED IN HISTORY, NONE MORE SO THAN THE ENGLISH PUB WITH ITS FASCINATING COLLECTION OF NAMES AND INN SIGNS AS WELL AS TRADITIONAL PUB GAMES. PUBS, BARS AND CAFÉS HAVE ALSO CONJURED UP SOME GREAT LITERATURE, AND GIVEN RISE TO SOME FUNNY AND RIBALD STORIES.

The Royal Oak at Langstone, Hampshire, a superb pub in an idyllic location

Pub signs are rich in history. The name of the Flask in Highgate, North London, stems from the time the pub sold flasks of spring water to ramblers

The Farriers Arms, St Albans, Hertfordshire, has an inn sign showing the coat of arms of the farriers' trade association

"We dined at an excellent inn at Chapel-house, where he expatiated on the felicity of England in its taverns and inns, and triumphed over the French for not having, in any perfection, the tavern life. 'There is no private house, (said he), in which people can enjoy themselves so well, as at a capital tavern'... He then repeated, with great emotion, Shenstone's lines:

Who'er has travell'd life's dull round,
Where'er his stages may have been,
May sigh to think he still has found
The warmest welcome at an inn."
James Boswell,
The Life of Samuel Johnson.

Every beer-drinking country has public places in which to drink the staple beverage. The reason why the English pub is always singled out as the quintessential environment in which to enjoy beer can be explained in one word: history. In most other countries, bars, bier kellers and cafés are modern buildings. They carry little historical baggage. But even though most English pubs go back no further than the late nineteenth century, and most are more recent, they have a direct lineage with the ale-houses, taverns and inns that date back as far as Roman and Saxon times. Even the design of the modern pub, with several rooms and corridors, replicates the earliest ale-houses, which were extensions of people's homes, chosen because the ale wife or brewster made the finest ale in the village.

WHAT'S IN A NAME
And while most bars in other countries carry the names of the owners by way of identification, the English pub comes with a fascinating variety of curious rubrics that delve deep into history. As the chain of ale-houses spread through England, it was no longer sufficient for the ale wife to stick an "ale stake" through a window or hang a garland of evergreens above the door to show that fresh ale was available. Ale-houses became commercial propositions and needed clear identities. Elaborate signs appeared outside them.

There were three men came out of the west,
Their fortunes for to try,
And these three men made a solemn vow,
John Barleycorn should die.
They ploughed, they sowed, they harrowed
    him in,
Throwed clods upon his head,
And these three men made a solemn vow,
John Barleycorn was dead.
Anon

As the people were largely illiterate, these signs had to be instantly recognizable. And as the people were frequently at war, many signs were taken from the crests of the "noble" families that organized the fighting. Some famous pub signs still in use, such as the Red Lion (John of Gaunt), Bear and Ragged Staff (Earl of Warwick), and Eagle and Child (Earl of Derby), have heraldic origins. Some names pre-date Christianity, such as the Chequers, of Roman origin – the sign indicated both a wine shop and a place where money could be exchanged – and the Green Man, a pagan man who covered himself in greenery and then attacked villagers. Pubs called the Green Man that use an idealized image of Robin Hood on their signs are wrong by several centuries.

The impact of Christianity can be seen in pubs called the Crossed Keys (the insignia of St Paul), the Mitre, the Lamb (a reference to Christ), the Bell, and the Hope and Anchor (Paul described hope as the "anchor of the soul") while the Bull is a corruption of "bulla", a monastic seal. New Inn is actually a very old name, a shortened form of Our Lady's Inn, the common name given to taverns built alongside churches and monasteries. During the brief Cromwellian republic, all Popish names were banned. The Salutation, a reference to the annunciation of the Virgin Mary, became the Flower Pot. Austere taverns of the time given the firmly Protestant name of God Encompasses Us were refashioned as the Goat and Compasses by opponents of Cromwell.

Publicans were always quick to touch their forelock to the monarch of the day, hence the profusion of Queen's and King's Heads. But as capitalism developed out of feudalism, inns were often the meeting places of trade associations that allowed their crests to be used, hence the survival of the Baker's Arms, the Dolphin (watermen), the Lamb and Flag (merchant tailors), the Three Compasses (carpenters), Noah's Ark (ship-wrights), and the Ram or Fleece (wool trade). In fact, in 1393 King Richard II brought in legislation that impelled landlords to erect signs to show they sold drink: "Whosoever shall brew ale in the town with intention of selling it must hang out a sign, otherwise he shall forefeit his ale".

DARTS

*D*arts is the success story of pub games this century, in the US as much as Britain and increasingly in other countries as well. Just about every single pub and club in Britain has a dartboard. It is played by millions and watched on television by even more.

According to legend, darts developed from a game in which archers practised their skills by firing arrows at a log or barrel end. But there isn't a shred of evidence to support the theory. There is no record of darts being played before the middle of the nineteenth century, when it first appeared as a fairground game using a blowpipe.

It quickly caught on, though. Log-end boards were straightforward enough for a local joiner to make. The game was easy enough to play passably but offered the real enthusiast a chance to develop a much higher level of skill. It was sociable enough to be played casually by a few friends, and competitive enough to become an inter-pub team game. From the publican's point of view a board was cheap to buy and didn't require a dedicated space as skittles did, but both casual and competitive play attracted custom.

Until the London board became universal, there were Yorkshire and Burton and Grimsby and Kent and Manchester and Lincoln and Norfolk boards, all with different values, sizes and numbers of beds, all of different diameters, all with different sequences of numbers. Which is exactly what one would expect if the game had first been played on a stall at a travelling fair.

For in an era before mass manufacture on the modern scale, each fair would have a different, hand-made, variant of the game. Then, local joiners would be commissioned by people who had played the game to produce as close to a copy as they could remember. Finally, local enthusiasts would invent flourishes of their own, such as the two diamonds worth 25 outside the scoring area on the Burton board.

The first mass-produced sisal boards – cheaper and more durable than a log-end, maintenance-free, and easier to get a dart to stick into – were of the London pattern, so a publican wanting a new board had to buy the London style to take advantage of the availability of a mass-produced type.

The board used around the world today was originally only one of two patterns common in the capital: the East London Fives board had bull, outer, trebles and doubles but had only 12 beds, three scoring five, three scoring 10, three scoring 15 and three scoring 20. A variant, Wide Fives, had enlarged five-scoring beds to help less-skilled players.

The London board which is now standard was chosen by the National Darts Association when it was formed in 1924 as its competition standard for no better reason than that it was dominant in the immediate area. In 1927 the NDA's national team championship won a big sponsorship from the *News of the World* newspaper, and any team which wanted to compete had to use the London board.

Success breeds success, and when the Clubs & Institutes Union and board manufacturer Nodor set up championships of their own they too settled on the London board. Then the first *News of the World* national individual championship in 1947 was played on the London board, and it was declared the national standard.

Darts is a remarkable game that can be played by people with great skill or people with none at all

Buying a round of beer in a British pub. If the round is a big one, drinkers will organize a kitty or "whip"

O Beer! O Hodgson, Guinness, Allsopp, Bass!
Names that should be on every infant's tongue!
Shall days and months and years and centuries pass,
And still your merits be unrecked, unsung?
Oh! I have gazed into my foaming glass,
And wished that lyre could yet again be strung.
Which once rang prophet-like through Greece, and
  taught her
Misguided sons that the best drink was water.

C. S. Calverley

Many pub names have a strong sporting theme, if fox hunting or cock fighting count as "sports". Cricket is far and away the most popular subject, with countless Cricketers. The Bat and Ball at Hambledon in Hampshire staged famous matches and is regarded as the home of the modern game. It was a brewpub where the landlord's ale "flared like turpentine". The most famous of all English cricketers, Dr W.G. Grace, has a pub named in his honour while The Yorker in London's Piccadilly commemorates a particularly wicked type of bowler's delivery. (There is no known American equivalent called The Spit Ball.) Although football (soccer) has a bigger following than cricket, it has less support on pub signs. Nevertheless the Gunners (Arsenal), the Spurs (Tottenham Hotspur), the Hammers (West Ham), the Saints (Southampton) and United (the internationally-recognized shorthand for Manchester United) all have pubs named after them.

THE DRINKER'S CODE OF HONOUR

The etiquette of pub drinking is also sharply different in English pubs. Whereas in most bars and cafés, drinkers will run up a tab, often marked by waiters on a beer mat or given as a receipt with each drink, in an English pub (or a Welsh or Scottish one for that matter) each beer is paid for as it is ordered. The British drink in "rounds", which means that each member of a group will take it in turns to buy drinks for the ensemble. The name is derived from "going the rounds", or serving everyone in turn with goods or services, which in turn probably comes from King Arthur's egalitarian round table. Woe betide any drinker who does not "stand his round". In order to avoid being considered a skinflint, a member of a round will declare his intention of buying drinks by declaring "It's my shout". The buying of beer in this fashion helps explain the comparative weakness of British draught beer. A group of six will get through six pints in the course of "a session" and will be glad, at the end, that the beer they were drinking was only around 3.5 per cent alcohol.

Waiter service is rare in an English or Welsh pub. The middle- and working-class inhabitants of the British Isles have never been at ease with the

"No wine," said Acton. "But I'd like to have a look at the beer-list, please." "I beg your pardon, Sir?" "Surely the biggest hotel in the biggest beer-drinking city in the world has a beer list?" "I'm afraid not, Sir!" "Incredible." Acton shook his head sadly. "Well, please ask the cellar-master if he has a bottle of '61 Foster's. It was a memorable year for Victorian beer, with that delicate flavour of bonfires in the hops. The '61 Foster's is a really superb lager, brut, mon, charnu, petillante, fino, pizzicato, and faintly amertume. It has that nobly fading straw-like pallor which is less a colour than a vestment, la robe: and an aroma that is distinctly Bouverie Street. The bouquet is a discreet cuir russe, or Old Harness. It is urbane but quietly persuasive, and with a notable wet finish, soft on the taste-buds, and on the pocket, too." The '61 Foster's was exhausted, but Acton found a tolerable '62 Melbourne Bitter to go with the coffee. He assured the wine-waiter that, though it lacked chiaroscuro and clangtint, it had a compensatory verve, good-humoured spritzig, and almost the panache of a pre-war Export Bass.

Cyril Pearl, *Pantaloons and Antics*

notion of being "waited on" and, apart from fish-and-chip takeaways, only started to eat out in large numbers when pubs offered food with buffet-style service. In Scotland the tradition is different: there are pubs in the "Borders", the areas abutting the boundary with England, and also in the great cities of Aberdeen, Dundee, Edinburgh and Glasgow. But elsewhere drinking is largely confined to hotels.

LAST ORDERS, GENTLEMEN, PLEASE

If drinking throughout Britain often seems frantic compared to the more measured style of bars and cafés, it is the lingering effect of the country's bizarre licensing laws that once restricted pub opening hours. The restrictions dated from the First World War when the teetotal Welsh politician David Lloyd George was convinced that drinking was harming the war effort. As part of the 1915 Defence of the Realm Act, pubs were only allowed to open for short periods around lunchtime and in the evening. Since the 1980s, many of these restrictions have been lifted and pubs can open all day from 11 a.m. until 11 p.m. if they wish. Even Sunday pub drinking laws were liberalized in 1995. But the British have yet to get used to this bibulous freedom and still tend to quaff pints as though the shade of Lloyd George is about to descend and deny them their pleasure.

> Up the street, in the Sailors Arms, Sinbad Sailors, grandson of Mary Ann Sailors, draws a pint in the sunlit bar. The ship's clock in the bar says half past eleven. Half past eleven is opening time. The hands of the clock have stayed still at half past eleven for fifty years. It is always opening time in the Sailors Arms.
> **Dylan Thomas,** *Under Milk Wood*

Irish pubs have a reputation for being more easy-going and laid-back than their British counterparts, mainly as a result of less restricted opening hours. Irish pubs open all day, though, being a Catholic country, do shut for a contemplative period in the afternoon, known as the "holy hour". The Irish, like the Welsh, tend to burst into song when they are "drink taken". Sometimes worse things happen. The famous writer-cum-

DOMINOES

The click of "doms" is one of the most soothing sounds in a pub or bar. The game is thought to have originated in Spain or France – certainly French prisoners of war in Britain at the end of the eighteenth century made pieces carved from bone. The game clearly developed from different forms of dice. The modern set of dominoes is made up of 28 pieces, ranging from double O to double six.

The standard game played in Britain uses six, nine or 12-spot dominoes. Four players – two sets of partners – are involved. The pieces are shuffled, each player draws out six unseen pieces and the game commences. Usually the player with double six begins. The next player must put down a piece whose spots match one side or the other of the first piece played. If the player cannot match the first piece, he "knocks" by rapping his piece on the table and play moves to the next person. The side with the least number of spots left is the winner. There are dozens of variations on the basic theme, all of them requiring considerable mathematical skill. Dominoes needs a quiet area and is not ideally suited to many large, one-bar and noisy pubs.

boozer Brendan Behan, an acknowledged expert on Dublin pubs, recorded a poem written by the owner of O'Meara's pub to commemorate a punch-up in the bar:

> *Then Hoolihan hit Hannaghan and Hannaghan hit McGilligan*
> *And everyone hit anyone of whom he had a spite,*
> *And Larry Dwyer, the cripple, who was sitting doing nothing,*
> *Got a kick that broke his jawbone for not indulging in the fight.*

Behan also recalled "Being in the Blue Lion in Parnell Street one day and the owner said to me: 'You owe me ten shillings', he said, 'you broke a glass the last time you were here'. 'God bless and save us,' I said, 'it must have been a very dear glass if it cost ten shillings. Tell us, was it a Waterford glass or something?' I discovered in double-quick time that it wasn't a glass that you'd drink out of he meant – it was a pane of glass and I'd stuck somebody's head through it."

EUROPEAN SOPHISTICATION

In mainland Europe there are occasional pastiches of the English pub – Japanese firms build them, complete with plastic beams – but a different culture prevails. The French café ranges from the large and plush to the small and overcrowded, dense with pungent cigarette smoke. In either, beer competes with wine, spirits and coffee, while food, ranging from the obligatory croque monsieur

The roistering Irish writer Brendan Behan admitted to being a "pane in the neck" in one Dublin bar

> When I die I want to decompose in a barrel of porter and have it served in all the pubs in Dublin. I wonder would they know it was me?
> **J. P. Donleavy,** *The Ginger Man*

JUKE-BOXES

Coin-operated music machines, in the form of musical boxes or player pianos, had existed in pubs and bars throughout the world from the nineteenth century. The juke-box is an American invention and was different because it offered a choice of phonographs or records. The first machine with an automatic changer system was the Gabriel Automatic Entertainer. It was primitive, had to be wound up and the sound came out of a horn.

Progress came in the 1920s with the advent of the electrically-recorded disc and by the end of that decade several companies were making juke-boxes. The most famous names, Wurlitzer and Rock-Ola, came on the scene in the early 1930s.

The heart of the juke-box is the changer system in which records are stored, selected and played on a turntable. Part of the fun lay not only in the music but in watching the selector process, with the disc rising up, being lowered on to the turntable and the pick-up arm coming down to produce the sound.

The name has several possible origins. Jook is an old black American slang word for dancing. A more vulgar theory is that "jook" meant sex and the first music machines were found in brothels. A third theory is that juke is a corruption of "jute" and jute joints were where jute pickers entertained themselves with music.

Juke-boxes became identified with speakeasies during Prohibition but they survived this poor image and became a focal part of the great upsurge in popular music in the 1930s and 1940s. The designs became ever more elaborate and entrancing, complete with flashing gaudy lights. Despite the arrival of television in the 1940s and 1950s, juke-boxes, by now exported all over the world, got a new lease of life with the enormous success of rock 'n' roll and stars such as Bill Haley and Elvis Presley. But the arrival of long-playing records, tapes and finally compact discs sent juke-boxes into a long, slow spin towards oblivion. They exist today in many bars as period pieces, delightful to the eye but silent on the ear.

The juke-box reached the zenith of its popularity during the rock 'n' roll era

Wenceslas Square, Prague, (inset) has superb hotels and bars serving world-class beers

to full meals, is always available. In northern France, where beer has deeper cultural roots, specialist bars, in common with those in Belgium, will offer beer menus with a wide range from several countries. The pace is slower than in a British pub and there is no pressure to drink up and leave – until waiters change shift and all tabs have to be cleared in a rush. Belgian cafés are often large, plush, multi-mirrored and with waiters well versed in the wonder and variety of beer – and ever-ready to offer chips with every dish.

There is no such thing as a German bar. There are Prussian bars and Bavarian bier kellers. The former tend to be formal and quiet, with service spilling out on to pavements in warm weather. In the Catholic south, bars and kellers are fun, large, roisterous barns of places, with waiters and waitresses often dressed in traditional lederhosen, serving beer at a fast and furious pace, accompanied by dishes in which the choice is pork, pork or, for a change, pork sausages.

Pork is also much in evidence in Czech bars. With the exception of the sumptuous fin de siècle hotels that ring Wenceslas Square in Prague, bars tend to be utilitarian by Western European standards but that will change as they meet the expectations of younger Czechs and tourists. Until the end of the old totalitarian regime, conversation tended to be limited for fear of police spies and informers. There was nothing new in that. The Good Soldier Schweik or Svejk was often in trouble for speaking his mind during the First World War in his favourite Prague bar, U Kalika (The Chalice). In one episode Schweik's drinking companion, Bretschneider, turns out to be an unwelcome one when he calls Schweik out into a corridor: "He showed him [Schweik] his eaglet and announced that he was arresting him and would take him at once to police headquarters. Schweik tried to explain that the gentleman must be mistaken, that he was completely innocent and that he had not uttered a single word capable of offending anyone. However, Bretschneider told him that he had in fact committed several criminal offences, including the crime of high treason. Then they returned to the pub and Schweik said to Palivec [the landlord]: 'I've had five beers, a

POOL

The biggest challenger to darts as the most popular pub game is pool. It's not the first table-game to enter the bar: billiards, bagatelle and shove-hapenny are well-attested in the eighteenth century, and devil among the tailors, in which a ball hung on a chain from a tall mast is swung at nine small skittles, is still played in many pubs and has caught on across Northern Europe.

Billiards evolved into its present form in the mid-eighteenth century, but primitive versions were current 100 years earlier, probably descending from a lawn game known in the fifteenth century and therefore a near cousin of pell-mell and croquet. Snooker and pool are both nineteenth-century descendants, the former emerging in the Indian Army in the 1870s, the latter advanced enough in its native US to be codified in 1900.

Bagatelle, the ancestor of pinball, developed as a cue game at about the same time as billiards and was just as popular, but now only really survives on any scale as a miniaturized version for children, played with a marble. Even in that form it is very much an antique, and although there are actually two or three pub bagatelle leagues still alive, it is probably best-known as the father of bar billiards.

The problem with most of these games is space. A standard billiards or snooker table is 12 feet by 6 feet, and requires a further 5 or 6 feet all round to give the players room. Even bagatelle, which is played from one end of the table only, has a board 6–10 feet long and again requires another 5 feet for the player. A patented variant of bagatelle, bar billiards, was invented in Flanders in the 1920s and was quickly exported all over Europe by keen businessmen.

Pool superseded all these table games at a stroke in the 1960s not because it takes up less space – it actually takes up more than a single-end game like bar billiards, and devil among the tailors takes up almost no space at all – nor because it is more flexible. There are far more games you can play on a full-size table than on a pool table. Pool took the nation's pubs and youth clubs by storm because of Paul Newman, who played Fast Eddie in *The Hustler*, released in Britain in 1961. By the time the sequel, *The Color of Money*, came out 25 years later there were 45,000 pool tables in pubs and clubs in Britain, there were local leagues, and there were regional, national and international championships.

Pool is as perfect a pub game as darts. It's sociable: you don't have to be too good to enjoy a knock-up. It's competitive, too: you can, if you choose, get to be as good as Fast Eddie himself. From the publican's point of view, the space problem is more than offset by the takings, and the fact that the vast majority of tables are leased cancels out their capital cost.

The last of the table games, **shove hapenny**, is making something of a comeback. It's a miniaturized cousin of an alley game played on an indoor court of 30 feet long or more by medieval, Tudor and Stewart aristocrats, and also a cousin of curling, ice-hockey and the shuffleboard still played on cruise ships.

Paul Newman has a lot to answer for. The success of the film "The Hustler" saw pool tables sprout in thousands of pubs and bars

couple of frankfurters and a roll. Now give me one more slivovice and I must go, because I'm under arrest.'"

OTHER NATIONAL IDIOSYNCRASIES

Australia and Scotland have two things in common: a lot of drinking is done in public houses euphemistically called "hotels" and both countries were once bedevilled by severe restrictions on opening hours. In Australia, when hotel bars were forced to close early in the evening, the "six o'clock swill" was a short period in which beer was poured down parched throats with indecent haste. In Scottish cities, a similar experience accompanied the "ten o'clock swill". Both countries are now more civilized places and their bars more pleasant since the shackles were removed.

> A fine beer may be judged with only one sip, but it is better to be thoroughly sure.
> **Czech proverb.**

The bar of the Hotel Belman, Mazatlan, Mexico
I wandered entirely unprepared into what seemed a vision of the past – a high, cool, scrupulous bar, presided over by angels in white, real bartenders with linen coats, affable exterior, everything. Two excellent English cock-fighting prints on the wall and the inevitable stoutish nude lady stepping over a brook, whose name used to be legion in the good old days. I stood hat in hand in the sanctified twilight of that spacious and cleanly haven, like a good Catholic would in a cathedral after his return from arid and heathen ports; and, after the proper genuflexion, ordered a glass of beer. It was hotter than blazes outside, real tropical, depleting heat. Here, within that exquisitely appointed grot, all was peace and zephyrous coolness. The beer arrived – draft beer – in a tall, thin, clean crystal of Grecian proportions, with a creamy head on it. I tasted it, dear reader, black or white. It was heaven. It was liquid manna. It had the frou-frou of ambrosia, the tender unctuousness of a melted pearl. The planets seemed to pause a moment in their circling to breathe a benediction on that Mexican brewer's head. One felt some great rubato, sweet yet vibrant, in the celestial orchestra of the revolving spheres. It was like a slight ecstatic sigh from the left lung of the Cosmos. Then the universe went on its wonted way again. Hot Dog! But that was a glass of beer!

John Barrymore, *Yachting log*

SKITTLES

*B*eer and skittles has become a cliché because the two really do go together so well, as an evening's play in a pub alley will quickly prove. Three regional forms of skittles survive. The commonest, **West Country**, is played by rolling a ball, as in American 10-pin bowling. **Long Alley**, more common in the East Midlands, is played on an alley anything from 27–36 feet long and usually with a hardwood "cheese" which is hurled but has to bounce. **Old English**, once common in London, now virtually extinct, is thought despite the name to have been introduced from the Low Countries. It too uses a cheese of anything up to 6lb, but unlike Long Alley the cheese should not bounce. The pins are mounted on a plinth and the alley is 21 feet long.

Minor local variants are **Rolly-Polly**, once common in Hertfordshire, played with 15 pins and a crescent-shaped projectile; and **Aunt Sally**, once common around Oxford, in which a single skittle has to be knocked off a special swivel by hurling a baton.

Unlike darts, there is no doubt about the antiquity of skittles: they are well documented in the fourteenth century. It is also interesting that the very same games are in many cases current in the Low Countries and surrounding areas of Germany and France: Rolly-Polly is known as Pierbol in Holland and is documented in seventeenth-century France and Spain; while Aunt Sally is known as Pagschieten in Holland and Flanders, Jukskei in South Africa, and Billons in France.

Bat & Trap, in which the player launches the ball into the air before hitting it as in a tennis serve, either by throwing it up or by a striking one end of a seesaw launcher with the bat, is even more ancient than skittles.

One variant, knurr and spell, descends from knurrenspiel, an Old Norse word meaning "ball game".

Another, tipcat, is the ancestor of rounders and hence baseball, while Kentish bat & trap is an identifiable cousin of cricket in that the striker stands before a miniature wicket at which an opponent gets a chance to bowl, and can be caught out by one of three fielders.

Like skittles, **quoits** is well-recorded in the fourteenth century and was popular enough in the late nineteenth century to have a regional association with standard tournament rules. It is still played in the north-east of England, on a 21-yard pitch with the pegs embedded in soft clay. A player can either try to ring the pegs or can defend them by landing his quoits upended in the clay to form an impenetrable hedge around the pegs.

Most bowling games have moved into the bar in various miniaturized forms.

The most common version of quoits is a parlour game, using a simple hook board and rubber rings. **Suffolk Caves** has five cups on a board into which the rings had to be tossed. **Ringing the Bull**, played in Belgium and France as well as Britain, survives more widely and involves pitching a quoit which is hung from the ceiling on a string over a hook stuck in the nose of a stuffed bull's head mounted on the wall.

In the United States, many bars tend to be dimly lit as though they still live in the shadow of Prohibition. They range from the spartan to the palatial, larger ones having areas set aside for the ubiquitous pool table. Service is usually highly attentive and polite, spoilt only by the shortage of choice and the wickedly low temperature at which beer is served. Sometimes drinkers are handed a frosted mug from the fridge to make the beer temperature even lower. It is difficult to decide whether this tendency is more or less distressing than drinking beer straight from the bottle.

BEER NICKNAMES

*B*eer drinkers love to both mix beers and give them strange nicknames. Most seem to be associated with Guinness and include:

Black and Tan: Guinness and bitter or Guinness and mild
Black Velvet: Guinness and champagne
Poor Man's Black Velvet: Guinness and cider
Black Russian: Guinness and vodka
Velvet Pussy: Guinness and port
Black Maria: Guinness and Tia Maria
Red Velvet: Guinness, cider and blackcurrant
Red Witch: Guinness, Pernod, cider and blackcurrant

In England, renowned for a laid-back and slightly ironic sense of humour, the following mixtures exist:

Mother-in-law: old and bitter
Granny: old and mild
Blacksmith: Guinness and barley wine
Boilermaker: brown and mild
Lightplater: light ale and bitter
Narfer narf: East London slang for half a pint of mild and half a pint of bitter. A half pint of this mixture is narfer narfer narf
Dragon's blood: barley wine and rum
Dog's nose: bitter and gin
Snake bite: lager and cider
Happy Days: In Scotland this is a mixture of beer and a Wee Heavy, a strong ale of the barley wine type

New York City has some fine old taverns dating from the nineteenth century

A game of table skittles

THE HISTORY OF BEER

"*I* FEEL WONDERFUL, DRINKING BEER IN A BLISSFUL MOOD, WITH JOY IN MY HEART AND A HAPPY LIVER." THESE WORDS WERE NOT WRITTEN BY SOMEONE IN THE CORNER OF A PUB ONE FRIDAY NIGHT BUT BY A SUMERIAN POET AROUND THE YEAR 3,000 BC. FOR BEER IS AS OLD AS HISTORY. GLASSES OF MODERN ALE, LAGER OR STOUT HAVE THEIR ROOTS DEEP IN ANCIENT CIVILIZATIONS STRETCHING BACK TO THE DAWN OF TIME.

The words of that Sumerian poet are revealing. He knew that beer not only made him feel cheerful, but was also good for his health. For most of recorded time, water was insanitary and unsafe. People could refresh themselves, however, by drinking alcohol, which contains antiseptic qualities, and in which water has been boiled. Fruit quickly perished in the ancient world, while grain could be stored for long periods. So beer, more than wine, became the drink of the people. Since it was made from a vitamin-rich porridge, beer made them content, flushed out their livers and kidneys, and kept both heart and skin diseases at bay. Along with bread, beer was a vital part of a staple diet.

Ancient Origins

Beer, according to some anthropologists, helped create civilized society. When people of the ancient world realized they could make bread and beer from grain, they stopped roaming and settled down to cultivate cereals in recognizable communities. The American anthropologist Alan Eames says: "Ten thousand years ago… barley was domesticated and worshipped as a god in the highlands of the southern Levant. Thus was beer the driving force that led nomadic mankind into village life." At that time, the world was a warmer place than today by two to three degrees Celsius. North Africa and the Middle East enjoyed a much heavier rainfall than they do today and the warm, moist climate encouraged the growth of cereals. It has been suggested by some experts that beer came before bread, that ancient people learned to make a pleasant, relaxing drink from soaked grain. It is more likely, however, that the reverse was the case: wet dough was left to rise in the open, starches turned to sugar by natural enzymic activity, and then wild yeasts in the air turned the sugars into alcohol.

Brewing became a major industry in the ancient world. Clay tablets with cuneiform writing discovered in Nineveh in the 1840s showed that beer was paid as a form of currency to stonemasons working on the great buildings of the pharoahs. The role of the brewer was sufficiently important for him or her – many women were brewers – to have their own hieroglyph: "fty". A drawing made with a stylus on wet clay shows a person bent over a vessel straining a cereal mash through a sieve. Spices and plants were added to primitive beer as flavourings and to prolong the life of the drink. In Egypt, beer was drunk by the upper classes through reeds to prevent the husks of the grain being swallowed.

Toby Fillpot, a legendary ale-drinker who was used as the enduring image on Toby jugs

The importance of brewing in the ancient world is shown by this cylinder seal from Egypt

A model of the bread and beer-making processes in Ancient Egypt. No one is certain how beer-making began: wet dough for baking may have fermented spontaneously, or beer may even pre-date baking. Either way, bread and beer encouraged nomads to settle down and grow grain

THE EARLY BEERS

The two main cereals used by ancient people in brewing were barley and a type of wheat called "emmer". The first beers were made from raw grain and would have been thin in alcohol, using the small amount of natural sugar present in the ears of wheat and barley. A giant step forward came in the second and third millenia, when brewers in Mesopotamia learned to turn barley into malt. Malting may have been accidental at first. Raw grain was left to soak and then dried in the sun. Magically, the grain had yielded up its starches and sugar caused a violent fermentation, resulting in a drink that was rich in alcohol. Malting rapidly became sophisticated and the Mesopotamians were able to produce dark, as well as light, beer by scorching the malt over fire.

The first brewers had no understanding of yeast. They knew only that when they made beer, the deposits from previous brews left in their clay vessels spontaneously turned the liquid into alcohol. Lactic acid bacteria in the vessels would also have attacked the sugary solution, giving a sour but quenching character to the beer, while wild airborne yeasts would also have had a role to play. No hops were used, as the plant was not known at the time. A major study of brewing in Babylon and Egypt, published in Germany in 1926, described the Babylonians as using unmalted emmer wheat and malted barley. It seems that from very early in the history of brewing, brewers discovered that barley malt produced the best extract of sugars, while wheat gave a fine tart and fruity character to beer. The brewers first made "beer bread", which was baked either light or dark brown, depending on the colour of beer required. A mash was then made by pouring heated water over the bread. It was filtered and left to ferment spontaneously. When fermentation finished, the rough beer was transferred to smaller vessels which were stored in cool cellars where a secondary fermentation occurred.

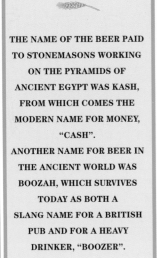

BEER-MAKING IN EGYPT

The Egyptians, on the other hand, used all malted grain and produced only dark-coloured beer. Plants, such as mandrake, and salt were added. The plants were used to balance the sweetness of the malt, while salt is a flavour-enhancer (it was still used in brewing until the nineteenth century AD.) Brewing in the ancient world was not, like modern home-brewing, a sideline, but a major industry. The Pharaoh Rameses gave 10,000 hectolitres a year of free beer to his temple administrators – and that amount was just the tip of the pyramid!

A MATTER OF TASTE

All the knowledge of brewing in the ancient world unearthed by anthropologists and Egyptologists left one tantalizing question unanswered, however: what did beer of the period taste like? The answer came thanks to the remarkable work of Fritz Maytag, owner of the Anchor Brewery in San Francisco. In the 1980s, Maytag contacted scholars throughout the world, who gave him detailed descriptions of how beer had been brewed in ancient civilizations. Maytag used recipes found on tablets from Sumeria in 3,000 BC and began by making 5,000 loaves of "bappir" bread from barley, roasted barley and barley malt. The loaves were baked twice to ensure they were dry in the centre, and were then cut into strips. The finished bread looked remarkably like Weetabix breakfast cereal.

The loaves were placed in the brewery's mash tun, along with some additional barley malt. Maytag had discovered – in a song dedicated to the goddess of brewing, Ninkasi – that sweetness was added twice to Sumerian beer. So he added honey to the mash and dates (for a touch of spiciness) to the beer. No hops were used. Ninkasi beer, as it was called, was not sold commercially but it was drunk at a banquet in the United States. Guests were invited to drink it through straws in the approved manner of the ancient world. It was five per cent alcohol and had an orange-red colour.

As the sweetness from the honey and dates had fermented, the beer was remarkably dry and refreshing. It was not bitter but, made from an ancient recipe almost lost in the dust of time, it was clearly and definably *beer*.

ISLAMIC INVASION

The art of brewing in Egypt and the surrounding lands was ended abruptly in the eighth century AD by the invasion of the Muslims and a Koran that banned the use of alcohol. But the secret was out. The Phoenicians, great sea-going traders, had taken cereals to other countries, and brewing developed in Bavaria and Bohemia, as well as spreading north to the Baltic and across the sea to the British Isles. As the world's climate changed yet again, wine-making was confined to the hot Mediterranean countries as grapes struggled to flourish in the cooler north. But from northern Spain to the Arctic circle hardy cereals grew in abundance, and the peoples of that vast territory brewed with vigour, not only to refresh themselves, but also to keep healthy with the aid of a drink that was rich in vitamin B.

The skill of brewers exceeded that of wine-makers. Cooperage – fashioning casks from heated and hooped staves of wood – allowed brewers to store their beers in large, air-tight containers. The Romans and the Greeks, by comparison, were still using the older technology of clay pots in which to store wine. In 21 AD, Strabo noted seeing wooden "pithoi" in Northern Europe. "The Celts are fine coopers," he wrote, "for their casks are larger than houses." As the Romans marched across Europe, they saw that from Spain northwards, the tribes made beer. "The nations of the west have their own intoxicant from grain soaked in water," wrote Pliny; "there are many ways of making it in Gaul or Spain and under different names, though the principle is the same. The Spanish have taught us that these liquors keep well." In Britain, the Celtic tribes made a beer they called "curmi". They also made cider from apples and mead from honey. In the Scottish Highlands, the tradition was to use heather, both as a flavouring and also to aid the fermentation of barley malt in brewing. The Romans, however, were unimpressed by beer and preferred to drink wine. But when supplies of wine ran out, they turned to brewing in order to keep their troops happy and healthy. Recent excavations of Roman sites in England have discovered large maltings, which suggests that brewing was carried out on a regular and organized basis.

There was no Roman diffidence about drinking beer when northern Europe was overrun by the Danes and Saxons, since they already had a great beer-drinking culture based on feasts – and every day seemed to offer the excuse for a feast of some type. From this period comes the expression "wassail" for a boozy celebration. Even Valhalla (paradise), according to Norse myth, was a great hall where the dead passed their time drinking beer, while in the living world, beer or malt were used to pay fines, tolls, rents and debts.

Coopers at work in the Middle Ages fashioning casks from wood and iron. The Romans marvelled at the ability of northern tribes to store their liquor in casks rather than the clay pots used for wine

IN ANGLO-SAXON TIMES, DRINKING GOBLETS WERE MARKED WITH PEGS TO SHOW HOW MUCH A PERSON HAD DRUNK. THIS GAVE RISE TO THE EXPRESSION "TO TAKE SOMEONE DOWN A PEG OR TWO". IN ENGLAND, INNS IN TOWNS HAD TO PAY A TAX KNOWN AS A "SCOT". DRINKERS WHO WENT OUT OF THE TOWN TO RURAL INNS WERE DESCRIBED AS DRINKING "SCOT FREE".

An ale wife in the full regalia of her craft. Women were the early brewers or brewsters as they made both bread and beer for their households

opened, a garland of evergreens is hung over the door for luck. But the Romans can lay claim to the first inn sign. A chequer board would be hung outside a building that both sold wine or beer and also changed money. There are still many English pubs called the Chequers.

The Nordic people called their beer öl or ealu, from which came the term "ale". Another Saxon term for beer was woet, which survives today as "wort", the sweet liquid made by mashing malt and water. For centuries, ale meant a drink made from the fermented sugars of malt and flavoured by plants, herbs and spices – but not hops. Beer, from the German bier, came later and was ale with the addition of hops. Today, both words are used in ale-drinking countries, but all modern beer – including mild ale, pale ale and winter ale – is made with hops. Ironically, the British could have used hops in their early ales, as the plant was eaten as a delicacy by the Romans. But the British, in common with brewers in mainland Europe, preferred to use other plants, such as bog myrtle, rosemary and yarrow.

The Germans and Scandinavians added a mixture of herbs called gruit. In Scandinavia, juniper was a common addition to beer. This use of spices and berries in brewing almost certainly influenced the first distillers of spirits from grain, such as gin and vodka.

The Early History of Beer

Throughout Europe, a small commercial brewing movement started to spread, almost always based on inns and taverns where the owners brewed ale. When the Normans invaded England, they brought with them a powerful love of wine and cider. But the locals went on doggedly brewing ale. The Norman Domesday Book in 1086, a remarkable survey of the lives of the English, recorded 43 *cervisiarii*, or commercial ale brewers, who could be fined four shillings or ducked in the village pond if they made *malam cerevisiam faciens* (bad ale).

Commercial brewers, however, soon found a major competitor – in the form of the Christian church. Archbishops, abbots and clerics had stepped in to cure the excesses of the Anglo-Saxons and to corner the market in ale. Ale was brewed for monks

THE FIRST PUB

Brewing was confined to the home and it was the responsibility of the woman of the house – the ale wife – to ensure the men were kept well supplied. A good ale wife was held in great esteem: Alreck, King of Hordoland, chose Geirhild to be his queen not because of her looks or her dowry, but because she brewed good ale. It was natural to make beer at the same time as bread, as key ingredients were common to both. Gradually, the best ale wives or brewsters became so celebrated in their communities that people would go to their houses to drink and, eventually, to buy ale. When a brew was ready, the ale wife would put a long pole covered in evergreens through a window. This "ale stake" was the first rudimentary ale-house sign. In England, pubs called the Bush or Hollybush commemorate the ale stake, and when a new pub is

as a staple part of their diet and it was also offered to the hordes of pilgrims who visited monasteries and sought food and drink. The Benedictines were the most enthusiastic brewers, though other orders were quick to emulate them. In medieval Germany there were 400-500 monastic breweries.

ECCLESIASTICAL HERITAGE

Monastic brewhouses were enormous. The Abbey of St Gaull in Switzerland in the ninth century had a malthouse, kiln, millroom for grinding the malt, as well as three brewhouses and storage cellars. The malthouse was big enough to allow four different "couches" of grain to be laid out for germination. To make beer, the monks used barley, oats and wheat. The partially germinated green malt was heated in a kiln, which had a central chimney round which were placed wickerwork platforms covered with material. The grain was spread out on the material and heated from below by wood fire. After kilning, the malt was ground by hand and then mixed with water in an open copper vessel that was heated by fire.

Monastic brewhouses were built near rivers. The Clairvaux Abbey in France used water power to grind the grain, provide liquor for the mash, and wash away the detritus after brewing. Smaller abbeys that didn't have malthouses would leave the grain on grassy ground overnight and the dew would start germination. When the grain sprouted, it was moved to a rudimentary kiln and heated by laying it on a hair cloth above a hearth. The malt was chewed to test it for softness and friability. The holy brewers preferred soft water and added soap to get the required effect. The mash was stirred with a wooden fork and when the wort simmered round the handle, it was estimated that saccharification (changing starch into sugar) had taken place. After this the wort was allowed to cool and then ladled into wooden casks which were known as "rounds". This was then mixed with yeast. When fermentation was complete, the tuns were sealed to allow the *cervoise* (from the Latin for ale, *cerevisia*) to mature and undergo a secondary fermentation.

The best record of medieval brewing came from the Queen's College brewhouse at Oxford University. It was built in 1340 and had changed little by the time it was destroyed by bombs in the Second World War. The mash tun was made of memel oak and had two outlet pipes covered with strainers to keep back the grain. The sugary extract – wort – flowed to an underback, or collecting vessel, below the mash tun and was then pumped manually to an open copper boiled by heat from a furnace.

Hops were not used when the brewery was first built, although boiling the wort was essential to kill bacteria. After boiling, the wort was cooled in large open wooden pans called cool ships, then ladled into a large wooden round where yeast was pitched. Once fermentation had started, the wort was taken in a vessel called a tun dish to casks in the cellar, where fermentation continued. Troughs were arranged below the casks to collect the yeast that frothed out of the bung holes – a modified version of the system survives in Marston's Brewery in Burton-on-Trent. When fermentation was finished, the casks were sealed and left to condition. The strength of this College Ale was around seven per cent alcohol by volume. A Chancellor's Ale of twice the strength was also brewed occasionally.

ELIZABETHAN TIMES

Ale brewing was different to modern practice in one key way: beers of different strength would be made from just one mash of malt. A strong beer would be made first, then the malt would be mixed with liquor for a second and third time to produce ales of declining strength. Monks called the strongest ale *prima melior* and kept it for the abbot and his distinguished guests. The second brew, *secunda*, was given to lay workers in the monasteries, while the brothers and poor pilgrims had to make do with a weak *tertia*. In Elizabethan times, Shakespeare immortalized *tertia* as "small beer". It was drunk by nursing mothers and children, as milk was unsafe. In 1512, the household records of the noble Percy

A stained-glass depiction of brewing as a commercial enterprise in Tournai Cathedral in Belgium

DURING THE MIDDLE AGES, GOVERNMENTS AND TOWN COUNCILS IN THE BRITISH ISLES AND MAINLAND EUROPE EMPLOYED OFFICIALS KNOWN AS "ALE CONNERS". THEIR JOB WAS TO TEST THE QUALITY OF THE ALE BREWED FOR COMMERCIAL SALE. THEY WOULD TEST IT BY POURING SOME ALE ON TO A WOODEN BENCH, THEN SITTING IN THE PUDDLE. IF THEIR LEATHER BREECHES STUCK TO THE SEAT, THEN THE ALE WAS CONSIDERED TO BE OF GOOD QUALITY.

family of Northumberland showed they consumed for breakfast each day during Lent a quart of ale for "my lord and lady", two pints for "my lady's gentle-woman" and one and half gallons for the gentlemen of the chapel and the children. Small beer would have been around three per cent alcohol or less. In seventeenth-century Amsterdam, children in the civic orphanage were given a pint of small beer a day as milk was thought to be infected with tuberculosis.

It should not, however, be thought that people in earlier times were in a state of perpetual drunkenness. Most of them were engaged in heavy manual labour and so would have quickly sweated off the alcohol. Moreover, houses were poorly heated and ale provided an easy form of internal warmth. Also, the overwhelming majority of the population lived lives of abject poverty. They had to sell cattle, poultry and eggs to the towns to survive and had a repetitive diet of thin vegetable soup and bread. So ale played a vital part in keeping them healthy.

The malthouse at Fountains Abbey in Yorkshire measured 60 square feet and the monks produced 60 barrels of strong ale every 10 days, the equivalent of almost 17,000 pints. The Domesday Book

recorded that the monks of St Paul's Cathedral in London brewed 67,814 gallons of ale a year, or 542,512 pints. English ale was considered to be of high quality. Thomas à Becket, who became Archbishop of Canterbury and was murdered in his cathedral, brewed ale as a young priest for the Benedictine monks of St Albans Abbey in Hertfordshire. In 1158, he took two chariot-loads of ale on a diplomatic mission to France. The ale was "decocted from choice fat grain as a gift for the French who wondered at such an invention – a drink most wholesome, clear of all dregs, rivalling wine in colour and surpassing it in flavour".

COMMERCIAL BREWING

At different periods of European history, the dissolution of monasteries broke the church's power over brewing. This was seen most dramatically in England when Henry VIII sacked the monasteries as part of his long-running dispute with Rome. Centuries later, monks forced out of France at the time of the revolution moved north into the Low Countries, started to brew and began the tradition of Trappist ales that survives to this day. In general, though, the decline of monastic brewing paved the way for the rise of a commercial brewing industry.

Commercial brewing was aided by the arrival of the hop plant. Hops were first noted as being grown in Babylon in 200 AD. The plant was taken to the Caucasus and then into parts of Germany by the Slavs following the migration of peoples after the fall of the Roman empire. Hop gardens were recorded in the Hallertau region of Bavaria in 736 AD. It is likely that at first hops were used as just another plant to balance the sweetness of malt, but brewers quickly grasped that they not only added a pleasing citric bitterness to ale, but also had antiseptic qualities that helped fight infections. Hopped beer had better keeping qualities, as was noted by Reynold Scott in his best-selling *A Perfitte Platforme for a Hoppe Garden* in 1574. As well as instructing growers in England on how to plant hops in the best soil and train them to climb up poles, he added: "Whereas you cannot make above eight to nine gallons of indifferent ale from one bushel of malt, you may draw 18–20 gallons of very good beer. If your ale may endure a fortnight, your beer through the benefit of the hop, shall continue a month, and what grace it yieldeth to the taste, all men may judge that have sense in their mouths." At

Brewing in the sixteenth century. By this period the hop was an essential element in beer production

a royal banquet in Windsor Park in 1528, 15 gallons of ale and 15 gallons of beer were ordered for the guests. The beer cost 20 pence, the ale two shillings and sixpence. The reason for the price difference was that less malt was needed to make hopped beer owing to its better keeping qualities. But ale did not disappear overnight and the hop was not universally welcomed.

WAGING WAR AGAINST THE HOP

The gruit market – the plants and spices added to ale before hops arrived – was a powerful one, often controlled by the church, and they saw that market threatened by the hop. The archbishop of Cologne, who controlled the sale of gruit through a decree known as the *Grutrecht*, attempted to outlaw the use of hops. In Russia, Archduke Vasili II banned the plant, as did Henry VIII in England. But consumer preference won the day. In fourteenth-century Holland, Amsterdamers demanded hopped beer from Hamburg and Bremen in preference to the local unhopped brews. Eventually, the controllers of gruit were bought out with substantial cash inducements.

The use of other plants did not immediately stop. In 1588, Jacob Theodor von Bergzabern, writing about brewing practice in Europe, said that while hops were used in the copper boil, "The English sometimes add to the brewed beer, to make it more pleasant, sugar, cinnamon, cloves and other good spices in a small bag. The Flemings mix it with honey or sugar and precious spices and so make a drink like claret or hippocras. Others mix in honey, sugar and syrup, which not only makes the beer pleasant to drink, but gives it a fine brown colour." He added that brewers had learned from "the Flemings and the Netherlanders" that adding laurel, ivy or Dutch myrtle to beer strengthens it, preserves it and prevents it going sour. London brewers were still using bog myrtle as late as the 1750s and Belgian wheat beers are spiced today with coriander and orange peel.

The hop arrived late in England when Flemish traders brought the plant to the south-east corner of the country. A century later, encouraged by the policy of land enclosure that created rich yeoman farmers, Kent became a major hop-growing region. The plant still met with lingering resistance, though. In an astonishing diatribe in his *Compendyous Regyment or Dyetary of Health* of 1542, Andrew Boorde almost burst with xenophobic rage: "Beer is made of malte, hoppes and water; it is the natural drynke for a Dutcheman, and nowe of lete dayes it is much used in England to the detryment of many Englysshe people; specyally it kylleth them the which be troubled with the colyke; and the stone and the strangulion; for the drynke is a colde drynke, yet it doth make a man fat, and doth inflate the bely, as it doth appere by the Dutche men's faces and belyes. If the bere be well served and fyned and not new, it doth qualify heat of the lyver." Ale, on the other hand, "is made of malte and water; and they the which do put any other thynge to ale than is rehersed, except yest, barme or godesgood, doth sofyticat theyr ale. Ale for an Englysche man is a naturell drinke. Ale must have these propertyes: it must be fresshe and clear, it muste not be ropy or smoky, nor it must have no weft or tayle. Ale should not be dronke under V [five] days olde". But the times were out of joint with Mr Boorde. Most "Englyschemen" preferred the cleaner, refreshing taste of hopped beer. By the middle of the sixteenth

A dish fit for a queen... Elizabeth I of England was fussy about her beer and often ordered London ale to be sent to her if provincial brews were not to her liking

century, a few years after Andrew Boorde had railed against the hop, there were 26 "common" or commercial brewers in London. They were undoubtedly brewing hopped beer, since most of them were based in Southwark, close to the major hop market.

A QUESTION OF TASTE

How did ale and beer taste in those times? We can get an idea from the far north of Norway, the old Norseland, where farmers still brew in the medieval manner. Juniper branches, rich with berries, are used as a filter in the mashing vessel and in the copper after the boil, though today hops are added alongside the juniper berries. Yeast is collected on a "totem stick" from one brew and then dipped in the fermenting vessel for the next one. The finished beer is around 10 per cent alcohol and has a rich, malty fruitiness with a distinct juniper character. In the north of Finland, a handful of brewers still produce the medieval beer style known as *sahti*. It is made from a mash of barley malt and rye, which is filtered over juniper. Hops are also added to the boil. The beer has a herbal, winey aroma, with a pronounced fruitiness in the mouth and a spicy finish.

The tiny Sint Martinus Brewery in Groningen in the far north of The Netherlands brews a beer called *Cluyn*, pronounced "clown", based on a 1340s' recipe for a strong wedding ale. The grist is a complex blend of malted barley, oats and wheat with unmalted versions of the three grains and some crystal malt for colour. As the beer is sold commercially, the brewery is forced by Dutch law to use hops; none was in the original recipe, which used

gruit instead. The beer is 8.8 per cent alcohol and is naturally conditioned in the bottle. It has a hazy copper colour and a fruity and herbal aroma. There is sour fruit in the mouth with hop bitterness, and more ripe fruit in the finish.

THE FIRST HOP BEERS

A recreation of an ale from 1503, based on a recipe in a book by Richard Arnold called *Customs of London*, is the earliest example of a beer that genuinely used hops. The original ingredients were listed as 10 quarters of malt, two quarters of wheat, two quarters of oats and 40 pounds of hops to make 60 barrels of beer. Home-brewing expert Graham Wheeler, who recreated the beer, smoked the malt over a wood fire in a garden barbeque. (At the time, all malt was kilned over wood fires.) Wheeler used Goldings hops, which did not exist at the time but there are no sixteenth-century varieties available today. The beer had an original starting gravity of 1065 degrees and finished with 6.7 per cent alcohol. As a result of the use of wheat, the beer had a hazy bronze colour and a pronounced smoky and herbal aroma. There was more smoked malt character on the palate, with a resiny underpinning from the hops, while the finish was intensely dry and bitter with dark fruit notes.

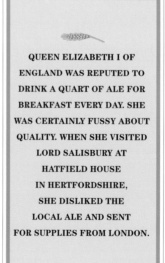

QUEEN ELIZABETH I OF ENGLAND WAS REPUTED TO DRINK A QUART OF ALE FOR BREAKFAST EVERY DAY. SHE WAS CERTAINLY FUSSY ABOUT QUALITY. WHEN SHE VISITED LORD SALISBURY AT HATFIELD HOUSE IN HERTFORDSHIRE, SHE DISLIKED THE LOCAL ALE AND SENT FOR SUPPLIES FROM LONDON.

THE INDUSTRIAL REVOLUTION

Most beer drinkers today would find the smoky character of Arnold's ale unacceptable. But it is likely that the beer is typical of its period. It was not until the Industrial Revolution of the late eighteenth and nineteenth centuries that coke became available as a source of fuel. Kilning malt by coal fire created noxious gases that tainted the grain, and coal fires were banned in many major cities because of the pollution they caused. Wood, on the other hand, was in plentiful supply in countries still largely covered by forests. In Britain, hornbeam was the preferred type of wood used in malt kilning. But wood fires were hard to control. They could flare suddenly and scorch the grain. As a result, all malt up until the turn of the nineteenth century was brown rather than pale. It produced a low level of sugary extract (10 per cent less than pale malt) and would, as Arnold's ale has shown, have had a pronounced smoky character.

The Early Development of Lager

But while all beer was brown, significant changes were taking place in brewing practice that were to fashion the future development of the industry. From the fifteenth century, attempts were made in central Europe to store beer at low temperatures so that it could survive the hot, torrid summers. In Germany, brewers started to keep their brews in ice-filled caves and discovered that at low temperatures the yeast would behave in a quite different manner. Instead of creating a deep, fluffy head on top of the wort and producing alcohol in a few days, it produced only a thin head and settled to the bottom of the vessel. Fermentation was also much slower and took several weeks. But, protected by both the cold and alcohol, the yeast was free from attack by wild, airborne strains. "Cold fermented beer" was mentioned in a report of Munich town council in Bavaria in 1420. A report from the city of Nabburg said: "One brews the warm or top fermentation; but first in 1474 one attempted to brew by the cold bottom fermentation and so preserve part of the brew for the summer."

It was not until the late nineteenth century that it was possible to culture a pure lager yeast strain, but the development of cold fermentation was of profound importance to brewers who had tussled with the problem of being unable to brew and thereby earn a living during the summer months. But it would be a mistake to over-emphasize the spread of lager brewing in the medieval period. As late as 1831 there were 16,000 breweries in Prussia

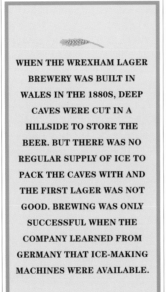

WHEN THE WREXHAM LAGER BREWERY WAS BUILT IN WALES IN THE 1880S, DEEP CAVES WERE CUT IN A HILLSIDE TO STORE THE BEER. BUT THERE WAS NO REGULAR SUPPLY OF ICE TO PACK THE CAVES WITH AND THE FIRST LAGER WAS NOT GOOD. BREWING WAS ONLY SUCCESSFUL WHEN THE COMPANY LEARNED FROM GERMANY THAT ICE-MAKING MACHINES WERE AVAILABLE.

producing top-fermenting beer. It was only from this date that cold fermentation began to dominate. By 1839, the number of Prussian brewers using top-fermentation had fallen to 12,000, and to 7,400 by 1865. Nor did every area of Germany accept lager brewing. In 1603, the city authorities of Cologne, in agreement with the brewers, banned cold fermentation. The people preferred top-fermenting beer and considered lager beer too intoxicating. Cologne has a mild climate and the brewers considered lagering unnecessary. Today, Cologne and neighbouring Düsseldorf still produce Kölsch and Alt beers by warm fermentation.

Bavaria was also to have a second impact on the future of brewing in the whole of Germany with the decision in 1516 by the Dukes Wilhelm IV and Ludwig X to introduce the Purity Pledge – known as the *Reinheitsgebot* – in the Assembly of the Estates of the Realm meeting in Ingolstadt. This stipulated that only barley malt, hops, yeast and water could be used to make beer. Similar decisions had been made for Munich in 1487 by Duke Albrecht IV and for the Landsheit area in 1493. These decisions were not entirely altruistic. The Bavarian royal family monopolized the growing and distribution of barley and they did not want that monopoly challenged by the use of other cereals or sugars.

It is significant that wheat was excluded from the terms of the *Reinheitsgebot* (though it was added later). Wheat beer, like white bread, was considered to be a delicacy fit only for the aristocracy. The *Reinheitsgebot* declared that the masses should drink pure beer, but it could only be barley-based beer – their rulers alone could enjoy the pleasures of wheat beer. The royal family, however, allowed commercial wheat beer brewing to develop on a limited scale in the nineteenth century and the family lost any power over brewing when it vacated the throne as a result of the First World War. The *Reinheitsgebot* covered the whole of Germany when the various principalities were united in 1871. In the 1980s the European Parliament, urged on by French brewers in the Strasbourg area who were anxious

The powerful temperance movement in Victorian Britain attacked the brewers for all manner of crimes – including death and murder, as this contemporary cartoon shows

to sell their beers across the border, declared the *Reinheitsgebot* a "restraint of trade". But a flood of what the Germans call *chemi-bier* did not pour into the country. Consumers supported brewers who declared their allegiance to the Purity Pledge.

The twin Bavarian developments of lagering and "pure beer" did not coalesce into a powerful force on the world stage until the nineteenth century. Before that, the shaping of a modern brewing industry came in England with the arrival of a beer style called "porter".

Porter

A major book on brewing techniques, *The London and Country Brewer*, published in 1754, contains no reference to porter. Yet four years later, H. Jackson, in his *Essay on Bread*, described porter as "the universal cordial of the populace". Porter came from nowhere to dominate first London, then British, brewing as the result of a number of changes in the drinks industry.

MOTHERS' RUIN
At the turn of the eighteenth century, the government had to act to combat the appalling deprivations caused by gin-drinking which was literally killing thousands of people. The tax on distilling corn increased the price of gin three

times, with the result that beer consumption increased dramatically.

The demand for beer also coincided with improvements in its production. Although coal fires were banned in London and coal itself was taxed, specialist country brewers were making pale ale that was carefully kilned over coal fires. When the tax on malt was increased to help pay for England's wars with France, brewers started to use less malt in their beers and more hops. But London drinkers missed their sweeter ales and started to mix the hoppier beers on sale with beer brought to London from the country by specialist wholesalers known as "ale drapers".

The country brewers had also cornered the market in the supply of "stale" beer. This was a beer that was matured for a year or more in large oak vats. During its long conditioning, lactic acid bacteria gave the beer a slightly sour character, a flavour that was much appreciated at the time. London brewers were mainly publicans who had neither the capital nor the space in their cellars to store beer for a long period. So, in order to blend beer to suit the taste of Londoners, they offered a mixture in their pubs known as "Three Threads" of pale, brown and stale. The name Three Threads comes from the fact that the beer was mixed from three casks into which spiggots or taps had been threaded. The blended beer became enormously popular, but the publicans realized they were losing money by having to buy pale and stale beers from the rich country brewers. The Londoners were determined to cut out the country brewers and corner the market for themselves.

"ENTIRE BUTT"
The breakthrough came in 1722, when Ralph Harwood, owner of the Bell Brewhouse in Shoreditch, produced a beer he called Entire Butt; this attempted to replicate the flavour of Three Threads. It is not known whether Harwood brewed three beers and then blended them in one cask or butt, or whether he brewed just the one ale, though the former theory is the more likely. He could even have advanced the ageing of the stale beer by innoculating it with a portion of genuine stale beer bought for the purpose. Whatever the method, Entire Butt became a sensation and was soon known as "porter" as a result of its popularity among street market

workers, who were a sizeable force in London at the time.

A retired brewer who used the pen name of Obadiah Poundage, writing in 1760, recorded that: "On this footing stood the trade until about the year 1722 when the Brewers conceived there was a method to be found preferable to any of these extremes [of buying beer for blending]; that beer be well brewed, kept its proper time, became racy and mellow, that is, neither new nor stale, such as would recommend itself to the public. This they ventured to sell for one pound three shillings per barrel that the victualling might retail at threepence per quart. The labouring people, porters etc, experienced its wholesomeness and utility, they assumed to themselves the use thereof, from whence it was called Porter or Entire Butt."

The early porters were blended beers, a mix of pale and brown, or pale, brown and stale. It was not until the nineteenth century that all porter was made from just one beer, and that only occurred when new technology made it possible to roast grain to a dark colour. The porters of the previous century would have been dark brown in colour. Different strengths of porter existed and the strongest versions were known as "porter stout" or "stout butt" beer. The term "stout" had been used for some time to denote the strongest (i.e. the stoutest) beer in a brewery, but gradually stout came to mean a strong version of porter.

SOCIAL CHANGE

The popularity of porter coincided with a major social upheaval in Britain, as the growth of land enclosure drove an army of people from the country into the towns. London's population grew at twice the rate of the rest of England and Wales and it soon became the most populous city in the world. A vast population of impoverished people, living in often squalid conditions, needed the solace of good beer in pleasant pubs. The success of porter and the Industrial Revolution, however, sent pub-brewing into terminal decline. By Victorian times, only four per cent of beer in London came from

brewpubs. The insatiable demand for porter – rich, fruity and heavily hopped – outstripped the ability of publicans to supply enough of it. So commercial brewers sprang up to meet the demand. Samuel Whitbread, for example, had a small ale brewery in Old Street in 1742, but he moved to new premises in Chiswell Street in the north perimeter of the City about six years later to concentrate on porter. He was able to invest in all the new technologies becoming available: steam engines, mechanical pumps, powered rakes for stirring the mash, and hydrometers for measuring the sugars in the wort and thermometers for registering temperatures – all beyond the means of publican brewers.

By 1760, Whitbread had built a Porter Tun Room at Chiswell Street, "the unsupported roof span of which is exceeded in its majestic size only by that of Westminster Hall". Before the tun room was opened, Whitbread had rented 54 different buildings throughout London to store porter. In Chiswell Street, porter could be stored in vast underground cisterns, the largest one containing the equivalent of 3,800 barrels of beer. The cisterns were cooled by internal pipes through which cold water was pumped, keeping the maturing beer in good condition in hot weather.

Brewing and storing beer in great bulk slashed the costs of production. Within less than a century, porter had moved from being an expensive beer made by blending to a cheap one produced in bulk, and in so doing it made the fortunes of the brewers. The likes of Whitbread would deliberately acetify a portion of their beer to give it a stale flavour and would then supply both young and stale, in different casks, to pubs. Publicans would then blend the beers to achieve the desired character demanded by their customers. Such a system still exists in

Giant storage vats were built to keep pace with the demand for porter and stout. Samuel Whitbread (left) built the first great porter brewery in London and became rich and powerful

THE CRAZE FOR PORTER ENCOURAGED LONDON BREWERS TO BUILD BIGGER AND BIGGER BREWERIES AND TO BOAST OF THEIR SIZE. IN 1814, A VAST PORTER VAT AT MEUX'S HORSE SHOE BREWERY IN TOTTENHAM COURT ROAD – WHERE THE DOMINION THEATRE NOW STANDS – BURST. THE DELUGE SWEPT AWAY BREWERY WALLS AND NEARBY BUILDINGS. EIGHT PEOPLE WERE KILLED BY "DROWNING, INJURY, POISONING BY THE PORTER FUMES OR DRUNKENNESS".

Belgium today, where lambic and gueuze beers are blended for individual bars.

By 1812, Chiswell Street was producing 122,000 barrels of porter and stout a year. Barclay Perkins brewed 270,000, Meux Reid 188,000 and Truman Hanbury 150,000. These were mighty, modern, capital intensive breweries, using great cast-iron vessels. They were the wonder of the rest of the world which, even in Germany, was a century behind Britain in brewing techniques.

ROASTED MALTS

The character of porter and stout changed dramatically in the early years of the nineteenth century with the invention of a roasting machine to produce roasted malts. With the ending of coal tax and the use of coke, brewers now had access to pale malt, with its higher level of sugary extract. But drinkers wanted a dark beer, which they believed to be stronger than a light one, and Daniel Wheeler's patent roasting machine, introduced in 1817, enabled the brewers to use black and chocolate malts for flavour and

A PORTER BREWED BY THE NETHERGATE BREWERY IN SUFFOLK IS CALLED OLD GROWLER, NAMED AFTER THE BREWER'S DOG. IT IS BASED ON A 1750S' LONDON RECIPE WHICH USED CORIANDER AND BOG MYRTLE AS WELL AS HOPS.

colour with the extract supplied by pale malt. In this way, the brewers were able to use less malt to make a greater volume of beer, with a resulting boost in profits.

Today, it is the porters and stouts of the nineteenth century that survive or are being recreated. There were so many variants on the theme in the previous century that even if a modern brewer took one recipe and reproduced it, it would be impossible to claim that it was a "typical" porter or entire butt of its day. And it must be remembered that a key constituent of the early porters was the use of a stale beer that had been matured for many months in oak vats.

THE SPREAD OF PORTER

The influence of porter was enormous. It spread from London to other towns and cities in Britain. Ireland, then under British control, was a ready market for porter and brewers there decided to make their own. Beamish & Crawford were brewing porter in Cork by 1792, while a young ale brewer named Arthur Guinness switched entirely to porter by the turn of the century. David Carnegie, a Scottish brewer, emigrated to Sweden to brew porter and it still survives today, made by top fermentation by the giant Pripps brewing group. Across the Baltic, the Sinebrychoff Brewery in Helsinki also brews a genuine porter.

Porter was also understandably popular with the settlers of North America. It was George Washington's favourite tipple and it was specially imported for him until the War of Independence. Strong "stout porters" were in great demand in Russia, including the court of Catherine the Great. This spawned a version of stout known as Russian Imperial. The Courage group still produces a bottle-conditioned Russian Imperial Stout. It is brewed by its Yorkshire subsidiary John Smiths in Tadcaster where, just down the road, a distant relation, Samuel Smith, also brews an Imperial Stout as well as a Taddy Porter.

Pale Ale Revolution

Porter and stout brewing went into sharp decline at the turn of the twentieth century. Drinkers were already showing a preference for both the new pale ales and the sweeter mild ales. But the death knell was sounded by government legislation during the First World War that stopped brewers using roasted malts because of the additional energy that was used. The government did not dare impose the same restrictions on Ireland, though, where the battle for Home Rule was reaching fever pitch. And so porter and stout became Irish specialities, and stout remains so to this day.

Porter's domination was already under attack in the previous century from the move to lighter-coloured beers. In Britain this was marked by the rise of pale ale. In central Europe, lager beer soared to success. Both were made possible by the new technologies of the Industrial Revolution and more should be made of the similarities of pale ale and lager rather than their differences. Both were made possible by the ability to produce pale malt, to culture pure yeast strains, to use better quality

hops, and to control fermentation temperatures with the aid of ice machines and refrigerators. The difference between them lay in the fact that British brewers remained faithful to warm fermentation – there was an undoubted jingoism and anti-Germanism about this – while the Europeans and Scandinavians embraced cold fermentation.

The pale-ale revolution began in Burton-on-Trent. The small Staffordshire town had been a renowned brewing centre since the twelfth century. Once the Trent Navigation Act of 1699 made the Midlands river navigable as far as Hull on the north-east coast, the Burton brewers began to export their sweet brown ales far and wide, and especially to the Baltic countries. But the lucrative Baltic trade was closed to the British during the Napoleonic Wars. Most of the Burton breweries closed and the handful of survivors searched desperately for new markets.

COLONIAL TRADE

Salvation came in the form of the colonial trade. Britain had first colonized India in 1772 and brewers had diligently exported ales to slake the thirsts of soldiers and civil servants. But mild ale and porter were not best suited to that climate. The word from India was simple: "We need light, well-hopped and refreshing beer." It had to be a special beer, though, to survive the three-month journey in the hold of a ship with the violent motion of the sea and sudden and severe fluctuations in temperature.

The first attempt at brewing a special beer for the India trade came, surprisingly, from London – surprising because London's soft waters were not ideal for making a light and hoppy beer. But George Hodgson, of Abbot & Hodgson's Bow Brewery, was based close to the East and West India Docks and Hodgson learnt that ships left for India virtually empty in order to pick up spices and silks for the return journey. Cargoes, therefore, were cheap on

Burton-on-Trent, a bucolic image at odds with its present position as the capital of British brewing. It is the hard spring waters of the area that made pale ale possible

Arthur Guinness (left), founder of both a brewing dynasty and a new beer style – dry Irish stout

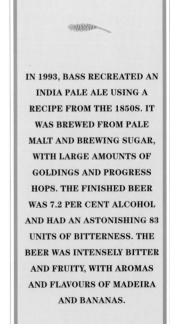

IN 1993, BASS RECREATED AN INDIA PALE ALE USING A RECIPE FROM THE 1850S. IT WAS BREWED FROM PALE MALT AND BREWING SUGAR, WITH LARGE AMOUNTS OF GOLDINGS AND PROGRESS HOPS. THE FINISHED BEER WAS 7.2 PER CENT ALCOHOL AND HAD AN ASTONISHING 83 UNITS OF BITTERNESS. THE BEER WAS INTENSELY BITTER AND FRUITY, WITH AROMAS AND FLAVOURS OF MADEIRA AND BANANAS.

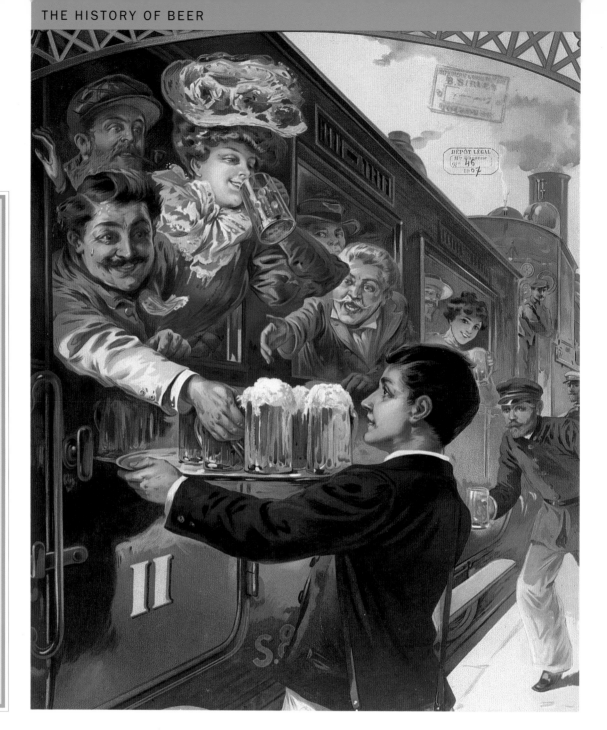

IN THE EIGHTEENTH AND NINETEENTH CENTURIES, ADULTERATION OF BEER WAS WIDESPREAD AS BREWERS SOUGHT TO MAKE QUICK PROFITS BY USING INFERIOR INGREDIENTS. IN ENGLAND, ALE WAS FOUND TO CONTAIN *COCCULUS INDICUS* BERRY, A POISON SIMILAR TO DEADLY NIGHTSHADE. LIMESTONE WAS WIDELY USED TO "FINE" OR CLEAR BEER, AS WERE BEAN FLOUR, TREACLE, OYSTER SHELLS, EGGSHELLS, CHALK AND SUGAR, AND LIME AND ISINGLASS. *FABIA ARMARA*, THE BITTER BEAN, WAS A POPULAR SUBSTITUTE FOR HOPS. MOLASSES, LIQUORICE, ELDERBERRY JUICE, CAPSICUM, CARAWAY SEEDS, GINGER AND SALT WERE ALL COMMONLY USED ADULTERANTS UNTIL BANNED BY THE GOVERNMENT.

Pale ale was the beer of the Railway Age. Trains transported beer from Burton to all parts of Britain. And as this postcard shows, pale ale refreshed passengers on long journeys

the outward run and Hodgson determined to fashion a beer that would make his fortune. No records remain of the brewery and no one can be certain what Hodgson's "India Ale" was like, save for the fact that the Burton brewers bought supplies in secret in an attempt to imitate it.

As their India Pale Ales were extremely light in colour, using just pale malt – in some cases lager malt – and brewing sugar, it is safe to assume that Hodgson's beer was similar. It was probably around 6 per cent alcohol, with twice the hop rate of other beers. The hops not only gave a tart and refreshing bitterness to the ale, but they also acted as a preservative on the long sea journey. Primed with brewing sugar in the casks, the beer would also have undergone a second fermentation, which

would have increased the level of alcohol. Hodgson's ale was successful and for years the Bow Brewery cornered the India trade. But the powerful East India Company, which handled Hodgson's beer, approached the Burton brewer Samuel Allsopp in 1821 and suggested he should provide choice and competition. Allsopp began to experiment with pale ale and was quickly followed by other Burton brewers, including William Bass.

THE BENEFITS OF CALCIUM

Within a decade, Allsopp and Bass were supplying more than half the beer shipped to India. Hodgson's fortunes duly waned and the company closed in 1885. The success of the Burton brewers lay in the remarkable mineral-rich waters of the town, with

calcium keeping yeast active in the cask and improving hop character. (Sulphate, on the other hand, increases bitterness.) The yeast strain developed by the Burton union system of fermentation also had a crucial role to play. It attacks malt and brewing sugars voraciously, producing a dry beer. It created a powerful second fermentation in the cask, producing more alcohol that helped fight off bacterial infection during the long sea journeys. India Pale Ales were also massively hopped, with three to four pounds in the copper and dry hopped in cask at around six ounces per barrel. The hops also acted as a preservative, prolonging the life of the beer. Units of bitterness would have been extremely high, around 70 to 80, but the beer would have softened during the long voyage.

The success of the Burton brewers encouraged competitors from London and other cities to open plants in the East Midlands town and avail themselves of the fine waters there. But India Pale Ales were a short-lived phenomenon, lasting from the 1830s until the 1880s. With the lager revolution sweeping Europe, it was natural that its proponents should seek markets overseas. The light, chilled and quenching beers suited the colonial climates better than pale ale, especially as lager beers were conditioned in the brewery, did not have to settle on arrival and did not have a sediment.

RAILWAYS AND CLASS

The Burton brewers switched to an internal market. With the arrival of the railway system, they could send their beers all over Britain. Pale ales became a sensation, particularly with the rising and aspiring new middle class who appreciated a beer that was too expensive for the working class.

Pale ale was the beer of the railway age, but the manner of its production began to change fundamentally. At the turn of the century, brewers started to buy pubs and create a "tied house" system. They could sell their beers direct to their outlets, but they could not wait several weeks or months for those beers to come into condition. As a result, India Pale Ales were replaced by "running beers". New strains of yeast were developed that settled out quickly and crystal malt, in which the starches had been turned to sugar in the maltings, started to be used to give flavour, colour and body to beer in an attempt to speed up maturity. These running beers are what we know today as "bitter". They developed out of the pale ale revolution, they are cask-conditioned in the pub cellar, but they are different in many ways to the amazing nineteenth-century style that spawned them.

The Advance of Lager Brewing

Outside of the British Isles, lager brewing was growing apace. A system tinkered with since the fifteenth century as a way of keeping beer free from infection became possible on a vast commercial scale with the development of ice-making machines.

The pace-setters in lagering were the great Munich brewers, especially Gabriel Sedlmayr II at Spaten. He had worked and studied in breweries throughout Europe, but returned to his family's company in 1834 to attempt to put his new theories into practice. Ice-making machines developed by Carl von Linde made it possible for brewers to store beer within their breweries, rather than transporting it to icy caves in the mountains. These machines were quickly followed by refrigerators and the technology was now in place to enable lager brewing to develop on a massive scale.

The advantages of lagering were three-fold: it gave brewers far greater control over fermentation,

A LINK WITH BAVARIA'S BREWING PAST COMES IN THE SHAPE OF PRINCE LUITPOLD'S BREWERY AT KALTENBERG. THE PRINCE (ABOVE) IS A DESCENDANT OF THE DUKES WHO INTRODUCED THE *REINHEITSGEBOT*. HIS SPECIALITY BEER IS A LAGER CALLED KÖNIG LUDWIG DUNKEL – KING LUDWIG'S DARK – LAGERED IN THE CASTLE'S CELLARS. JOUSTING TOURNAMENTS ARE HELD IN THE CASTLE GROUNDS DURING THE SUMMER.

Gabriel Sedlmayr II of the Spaten Brewery in Munich worked to develop lager-brewing on a commercial scale – though his first lagers were brown, not golden

Jan Primus (centre), a thirteenth-century Flemish duke with a remarkable capacity for beer-drinking. A corrupted version of his name – Gambrinus – is used by several breweries, including one in Pilsen

avoiding bacterial infection; it produced beers with a cleaner, less fruity character; and, because the beers were filtered and conditioned in the brewery, they were less prone to being affected by poor and unskilful service in cafés and bars. Lagering was capital-intensive, with major investment needed in conditioning tanks and cooling equipment, and with the beer tied up for months in brewery cellars before it could be released for sale. Spaten, Paulaner, Löwenbräu and the other Munich brewers aided the lagering technique by using hops predominantly for aroma rather than bitterness and varieties of barley that produced clean, malty aromas and flavours. They were also restrained by the *Reinheitsgebot* and could use only malt in their beers, with no sugars or roasted grain.

It comes as something of a shock, then, to realize that the first commercial lagers were dark in colour. Coal was expensive in Bavaria and brewers had continued to kiln their malt over wood fires. The beers were rounded, clean-tasting with hints of spice, chocolate and coffee: the style is still brewed in considerable quantities in the Franconia region of Bavaria, centred on the town of Kulmbach. A dark beer is known in Bavaria as a *dunkel* or a *dunkles*, and beers of this style continued to dominate the market there – rather as English mild ale did – until the 1950s.

A GIFT FROM BOHEMIA

The first golden lager came not from Bavaria, but from neighbouring Bohemia. Pilsen had been an important brewing centre since the foundation of the town in 1295, when King Wenceslas II gave 260 citizens the right to brew. In the sixteenth century, a treatise on scientific brewing was written in Latin by Tadeas Hajek, while the research of Frantisek Ondrej Poupé in the late eighteenth century spurred the use of modern methods of malting and control of the mash with the use of a hydrometer. Professor Karel Balling, whose name was later used to measure the strength of beer, began to lecture on brewing chemistry in Prague in 1833. A Czech

brewing school was opened in 1869 and a maltsters' school followed in 1897. For all its bucolic charms, Bohemia was not a brewing backwater.

The variable nature of Bohemian beer, in a country with severe winters but blazing summers, had long been a problem. When an entire batch of beer was poured down the Pilsen drains in 1838 after it had been declared unfit for consumption, a group of citizens who still held the seal of Wenceslas decided to take emergency action. They set up a "citizen's brewery" and invited a Bavarian brewer named Josef Groll to work for them.

Groll brought with him the knowledge of cold fermentation, but he decided to use only the finest Bohemian malt, local Zatec hops and the soft water of Pilsen. Groll's golden beer may have been an error – according to legend, he had intended to make a *dunkel* but the maltsters made a mistake with the kilning temperature – but it was an immediate sensation and has since been copied throughout the world.

At the end of the century, the beer was renamed Pilsner Urquell in German (*Plzensky Prazdroj* in Czech), meaning "original source Pilsner beer". But it was a classic case of locking the stable door after the dray horse had bolted. Pilsner – often spelt Pilsener or shortened to Pils – is the most abused beer style in the world and too often stands for a pale, thin, undistinguished beer lagered for a short period of a few weeks. The only two beers that deserve the name Pilsner are Pilsner Urquell and Gambrinus, both brewed in Pilsen.

LAGER'S INEXORABLE RISE

Lager brewing spread like a forest fire throughout the world. In Scandinavia, where the first pure lager yeast culture was isolated at the Carlsberg Brewery in Copenhagen, wheat beers and such medieval styles as *sahti* were dumped in favour of the new style. The Germans, with their colonial foothold in Africa, busily introduced lagering to that vast continent, and also to China. In Japan, meanwhile, there was no brewing tradition at all until the Americans

and the Germans helped set up breweries there. The Germans also introduced lagering to South America, though the major influence in Mexico was Austrian: the country was briefly part of the Austrian Empire. The Viennese style of brewing was to use well-kilned "red" malt and the style survives today in Mexico in such beers as Dos Equis and Negra Modelo.

THE BEERS THAT REPUTEDLY MADE MILWAUKEE FAMOUS

Lager reached the United States with the second wave of immigrants from central Europe. Germans who settled in Milwaukee found a plentiful supply of ice from a nearby lake and were able to start brewing. The Americans grasped new technology with enthusiasm and, with the aid of refrigeration, lager brewing spread rapidly.

The particular type of six-row barley that grows in the United States is rich in enzymes and allowed brewers to use large amounts of unmalted cereals, such as rice and corn, in their beers to cheapen production costs. The result has been the rise of bland, refreshing but uninteresting interpretations of the lager style. This development was aided by Prohibition, the total ban on the manufacture and sale of alcohol in the US that lasted from 1920 to 1933. The effect, though, was quite the opposite to the one wanted by the legislators. Alcohol was still freely available in illegal drinking places and was of a low and often dangerous quality. Increasingly, "bootleg" liquor came under the control of the Mafia, who even set up their own breweries and distilleries. Most commercial breweries went out of business. Only the biggest survived by producing soft drinks and legal "near beer" constituted of less than three per cent alcohol.

When Prohibition ended, a handful of giant brewers had the market to themselves and started to fashion a new industry based on bland lagers. This move intensified during the Second World War: with a vast number of men abroad on active service, the brewers set out to woo women with even lighter concoctions.

MODERN DEVELOPMENTS

Since the 1980s, brewers in North America and Japan have tinkered with such new versions of light lager as "dry beer" and "ice beer". The former – developed in Japan – is filtered to remove most of the "beery" taste, especially hop bitterness, while the latter – a Canadian invention – is produced by a complex system, similar to distillation, in which the beer is frozen to form ice crystals and then slowly warmed up until it liquefies. These are likely to be transitory brews, however, aimed essentially at people who do not like the taste of beer.

Dry beer and ice beer seem to deny the fact that the last decade of the twentieth century has seen a remarkable revival of older beer styles and a greater appreciation of quality by consumers. In Britain, cask-conditioned "real ale" is the beer of the moment, while porters and stouts are once more in demand.

The ales of Belgium are reaching an ever-growing audience, the *bières de garde* of Northern France have emerged from the long shadow cast by wine, and even in Germany top-fermenting wheat beers are challenging the hegemony of lager.

It has been a long journey for beer from the ancient world of the Pharaohs, but it has survived the voyage and looks set to find even greater appreciation in the twenty-first century.

GLOSSARY: THE LANGUAGE OF BEER

ERE ARE THE KEY TERMS YOU NEED TO HELP YOU WIDEN AND DEEPEN YOUR APPRECIATION OF ALE AND LAGER. BY SPEAKING THE LANGUAGE OF BEER, YOU CAN BETTER GRASP BOTH ITS MANY STYLES AND THE CENTURIES-OLD TECHNIQUES USED TO MAKE THEM.

Abbey
Commercial Belgian beers licensed by abbeys. Not to be confused with Trappist ales.

Adjuncts
Materials used in place of traditional grains for cheapness or lightness of flavour. Common adjuncts are rice, maize (corn) and brewing sugar.

Ale
The world's oldest beer style produced by top or warm fermentation.

Alpha acid
The main component of the bittering agent in the hop flower.

Alt
Literally Old in German, a top-fermenting beer mainly confined to the city of Düsseldorf.

Attenuation
The extent to which brewing sugars turn to alcohol and carbon dioxide.

Beer
Generic term for an alcoholic drink made from grain; includes both ale and lager.

Bitter
British term for the pale, amber or copper-coloured beers that developed from the pale ales of the nineteenth century.

Bock or Bok
Strong beer style of Germany and the Netherlands.

Bottle-conditioned
A beer that undergoes a secondary fermentation in the bottle.

Cask-conditioned
Beer that undergoes a secondary fermentation in the cask, a style closely identified with British beers. Popularly known as "real ale".

Copper
Vessel used to boil the sugary wort with hops. Also known as a brew kettle.

Decoction mashing
A system mainly used in lager brewing in which portions of the wort are removed from the mashing vessel, heated to a higher temperature and then returned. Improves enzymic activity and the conversion of starch to sugar in poorly modified malts.

Dry-hopping
The addition of a small amount of hops to a cask of beer to improve aroma and bitterness.

Dunkel
A dark lager beer in Germany, a Bavarian speciality that predated the first pale lagers.

EBC
European Beer Convention that indicates the colour in malts and beers.

Entire
The earliest form of porter, short for "entire butt".

Ester
Flavour compounds produced by the action of yeast turning sugars into alcohol and carbon dioxide. Esters may be fruity or spicy.

Fining
Substance that clarifies beer, usually made from the swim bladder of sturgeon fish; also known as isinglass.

Framboise or frambozen
Raspberry-flavoured lambic beer.

Grist
The coarse powder derived from malt that has been milled or "cracked" in the brewery prior to mashing.

Gueuze
A blend of Belgian lambic beers.

Helles or Hell
A pale Bavarian lager beer.

IBU
International Units of Bitterness, scale for measuring the bitterness of beer.

Infusion
Method of mashing used mainly in ale-brewing where the grains are left to soak with pure water while starches convert to sugar, usually carried out at a constant temperature.

Kölsch
Top-fermenting golden beer from Cologne.

Kräusen
The addition of partially-fermented wort during lagering to encourage a strong secondary fermentation.

Kriek
Cherry-flavoured lambic beer.

Lager
From the German meaning "store". The cold-conditioning

of beer at around 0 degrees Centigrade to encourage the yeast to settle out, increase carbonation and produce a smooth, clean-tasting beer.

Lambic
Belgian beer made by spontaneous fermentation.

Lauter tun
Vessel used to clarify the wort after the mashing stage.

Malt
Barley or other cereals that have been partially germinated to allow starches to be converted into fermentable sugars.

Mash
First stage of the brewing process, when the malt is mixed with pure hot water to extract the sugars.

Märzen
Traditional Bavarian lager brewed in March and stored until autumn for the Munich Oktoberfest.

Mild
Dark brown (occasionally pale) English and Welsh beer, lightly hopped. The oldest style of beer that once derived its colour from malt cured over wood fires. One of the components of the first porters.

Milk stout
Stout made with the addition of lactose, which is unfermentable, producing a beer low in alcohol with a creamy, slightly sweet character.

Pilsner or Pilsener or Pils
International brand name for a light-coloured lager. In the Czech Republic the term is confined to beers brewed in Pilsen or Pilzen where the style was perfected.

Porter
Dark – brown or black – beer originating in London, deriving its name from its popularity with street-market porters.

Priming
The addition of sugar to encourage a secondary fermentation in beer.

Reinheitsgebot
Bavarian beer law of 1516 , the "Purity Pledge", that lays down that only malted grain, hops, yeast and water can be used in brewing. Now covers the whole of Germany.

Shilling
Ancient method of invoicing beer in Scotland based on strength. Beers are called 60, 70 or 80 shilling.

Sparging
Sprinkling or spraying the spent grains in the mash tun or lauter tun to flush out any remaining malt sugars. From the French esparger, to sprinkle.

Square
A traditional open fermenting vessel.

Steam beer
American beer style saved by the Anchor Brewery in San Francisco.

Stout
Once an English generic term for the strongest or "stoutest" beer in a brewery; came to be identified with porter. Porter Stout eventually became modified to just stout. Now considered a quintessentially Irish style.

Trappist
Ales brewed by monks of the Trappist order in Belgium and The Netherlands.

Union
Method of fermentation developed in Burton-on-Trent using large oak casks.

Ur or Urtyp
German for original. Urquell as in Pilsner Urquell means "original source Pilsner".

Weizen or weisse
German term meaning wheat or white beer. Wit in Flemish.

Wort
Liquid resulting from the mashing process, rich in malt sugars.

LAST ORDERS...

Getting drunk is stupid and often offensive and does not improve the appreciation of good beer. But it happens to all drinkers from time to time. If you know you may be drinking several beers, eat a good meal first to line the stomach, eat snacks during the course of the drinking session and then drink several glasses of water before going to bed.

If you have a hangover, ignore the offer of black coffee. Caffeine is a stimulant and gets the alcohol in your bloodstream working again. If you are dehydrated drink water or weak tea, which is much lower in caffeine than coffee. Avoid milk.

The traditional cure for a hangover is a Prairie Oyster: blend together a beaten raw egg, brandy, tabasco or Worcester sauce. Beef consommé with vodka is another recommended cure.

Proprietary cures such as Underberg or Fernet Branca bitters contain alcohol and may not necessarily make you feel better.

But the "hair of the dog" is often recommended as a cure. Two legendary American soaks had famous cures. W.C. Fields' cure was "A martini made of one part vermouth, four parts gin and one olive, to be taken round the clock" while jazz musician Eddie Condon's was: "Take the juice of two quarts of whiskey".

INDEX

PICTURE CREDITS

The publishers would like to thank the following sources for their kind permission to reproduce the pictures in this book:

P Lauritz Aass; Adnams & Co Ltd; AKG London/Germanisches National Museum, Nuremberg, Schloss Ambras, Innsbruck; Allsport/Howard Boylan; Anchor Brewing Company; Anheuser-Busch/GCI Ltd; Asahi Breweries/Courage Ltd; Bank's/Welbeck Golin/Harris; Bass Brewers Ltd; Belhaven Brewery; Bitburger Brauerei Theo Simon/ Benton Associates; The Anthony Blake Photo Library/G Buntrock; Boon Rawd Brewery; Boston Brewing Company; S A Brain & Co Ltd; Bridgeman Art Library/ Fitzwilliam Museum, Cambridge; BridgePort Brewing Company; Brooklyn Brewery; Broughton Brewery Ltd; Budvar/Ryan & Cox PR; Charlotte Bush; The Caledonian Brewing Company/ Arbus; Camera Press/Anthony Armstrong-Jones; CAMRA; Brasserie Cantillon; Carlsberg Tetley; Carlton & United/Foster's; Cascade Brewery; Castlemaine Perkins Ltd; Celis Brewery; Jean-Loup Charmet; Cölner Hofbräu; Colorsport; Coors; Coopers Brewery/The Impact Agency; Courage Ltd; CPC (UK) Ltd; Brasserie Debuisson; De Koninck; Diebels; Dock Street Brewery; Dortmunder Actien Brauerei; Brasserie Duyck; Einbecker Brauhaus; Eldridge, Pope & Company; Erste Kulmbacher Actienbrauerei; Mary Evans Picture Library; Simonds, Farsons, Cisk; Felinfoel Brewery; Brasserie Fischer; French & Jupps Ltd/Palmer Bremner Associates Ltd; Greene King; Guinness Brewing GB; Guinness Ireland Ltd; Hall & Woodhouse; Robert Harding Picture Library/Duncan Maxwell; Edwards Harvey Associates; Heineken N V; Brauerei Heller-Trum; Henninger;

Michael Holford; Holsten Brauerei AG; Hulton Deutsch Collection Ltd; Hürlimann; The Image Bank/Skip Dean, Michael Skott, Richard Stradtmann; Images Colour Library; Image Select/Ann Ronan Picture Library; Brauerei Inselkammer; Interbrew/Emerson & Co; Michael Jackson; Friesisches Bräuhaus zu Jever; James Johnson; Schlossbrauerei Kaltenberg/Richard Horton; Kona Brewing Company; Labatt's/Lexis Public Relations; Lees; Löwenbräu; Iain MacLaren; Barbara Maggs; Zoë Maggs; Maisel's; Maison Caurette; Marston, Thompson & Evershed; Ken McClymont; McMullen & Sons, Ltd; Miller Brewing; Grupo Modelo, SA de CV; Molson; Brouwerij Moortgat; Munich Tourist Office; Murphy/Berners Place Consultancy; Benjamin Myers; Shepherd Neame Ltd/Edwards Harvey Associates; Orkney Brewery; Abbaye de Notre-Dame d'Orval/Lagoon; Pabst; Paul's Malt; Pete's Brewing Company/The Bright Partnership; Brauerei Pinkus Müller; Plzensky Prazdroj; Roger Protz; Range/Bettmann; The Redhook Ale Brewery/Dan Lamont; Rex/Nils Jorgensen, Ray Roberts, S M Rosenlun, Mike Toy; Brouwerij Rodenbach; Sapporo Breweries/Marblehead; Bierbrouwerij St Christoffel B V; Privatbrauerei G Schneider & Sohn/Brewers Imports; Sarah Schuman; Brasserie Schutzenberger; Scottish & Newcastle Breweries/The Boroughloch Consultancy/Lowe Bell Financial Ltd; Abbaye de Notre-Dame de Scourmont; Science Photo Library/Manfred Kage; Conrad Seidl; Sierra Nevada Brewing Company; Samuel Smith; E Smithwick & Sons Ltd; South Pacific Brewery; Spaten-Franziskaner-Bräu; The Stroh Brewing Company; The Swan Brewery; Tempo Beer Industries; Toohey's Ltd; Charles Wells Ltd/Laing Henry Ltd; Nicholas Redman, Archivist/Whitbread PLC; Whitbread PLC/Robert Hinton & Partners; Wye College/Hop Research/Peter Derby; Yakima Brewing & Malting Company; Young's & Co's Brewing PLC; Zefa.

Thanks are due in particular to Roger Protz for help and advice, and to Nicholas Redman at the Whitbread Archive and Thomas Lange of Brewers Imports.

Every effort has been made to acknowledge correctly and contact the source and/or copyright holder of each picture, and Carlton Books Limited apologises for any unintentional errors or omissions which will be corrected in future editions of this book.